Lecture Notes in Computer Science   13145

More information about this subseries at https://link.springer.com/bookseries/7409

Raju Bapi · Sandeep Kulkarni · Swarup Mohalik ·
Sathya Peri (Eds.)

Distributed Computing and Intelligent Technology

18th International Conference, ICDCIT 2022
Bhubaneswar, India, January 19–23, 2022
Proceedings

Editors
Raju Bapi
International Institute of Information
Technology
Hyderabad, India

Sandeep Kulkarni
Michigan State University
East Lansing, MI, USA

Swarup Mohalik ⓘ
Ericsson India Global Services Private Ltd.
Bangalore, India

Sathya Peri
Indian Institute of Technology Hyderabad
Kandi, Telangana, India

ISSN 0302-9743   ISSN 1611-3349 (electronic)
Lecture Notes in Computer Science
ISBN 978-3-030-94875-7   ISBN 978-3-030-94876-4 (eBook)
https://doi.org/10.1007/978-3-030-94876-4

LNCS Sublibrary: SL3 – Information Systems and Applications, incl. Internet/Web, and HCI

This Springer imprint is published by the registered company Springer Nature Switzerland AG
The registered company address is: Gewerbestrasse 11, 6330 Cham, Switzerland

Preface

This volume contains the papers selected for presentation at the 18th International Conference on Distributed Computing and Intelligent Technology (ICDCIT 2022) held during January 19–23, 2022, in Bhubaneswar, India.

From its humble beginnings, the ICDCIT conference series has grown to a conference of international repute and has become a global platform for computer science researchers to exchange research results and ideas on the foundations and applications of distributed computing and intelligent technology. An additional goal of ICDCIT is to provide an opportunity for students and young researchers to get exposed to topical research directions of distributed computing and intelligent technology. Given the importance of learning-related topics such as artificial intelligence, machine learning, and computer vision, the title of the conference was revised to 'International Conference on Distributed Computing and Intelligent Technology'.

This year we received 50 full paper submissions. Each submission considered for publication was reviewed by three or four Program Committee (PC) members with the help of reviewers outside of the PC. Based on the reviews, the Program Committee decided to accept 15 papers - 11 regular papers and four short papers - for presentation at the conference, with an acceptance rate of 22% for full papers.

We would like to express our gratitude to all the researchers who submitted their work to the conference. Our special thanks go to all colleagues who served on the Program Committee, as well as the external reviewers, who generously offered their expertise and time which helped us select the papers and prepare the conference program.

We were fortunate to have six invited speakers – Hagit Attiya (Technion, Israel), Philippas Tsigas (Chalmers University, Sweden), Roger Wattenhofer (ETH Zurich, Switzerland), Matthew E. Taylor (University of Alberta, Canada), Michael Cashmore (University of Strathclyde, Glasgow), and U. Deva Priyakumar (IIIT Hyderabad, India). Their talks provided us with the unique opportunity to hear the leaders of various fields. The papers related to the invited talks were also included in this volume.

A number of colleagues have worked very hard to make this conference a success. We wish to express our thanks to the local Organizing Committee, the organizers of the satellite events, and the many student volunteers. The School of Computer Engineering, Kalinga Institute of Industrial Technology (KIIT), the host of the conference, provided various support and facilities for organizing the conference and its associated events.

Finally, we enjoyed institutional and financial support from the Kalinga Institute of Industrial Technology (KIIT), Bhubaneswar for which we are thankful. In particular, we express our sincere thanks to Achyuta Samanta, the Founder of KIIT University, for his continuous support to ICDCIT since its inception. We express our appreciation to all the Steering Committee members, and in particular Hrushikesha Mohanty, DN Dwivedy, Subhasis Das, and Samaresh Mishra, whose counsel we frequently relied on. Thanks is also due to the faculty members and staff of the School of Computer Engineering, KIIT University, for their timely support.

January 2022

Sandeep Kulkarni
Swarup Mohalik
Sathya Peri
Raju Bapi

Organization

General Chair

Swarup Mohalik   Ericsson, Bangalore, India

Program Committee Chairs

Sathya Peri   IIT Hyderabad, India
Sandeep Kulkarni   Michigan State University, USA
Raju Bapi   IIIT Hyderabad, India

Conference Management Chair

Samaresh Mishra   KIIT, India

Organizing Chair

Subhasis Dash   KIIT, India

Finance Chairs

Manoj Kumar Mishra   KIIT, India
Kunal Anand   KIIT, India

Publicity Chairs

Bindu Agarwalla   KIIT, India
Abhaya Kumar Sahoo   KIIT, India

Registration Chairs

Sital Dash   KIIT, India
Kamakhya Narain Singh   KIIT, India

Session Management Chairs

Ajay Kumar Jena   KIIT, India
Amiya Kumar Dash   KIIT, India

Publications Chairs

Saurabh Bilgaiyan   KIIT, India
Santwana Sagnika   KIIT, India

Student Symposium Chairs

Pradeep Kumar Mallick   KIIT, India
Amiya Ranjan Panda   KIIT, India

Industry Symposium Chairs

Debasish Das   TCS, India
Jagannath Singh   KIIT, India

Project Innovation Contest Chairs/Innovation Chairs

Chittaranjan Pradhan   KIIT, India
Junali Jasmine Jena   KIIT, India

Workshop Chairs

Sapna P. G.   ikval Softwares, India
Siddharth Swarup Rautaray   KIIT, India
Krishna Chakravarty   KIIT, India

Ph.D. Symposium Chairs

Satya Ranjan Dash   KIIT, India
Manas Ranjan Lenka   KIIT, India

Steering Committee

Maurice Herlihy   Brown University, USA
Gérard Huet   Inria, France
Bud Mishra   Courant Institute of Mathematical Sciences,
                                     NYU, USA
Hrushikesha Mohanty   KIIT, India
Raja Natarajan   Tata Institute of Fundamental Research, India
David Peleg   Weizmann Institute of Science, Israel
R. K. Shyamasundar   IIT Bombay, India

Program Committee

Distributed Computing Track

Kishore Kothapalli	IIIT Hyderabad, India
Neeraj Mittal	University of Texas at Dallas, USA
Archit Somani	Huawei Research, India
Sweta Kumari	Huawei Research, India
Muktikanta Sa	Telecom Paris, France
Elad Schiller	Chalmers University of Technology, Sweden
Achour Mostefaoui	University of Nantes, France
Binoy Ravindran	Virginia Tech, USA
Sebastien Tixeuil	Sorbonne University, France
Matthieu Perrin	University of Nantes, France
Xavier Defago	Tokyo Institute of Technology, Japan
Ajay Kshemkalyani	University of Illinois Chicago, USA
Toshimitsu Masuzawa	Osaka University, Japan
Maria Potop-Butucaru	Sorbonne University, France
Gokarna Sharma	Kent State University, USA
Vidhya Tekken Valapil	GE Research, USA
Bapi Chatterjee	IST Austria, Austria
Matthieu Perrin	University of Nantes, France
Meenakshi D'Souza	IIIT Bangalore, India
Stéphane Devismes	Grenoble Alpes University, France
John Augustine	IIT Madras, India
Silvia Bonomi	Sapienza University of Rome, Italy
R. Ramanujam	Institute of Mathematical Sciences, Chennai, India
Anisur Rahaman	ISI Kolkata, India

Intelligent Technology Track

Ansuman Banerjee	ISI Kolkata, India
Assad Alam	Ericsson Research, Sweden
Atul Negi	University of Hyderabad, India
Chandra Shekar Lakshminarayanan	IIT Palakkad, India
Chiranjeevi Yarra	IIIT Hyderabad, India
Chittaranjan Hota	BITS-Pilani Hyderabad, India
Debi Prasad Dogra	IIT Bhubaneswar, India
Krishna Prasad	IIT Gandhinagar, India
Manoranjan Satpathy	IIT Bhubaneswar, India
Niladri Bihari Puhan	IIT Bhubaneswar, India

Padmanabhuni Srinivas	IIT Tirupati, India
Pradeep Kumar	IIM Lucknow, India
Puneet Goyal	IIT Ropar, India
Radhakrishna P.	NIT Warangal, India
Raghava Mutharaju	IIIT Delhi, India
Sai Prasad P. S. V. S.	University of Hyderabad, India
Srinath Srinivasa	IIIT Bangalore, India
Subba Reddy Oota	Inria Bordeaux, France
Sumit Jha	University of Texas at San Antonio, USA
V. Ravi	Institute for Development and Research in Banking Technology, India
Vinod P. K.	IIIT Hyderabad, India
Naveen Nekuri	University of Hyderabad, India
Asif Ekbal	IIT Patna, India
Himadri S. Paul	TCS Research, India
Moumita Das	Ericsson, India
Arani Bhattacharya	IIIT Delhi, India

Additional Reviewers

Kaushik Majumdar
Aliva Bakshi
Sumit Tetarave
Sunny Raj
Julien Aimonier-Davat
Yoann Dieudonné
Subhash Bhagat
Chaitali Diwan
Tanik Saikh
Yash Khare
Kamalakar Dadi

Abdullah Alourani
Soumitra Ghosh
Bernard Nongpoh
Sravanthi Upadrasta
Vivek Talwar
Chayan Sarkar
Chitra Babu
Pascal Lafourcade
Parwat Singh Anjana
Karine Altisen

Contents

Intelligent Technology

Invited Papers

Modern AI/ML Methods for Healthcare: Opportunities and Challenges

Akshit Garg, Vijay Vignesh Venkataramani, Akshaya Karthikeyan,
and U. Deva Priyakumar⁽✉⁾

Center for Computational Natural Sciences and Bioinformatics, International
Institute of Information Technology, Hyderabad, Hyderabad 500 032, India
deva@iiit.ac.in

Abstract. Artificial Intelligence has seen a significant resurgence in
the past decade in wide ranging technology and domain areas. Recent
progress in digitisation and high influx of biomedical data have led to an
unparalleled success of Machine Learning systems in healthcare, which
is perceived to be a possible game changer for 'healthcare to all'. This
article gives an account of some of the current applications of AI solutions in the medical domains of diagnosis, prognosis and treatment. The
article will also illustrate the implications of AI in the fight against the
COVID-19 pandemic. Lastly, the article will summarise the challenges
AI currently faces in its wide-scale adoption in the healthcare industry
and how they can possibly be dealt with to move towards a more intelligent medical future. This may enable moving towards quality healthcare
for all.

Keywords: Healthcare · Artificial Intelligence · Machine Learning ·
Deep Learning · Diagnosis · Prognosis

1 Introduction

At its simplest, Artificial Intelligence (AI) is essentially a branch of computer science that aims to build intelligent machines that can think and learn like humans.
Even though the idea of AI has been around for a long time, the term "Artificial Intelligence" was first coined in 1956 at a conference in Dartmouth College [75]. Due to breakthroughs in computational hardware, algorithms, libraries
and datasets, AI has seen a significant resurgence in the past decade and has
seeped through into various domains. With the digital revolution, the generation
of big datasets has been made possible, leading to the significant success of the
data-hungry AI techniques of Machine Learning (ML) and Deep Learning (DL).

The healthcare sector, in particular, is responsible for the maintenance and
improvement of health for the people through various means like prevention,

A. Garg and V. V. Venkataramani—Contributed equally.

diagnosis, treatment and cure of illness (both mental and physical). But with the industry facing a severe shortage of medical staff [77] to treat an ever grow-ing population, this becomes a very challenging task. The advent of AI into the industry can help physicians, assisting them in difficult areas like diagnosis, prognosis and help them make decisions quickly and efficiently. As various hos-pital records get digitised, researchers have seen a sharp increase in the amount of viable data that can be used for AI, which has been a severely limiting factor in the past. Due to this high influx of biomedical data, AI in healthcare is cur-rently being dominated by ML and DL. Researchers can now use Machine/Deep learning studies and apply them to existing medical practices to come up with innovative solutions to solve issues faced by the healthcare industry. Multimodal data plays an important role in success of AI in Healthcare. Figure 1 shows how AI utilizes data from different modalities to assist in various sectors of healthcare. This article will look at a few applications of AI techniques in various medical domains like diagnosis, prognosis and treatment. We will also look into how AI has played a pivotal role in the COVID-19 pandemic. Lastly, we will discuss about some of the challenges AI in Healthcare faces and how these challenges can be overcome to move towards a brighter and intelligent medical future.

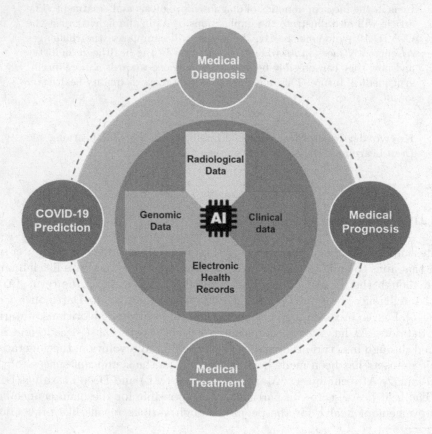

Fig. 1. A schematic of use of multimodal data and AI for different aspects of healthcare problems

2   AI in Medical Diagnosis

One of the essential steps for providing good medical care is to identify the underlying disease. Diagnosis refers to this process of assessing and identifying the underlying condition from the patient's symptoms. Health practitioners may take the help of several methods ranging from patients health history, imaging tests, blood tests etc. to conduct an efficient diagnosis. ML and DL, in particular, have revolutionised the field of Medical Diagnosis and one can argue that the applications of AI in Diagnosis are the most wide-ranging and successful. Figure 2 demonstrates various medical fields where AI is being used for diagnosis. In the following section, we will summarize the advances of AI for diagnosis in these fields.

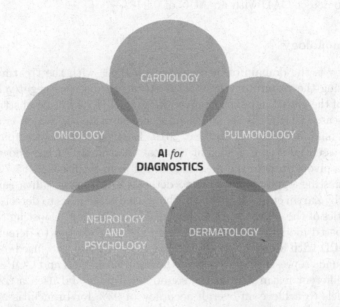

Fig. 2. Five major medical domains where modern AI/ML methods have been used for disease diagnosis

2.1   Cardiology

Cardiology refers to the branch of medicine that involves studying and treating conditions affecting the heart and circulatory system. Cardiovascular diseases (CVDs) are one of the leading causes of global deaths, World Health Organization (WHO) estimates 17.9 million lives are lost annually due to CVDs. Several AI applications have been proposed to help in the early detection of various cardiac diseases through the anomaly detection in cardiac imaging, electrocardiogram (ECG) signals and blood parameters.

Hussain et al. [36] proposed Linear Kernel Support Vector Machine which analysed the heart rate variability signals to detect Congestive Heart Failure with an area under the receiver operating characteristic curve (AUC) of 0.97. Qu et al. [69] proposed ML methods to detect congestive heart failure with an accuracy of 84.0%. Than et al. [93] introduced an ML algorithm MI^3 which used Gradient boosting to generate a score suggesting probability of Myocardial Infarction (MI). MI^3 was trained on a cohort of 3013 patients and used the combination of age, sex and paired high-sensitivity cardiac troponin I concentrations to detect MI. Sharma et al. [80] proposed an ML model which utilised the full length multilead ECG signal to detect MI with an AUC of 0.9945 while Weiss et al. [109] utilised Statistical Relation Learning Algorithms to detect MI from Electronic Health Records. Akella et al. [3] trained a Neural Network on a cohort of 303 patients to detect Coronary Artery Disease (CAD) with an accuracy of 93% using 14 different medical parameters. Wang et al. [104] used Random Forest Classifier to detect CAD with an AUC of 0.948.

2.2 Pulmonology

Pulmonology is the domain of medicine which deals with the treatment of diseases affecting the respiratory system. Respiratory diseases negatively affect a large part of the global population. According to WHO, chronic obstructive pulmonary disease (COPD) is the 3rd leading cause of death, which is attributed to over 3.2 million deaths in the year 2019. Early detection of respiratory diseases is an essential step for efficient medical treatment. AI has shown promise in playing a pivotal role in the diagnosis of respiratory diseases [65, 72, 85, 88].

An interesting application of AI to detect COPD using saliva samples was introduced by Zarrin et al. [115]. The authors used biosensors to detect the dielectric properties of the saliva samples. The eXtreme Gradient Boosting (XGBoost) algorithm based model is then trained upon these properties to detect the presence of COPD with an accuracy of 91.25%. Porieva et al. [68] used a dataset of 296 lung sounds representing 3 classes of normal, bronchitis and COPD. Authors extracted different features from the sound recordings and used a combination of ML models to achieve an overall accuracy of 93% for bronchitis and COPD detection. Recent advances in deep learning and computer vision have lead to an emergence of models which can detect pulmonary fibrosis [24], pulmonary arterial hypertension [89], pneumonia [94] using different chest imaging data.

2.3 Dermatology

Dermatology is the branch of medicine involving the study and treatment of skin, hair and nails. Visual inspection is one of the essential steps in diagnosing a dermatological problem. The advancements of computer vision has opened up new horizons for the field of AI in dermatology and have led to some of the recent DL models which can provide a diagnosis which is at par with some of the field's leading experts [31, 96]. With the help of AI, mobile devices can provide easy and cheap access to high-quality medical diagnosis to the parts of population who were previously left behind [19, 98].

Kim et al. [44] trained a Convolutional neural network (CNN) using clinical images belonging to 90 different patients. The CNN was able to detect Onychomycosis with a positive predictive value/negative predictive value of 73.4%/61.5% which was comparable with the results of 5 dermatologists with positive predictive value/negative predictive value of 69.3%/66.7%. EczemaNet [64] is a CNN trained on clinical images to predict the severity and presence of Atopic Dermatitis with a high accuracy. Gustafson et al. [34] proposed a Natural Language Processing (NLP) based algorithm for Electronic Health Record based phenotyping to identify Atopic Dermatitis in adults. Ros-Net [15] is an Inception-ResNet-v2 trained to detect rosacea with an accuracy of 89.8%. AI based solutions for diagnosis of Psoriasis [99], Onychomycosis [44] are also being proposed. Recent advancements in AI in Dermatology will improve the overall well being of global population.

2.4 Neurology and Psychiatry

Neurology is the science of treating and diagnosing the diseases of the nervous system. Early detection of neurological diseases can help in improvement of provided medical care. AI plays an important role in early detection of neurological disorders [8,27,59,73,78,87,91]. Recent studies have aimed for early detection of neurodegenerative diseases using non-coding RNAs and MicroRNAs [29,50,51,117]. AI solutions for early detection of Alzheimer's disease using Electroencephalography (EEG) [83,97] are also being put forward. Liu et al. [48] proposed a new method which uses speech data to extract spectrogram features to detect Alzheimer's disease. Recent studies have tried to exploit gait for early detection of Parkinson's disease [5,13]. Several DL based solutions have also been proposed which can help in accurate and precise detection of brain hemorrhage in brain CT images [16,40]. Dammu et al. [26] developed an ML model to classify Autism Spectrum Disorder with an accuracy of 73.6% using the resting state functional magnetic resonance imaging (rs-fMRI).

Psychiatry is the branch of medicine associated with the diagnosis, prevention and treatment of mental disorders. Diagnosis of mental illness is an inaccurate and challenging process where a psychiatrist or psychologist tries to evaluate a patients mental health. A large part of the global population does not have access to good psychiatric diagnosis. WHO estimates depression alone affects 5% of the worldwide population, and early detection of depression can make enormous improvements in its medical treatment. AI based depression detection models are being deployed, which use NLP and emotion detection to detect potential patients of depression from their social media feeds [7,28,37,61]. Sato et al. [76] developed ML model to detect people susceptible to major depression using the functional magnetic resonance imaging (fMRI) data. Schizophrenia (SCZ) affects 20 million people worldwide and early detection can help in providing patients with better medical care. ML and DL models are being developed to detect SCZ using the EEG signals [21,116], genomic data [95] and fMRI data [86] for early and accurate detection of SCZ.

2.5   Oncology

Cancer is the second leading cause of death and led to one in six deaths in 2018. Oncology is the branch of medicine associated with the treatment of cancer. AI can play an important role in early and accurate cancer diagnosis. Mobile devices equipped with AI can provide a low cost and easy diagnosis to the remote population [30]. Esteva et al. [31] trained a deep Convolution Neural Network (CNN) on a dataset of 129,450 clinical images to detect skin cancer. The CNN was able to achieve performance on par with 21 board-certified Dermatologists. DL models are being proposed which can detect and classify brain cancer [20,101], breast cancer [43,100] and renal cancer [90] from radiological and histopathological images. Whole genome sequencing data is also being used to train ML models which can enable early detection of different cancers [22,103].

3   AI in Medical Prognosis

After successful diagnosis of a patient's underlying condition, health professionals move on to determine their prognosis. Medical prognosis refers to the process of predicting or forecasting the expected developments and even the outcome of a medical condition for a given patient. Determining an accurate prognosis can be very difficult due to the various factors involved. Healthcare professionals look at factors like disease progression, patient's current health and patient's medical history to determine a suitable prognosis. Recent developments in ML and DL in the healthcare industry has helped healthcare professionals greatly increase the accuracy and their confidence in their prognosis. In further sub-sections we discuss how AI has helped prognosis prediction in different kinds of studies.

3.1   Cancer Progression Studies

Once a patient is diagnosed with cancer, determining a suitable prognosis is very important as it helps determine the next course of action medically. Cancer is estimated to affect 1 in 10 people on average in the USA [81], making the task of predicting cancer progression very important. Nie et al. [60] developed a 3D deep learning framework to automatically extract features from pre-operative multi-modal images like MRI, fMRI, DTI of high-grade glioma patients (i.e., patients suffering from a type of brain tumors), achieving accuracies as high as 89.9%. CNNs are being used to segment a brain tumor from healthy tissue, once the tumor data is extracted, regression is used to predict the number of days of overall survival [38]. Boeri et al. [17] built an ML model to predict outcomes after surgery for breast cancer patients with an accuracy of 95%. Using various deep learning techniques, survival prediction for Non-small cell lung cancer (NSCLC) is being predicted with good accuracy [47,114]. Tang et al. [92] came up with a novel approach for predicting prognosis of Kidney renal clear cell carcinoma (KIRC). Using lasso regression, a prognosis model on the basis of methylation-driven genes was developed. The survival rates of patients were then predicted using both clinical information and the methylated prognosis model, finally giving a C-index value of 0.838 for the test data. Instead of targeting a specific type of cancer, there has been research using multi-modal data for pan-cancer prognosis. These papers make use of DL techniques on histopathology slides and other clinical information to finally predict single cancer and pancancer overall survival [23, 82].

3.2   Mortality Prediction Studies

Mortality prediction refers to the process of predicting the risk of a critically ill patient's mortality or death. Building an accurate mortality predictor using AI can assist physicians perform appropriate clinical interventions for critically ill patients, thus helping them improve the patient's medical care.

Kong et al. [46] were able to use ML to predict the mortality of sepsis patients in the ICU with moderate success. They built four different kinds of machine-learning based classifier models and trained them on the medical information mart for intensive care (MIMIC) III dataset. They found the gradient boosting machine (GBM) performed the best, giving an AUC of 0.845. Using gradient boosting, Parikh et al. [66] were able to predict 6-month mortality for patients with cancer successfully with an AUC of 0.87. Studies of mortality prediction is also being done for different kinds of cancer specifically like advanced hepatocellular carcinoma (HCC) [52] and metastatic colorectal cancer (mCRC) [74].

The need for calculating mortality risk for traumatic patients admitted to the ICU is very high, Servia et al. [79] conducted a series of experiment using the RETRAUCI database which is the national trauma registry of 52 Spanish ICUs from the period of 2015–2019. The 9 different ML models they developed used a set of variables derived from the deviation of both physiological and anatomical parameters to predict the death risk of a given traumatised patient. Elderly trauma patients generally have a very high risk or mortality, Morris et al. [58] present a set of novel outcome scores, quick elderly mortality after trauma (qEMAT) score and a full elderly mortality after trauma (fEMAT) score, for predicting mortality of elderly trauma patients. They achieve an AUC of 0.84 for the qEMAT and 0.86 for fEMAT.

Stillbirth can be defined as death of a fetus after 20 or 28 weeks of pregnancy. It is a devastating outcome which accounts to two-thirds of perinatal mortality or live-born children who are yet to complete 7 days of life [32, 57]. Using a combination of features like current pregnancy complications, congenital anomalies, maternal characteristics, and medical history, researchers were able to use regularised logistic regression, decision tree based on classification and regression trees, random forest, extreme gradient boosting, and a multilayer perceptron neural network which could predict the risk of stillbirth with mild success, i.e., the best performing classifier XGBoost was able to predict 45% of stillbirths among all women in the dataset [55].

Mortality prediction studies in the field of cardiology has been very active, as cardiovascular diseases account for a large amount of deaths worldwide. Adler et al. [1] trained a boosted decision tree on a cohort of 5822 hospitalized patients with Heart Failure (HF). Using eight key variables the model was able to give a risk score with an AUC of 0.88. Wang et al. [108] proposed a feature rearrangement based DL system for heart failure mortality prediction, which works well even on imbalanced datasets. The researchers also propose a method called Feature rearrangement based convolutional layer, where they show that the order of the input features is also essential for the convolutional network. Numerous studies on the risk stratification and mortality prediction for COVID-19 patients have been reported in the last one and a half years, which are discussed later.

4   AI in Medical Treatment

In the previous sections we discussed how AI has greatly impacted the way healthcare professionals accurately diagnose and give prognosis to patients. In this section, we will look at how AI techniques like ML and DL have helped improve the quality of the treatment they provide to their patients.

The development of a emergency department (ED) triage systems that are able to differentiate patients according to care they need remains a challenging task. Raita et al. [70] were able to build a deep neural network to predict if patients coming to the ED were critically ill with an AUC of 0.86. As the leading cause of mortality and morbidity, CVDs are very time sensitive in nature, especially if the patient suffering from it is admitted to the ED. Using data from about 17,661 ED patients with suspected CVDs, researchers used a set of ML models like multinomial logistic regression, extreme gradient boosting, random forest and gradient-boosted decision tree to train on 80% of the data, keeping the rest for testing. They achieved AUC of 0.937 for XGBoost, 0.921 for gradient-boosted decision tree, 0.919 for random forest and 0.908 for multinomial logistic regression [39]. Klang et al. [45] developed a novel prediction model to find patients in who require head CT exam during Emergency Department (ED) triage. Using a gradient boosting model with a dataset containing 595,561 ED visits, the model showed an AUC of 0.93, with sensitivity of 88.1% and specificity of 85.7%.

AI in robotics has greatly influenced the healthcare industry, we can see that even though AI controlled robotic systems are used proficiently in healthcare laboratories and for manufacturing healthcare equipment with precision [110], it's adoption into mainstream medical practices like surgery has been scarce. Minimally invasive surgery is a great alternative to open surgery options as it reduces surgical trauma and eases post-surgery rehabilitation, but it comes with its own set of disadvantages as surgeons now need to handle a confined work space, loss of depth perception, and compromised hand-eye coordination. There has been console operated robotic systems, like the da Vinci surgical system which is able to perform minimally invasive surgery by replication the hand movements of a surgeon with high precision [33]. Concentric Tube Robots (CTRs) which are a special class of continuum robots (i.e., a type of robot characterised by infinite degrees of freedom and number of joints [84]) has shown great potential for minimally invasive surgery due to its miniaturization potential and maneuverability [4].

The advent of AI in healthcare has also come as a boon for hospitals themselves. Re-admission in hospitals is generally defined as admitting a patient again within, generally, 30 days of initial admission. Ajay et al. [2] showed the cons of re-admission in hospitals and proposed how it can be prevented using ML techniques. Vivanco et al. [102] used ML techniques to identify patients likely to overstay in hospitals, these patients are partly responsible for high waiting times and bed shortages in the hospital. Using a decision tree classifier, they were able to achieve a F-Measure of 0.826 for patients at a tertiary teaching hospital and an F-Measure of 0.784 at a community hospital. Yala et al. [112] built a classifier to parse classical breast pathology reports automatically by extracting pertinent tumor characteristics into readily available data with an average accuracy of 97% of individual categories.

Hypoxaemia is the condition where there is an abnormally low concentration of oxygen in the blood. Researchers were able to use a ML based system to predict the prevention of hypoxaemia during surgery. They were effectively able to double the rate of prediction of hypoxaemia by anesthesiologists from 15% originally to 30% with the use of their system [53]. Wijnberge et al. [111] used a ML algorithm that predicts hypotension during surgery in combination with personalized treatment. Hatib et al. [35] built a custom ML based algorithm to predict intraoperative hypotension, they were able to achieve a sensitivity of 88% and specificity of 87% 15 min before a hypotensive event with an AUC of 0.95.

5   AI in COVID-19

Coronavirus Disease 2019 (COVID-19) is an infectious disease caused by Severe Acute Respiratory Syndrome Coronavirus 2 (SARS-CoV-2) Virus. The outbreak of COVID-19 originated from Wuhan, China and rapidly spread across the world, bringing the global population to a standstill. Severe cases of COVID-19 can lead to serious respiratory disease and pneumonia, which might even lead to death. By the end of October 2021, WHO has confirmed over 4.9 million deaths due to COVID-19. AI interventions can help in controlling the pandemic. AI models are being used to quickly and accurately identify individuals who are not wearing face masks [12,49]. COVID-19 is an infectious disease that spreads very rapidly and poses immense pressure on the existing health infrastructure of the world. Early prediction of an upcoming surge in the COVID-19 positive cases can help the authorities in taking proactive measures that can save thousands of lives. Researchers have developed AI based models for epidemic waves forecasting [10,67,107]. These models can predict the approximate time and intensity of the forthcoming surge of positive cases. Several prognostic and diagnostic applications of AI for COVID-19 are also being developed, proving the immense significance of AI in this fight.

5.1   AI Based COVID-19 Diagnosis

Early detection of COVID-19 is an essential step to stop the spread of the virus. Several studies tried to use AI based solutions to help in accurate and fast COVID-19 diagnosis. Many studies trained ML models using chest X-rays [11,71,105], while others tried to exploit the chest CT images [14,42] for the early detection of COVID-19. Although radiological imaging based solutions tend to perform well, they are expensive and complex. Some studies proposed using cough or respiratory sound recordings for COVID-19 detection [56,62,63]. Aly et al. [9] used a dataset of 1299 sound samples to train an ML model that detected COVID-19 positive samples with an AUC of 0.96. Zoabi et al. [118] proposed an ML model trained on records of 51,831 individuals. The model could detect COVID-19 positive cases with a high accuracy by just using the symptoms and basic patient information like age and sex.

5.2   AI Based COVID-19 Prognosis

COVID-19 has posed an unprecedented pressure on global health infrastructure due to the enormous inflow of patients demanding medical care. In times of distress, efficient utilisation of critical resources like oxygen and ventilators becomes an important step, which, if not appropriately enacted, can lead to the deaths of many. The efficient prognosis of COVID-19 patients can help in the early identification of high-risk patients. Authorities can then provide preferred medical care to individuals who stand a chance of developing severe complications, which might help in saving thousands of lives. Many AI solutions for early and quick COVID-19 prognosis are being developed. Wang et al. [106] proposed ML models based on clinical and laboratory features to predict mortality of COVID-19 patients with an AUC of 0.83. Bolourani et al. [18] developed an ML model that utilised features like age, respiratory rate, serum lactate to predict respiratory failure with an accuracy of 91.9%. ML models to predict mortality and severity of patients using chest X-rays and CT scans have also been proposed [25,54].

   In further sections, we will look at two different COVID-19 risk stratification and mortality prediction studies to get an in-depth understanding of the research in the domain of AI for COVID-19.

5.3   Machine Learning Based Clinical Decision Support System for Early COVID-19 Mortality Prediction

Karthikeyan et al. [41] proposed an ML model to predict COVID-19 patient Mortality. The model uses a combination of five readily available features: neutrophils, lymphocytes, lactate dehydrogenase (LDH), high-sensitivity C-reactive protein (hs-CRP), and age to predict mortality with an accuracy of 96%. Various ML models like Support Vector Machine, XGBoost, random forests, logistic regression, neural network and decision trees were trained and tested to get the best performing model. The neural network performed the best with an ability

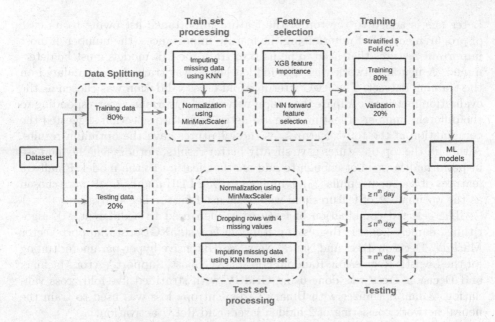

Fig. 3. ML pipeline used by Karthikeyan et al.

to predict mortality with an accuracy of 90% as early as 16 days before the outcome. Figure 3 depicts the ML pipeline used for the study.

For the study, the authors used the publicly available dataset provided by Yan et al. [113]. The dataset is a time-series data of 375 COVID-19 patients from Tongji Hospital in Wuhan, China. It contains the information corresponding to 74 biomarkers and data sample time, admission time, discharge time and outcome. After data cleaning, K-Nearest Neighbour algorithm was used to impute the missing values followed by Min-Max scaling. The pre-processed dataset consisted of 1,766 data points coming from 370 different patients. Since the dataset is time series, a single patient had multiple data points corresponding to different days of hospital stay. To ensure exclusive patients for train and test set, authors divided the dataset such that all the data points corresponding to 80% of the randomly chosen patients were considered for the training set while all the data points of the remaining 20% of the patients were considered for the testing dataset. The test set had a balanced distribution, where 56.3% of data points correspond outcome as 'died' while 43.7% data points had 'survived' as the outcome.

After the data pre-processing and data splitting, XGBoost classifier was used to get the relative feature importances of all the available features. The average importance of features was found by taking the arithmetic mean of feature importance of 100 different runs, where each run takes a random 80% of the training data points. XGBoost feature importance produced the list with the top 4 features being neutrophils (%), lymphocyte (%), LDH and hs-CRP.

Later age is added to the top of the feature importance list owing to its ease of procurement. After determining the feature importances, the number of most important features that need to be used to train the ML models must be determined. A neural network with two hidden layers was trained and validated on the training dataset. The AUC after five-fold cross validation was chosen as the evaluation metric to compare the neural network's performance corresponding to the different number of features. Neural network feature selection suggested the combination of the top 5 features, as these features gave the optimum results. Although the top 6 features gave slightly better results, authors felt the increase in performance was not enough to add another feature to the model. Finally, 5 features of age, neutrophils (%), lymphocyte (%), LDH and hs-CRP were chosen as the optimal set of features and were thus used for further analysis.

The selected combination of features is then used to 6 different ML algorithms, namely Logistic Regression, Random Forests, XGBoost, Support Vector Machine, Decision Trees and Neural Network. Extensive hyper-parameter tuning for the Logistic Regression, Random Forests, XGBoost, Support Vector Machine, and Decision Trees was done using GridCV with stratified five-fold cross validation. Adam optimizer with Binary Cross Entropy loss was used to train the neural network consisting of 2 hidden layers and ReLU activation.

Figure 4 shows comparison of overall test accuracy, F1 score and AUC of different ML algorithms used in the study. The graphs suggest neural network performs the best with an overall accuracy of 96.53% (±0.64%), F1 score of 0.969 (±0.006) and AUC of 0.989 (±0.006). Neural network was hence chosen as the ML model for all the further analysis.

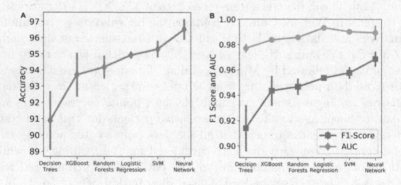

Fig. 4. Comparison of the performance of different ML algorithms. Standard deviation is denoted by the vertical lines.

The authors of the study also tested the model's capacity to predict mortality with respect to number of days to outcome. Figure 5 shows the analysis where model is tested on different datasets varied with respect to different cutoff for days to outcome. For the value of cutoff set as 'n' a new dataset is generated where only the data points which have the number of days to outcome '≥ n' are selected. The Fig. 5 suggests model was able to achieve an accuracy of 90% for cutoff set as 16 days, hence model is able to predict mortality with an accuracy of 90% as early as 16 days in advance to day of outcome.

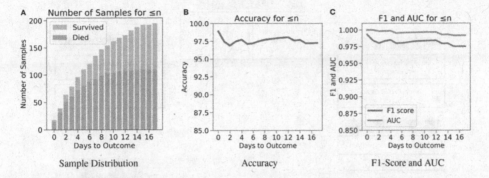

Fig. 5. The performance of neural net on the test data when only data points with days to outcome ≥n are chosen. (A) Class wise distribution of varying dataset. (B) Accuracy of the model with respect to varying dataset. (C) F1-score and AUC of the model with respect to varying dataset.

5.4 COVID-19 Risk Stratification and Mortality Prediction in Hospitalized Indian Patients

Even though studies regarding COVID-19 had been done in the past, analysis of Indian COVID-19 patients was required. Alle et al. [6] conducted a detailed study to understand the COVID-19 disease progression in the Indian cohort. The data for the study was collected from the Max Group of Hospitals, New Delhi, India. The authors developed XGboost based ML model for risk stratification with an F1 score of 0.81, while a logistic regression classifier was used for mortality prediction with an F1 score of 0.71. The study also tried to investigate the differences between disease progression in Wuhan and New Delhi cohorts.

A time-series data of 544 COVID-19 cases was collected by the MAX group of hospitals, New Delhi, between June 3rd and October 23rd, 2020. Patient data was anonymised at the data warehouse of CSIR-IGIB, New Delhi, to ensure patient privacy. The data comprised 357 different biomarkers, including vitals, symptoms, comorbidities, blood biomarkers, and medicines administered. The authors categorised the patients into different risk levels. They created three sets of different labels based on mortality, quaternary stratification and binary stratification. Mortality comprised of outcome labels of died and survived. Quaternary stratification had four outcome labels of home quarantined, hospitalised but not on respiratory support, on respiratory support, died based on patient's severity during the disease. Binary stratification had output labels of mild and severe, where mild risk represented home quarantined or hospitalised patients

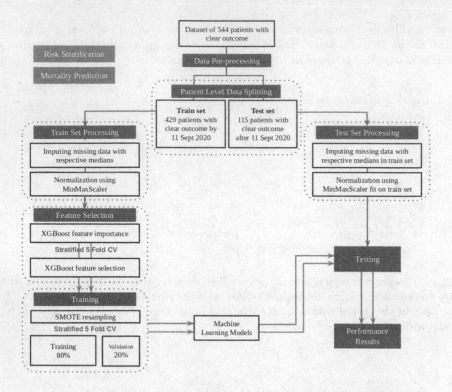

Fig. 6. ML pipeline used by Alle et al.

without respiratory support. The severe risk category comprised patients who were either on respiratory support during their hospital stay or succumbed to the disease.

As the data for the study was a time-series dataset, a single patient had multiple records of data with respect to blood parameters and vitals. For the study, authors considered each blood sample recording as a separate data point. The missing values for a parameter were imputed with the nearest value of the parameter from the patient's past results. All the numerical parameters were scaled within a range of 0–1 using min-max scaler. To ensure patient-level segregation between train and test set, all the 429 patients who had a clear outcome before 11th September 2020 were considered for the training set while the data of other 115 patients was used for the generation of the holdout test set.

Figure 6 depicts the flowchart for ML pipeline. Different sets of features were selected for mortality prediction and risk stratification. These features were then used for training and testing of various ML algorithms. The explanation about feature selection and training is discussed below.

To identify the most important features, the relative importances of all the features were identified using XGBoost algorithm. The number of features to be used for training the ML model was then determined by training XGBoost with different number of features, with features being added in the order of their relative importance. The smallest cluster of features giving the optimal performance was then chosen for model training. To account for high class imbalance of training set, SMOTE algorithm was used for synthetic generation of samples belonging to the minority class. XGBoost, Random Forest, SVM, Logistic Regression based models were then trained for mortality and risk prediction.

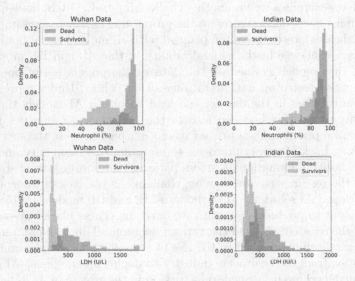

Fig. 7. Density histogram to compare Indian and Wuhan cohort

11 features were selected for the risk stratification task: absolute neutrophil count, LDH, lymphocyte (%), neutrophil (%), record of diabetes comorbidity, ferritin, INR, interleukin-6 (IL-6), oxygen saturation level, absolute eosinophil count and packed cell volume. XGboost algorithm performed best with an F1 score of 0.810 ± 0.01 and AUC of 0.833 ± 0.01. For mortality prediction, a set of 9 features were selected: D-Dimer, Ferritin, Lymphocyte (%), Neutrophil to Lymphocyte ratio (NLR), WBC, Trop I, INR, IL-6 and LDH. Logistic regression performed the best for the task with an AUC and F1 score of 0.927 ± 0.01 and 0.710 ± 0.02.

The authors tried to identify differences between Wuhan and the Indian cohort, for which data provided by Yan et al. was used to understand the disease progression for the Wuhan cohort. Authors plotted density histograms for five different parameters like neutrophil (%), LDH to understand the differences between people who survived and those who did not. From Fig. 7 we can observe that for the Wuhan cohort, the neutrophil (%) and LDH had really high variation between the people who died and those who survived. The Indian cohort did not show such a stark variation.

6   Summary and Outlook

Although AI in Healthcare has shown excellent prospects, it faces many challenges. ML models are data-hungry systems that require enormous amounts of data for training. Healthcare data collection is an arduous task, and often healthcare datasets are inadequate and biased. Data scarcity poses a significant challenge to the success of AI in healthcare. Developing an AI for healthcare solution that generalises well is another challenging task. Often, inadequate and biased training data fails to represent the proper and complete subsample of the data. Healthcare datasets are often plagued with ethnic and racial biases, which pose a severe challenge in the generalizability of the ML and DL models. It is often seen that models trained on the data of the population of one subcontinent fail when tested on data from some other cohort. Under representation of the minority class in the dataset can lead to biased AI models that overfit the majority class. This bias can lead to the seclusion of minorities from the general medical practice. Data privacy is another big hurdle in the success of AI in healthcare. Lack of proper protocols to maintain the anonymity and privacy of intimate health information dissuades patients and hospitals from sharing the data with the researchers. Another big challenge is the lack of interpretability in the developed AI solutions. Most modern ML and DL models are black boxes that take input to produce a quantitative outcome. These black box models fail to explain the reasoning behind the various decisions. This lack of interpretability and generalisability has led to the loss of trust of the medical community in AI. Hesitation from the healthcare industry to deploy and augment AI solutions at the ground level has developed some friction in the growth of AI in healthcare.

Even though many challenges loom ahead of the success of AI in healthcare, we believe in the coming future, AI will play a pivotal role in revolutionising the healthcare industry for good. Cumulative efforts of academia, industry and government authorities might help in the generation of more extensive and unbiased healthcare datasets. Development and training of the AI models which are uninhibited from racial and ethnic biases will play a crucial role in the success of AI in healthcare. Proper protocols and regulations need to be established to dismiss the concerns regarding data privacy and security. Developing trust toward the AI solution is also an essential attribute in the widescale adoption of AI in healthcare. We believe AI would not eliminate the need for human intervention; instead, it will assist radiologists and clinicians in providing more reliable, cheaper and easily accessible medical care to all.

Acknowledgements. We thank IHub-Data, IIIT Hyderabad for financial support.

References

1. Adler, E.D., et al.: Improving risk prediction in heart failure using machine learning. Eur. J. Heart Fail. **22**(1), 139–147 (2020)
2. Ajay, S., Deshpande, P.: Preventive readmission in hospitals using machine learning. In: 2020 IEEE International Conference for Innovation in Technology (INOCON), pp. 1–5. IEEE (2020)
3. Akella, A., Akella, S.: Machine learning algorithms for predicting coronary artery disease: efforts toward an open source solution. Future Sci. OA **7**(6), FSO698 (2021)
4. Alfalahi, H., Renda, F., Stefanini, C.: Concentric tube robots for minimally invasive surgery: current applications and future opportunities. IEEE Trans. Med. Robot. Bionics **2**(3), 410–424 (2020)
5. Alle, S., Priyakumar, U.D.: Linear prediction residual for efficient diagnosis of Parkinson's disease from gait. In: de Bruijne, M., et al. (eds.) MICCAI 2021. LNCS, vol. 12905, pp. 614–623. Springer, Cham (2021). https://doi.org/10.1007/978-3-030-87240-3_59
6. Alle, S., et al.: COVID-19 risk stratification and mortality prediction in hospitalized Indian patients. medRxiv (2020)
7. AlSagri, H.S., Ykhlef, M.: Machine learning-based approach for depression detection in Twitter using content and activity features. IEICE Trans. Inf. Syst. **103**(8), 1825–1832 (2020)
8. Álvarez, J.D., Matias-Guiu, J.A., Cabrera-Martín, M.N., Risco-Martín, J.L., Ayala, J.L.: An application of machine learning with feature selection to improve diagnosis and classification of neurodegenerative disorders. BMC Bioinform. **20**(1), 1–12 (2019). https://doi.org/10.1186/s12859-019-3027-7
9. Aly, M., Rahouma, K.H., Ramzy, S.M.: Pay attention to the speech: COVID-19 diagnosis using machine learning and crowdsourced respiratory and speech recordings. Alexandria Eng. J. **61**(5), 3487–3500 (2021)
10. Ardabili, S.F., et al.: COVID-19 outbreak prediction with machine learning. Algorithms **13**(10), 249 (2020)
11. Asif, S., Wenhui, Y.: Automatic detection of COVID-19 using X-ray images with deep convolutional neural networks and machine learning. medRxiv (2020)
12. Asif, S., Wenhui, Y., Tao, Y., Jinhai, S., Amjad, K.: Real time face mask detection system using transfer learning with machine learning method in the era of COVID-19 pandemic. In: 2021 4th International Conference on Artificial Intelligence and Big Data (ICAIBD), pp. 70–75. IEEE (2021)
13. Aversano, L., Bernardi, M.L., Cimitile, M., Pecori, R.: Early detection of Parkinson disease using deep neural networks on gait dynamics. In: 2020 International Joint Conference on Neural Networks (IJCNN), pp. 1–8. IEEE (2020)
14. Barstugan, M., Ozkaya, U., Ozturk, S.: Coronavirus (COVID-19) classification using CT images by machine learning methods. arXiv preprint arXiv:2003.09424 (2020)
15. Binol, H., Plotner, A., Sopkovich, J., Kaffenberger, B., Niazi, M.K.K., Gurcan, M.N.: Ros-NET: a deep convolutional neural network for automatic identification of rosacea lesions. Skin Res. Technol. **26**(3), 413–421 (2020)
16. Bobby, J.S., Annapoorani, C.: Analysis of intracranial hemorrhage in CT brain images using machine learning and deep learning algorithm. Ann. Rom. Soc. Cell Biol. **25**(6), 13742–13752 (2021)

17. Boeri, C., et al.: Machine learning techniques in breast cancer prognosis prediction: a primary evaluation. Cancer Med. **9**(9), 3234–3243 (2020)
18. Bolourani, S., et al.: A machine learning prediction model of respiratory failure within 48 hours of patient admission for COVID-19: model development and validation. J. Med. Internet Res. **23**(2), e24246 (2021)
19. Brewer, A.C., et al.: Mobile applications in dermatology. JAMA Dermatol. **149**(11), 1300–1304 (2013)
20. Brunese, L., Mercaldo, F., Reginelli, A., Santone, A.: An ensemble learning approach for brain cancer detection exploiting radiomic features. Comput. Methods Programs Biomed. **185**, 105134 (2020)
21. Buettner, R., Hirschmiller, M., Schlosser, K., Rössle, M., Fernandes, M., Timm, I.J.: High-performance exclusion of schizophrenia using a novel machine learning method on EEG data. In: 2019 IEEE International Conference on E-Health Networking, Application & Services (HealthCom), pp. 1–6. IEEE (2019)
22. Chabon, J.J., et al.: Integrating genomic features for non-invasive early lung cancer detection. Nature **580**(7802), 245–251 (2020)
23. Cheerla, A., Gevaert, O.: Deep learning with multimodal representation for pancancer prognosis prediction. Bioinformatics **35**(14), i446–i454 (2019)
24. Christe, A., et al.: Computer-aided diagnosis of pulmonary fibrosis using deep learning and CT images. Invest. Radiol. **54**(10), 627 (2019)
25. Cohen, J.P., et al.: Predicting COVID-19 pneumonia severity on chest X-ray with deep learning. Cureus **12**(7), e9448 (2020)
26. Dammu, P.S., Bapi, R.S.: Employing temporal properties of brain activity for classifying autism using machine learning. In: Deka, B., Maji, P., Mitra, S., Bhattacharyya, D.K., Bora, P.K., Pal, S.K. (eds.) PReMI 2019. LNCS, vol. 11942, pp. 193–200. Springer, Cham (2019). https://doi.org/10.1007/978-3-030-34872-4_22
27. Dammu, P.S., Bapi, R.S.: Temporal dynamics of the brain using variational bayes hidden Markov models: application in autism. In: Deka, B., Maji, P., Mitra, S., Bhattacharyya, D.K., Bora, P.K., Pal, S.K. (eds.) PReMI 2019. LNCS, vol. 11941, pp. 121–130. Springer, Cham (2019). https://doi.org/10.1007/978-3-030-34869-4_14
28. Deshpande, M., Rao, V.: Depression detection using emotion artificial intelligence. In: 2017 International Conference on Intelligent Sustainable Systems (ICISS), pp. 858–862. IEEE (2017)
29. Dos Santos, M.C.T., et al.: miRNA-based signatures in cerebrospinal fluid as potential diagnostic tools for early stage Parkinson's disease. Oncotarget **9**(25), 17455 (2018)
30. Emuoyibofarhe, J.O., Ajisafe, D., Babatunde, R.S., Christoph, M.: Early skin cancer detection using deep convolutional neural networks on mobile smartphone. Int. J. Inf. Eng. Electron. Bus. **12**(2), 21–27 (2020)
31. Esteva, A., et al.: Dermatologist-level classification of skin cancer with deep neural networks. Nature **542**(7639), 115–118 (2017)
32. Flenady, V., et al.: Major risk factors for stillbirth in high-income countries: a systematic review and meta-analysis. The Lancet **377**(9774), 1331–1340 (2011)
33. Gomes, P.: Surgical robotics: reviewing the past, analysing the present, imagining the future. Robot. Comput.-Integr. Manuf. **27**(2), 261–266 (2011)
34. Gustafson, E., Pacheco, J., Wehbe, F., Silverberg, J., Thompson, W.: A machine learning algorithm for identifying atopic dermatitis in adults from electronic health records. In: 2017 IEEE International Conference on Healthcare Informatics (ICHI), pp. 83–90. IEEE (2017)

35. Hatib, F., et al.: Machine-learning algorithm to predict hypotension based on high-fidelity arterial pressure waveform analysis. Anesthesiology **129**(4), 663–674 (2018)
36. Hussain, L., et al.: Detecting congestive heart failure by extracting multimodal features and employing machine learning techniques. BioMed Res. Int. **2020** (2020). Article ID: 4281243
37. Islam, M.R., Kabir, M.A., Ahmed, A., Kamal, A.R.M., Wang, H., Ulhaq, A.: Depression detection from social network data using machine learning techniques. Health Inf. Sci. Syst. **6**(1), 1–12 (2018). https://doi.org/10.1007/s13755-018-0046-0
38. Islam, M., Jose, V.J.M., Ren, H.: Glioma prognosis: segmentation of the tumor and survival prediction using shape, geometric and clinical information. In: Crimi, A., Bakas, S., Kuijf, H., Keyvan, F., Reyes, M., van Walsum, T. (eds.) BrainLes 2018. LNCS, vol. 11384, pp. 142–153. Springer, Cham (2019). https://doi.org/10.1007/978-3-030-11726-9_13
39. Jiang, H., et al.: Machine learning-based models to support decision-making in emergency department triage for patients with suspected cardiovascular disease. Int. J. Med. Inform. **145**, 104326 (2021)
40. Jnawali, K., Arbabshirani, M.R., Rao, N., Patel, A.A.: Deep 3D convolution neural network for CT brain hemorrhage classification. In: Medical Imaging 2018: Computer-Aided Diagnosis, vol. 10575, p. 105751C. International Society for Optics and Photonics (2018)
41. Karthikeyan, A., Garg, A., Vinod, P., Priyakumar, U.D.: Machine learning based clinical decision support system for early COVID-19 mortality prediction. Front. Public Health **9**, 626697 (2021)
42. Kassania, S.H., Kassanib, P.H., Wesolowskic, M.J., Schneidera, K.A., Detersa, R.: Automatic detection of coronavirus disease (COVID-19) in X-ray and CT images: a machine learning based approach. Biocybern. Biomed. Eng. **41**(3), 867–879 (2021)
43. Khuriwal, N., Mishra, N.: Breast cancer detection from histopathological images using deep learning. In: 2018 3rd International Conference and Workshops on Recent Advances and Innovations in Engineering (ICRAIE), pp. 1–4. IEEE (2018)
44. Kim, Y.J., Han, S.S., Yang, H.J., Chang, S.E.: Prospective, comparative evaluation of a deep neural network and dermoscopy in the diagnosis of onychomycosis. PLoS ONE **15**(6), e0234334 (2020)
45. Klang, E., et al.: Promoting head CT exams in the emergency department triage using a machine learning model. Neuroradiology **62**(2), 153–160 (2020). https://doi.org/10.1007/s00234-019-02293-y
46. Kong, G., Lin, K., Hu, Y.: Using machine learning methods to predict in-hospital mortality of sepsis patients in the ICU. BMC Med. Inform. Decis. Mak. **20**(1), 1–10 (2020). https://doi.org/10.1186/s12911-020-01271-2
47. Lai, Y.H., Chen, W.N., Hsu, T.C., Lin, C., Tsao, Y., Wu, S.: Overall survival prediction of non-small cell lung cancer by integrating microarray and clinical data with deep learning. Sci. Rep. **10**(1), 1–11 (2020)
48. Liu, L., Zhao, S., Chen, H., Wang, A.: A new machine learning method for identifying Alzheimer's disease. Simul. Model. Pract. Theory **99**, 102023 (2020)
49. Loey, M., Manogaran, G., Taha, M.H.N., Khalifa, N.E.M.: A hybrid deep transfer learning model with machine learning methods for face mask detection in the era of the COVID-19 pandemic. Measurement **167**, 108288 (2021)
50. Ludwig, N., et al.: Machine learning to detect Alzheimer's disease from circulating non-coding RNAs. Genomics Proteomics Bioinform. **17**(4), 430–440 (2019)

51. Lugli, G., et al.: Plasma exosomal miRNAs in persons with and without Alzheimer disease: altered expression and prospects for biomarkers. PLoS ONE **10**(10), e0139233 (2015)
52. Lui, T.K., Cheung, K.S., Lui, K.L.: Machine learning models in the prediction of one-year mortality in patients with advanced hepatocellular cancer on immunotherapy. SSRN 3885156 (2021)
53. Lundberg, S.M., et al.: Explainable machine-learning predictions for the prevention of hypoxaemia during surgery. Nat. Biomed. Eng. **2**(10), 749–760 (2018)
54. Mahmud, T., et al.: CovTANet: a hybrid tri-level attention-based network for lesion segmentation, diagnosis, and severity prediction of COVID-19 chest CT scans. IEEE Trans. Ind. Inform. **17**(9), 6489–6498 (2020)
55. Malacova, E., et al.: Stillbirth risk prediction using machine learning for a large cohort of births from Western Australia, 1980–2015. Sci. Rep. **10**(1), 1–8 (2020)
56. Mohammed, E.A., Keyhani, M., Sanati-Nezhad, A., Hejazi, S.H., Far, B.H.: An ensemble learning approach to digital corona virus preliminary screening from cough sounds. Sci. Rep. **11**(1), 1–11 (2021)
57. Monk, A., et al.: Perinatal deaths in Australia 1993–2012 (2016)
58. Morris, R.S., et al.: Predictors of elderly mortality after trauma: a novel outcome score. J. Trauma Acute Care Surg. **88**(3), 416–424 (2020)
59. Myszczynska, M.A., et al.: Applications of machine learning to diagnosis and treatment of neurodegenerative diseases. Nat. Rev. Neurol. **16**(8), 440–456 (2020)
60. Nie, D., Zhang, H., Adeli, E., Liu, L., Shen, D.: 3D deep learning for multi-modal imaging-guided survival time prediction of brain tumor patients. In: Ourselin, S., Joskowicz, L., Sabuncu, M.R., Unal, G., Wells, W. (eds.) MICCAI 2016. LNCS, vol. 9901, pp. 212–220. Springer, Cham (2016). https://doi.org/10.1007/978-3-319-46723-8_25
61. Orabi, A.H., Buddhitha, P., Orabi, M.H., Inkpen, D.: Deep learning for depression detection of Twitter users. In: Proceedings of the Fifth Workshop on Computational Linguistics and Clinical Psychology: From Keyboard to Clinic, pp. 88–97 (2018)
62. Pahar, M., Klopper, M., Warren, R., Niesler, T.: COVID-19 cough classification using machine learning and global smartphone recordings. Comput. Biol. Med. **135**, 104572 (2021)
63. Pahar, M., Niesler, T.: Machine learning based COVID-19 detection from smartphone recordings: cough, breath and speech. arXiv preprint arXiv:2104.02477 (2021)
64. Pan, K., Hurault, G., Arulkumaran, K., Williams, H.C., Tanaka, R.J.: EczemaNet: automating detection and severity assessment of atopic dermatitis. In: Liu, M., Yan, P., Lian, C., Cao, X. (eds.) MLMI 2020. LNCS, vol. 12436, pp. 220–230. Springer, Cham (2020). https://doi.org/10.1007/978-3-030-59861-7_23
65. Pankratz, D.G., et al.: Usual interstitial pneumonia can be detected in transbronchial biopsies using machine learning. Ann. Am. Thorac. Soc. **14**(11), 1646–1654 (2017)
66. Parikh, R.B., et al.: Machine learning approaches to predict 6-month mortality among patients with cancer. JAMA Netw. Open **2**(10), e1915997 (2019)
67. Pinter, G., Felde, I., Mosavi, A., Ghamisi, P., Gloaguen, R.: COVID-19 pandemic prediction for Hungary; a hybrid machine learning approach. Mathematics **8**(6), 890 (2020)

68. Porieva, H., Ivanko, K., Semkiv, C., Vaityshyn, V.: Investigation of lung sounds features for detection of bronchitis and COPD using machine learning methods. Visnyk NTUU KPI Seriia-Radiotekhnika Radioaparatobuduvannia (84), 78–87 (2021)

69. Qu, Z., Liu, Q., Liu, C.: Classification of congestive heart failure with different New York heart association functional classes based on heart rate variability indices and machine learning. Expert. Syst. **36**(3), e12396 (2019)

70. Raita, Y., Goto, T., Faridi, M.K., Brown, D.F., Camargo, C.A., Hasegawa, K.: Emergency department triage prediction of clinical outcomes using machine learning models. Crit. Care **23**(1), 1–13 (2019)

71. Rasheed, J., Hameed, A.A., Djeddi, C., Jamil, A., Al-Turjman, F.: A machine learning-based framework for diagnosis of COVID-19 from chest X-ray images. Interdisc. Sci. Comput. Life Sci. **13**(1), 103–117 (2021). https://doi.org/10.1007/s12539-020-00403-6

72. Razavi-Termeh, S.V., Sadeghi-Niaraki, A., Choi, S.M.: Asthma-prone areas modeling using a machine learning model. Sci. Rep. **11**(1), 1–16 (2021)

73. Rowtula, V., Oota, S., Gupta, M., Surampudi, B.R.: A deep autoencoder for near-perfect fMRI encoding (2018)

74. Rumpold, H., et al.: Prediction of mortality in metastatic colorectal cancer in a real-life population: a multicenter explorative analysis. BMC Cancer **20**(1), 1–9 (2020)

75. Russell, S., Norvig, P.: Artificial intelligence: a modern approach (2002)

76. Sato, J.R., Moll, J., Green, S., Deakin, J.F., Thomaz, C.E., Zahn, R.: Machine learning algorithm accurately detects fMRI signature of vulnerability to major depression. Psychiatry Res. Neuroimaging **233**(2), 289–291 (2015)

77. Scheffler, R.M., Liu, J.X., Kinfu, Y., Dal Poz, M.R.: Forecasting the global shortage of physicians: an economic-and needs-based approach. Bull. World Health Organ. **86**, 516-523B (2008)

78. Senturk, Z.K.: Early diagnosis of Parkinson's disease using machine learning algorithms. Med. Hypotheses **138**, 109603 (2020)

79. Serviá, L., et al.: Machine learning techniques for mortality prediction in critical traumatic patients: anatomic and physiologic variables from the RETRAUCI study. BMC Med. Res. Methodol. **20**(1), 1–12 (2020)

80. Sharma, L.D., Sunkaria, R.K.: Inferior myocardial infarction detection using stationary wavelet transform and machine learning approach. SIViP **12**(2), 199–206 (2017). https://doi.org/10.1007/s11760-017-1146-z

81. Siegel, R.L., Miller, K.D., Jemal, A.: Cancer statistics, 2019. CA: A Cancer J. Clin. **69**(1), 7–34 (2019)

82. Silva, L.A.V., Rohr, K.: Pan-cancer prognosis prediction using multimodal deep learning. In: 2020 IEEE 17th International Symposium on Biomedical Imaging (ISBI), pp. 568–571. IEEE (2020)

83. Simpraga, S., et al.: EEG machine learning for accurate detection of cholinergic intervention and Alzheimer's disease. Sci. Rep. **7**(1), 1–11 (2017)

84. Singh, P.K., Krishna, C.M.: Continuum arm robotic manipulator: a review. Univers. J. Mech. Eng. **2**(6), 193–198 (2014)

85. Spathis, D., Vlamos, P.: Diagnosing asthma and chronic obstructive pulmonary disease with machine learning. Health Inform. J. **25**(3), 811–827 (2019)

86. Steardo, L., Jr., et al.: Application of support vector machine on fMRI data as biomarkers in schizophrenia diagnosis: a systematic review. Front. Psychiatry **11**, 588 (2020)

87. Surampudi, S.G., Naik, S., Surampudi, R.B., Jirsa, V.K., Sharma, A., Roy, D.: Multiple kernel learning model for relating structural and functional connectivity in the brain. Sci. Rep. **8**(1), 1–14 (2018)

88. Sweatt, A.J., et al.: Discovery of distinct immune phenotypes using machine learning in pulmonary arterial hypertension. Circ. Res. **124**(6), 904–919 (2019)

89. Swift, A.J., et al.: A machine learning cardiac magnetic resonance approach to extract disease features and automate pulmonary arterial hypertension diagnosis. Eur. Heart J.-Cardiovasc. Imaging **22**(2), 236–245 (2021)

90. Tabibu, S., Vinod, P., Jawahar, C.: Pan-Renal Cell Carcinoma classification and survival prediction from histopathology images using deep learning. Sci. Rep. **9**(1), 1–9 (2019)

91. Tagaris, A., Kollias, D., Stafylopatis, A., Tagaris, G., Kollias, S.: Machine learning for neurodegenerative disorder diagnosis-survey of practices and launch of benchmark dataset. Int. J. Artif. Intell. Tools **27**(03), 1850011 (2018)

92. Tang, W., Cao, Y., Ma, X.: Novel prognostic prediction model constructed through machine learning on the basis of methylation-driven genes in kidney renal clear cell carcinoma. Biosci. Rep. **40**(7), BSR20201604 (2020)

93. Than, M.P., et al.: Machine learning to predict the likelihood of acute myocardial infarction. Circulation **140**(11), 899–909 (2019)

94. Toğaçar, M., Ergen, B., Cömert, Z., Özyurt, F.: A deep feature learning model for pneumonia detection applying a combination of mRMR feature selection and machine learning models. Irbm **41**(4), 212–222 (2020)

95. Trakadis, Y.J., Sardaar, S., Chen, A., Fulginiti, V., Krishnan, A.: Machine learning in schizophrenia genomics, a case-control study using 5,090 exomes. Am. J. Med. Genet. B Neuropsychiatr. Genet. **180**(2), 103–112 (2019)

96. Tschandl, P., et al.: Comparison of the accuracy of human readers versus machine-learning algorithms for pigmented skin lesion classification: an open, web-based, international, diagnostic study. Lancet Oncol. **20**(7), 938–947 (2019)

97. Tzimourta, K.D., et al.: Machine learning algorithms and statistical approaches for Alzheimer's disease analysis based on resting-state EEG recordings: a systematic review. Int. J. Neural Syst. **31**(5), 2130002 (2021)

98. Udrea, A., et al.: Accuracy of a smartphone application for triage of skin lesions based on machine learning algorithms. J. Eur. Acad. Dermatol. Venereol. **34**(3), 648–655 (2020)

99. Umapathy, S., Sampath, M., Nelufer, Srivastava, S.: Automated segmentation and classification of psoriasis hand thermal images using machine learning algorithm. In: Thakkar, F., Saha, G., Shahnaz, C., Hu, Y.C. (eds.) Proceedings of the International e-Conference on Intelligent Systems and Signal Processing. AISC, vol. 1370, pp. 487–496. Springer, Singapore (2022). https://doi.org/10.1007/978-981-16-2123-9_37

100. Vaka, A.R., Soni, B., Reddy, S.: Breast cancer detection by leveraging machine learning. ICT Express **6**(4), 320–324 (2020)

101. Vijayakumar, T.: Classification of brain cancer type using machine learning. J. Artif. Intell. **1**(02), 105–113 (2019)

102. Vivanco, R., Roberts, D.: Predicting patients likely to overstay in hospitals. In: 2011 10th International Conference on Machine Learning and Applications and Workshops, vol. 2, pp. 168–171. IEEE (2011)

103. Wan, N., et al.: Machine learning enables detection of early-stage colorectal cancer by whole-genome sequencing of plasma cell-free DNA. BMC Cancer **19**(1), 1–10 (2019). https://doi.org/10.1186/s12885-019-6003-8

104. Wang, C., et al.: Development and validation of a predictive model for coronary artery disease using machine learning. Front. Cardiovasc. Med. **8**, 43 (2021)
105. Wang, D., Mo, J., Zhou, G., Xu, L., Liu, Y.: An efficient mixture of deep and machine learning models for COVID-19 diagnosis in chest X-ray images. PLoS ONE **15**(11), e0242535 (2020)
106. Wang, K., et al.: Clinical and laboratory predictors of in-hospital mortality in patients with COVID-19: a cohort study in Wuhan. China. Clin. Infect. Dis. **71**(16), 2079–2088 (2020)
107. Wang, P., Zheng, X., Li, J., Zhu, B.: Prediction of epidemic trends in COVID-19 with logistic model and machine learning technics. Chaos, Solitons Fractals **139**, 110058 (2020)
108. Wang, Z., Zhu, Y., Li, D., Yin, Y., Zhang, J.: Feature rearrangement based deep learning system for predicting heart failure mortality. Comput. Methods Programs Biomed. **191**, 105383 (2020)
109. Weiss, J.C., Natarajan, S., Peissig, P.L., McCarty, C.A., Page, D.: Machine learning for personalized medicine: predicting primary myocardial infarction from electronic health records. AI Mag. **33**(4), 33–33 (2012)
110. Wheeler, M.: Overview on robotics in the laboratory. Ann. Clin. Biochem. **44**(3), 209–218 (2007)
111. Wijnberge, M., et al.: The use of a machine-learning algorithm that predicts hypotension during surgery in combination with personalized treatment guidance: study protocol for a randomized clinical trial. Trials **20**(1), 1–9 (2019)
112. Yala, A., et al.: Using machine learning to parse breast pathology reports. Breast Cancer Res. Treat. **161**(2), 203–211 (2016). https://doi.org/10.1007/s10549-016-4035-1
113. Yan, L., et al.: An interpretable mortality prediction model for COVID-19 patients. Nat. Mach. Intell. **2**(5), 283–288 (2020)
114. Yuan, Q., et al.: Performance of a machine learning algorithm using electronic health record data to identify and estimate survival in a longitudinal cohort of patients with lung cancer. JAMA Netw. Open **4**(7), e2114723 (2021)
115. Zarrin, P.S., Roeckendorf, N., Wrenger, C.: In vitro classification of saliva samples of COPD patients and healthy controls using machine learning tools. IEEE Access **8**, 168053–168060 (2020)
116. Zhang, L.: EEG signals classification using machine learning for the identification and diagnosis of schizophrenia. In: 2019 41st Annual International Conference of the IEEE Engineering in Medicine and Biology Society (EMBC), pp. 4521–4524. IEEE (2019)
117. Zhou, M., Zhao, H., Wang, X., Sun, J., Su, J.: Analysis of long noncoding RNAs highlights region-specific altered expression patterns and diagnostic roles in Alzheimer's disease. Brief. Bioinform. **20**(2), 598–608 (2019)
118. Zoabi, Y., Deri-Rozov, S., Shomron, N.: Machine learning-based prediction of COVID-19 diagnosis based on symptoms. npj Digit. Med. **4**(1), 1–5 (2021)

An Introduction to Graph Neural Networks from a Distributed Computing Perspective

Pál András Papp and Roger Wattenhofer[⊠]

ETH Zürich, Zürich, Switzerland
{apapp,wattenhofer}@ethz.ch

Abstract. The paper provides an introduction into the theoretical expressiveness of graph neural networks. We discuss the basic properties and main applications of standard GNN models, and we show how these constructions are both upper and lower bounded in expressive power by the Weisfeiler-Lehman test. We then outline a wide variety of approaches to increase the expressiveness of GNNs above this theoretical limit, and discuss the strengths and weaknesses of these methods.

Keywords: Graph Neural Network · Distributed computing · Weisfeiler-Lehman test · Expressive power

1 Introduction

Graph Neural Networks (GNNs) are one of the recent success stories in machine learning. They have first been developed in [6,16], and have been the subject of intensive study in the past few years [8]. GNNs have achieved remarkable results in a very wide range of applications, such as chemistry, physical systems, social science or recommendation systems [5,13,19].

This paper provides a brief introduction into GNNs from a distributed computing perspective. While the practical properties and concrete applications of GNNs are also interesting and extensively studied topics, we mostly focus on the theoretical capabilities of GNNs, and in particular: (i) what GNNs can learn in theory, (ii) what is beyond their expressive power, (iii) and how we can extend the GNN concept in order to increase this expressive power. It turns out that these questions are closely related to some variants of classical message passing model in distributed computing.

2 Model and Background

2.1 Preliminaries

Similarly to distributed message passing algorithms, GNNs operate on graphs. For simplicity, we will assume that these graphs are simple, unweighted, undirected.

R. Bapi et al. (Eds.): ICDCIT 2022, LNCS 13145, pp. 26–44, 2022.
https://doi.org/10.1007/978-3-030-94876-4_2

We denote the set of nodes and edges by V and E, respectively. Individual nodes of the graph are mostly denoted by u or v, the number of nodes in the graph by $n = |V|$.

The neighborhood of u is denoted by $N(u)$, the degree of u by $\delta(u) = |N(u)|$. We assume for convenience that the graph has a bounded degree, i.e. $\delta(u) \leq \Delta$ for all $u \in V$ and some global constant Δ; this is indeed realistic e.g. in many chemical or biological applications.

In contrast to most message passing models, nodes in a GNN do not have identifiers; instead they have input *features*, which describe some properties of the node. We can assume that features are represented as real numbers. Unlike IDs, these features might not be unique. To make our examples simpler, we will assume that a node only has a single feature. However, in most applications, nodes actually have d different features, and thus the features of a node are stored as a vector $\in \mathbb{R}^d$.

We also apply the double brackets notation $\{\{\cdot\}\}$ to denote a multiset, i.e. where the same element can appear multiple times.

2.2   Graph Neural Networks

A GNN is similar to the popular message passing model in distributed computing: the GNN operates in rounds, and nodes communicate with their neighbors in each round.

Definition 1. *A Graph Neural Network (GNN) operates in synchronous rounds. In each round, every node v independently computes a new state; we denote the state of v after time step t by $h_v^{(t)}$. The initial state $h_v^{(0)}$ is the node feature(s) of v.*

The state in time step t is always computed from (i) the node's own state $h_v^{(t-1)}$ in the previous time step, and (ii) the state $h_u^{(t-1)}$ of the nodes' neighbors $u \in N(v)$ in the previous time step. More specifically, GNNs are described in terms of two functions:

$$a_v^{(t)} = \text{AGGREGATE}\left(\{\{h_u^{(t-1)} \mid u \in N(v)\}\}\right)$$

and

$$h_v^{(t)} = \text{UPDATE}\left(h_v^{(t-1)}, a_v^{(t)}\right),$$

where AGGREGATE *is a permutation-invariant function.*

In the machine learning literature, the states of nodes are usually called embeddings. Furthermore, the rounds of computation are also called *layers*. We will denote the number of rounds/layers by r, where r is usually a small constant.

In more sophisticated GNN models, the AGGREGATE and UPDATE functions may also depend on the time step t. However, they cannot depend on the node v, since each node uses the same function (similarly to an orthodox distributed model, where each node executes the same program).

One of the key concepts in this definition is the permutation-invariance of the AGGREGATE function; intuitively, this means that if the same multiset of states was distributed in any other way among the neighbors, then the function would still return the same value. It is very natural to wonder how one can implement an AGGREGATE function in practice that is permutation-invariant on the one hand, but still sufficiently expressive.

Example 1. Aggregation is often implemented as

$$\text{AGGREGATE}(M) := \mathcal{A}\left(\{\{f(i) \mid i \in M\}\}\right),$$

where f is some transformation $f : \mathbb{R} \to \mathbb{R}$, and $\mathcal{A}$ is one of the following permutation-invariant functions: MAX, MEAN, SUM.

In the simplest case, the transformation f is implemented as

$$f(x) := \sigma(w \cdot x),$$

where $w \in \mathbb{R}$ is a learnable weight, and σ is a simple non-linearity. The input x of the function commonly also includes a constant value 1.

Executing a transformation f before $\mathcal{A}$ ensures that the GNN can represent a large class of functions. The non-linearity σ is usually a simple function such as the step function ($\sigma(x) = 0$ for $x < 0$, $\sigma(x) = 1$ for $x \geq 0$), a ReLU ($\sigma(x) = 0$ for $x < 0$, $\sigma(x) = x$ for $x \geq 0$), or some kind of a sigmoid. Note that if the states are in $\mathbb{R}^d$ instead of just $\mathbb{R}$, then the transformation is a function $f : \mathbb{R}^d \to \mathbb{R}^d$, $W \in \mathbb{R}^{d \times d}$ is a matrix, and σ is applied element-wise on each cell of $w \cdot x$.

The main idea behind GNNs is that the functions defining a GNN are not all hard-coded. That is, while $\mathcal{A}$ and σ are usually decided in advance, the weight w is *learnt* by the neural network on a large set of data; that is, weights are adjusted repeatedly during training, until the output of the GNNs (the final state) is of good enough quality. Discussing the details of this standard training procedure (backpropagation) is beyond the scope of this paper.

Applications often use a more sophisticated function f; for example, a so-called multi-layer perceptron (MLP), which is a neural network formed from the repeated application of the transformation $f(x) = \sigma(w \cdot x)$, with a different choice of weights on different levels. It is known that MLPs can approximate any continuous $\mathbb{R} \to \mathbb{R}$ function, which hints that with such a powerful f, GNNs are rather expressive.

Example 2. Let us construct an example GNN to decide if a node v is adjacent to a leaf node. Assume for convenience that the initial node features are the degrees: $h_v^{(0)} = \delta(v)$. Then we can easily solve this task by a 1-layer GNN that has

$$\text{AGGREGATE}(N(v)) = \text{MAX}(-h_u^{(t-1)} \mid u \in N(v))$$

and

$$\text{UPDATE}(h_v^{(t-1)}, a_v^{(t)}) = -a_v^{(t)}.$$

This ensures that if $h_v^{(1)} = 1$, then v has an adjacent leaf neighbor, whereas if $h_v^{(1)} \neq 1$, then this is not the case.

2.3   Comparison to Distributed Algorithms

GNNs are in many ways similar to our distributed algorithms in the message passing model: for a given number of rounds r, they aggregate messages from their neighbors, execute a computation, and then they pass on the new states to their neighbors again. However, there are also some key differences.

- The most obvious difference is that GNNs do not have infinite computational power: they can only compute the next state with the formulas above.
- Furthermore, GNNs do not have the ability to send different, specialized messages to different neighbors: their current node state is essentially their entire view of the world, and they can only pass on this node state to each of their neighbors in each round.
- As mentioned before, nodes do not have unique identifiers in the GNN setting. Hence symmetry breaking and distinguishing specific structures are some of the main challenges.
- Finally, nodes do not have a *port numbering*, i.e. they cannot distinguish their different neighbors. This means that if the neighbor states form a multiset $M = \{\{h_u^{(t)} \mid u \in N(v)\}\}$, then any other permutation of M along the neighbors would also produce the same next state $h_v^{(t+1)}$. In this framework, a node might not even be able to execute simple tasks that are fundamental steps in classical distributed algorithms, e.g. decide if it has received the same message from a specific neighbor in two consecutive rounds.

2.4   Applications of GNNs

So what kind of graph-related questions do we want to answer with a GNN? We know that GNNs compute a final state $h_v^{(r)}$ for each node v. In the simplest case, node labels are already what we are looking for in the first place.

Definition 2. *In a node classification task, we want to compute (or approximate) a function $V \to \mathbb{R}$. For example, we want to compute some property of the nodes (represented as a real number or vector), or we want to partition the nodes into different classes.*

The final state of the node can be interpreted as the value of this property, or the label of the class we sort the node into. As such, a GNN can be directly applied to solve a node classification task. For a more sophisticated classification, it is also a common method to apply a function $g(h_v^{(0)}, h_v^{(1)}, \ldots, h_v^{(r)})$ which predicts the final label of v from all the states it had during the different rounds.

In other applications, however, node states are not even the end of the story.

Definition 3. *In a graph classification task, we want to estimate a function that is dependent on the entire graph; i.e. a function $\mathcal{G} \to \mathbb{R}$, where $\mathcal{G}$ denotes the set of all possible input graphs.*

For example, given the structure of a specific molecule, we want to estimate some physical or chemical property of the molecule.

In case of graph classification, we can collect the set of states of each node into a multiset M with $|M| = n$, and learn a so-called READOUT function $\mathcal{M} \to \mathbb{R}$ for the graph classification task, where $\mathcal{M}$ denotes the set of all multisets of size n. E.g. if each state $h_u^{(r)}$ describes how faulty node u is, then we could simply compute $\sum_{u \in V} h_u^{(r)}$ as the total "faultiness" of the entire network. For a classification task, we could also introduce a threshold θ, e.g. $\theta = 3$ or $\theta = \frac{1}{5} \cdot n$, and classify a network as too faulty if $\sum_{u \in V} h_u^{(r)} \geq \theta$. For another example, if we compute an state where $h_u^{(r)} = 1$ if node u satisfies some (local) constraint and $h_u^{(r)} = 0$ otherwise, then a READOUT aggregation with $\text{AND}_{u \in V}$ allows us to decide if the constraint is fulfilled at every node in the graph.

Finally, another popular task is link prediction.

Definition 4. *In a* link prediction *task, there is an original graph G, but we only see a subset of the edges, i.e. we see another graph G' where some of the edges of G are missing. Given a specific pair of nodes u and v, our task is to predict whether the edge (u, v) is present in the original graph G.*

In this case, we can learn a function $\mathbb{R} \times \mathbb{R} \to [0, 1]$ which takes the states $h_u^{(r)}$ and $h_v^{(r)}$ of u and v as inputs, and outputs the estimated probability of the edge (u, v) being present in the graph.

3 Limits of GNNs: The WL-Test

Given this overview of the GNN framework, it is very natural to wonder what GNNs can or cannot compute.

3.1 Different Aggregation Methods

Recall from Example 1 that some of the popular permutation-invariant aggregation functions for $\mathcal{A}$ are MAX, MEAN and SUM. One might wonder which of these three functions is the best choice. Not surprisingly, this depends on the concrete application. The example below already shows that their expressive power is somewhat different.

Example 3 (from [18]). In the example graphs of Fig. 1, consider the state of v after using a GNN with a single layer ($r = 1$). The different node features are shown by colors; for simplicity, assume that the orange feature corresponds to 1, and the green feature corresponds to 2. Also, assume that we execute no transformation before aggregating the values, i.e. $f(x) = x$ in the formula of Example 1.

MAX aggregation cannot even distinguish the left and middle graphs, since it returns 2 in both cases. However, MEAN can distinguish them: it returns 1.66 for the first graph, and 1.5 for the second.

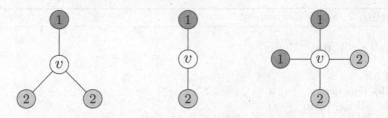

Fig. 1. An example for the limits of different aggregators. (Color figure online)

However, even MEAN aggregation cannot distinguish the middle and right examples: it returns 1.5 in both cases. On the other hand, SUM can distinguish these, too: it returns 3 for the middle graph, and 6 for the right-hand graph.

Note that the choice of f does not matter for the example above: for two nodes with the same feature $h_v^{(0)}$, the value of $f(h_v^{(0)})$ is the same as well.

This example suggests that MEAN aggregation is more expressive than MAX, and SUM is more expressive than MEAN. It is indeed true that in terms of representative power, SUM is the strongest one of these options. However, SUM might not always be the best choice in practice. For example, MEAN has the useful property that the output does not scale with the number of neighbors. One can also find simple examples where MAX provides an easy solution.

3.2 The Weisfeiler-Lehman Algorithm

So let us now revisit our original, general question: how can we describe the functions that GNNs can compute? In order to answer this, we first make a brief detour to the so-called Weisfeiler-Lehman algorithm on graphs, also known as the state refinement (or color refinement) algorithm.

In the beginning of this algorithm, each node v has the same initial state $s_v^{(0)}$, and these states are refined through multiple rounds. Throughout the algorithm, the state of a given node essentially represents its current knowledge about its local neighborhood.

The pseudocode of the algorithm is shown in Algorithm 1. The RELABEL function is essentially a hash function which assigns a different state to each possible configuration in the neighborhood of the node. More formally, RELABEL is an injective function $\mathbb{R} \times \mathcal{M} \to \mathbb{R}$, where $\mathcal{M}$ denotes all possible multisets of $\mathbb{R}$. Intuitively speaking, this means that if two nodes u and v have the same state in iteration t, then they will receive a different state in the next time step if and only if there exists a state s such that u and v have a different number of neighbors that are in state s at time step t. E.g. after the first round of the algorithm, two nodes have the same state if and only if they have the same degree.

Note that there is no termination condition in the pseudocode: the algorithm runs forever. However, in practice, we are only interested in further refinement steps as long as the algorithm actually makes progress, i.e. it distinguishes more nodes from each other.

Algorithm 1. State Refinement

1: $t = 0$
2: **for all** $v \in V$ **do**
3:     $s_v^{(0)} = 0$
4: **end for**
5: **while** True **do**
6:     **for all** $v \in V$ **do**
7:         $s_v^{(t+1)} = \text{RELABEL}\left(s_v^{(t)}, \{\{s_u^{(t)} \mid u \in N(v)\}\} \right)$
8:     **end for**
9:     $t = t + 1$
10: **end while**

Definition 5. *We say that state refinement has finished in time step t if there exist no pair of vertices u, v such that $s_u^{(t)} = s_v^{(t)}$, but $s_u^{(t+1)} \neq s_v^{(t+1)}$.*

Theorem 1. *The state refinement algorithm finishes in at most n rounds.*

Proof. If the algorithm has not terminated after round t, then this means that there are two vertices u and v such that $s_u^{(t-1)} = s_v^{(t-1)}$, but $s_u^{(t)} \neq s_v^{(t)}$. On the other hand, if nodes u and v have different states in round t, then they also have different states in all subsequent rounds $t' > t$.

Hence the number of different states that are present in the graph strictly increases in each round. Since this can be at most n, the algorithm finishes after at most n rounds.

This state refinement algorithm is commonly known as the *Weisfeiler-Lehman (WL) algorithm*. The algorithm was developed as a fundamental heuristic to test the isomorphism of graphs. Graph isomorphism is a fundamental problem in theoretical computer science: intuitively, if two graphs are isomorphic, then they are "essentially the same", but the nodes are (possibly) presented in a different order.

Definition 6. *Two graphs $G_1(V_1, E_1)$ and $G_2(V_2, E_2)$ are isomorphic if there exists a bijection $\pi : V_1 \to V_2$ such that for any $u, v \in V_1$, we have $(u, v) \in E_1$ if and only if $(\pi(u), \pi(v)) \in E_2$.*

Deciding if G_1 and G_2 are isomorphic is a fundamental problem, but it is rather difficult: we do not know how to solve it in polynomial time, even in a centralized setting. Think about a naive algorithm that checks all possible bijections π: this would take $\Omega(n!)$ time.

After running the state refinement algorithm on both G_1 and G_2, we can test isomorphism with the function in Algorithm 2. The equality of multisets can be checked, for example, by sorting both multisets, and then comparing the corresponding elements. If these so-called *canonical forms* of two graphs are not equivalent, then the two graphs are certainly not isomorphic. However, if the canonical forms are equivalent, then it is still possible that the graphs are not isomorphic, but the test was unable to detect this. In other words, the algorithm is a one-sided isomorphism test.

Algorithm 2. Isomorphism testing after state refinement

1: $M_1 = \{\{s_v \mid v \in V_1\}\}$ and $M_2 = \{\{s_v \mid v \in V_2\}\}$
2: **if** $M_1 = M_2$ **then**
3:   output "maybe isomorphic"
4: **else**
5:   output "not isomorphic"
6: **end if**

Some examples for non-isomorphic graphs that are not distinguished by the Weisfeiler-Lehman algorithm are as follows.

Example 4. The two 8-node graphs in Fig. 2 are non-isomorphic: one of them consists of two 4-cycles, the other consists of a single 8-cycle.

Since each node begins with the same state s and each node has exactly two neighbors in state s, RELABEL assigns the same new state to each node. Hence the algorithm already terminates in the first round on both graphs, and the multisets M_1 and M_2 are identical; the algorithm outputs "maybe isomorphic".

Example 5. The two graphs in Fig. 3 are again non-isomorphic; for example, one of them has a triangle, but the other one does not.

In the first state refinement step, nodes receive different states based on their degree. In the second step, however, nodes in the same state already all have the same multiset of states in their neighborhoods, so the algorithm terminates. The multiset of states is the same in the two graphs.

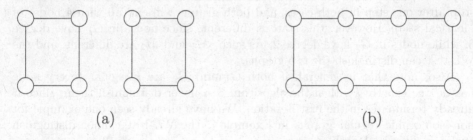

(a)   (b)

Fig. 2. Two graphs on 8 nodes, consisting of cycles of different length.

Example 6. Figure 4 is a slight variation of Fig. 3, where the process goes on for three iterations instead of two, again outputting "maybe isomorphic". The graphs in this case correspond to two different molecules, Decalin and Bicyclopentyl.

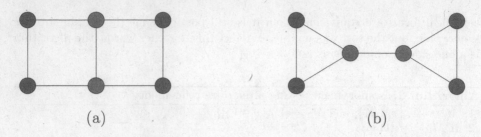

Fig. 3. Two graphs that cannot be distinguished by the WL algorithm.

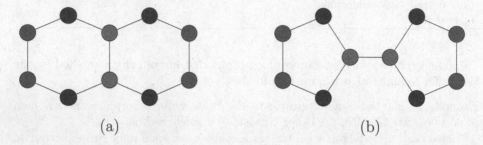

Fig. 4. Two graphs that cannot be distinguished by the WL algorithm.

The WL-test is one of the most well-known heuristics for isomorphism testing, and it has been the subject of intensive study for decades [3,7,17]. The algorithm is also one of the main ingredients of Babai's celebrated result on the complexity of the isomorphism problem [1].

We point out that for the full power of the algorithm, it is important that we compare the actual states in M_1 and M_2, and not just the number of the occurrences of each state. For example, consider a clique on 4 nodes as G_1, and a cycle of length 4 as G_2. Both graphs are regular, so the refinement process will stop after one step in both cases, and both graphs will end up with 4 nodes of identical state. However, this state is different, since nodes in G_1 have degree 3, while nodes in G_2 have degree 2. As such, M_1 and M_2 are different, and the WL-test can distinguish the two graphs.

Also, note that in general, if both G_1 and G_2 are k-regular (every node has degree exactly k), then the algorithm can never distinguish them, since it already terminates in the first iteration. We have already seen one example for non-isomorphic regular graphs in Example 4: the WL-test cannot distinguish cycles of different length.

On the positive side, it was shown that the majority of graphs can indeed be distinguished by the algorithm, and the algorithm can also always distinguish some special kinds of graphs such as trees [3].

3.3 The WL-Test and GNNs

It turns out that the WL-test is closely related to GNNs. Let us assume that a GNN begins with no information on the nodes, i.e. any two nodes u, v have the same features $h_u^{(0)} = h_v^{(0)}$.

Theorem 2 (from [18]). *If two nodes u and v in G have the same state $s_u^{(r)} = s_v^{(r)}$ after r rounds of the state refinement algorithm, then any r-layer GNN on G will compute the same final states for the nodes: $h_u^{(r)} = h_v^{(r)}$.*

Proof. We can prove this by induction, showing that the states $h_u^{(t)}$ and $h_v^{(t)}$ are identical after each time step $t \in \{0, ..., r\}$. For $t = 0$, this is straightforward, since all nodes begin with the same feature.

For a general t, assume that the statement is already proven for $t-1$. Assume that u and v still have the same state in round t; due to the state refinement algorithm, this implies that they had the same state $s_u^{(t-1)} = s_v^{(t-1)}$ at time $t - 1$, and the same multiset of states in their neighborhood: $\{\{s_{u'}^{(t-1)} \mid u' \in N(u)\}\} = \{\{s_{v'}^{(t-1)} \mid v' \in N(v)\}\}$. Due to the induction hypothesis, this means that $h_{u'}^{(t-1)} = h_{v'}^{(t-1)}$ and $\{\{h_{u'}^{(t-1)} \mid u' \in N(u)\}\} = \{\{h_{v'}^{(t-1)} \mid v' \in N(v)\}\}$ in our GNN. However, then according to the formulas in Definition 1, the nodes will also have the same state $h_u^{(t)} = h_v^{(t)}$.

This shows that the expressive power of GNNs is *at most as high* as that of the WL-test: if the WL algorithm fails two distinguish two graphs, then a GNN will also produce the same result on these graphs. For example, for several applications, it is important to know whether a node is contained in a triangle. However, as Example 5 shows, GNNs are unable to decide this from the final state of a node: the blue nodes in the left graph are contained in a triangle, while the blue nodes in the right graph are not. According to Theorem 2, these blue nodes will end up with the same final state in the two graphs.

It is natural to wonder about the other direction: are GNNs indeed as powerful as the WL-test? It turns out that they are.

Theorem 3 (from [18]). *There exists an r-layer GNN that fulfills the following property: if two nodes u and v have a different state $s_u^{(r)} \neq s_v^{(r)}$ after r rounds of state refinement, then the GNN assigns different final states $h_u^{(r)} \neq h_v^{(r)}$ to u and v.*

Proof Sketch. We only outline the main idea of the proof, which is quite natural: if both AGGREGATE and UPDATE are injective on their domain, then whenever two nodes receive a different state in the state refinement, they also receive a different state in the GNN. Through another induction, this shows that if the final states of u and v are different, then also $h_u^{(r)} \neq h_v^{(r)}$. It only remains to show an example for an injective AGGREGATE and UPDATE function.

In case of AGGREGATE, we show that there exists a function f such that $\sum_{x \in M} f(x)$ is different for every multiset M over the possible states. As a technicality, the theorem assumes that node features come from a countable set X, i.e. there is a mapping $Z : X \to \mathbb{Z}^+$. Since the degree of the graph is bounded by Δ, we can select a large integer $\ell > \Delta$; this ensures that for any multiset M we encounter, we have $|M| < \ell$.

Now let us define $f(x) = \ell^{Z(x)}$ for any $x \in X$. This ensures that $\sum_{x \in M} f(x)$ is indeed unique for any multiset M: it essentially encodes the multiset as a number in ℓ-ary format, where each position corresponds to a specific value in $x \in X$, and the digit at the position describes the multiplicity of x in M. Hence this AGGREGATE function is indeed injective.

Given this sum, an injective UPDATE function can be created in several ways. A simple solution is to define it as $\alpha \cdot h_v^{(t-1)} + a_v^{(t)}$, where α is a freely chosen irrational number. A specific $h_v^{(t)}$ then uniquely determines the corresponding $h_v^{(t-1)}$ and $a_v^{(t)}$.

Finally, it follows from classical results in machine learning (the so-called universal approximation theorem) that if this function exists, then a GNN can indeed learn this function if AGGREGATE and UPDATE are implemented by, for example, a multi-layer perceptron.

This means that the most powerful GNNs we can design are exactly as powerful as the state refinement algorithm!

Intuitively speaking, the construction of injective functions also shows that whenever we can describe an algorithm in the corresponding message passing model (constantly many rounds, not distinguishing a node's neighbors, no node IDs), then a GNN can indeed express the function computed by the algorithm. This allows us to discuss the expressiveness of GNNs on a higher abstraction level, and ignore the details of the actual implementation. Of course, this only describes the theoretical capabilities of a GNN – whether a GNN in practice can indeed *learn* such complicated functions is another question.

4   More Expressive GNNs

The examples in Figs. 2, 3 and 4 show that some neighborhoods cannot be distinguished by the WL algorithm, and hence also not by GNNs. This raises a natural question: how can we make GNNs more expressive?

4.1   Port Numbers

One natural approach is to introduce port numbers into our model [14].

Definition 7. *In a GNN with port numbers, each node v numbers its incident edges from 1 to $\delta(v)$, and the domain of* AGGREGATE *is not a multiset as before, but a vector $\mathbb{R}^\Delta$, which allows the result to depend on the different neighbors in a different way.*

More formally, the domain of the AGGREGATE *function is $\hat{\mathbb{R}}^\Delta$, where $\hat{\mathbb{R}} = \mathbb{R} \cup \{\perp\}$, and $\perp$ is a special symbol denoting that the node does not have a neighbor with the given port number.*

Of course, there are multiple ways a node can number its incident edges. Hence in these GNNs, the final state also depends on the port numbers assigned to the edges: for a different assignment of port numbers in the same graph, the nodes might compute a different state! As such, besides the challenge of distinguishing non-isomorphic graphs from each other, this setting also raises a dual problem: to ensure that isomorphic graphs are not distinguished accidentally.

Also, port numbers are still not always enough to distinguish our examples.

Theorem 4 (from [4]). *GNNs with port numbers are still unable to distinguish some of the previous examples in case of an unlucky port numbering.*

Proof. Consider Fig. 5, which is an extension of the graph in Fig. 2 with port numbers and some node features (colors). However, port numbers and features are chosen such that the two graphs still cannot be distinguished by a GNN.

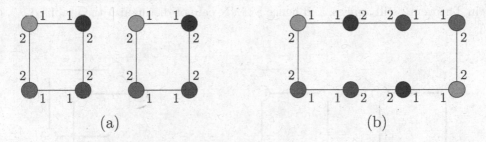

(a)   (b)

Fig. 5. Graphs that cannot be distinguished even with port numbers.

Note that introducing port numbers brings our setting significantly closer to classical distributed algorithms. In particular, one can adapt the construction of injective functions in Theorem 3 to this model with port numbers; this essentially means that the resulting GNNs have the same expressive power as the so-called anonymous model of distributed computing. It also follows that upper and lower bounds for the solvability of combinatorial problems in the anonymous model also carry over to this GNN model [14].

4.2   Domain-Specific Extra Features

A more practice-oriented approach is to apply further insights from the given application area, e.g. by adding more node features which help us distinguish the different cases. For example, in molecule modelling, one possibility is to also measure the angles of the different edges between the graphs, and add this as an extra node feature to each node [9].

Definition 8. *In a GNN with angles, we assume that there is a given position for each node in a 2- or 3-dimensional space. The angles between the incident edges of v are added to $h_v^{(0)}$ as node features.*

Note that this raises some difficult representation questions about storing these angles: we either have to tie these features to pairs of edges, or we have to come up with a structured way to store all the $\binom{\delta(v)}{2}$ angles at each node v. For simplicity, we will only consider some specific graphs now where each node has degree two; this means that each node only needs to store exactly 1 angle parameter, i.e. a single extra feature.

However, given an unlucky geometric embedding, there are graphs that still cannot be distinguished with this method.

Theorem 5 (from [4]). *Even if we add the angles of edges as extra features, there are non-isomorphic graphs G_1, G_2 that cannot be distinguished by GNNs.*

Proof. Consider the graphs in Fig. 6, which are embeddings of the (non-isomorphic) graphs in Fig. 2 in 3-dimensional space. For all nodes in both graphs, the two incident edges have an angle of 90° between them, so in any representation, all nodes begin with the same feature. This means that the upper bound in Theorem 2 still applies, and hence a GNN cannot distinguish the graphs.

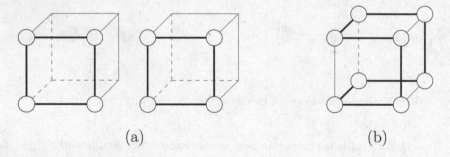

(a)   (b)

Fig. 6. Two graphs that cannot be distinguished even with angle features.

4.3   Random Features

Another approach from the theoretical side is to do symmetry breaking by introducing random features to each node. That is, we increase the dimension d of the feature vector by 1, and into this final slot of the vector, we insert a uniform random integer in $\{1, ..., L\}$ (for some constant L), which is chosen independently for each node. This approach was introduced in [15].

Definition 9. *In a GNN with random features, we assign a new random feature to each node, i.e. an integer chosen uniformly at random from $\{1, ..., L\}$ (for some constant limit L), independently from other nodes.*

With this approach, an algorithm can now recognize that two nodes observed on two different paths actually correspond to the same node. That is, if the random features are more-or-less unique in the neighborhood (which becomes probable if the neighborhood has bounded size and L is large enough), then we can essentially use them as pseudoIDs, and we obtain a model that is again quite close to classical distributed algorithms.

Example 7. Random IDs already allow us to separate cycles of different length. Consider a graph G_1 that consists of 2 disjoint 3-cycles, versus a graph G_2 which consists of a single 6-cycle, as in Fig. 7. Both in G_1 and G_2, a standard GNN with 3-layers will observe the same structure.

However, let us add a random feature to each node, and assume that L is high enough such that all the six nodes receive a different pseudoID with decent probability. In this case, a node in G_1 will always see a node with the same pseudoID in a 3-hop distance, whereas in G_2, this will not happen when the pseudoIDs are unique. Based on this information, a sufficiently powerful GNN can distinguish the two graphs.

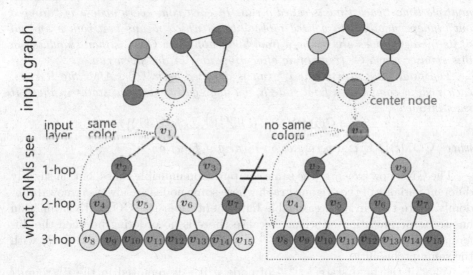

Fig. 7. (from [15]) Distinguishing cycles of different length with random features.

For this GNN variant, one can prove an even stronger result: in theory, it can distinguish any two distinct neighborhoods.

Theorem 6 (from [15]). *For any set of bounded-degree local neighborhoods S, there exists a GNN with weights such that for each node v,*

- *if the r-hop neighborhood of v is isomorphic to a graph in S, then $h_v^{(r)} > 0.5$ with high probability.*

– if the r-hop neighborhood of v is not isomorphic to any graph in S, then $h_v^{(r)} < 0.5$ with high probability.

However, while this sounds convincing in theory, the approach has some notable drawbacks when applied in practice. In particular, if we train a GNN with random features, it often learns to distinguish different structures by learning how the different random features relate to each other. If we apply these learnt functions later in a situation where the random features happen to have a different relation to each other, then our learnt functions might return something that is not useful. Therefore, while random features often yield good results on the training data, the approach might not generalize so well to new test data.

4.4   GNNs with Dropouts

Another method of introducing randomization is to use dropouts; that is, to randomly remove some nodes from our input graph. GNNs with dropouts were introduced and studied in [12].

Definition 10. *A GNN with dropouts executes the same r-round computation multiple times; each time is called a run. In each run, every node v is "dropped out" independently with a fixed probability p, which means that both v and all of its incident edges are removed from the graph. The GNN is then simulated in this smaller graph G' (remaining after dropouts) in the given run.*

The final state of v in the ith run is denoted by $h_v^{(r)\,[i]}$. After the R runs, each node v computes a final state $\hat{h}_v$ by aggregating its final states in these R runs through

$$\hat{h}_v = \text{COMBINE}\,(\{\!\{\, h_v^{(r)\,[1]}, ..., h_v^{(r)\,[R]} \,\}\!\}),$$

where COMBINE *is a permutation-invariant function.*

The GNN now executes the same computation multiple times, but on slightly different variants of the original graph where some nodes are always removed randomly. Note that in any reasonable implementation, the COMBINE function has to be permutation-invariant, because there is no ordering between the different runs: a given final state $h_v^{(r)\,[i]}$ is obtained in each run $i \in \{1, ..., R\}$ with the same probability.

What if the final state $h_v^{(r)\,[i]}$ of node v if v is removed in the ith round? This is just a technical question. We can conveniently assume that $h_v^{(r)\,[i]} = 0$ in this case, or that $h_v^{(r)\,[i]}$ is then left out from the multiset $\{\!\{\, h_v^{(r)\,[1]}, ..., h_v^{(r)\,[R]} \,\}\!\}$ altogether.

The main idea of this approach is that even if two neighborhoods cannot be distinguished by the WL-test, the modified neighborhoods (when some nodes are removed) are often still distinguishable. Note that in order to use this method, we not only have to execute multiple runs while training the GNN, but also during testing, i.e. every time when we want to apply the GNN on a new graph.

Example 8. Recall that the graphs in Fig. 2 cannot be distinguished by standard GNNs. However, consider a GNN with dropouts, $r = 2$ layers, and a simple choice of $a_v^{(t)} = \sum_{u \in N(v)} h_u^{(t-1)}$ and $h_v^{(t)} = h_v^{(t-1)} + a_v^{(t)}$. For example, if no node is removed in a run, then each node ends up with a final state of $h_v^{(2)} = 9$.

Now consider the probability of having a final state $h_v^{(r)} = 7$ in a run for any of the nodes v (in a run where v itself is not removed). In the left graph of Fig. 2, this can already happen if the node at distance 2 from v is removed, which happens with probability p in each run. However, in the 8-cycle, this only happens if both of the nodes at distance 2 from v are removed, which happens with probability p^2.

This means that if R is large enough, then the expected occurrences of 7 as a final state after R runs in the two graphs is $p \cdot R$ and $p^2 \cdot R$, respectively. As such, the COMBINE function can separate these cases based on the frequency of the value 7 in the multiset (with a decent probability).

Example 9. Recall that the middle and right graphs in Fig. 1 cannot be distinguished with $\mathcal{A} =$ MEAN in case of $r = 1$.

However, in case of dropouts, the right graph can produce a final $h_v^{(1)}$ value of 1.33 or 1.66 in case a neighbor of v is dropped out. These final states can never occur in the middle graph; as such, if the multiset $\{\!\{ h_v^{(r)\,[1]}, ..., h_v^{(r)\,[R]} \}\!\}$ contains either 1.33 or 1.66, then we know that v has the right-hand neighborhood instead of the one in the middle.

In case of dropouts, v essentially observes a probability distribution of final states. If two such probability distributions are different, then a sophisticated COMBINE function can separate the two cases. Of course, this only holds if R is large enough. But how large does R have to be?

Note that asymptotically speaking, if $p, \Delta, r \in \mathcal{O}(1)$, then the maximal size of the r-hop neighborhood is $\mathcal{O}(\Delta^r)$, and the number of possible dropout patterns is $2^{\mathcal{O}(\Delta^r)} = \mathcal{O}(1)$, each happening with a constant probability. However, ensuring that we observe all such configurations is usually not viable in practice.

One simpler objective is to observe all the possible 1-dropouts.

Definition 11. *Given the r-hop neighborhood $N^r(v)$ of v, we say that a specific run is a 1-dropout if exactly 1 node is removed from $N^r(v)$, and v is not removed.*

A simple technical argument shows that if $n_0 := |N^r(v)|$, then in order to maximize the probability of any 1-dropout for v, we should select $p = \frac{1}{n_0}$. Note that different nodes have a different r-hop neighborhood size (i.e. different n_0), while p is a global parameter; however, if the neighborhood sizes are not so different, then this is not a problem in practice.

With this choice of p, one can already investigate the number of runs it take to ensure that we observe all the possible 1-dropouts. The following lower bound can be shown by applying a Chernoff bound.

Theorem 7 (from [12]). *Let $p = \frac{1}{n_0}$. Then with $R = \mathcal{O}(n_0 \cdot \log n_0)$ runs, v observes all the possible 1-dropouts in $N^r(v)$ with high probability.*

Requiring $\mathcal{O}(n_0 \cdot \log n_0)$ distinct runs is not too high from a theoretical perspective; however, this might already be too high to be feasible in practice.

Are 1-dropouts already enough to distinguish any two distinct r-hop neighborhoods? Unfortunately not.

Theorem 8 (from [12]). *There is a pair of non-isomorphic neighborhoods that cannot be distinguished based on the 1-dropouts.*

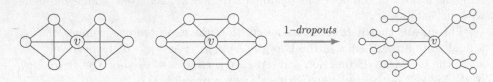

Fig. 8. (from [12]) Example of two graphs that are not separable by 1-dropouts (left side). In both of the graphs, for any of the 1-dropouts, v observes the same tree structure for $r = 2$, shown on the right side.

Proof. Consider the left and middle graphs in Fig. 8, obtained by connecting v to each node in two 3-cycles or a 6-cycle, respectively, and assume that $r = 2$. Note that in both cases, v can observe all the nodes and edges of the graph in 2 hops; a classical message passing algorithm could easily distinguish these cases.

However, a GNN without dropouts always computes the same state in both graphs. Furthermore, in case of any of the 6 possible 1-dropouts (in either of the graphs), v also observes the same tree structure (shown on the right side of the figure), so it also computes the same $h_v^{(2)}$. As such, the two graphs cannot be distinguished from the 1-dropouts.

4.5   Metagraph-Based Approaches

Other notable methods to increase the expressive power of GNNs use another interesting approach: they first transform the original input graph into a more sophisticated meta-graph (in order to capture structural properties that cannot be recognized by the WL-test), and then they run a GNN on this new graph. We also mention these GNN variants for completeness; however, since they operate on modified variants of the input graph, they are not so closely related to classical message passing models.

One such approach for more powerful GNNs is based on a higher-order WL-test. In this paper, we only discussed the so-called 1-WL algorithm, but WL is in fact a hierarchy of isomorphism-heuristics. That is, for each $k \in \mathbb{Z}^+$, there is also a more sophisticated k-WL algorithm which essentially operates on the different k-tuples of nodes in the original graph, and it is known that $(k+1)$-WL is always strictly more expressive than k-WL. There are also more powerful GNN variants that are based on these higher-order WL algorithms [10,11]; however, these

GNNs have at least $\Omega(n^k)$ space and sometimes even higher time complexity, so they are often not applicable in practice.

Another similar approach is to use so-called cell complexes [2]; intuitively speaking, this method finds specific substructures (such as cycles or cliques) in the graph, and adds new extra nodes to the graph representing these structures; these nodes are then connected to the original nodes and smaller structures that they contain. This method also comes with increased complexity.

5   Conclusion

In this paper we discussed the connection between distributed message passing algorithms and graph neural networks. We believe that this connection will advance the state of the art in both areas.

References

1. Babai, L.: Graph isomorphism in quasipolynomial time. In: Proceedings of the Forty-Eighth Annual ACM Symposium on Theory of Computing (STOC), pp. 684–697. ACM, New York (2016)
2. Bodnar, C., et al.: Weisfeiler and Lehman go cellular: CW networks (2021). arXiv preprint 2106.12575
3. Cai, J.Y., Fürer, M., Immerman, N.: An optimal lower bound on the number of variables for graph identification. Combinatorica **12**(4), 389–410 (1992). https://doi.org/10.1007/BF01305232
4. Garg, V., Jegelka, S., Jaakkola, T.: Generalization and representational limits of graph neural networks. In: Proceedings of the 37th International Conference on Machine Learning (ICML), vol. 119, pp. 3419–3430. PMLR (2020)
5. Gilmer, J., Schoenholz, S.S., Riley, P.F., Vinyals, O., Dahl, G.E.: Neural message passing for quantum chemistry. In: Proceedings of the 34th International Conference on Machine Learning, pp. 1263–1272 (2017)
6. Gori, M., Monfardini, G., Scarselli, F.: A new model for learning in graph domains. In: Proceedings of the 2005 IEEE International Joint Conference on Neural Networks, vol. 2, pp. 729–734 (2005)
7. Grohe, M., Kersting, K., Mladenov, M., Selman, E.: Dimension reduction via colour refinement. In: Schulz, A.S., Wagner, D. (eds.) ESA 2014. LNCS, vol. 8737, pp. 505–516. Springer, Heidelberg (2014). https://doi.org/10.1007/978-3-662-44777-2_42
8. Hamilton, W.L.: Graph representation learning. In: Synthesis Lectures on Artificial Intelligence and Machine Learning, vol. 14, no. 3, pp. 1–159 (2020)
9. Klicpera, J., Groß, J., Günnemann, S.: Directional message passing for molecular graphs. In: 8th International Conference on Learning Representations (ICLR) (2020)
10. Maron, H., Ben-Hamu, H., Serviansky, H., Lipman, Y.: Provably powerful graph networks. In: Advances in Neural Information Processing Systems (NeurIPS), vol. 32. Curran Associates, Inc. (2019)
11. Morris, C., et al.: Weisfeiler and Leman go neural: higher-order graph neural networks. In: Proceedings of the AAAI Conference on Artificial Intelligence, vol. 33, pp. 4602–4609 (2019)

12. Papp, P.A., Martinkus, K., Faber, L., Wattenhofer, R.: DropGNN: random dropouts increase the expressiveness of graph neural networks. In: 35th Conference on Neural Information Processing Systems. Curran Associates, Inc. (2021)
13. Park, N., Kan, A., Dong, X.L., Zhao, T., Faloutsos, C.: Estimating node importance in knowledge graphs using graph neural networks. In: Proceedings of the 25th ACM SIGKDD International Conference on Knowledge Discovery & Data Mining, pp. 596–606. Association for Computing Machinery (2019)
14. Sato, R., Yamada, M., Kashima, H.: Approximation ratios of graph neural networks for combinatorial problems. In: Advances in Neural Information Processing Systems (NeurIPS), vol. 32. Curran Associates, Inc. (2019)
15. Sato, R., Yamada, M., Kashima, H.: Random features strengthen graph neural networks. In: Proceedings of the 2021 SIAM International Conference on Data Mining (SDM), pp. 333–341 (2021). https://doi.org/10.1137/1.9781611976700.38
16. Scarselli, F., Gori, M., Tsoi, A.C., Hagenbuchner, M., Monfardini, G.: The graph neural network model. IEEE Trans. Neural Netw. **20**(1), 61–80 (2009)
17. Weisfeiler, B., Leman, A.: The reduction of a graph to canonical form and the algebra which appears therein. Nauchno-Technicheskaya Informatsi Ser. **2**(9), 12–16 (1968)
18. Xu, K., Hu, W., Leskovec, J., Jegelka, S.: How powerful are graph neural networks? In: 7th International Conference on Learning Representations (ICLR) (2019)
19. Ying, R., He, R., Chen, K., Eksombatchai, P., Hamilton, W.L., Leskovec, J.: Graph convolutional neural networks for web-scale recommender systems. In: Proceedings of the 24th ACM SIGKDD International Conference on Knowledge Discovery & Data Mining, pp. 974–983. Association for Computing Machinery (2018)

Towards Temporally Uncertain Explainable AI Planning

Andrew Murray[1], Benjamin Krarup[2], and Michael Cashmore[1(✉)]

[1] Strathclyde University, Glasgow, UK
{a.murray,michael.cashmore}@strath.ac.uk
[2] King's College London, London, UK
benjamin.krarup@kcl.ac.uk

Abstract. Automated planning is able to handle increasingly complex applications, but can produce unsatisfactory results when the goal and metric provided in its model does not match the actual expectation and preference of those using the tool. This can be ameliorated by including methods for explainable planning (XAIP), to reveal the reasons for the automated planner's decisions and to provide more in-depth interaction with the planner. In this paper we describe at a high-level two recent pieces of work in XAIP. First, plan exploration through model restriction, in which contrastive questions are used to build a tree of solutions to a planning problem. Through a dialogue with the system the user better understands the underlying problem and the choices made by the automated planner. Second, strong controllability analysis of probabilistic temporal networks through solving a joint chance constrained optimisation problem. The result of the analysis is a Pareto optimal front that illustrates the trade-offs between costs and risk for a given plan. We also present a short discussion on the limitations of these methods and how they might be usefully combined.

1 Introduction

Automated Planning is the process of considering and organising actions to achieve goals before starting to execute them. In automated planning, the actions that must be performed are not predetermined by the goals, but are selected and scheduled from a typically large number of alternative actions. The choice is guided by an effort to achieve the goals whilst optimising various metrics. Ordering choices and resource allocations are made, and evaluated, as part of the selection process. The consequence of this approach is that neither the number of actions in a plan, nor resource allocation of the plan, are predetermined. This distinguishes planning from scheduling, where the actions to be performed are predetermined but the timing of actions, and the allocation of resources to them, are not [16].

As automated planning is being used in increasingly complex applications, explanation plays a crucial role in building trust – both in automated planners and in the plans that they produce. A plan is a set of instructions that can be carried out by humans or autonomous agents. In either case, the plan conveys the means by which a goal is to be achieved, but not the reasons for the choices it embodies. When the audience for a plan

© Springer Nature Switzerland AG 2022
R. Bapi et al. (Eds.): ICDCIT 2022, LNCS 13145, pp. 45–59, 2022.
https://doi.org/10.1007/978-3-030-94876-4_3

includes humans then it is natural to suppose that some users might wish to question the reasoning, intention and underlying assumptions that lead to those choices.

As a result of this, there has been growing interest in investigating the explanation of plans [3], developing various approaches to building trust and understanding in the decisions made by an automated planner. Automated planning presents a distinct advantage in the context of explainable AI (XAI) in that it relies on the use of a model of the available actions. The model supports both prediction of action effects on a state and the identification of states from which the actions are applicable. However, in the context of explanation, the model becomes a shared vocabulary between the system and the user, enabling a depth and specificity of communication that is more difficult to obtain when explaining the decisions of systems such as deep-neural nets [31].

In this paper we describe recent work in two distinct areas of explainable automated planning (XAIP). First, in Sect. 2 we report on recent work in plan negotiation and the use of *contrastive explanations* to explore a space of plans. Then, in Sect. 3 we report on an approach to optimisation under one kind of uncertainty: *temporal uncertainty* about how long actions will take to complete. This approach can be used to generate analyses of the trade-offs between plan costs and risks. In Sect. 4 we discuss how this approach might be embedded within iterative plan exploration.

Both of these approaches share the idea of exploring a space of solutions, and by so doing gain a deeper understanding about the structure of the underlying problem. The motivation behind these approaches is that the user, with increased understanding, will either (i) gain trust in the decisions made by the automated planner, (ii) identify where the planner is operating outside of its competency, or (iii) identify where the planner is unaware of the user's preferences. In whichever case, the process of automated planning becomes a more useful interactive process that has the potential to converge towards a more satisfactory plan. In Sect. 4 we discuss how these different strands could be brought together to form a comprehensive suite of tools for plan explanation, which could be used by a human operator to better understand the problem, constraints, and converge to a more preferred solution.

1.1 Explainable AI Planning in Literature

Meuller et al. [26] provide an overview of the landscape of research into XAI. This work spans several decades, and includes work carried out with intelligent tutoring systems, XAI hypotheses and models, and explanation in expert systems. The early work on explanation in expert systems provided causal explanation for conclusions, often in the form of chains of rules contributing to the conclusion [38]. Recently, there has been a resurgence of interest in explanation in XAI, both when the model is and is not interpretable. This is, in large part, due to the difficulty of understanding the results of deep learning systems [31].

While there is a long history of work on explanation in AI, most work on explanation of plans (XAIP) is relatively recent. In a challenge paper, Smith [33] argues for the importance of plan explanation in mission planning, and suggests that questioning and explanation is part of an iterative process that helps elucidate and refine the preferences for a planning problem. Fox et al. [14] highlight contrastive 'why' questions as being important for plan explanation, and describe a number of different types of these questions and possible responses. Chakraborti et al. [3] survey recent work in XAIP and categorise the different approaches that have emerged in the last several years, including three important areas:

- *model reconciliation* - namely, that the need for explanation is due to differences between the agent's and the human's model of the planning problem. The planning system therefore "suggests changes to the human's model, so as to make its plan be optimal with respect to that changed human model" [2,23,34].
- *contrastive explanations* - an approach answering local contrastive questions; explaining the reason that a contrast case B was not a feature of the plan by revealing the consequences that would hold if B *were* the case [1,7,14,19,20,22].
- and *explanation of unsolvability* for planning problems [8,9,17,35].

2 Contrastive Explanations in Plan Exploration

Fundamentally, the need for plan explanation is driven by the fact that a human and a planning agent may have different models of the planning problem and different computational capabilities. In this section we describe our approach to plan explanation through *exploration*. Through asking contrastive questions, a human user can impose iterative restrictions upon the model of the automated planner in order to generate different plans. In so doing, the user gains a better understanding of the problem and capabilities of the automated planner. An in-depth description of this process, including a formal definition of model restrictions, is presented in Krarup et al. [21].

2.1 Planning Model and Capability

A standard modelling language for autonomous planning is the Planning Domain Description Language (PDDL), originally developed in 1998 by a committee led by Drew McDermott [25] and later extended to support more expressive features such as time [6,13], preferences [15], continuous change and exogenous events [12]. To describe our approach to plan exploration, we'll use PDDL2.1 as an example planning formalism. Our definition follows the definition of PDDL2.1 given by Fox and Long [13], extended by a set of time windows and explicit record of the plan metric. A more detailed description can be found in Krarup et al. [21].

Definition 1 (Planning model). *A planning model is a pair $\Pi = \langle D, Prob \rangle$. The domain $D = \langle Ps, Vs, As, arity \rangle$ is a tuple where Ps is a finite set of predicate symbols, Vs is a finite set of function symbols, As is a set of action schemas, called operators, and $arity$ is a function mapping all of these symbols to their respective arity. The problem $Prob = \langle Os, I, G, M, W \rangle$ is a tuple where Os is the set of objects in the planning instance, I is the initial state, G is the goal condition, M is a plan-metric function from plans to real values (plan costs) and W is a set of time windows.*

A solution for a planning model is called a *plan*. A plan is a sequence of grounded actions, $\pi = \langle a_1, a_2, \ldots, a_n \rangle$ each with a respective time denoted by $Dispatch(a_i)$. The execution of a plan consists of a sequence of *happenings* corresponding to the effects of actions and exogenous effects in the world [13]. This sequence describes a trace of times, $t_{i=0\ldots k}$ and states, $s_{i=0\ldots k+1}$ such that $s_0 = I$ and for each $i = 0 \ldots k$, s_{i+1} is the result of executing the happening at time t_i from state s_i. The plan is valid if $s_{k+1} \models G$ (that is, the goal is satisfied in the final state reached by the plan).

We assume that the human's planning model Π^H, and planning agent's model Π^P share the same vocabulary, namely the same predicate symbols Ps, function symbols Vs, and actions As from the domain D, and objects Os from the problem. However, the action durations, conditions, and effects may be different, and the initial states I, goals G, and plan metric M may be different.

Even when a human and a planning agent have the same planning models $\Pi^H = \Pi^P$, there are typically multiple plans satisfying this planning model. Although a planner is intended to optimise the plan with respect to the plan metric, it is common to produce only one of the valid plans, rather than an optimal plan for a model. For some problems a planner might even fail to produce a plan at all. In part, this is an inevitable consequence of the undecidability of planning problems with numeric variables and functions [18], but it is also a consequence of the practical limits on the computational resources available to a planner (time and memory). These observations are equally valid for automated and human planners. In order to discuss the process of developing plan explanations, it is helpful to define the planning abilities of both the planner and the user. We model the planning capability of an agent as a partial function from planning models to plans:

Definition 2. *The* **planning capability** *of an agent A (human or machine), is a partial function, $\mathbb{C}^A$, from planning models to plans. Given the agent's planning model, Π^A, if $\mathbb{C}^A(\Pi^A)$ is defined, then it is a candidate plan π^A for the agent.*

The part of the function domain on which $\mathbb{C}^A$ is defined determines the planning competency of the agent – domain-problem pairs for which the agent cannot find a plan lie outside this competency. Note that the planning competency of an agent can be restricted by a bound on the computational resources the agent is allowed to devote to the problem, as well as by the capabilities of the agent in constructing and adequately searching the search space that the problem defines.

When A is an automated AI planner P, the computational ability is determined by the search strategy implemented in the planner and the resources allocated to the task. When A is a human planner H, the planning capability is determined by the understanding that the human has of the planning model and the patience and problem-solving effort they are willing to devote to solving the problem. It cannot be assumed that, if $\mathbb{C}^H(\Pi^H)$ is defined, that the human's model Π^H accurately reflects the world, or that the reasoning $\mathbb{C}^H$ is sound. This means that the plan may not be valid.

One aspect of the process of planning and explanation is that the user can revise their model Π^H as the process unfolds. However, it is also possible that the user can change their planning capability $\mathbb{C}^H$, by coming to a greater understanding of the model, by engaging in more reasoning, or by simply concluding that the solution provided by an automated system is satisfactory. It is also possible that the planner responses lead to the user changing their view of what might be a good plan to solve a problem, while still not adopting the solution offered by the planner.

2.2 Iterative Plan Exploration

We adopt the approach that the human user asks contrastive questions that impose additional restrictions ϕ on the agent's planning problem Π^P to generate a succession of hypothetical planning problems. The object of these questions and the resulting hypothetical plans is for the user to understand and ultimately arrive at a satisfactory plan. We call this process *Iterative Plan Exploration*.

Given the planning models Π^H and Π^P, and planning capabilities $\mathbb{C}^H$ and $\mathbb{C}^P$ of a human and planning agent, the two agents disagree when $\mathbb{C}^H(\Pi^H) \neq \mathbb{C}^P(\Pi^P)$, which can arise in the case that either of these terms is undefined, or if both terms are defined and yield different plans. We assume that the user is able to inspect the planner output and determine a question that will expose some part of the explanation for this difference. By questioning why certain decisions were made in the plan and receiving contrastive explanations the user can gain an initial understanding. As their understanding of the plan develops they can ask more educated questions to gain a deeper understanding or try to arrive at an alternative plan that they consider more satisfactory. This process concludes when the user is satisfied with some plan.

We formalise the iterative process of questioning and explanation as one of successive *model restriction*, in which the user asks contrastive questions in an attempt to understand the planning agent's plan and potentially steer the planning agent towards a satisfactory solution. We suppose that, when $\mathbb{C}^H(\Pi^H) \neq \mathbb{C}^P(\Pi^P)$, the user can construct a *foil*, ϕ, in the form of a constraint that $\mathbb{C}^P(\Pi^P)$ does not satisfy, so that seeking an explanation for the plan, $\mathbb{C}^P(\Pi^P)$, can be seen as seeking a plan for Π^P that also satisfies ϕ. This requirement acts as a restriction on Π^P and is captured as follows.

Definition 3. *A **constraint property** is a predicate, ϕ, over plans.*
*A **constraint operator**, $\times$ is defined so that, for a planning model Π and any constraint property ϕ, $\Pi \times \phi$ is a model Π', called a **model restriction** of Π, satisfying the condition that any plan for Π' is a plan for Π that also satisfies ϕ.*

The process in which the user interacts with a planner is an iterative one – the user successively views plans and seeks explanations by generating foils that impose additional restrictions on the planning problem. The collection of model restrictions forms a tree, rooted at the original model and extended by the incremental addition of new constraint properties, as shown in Fig. 1. As the user inspects the result of applying $\mathbb{C}^P$ to a node in this tree, their own planning model and capability, Π^H and $\mathbb{C}^H$, may change, reflecting accumulating understanding of the plans that can be constructed for the model. It is worth emphasising that any constraint, ϕ, may be added to any model, so that the user is not forced to develop a tree of models in any particular way to arrive at the consequence of adding any specific constraint to a model.

It should be noted that, depending on the planning models and capabilities of the two participants, there might not exist any constraint achieving a common solution. For example, in the degenerate case in which $\mathbb{C}^P$ produces no plan at all, for any value of ϕ, then there can be no mutually satisfactory plan. Typically, the greater the differences between the planning models and capabilities of the two agents, the more likely it will be that there is no common satisfactory plan.

We formally capture the iterative process of model restriction and planning as:

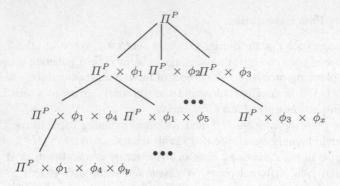

Fig. 1. A fragment of a tree of model restrictions for a planner P. Each node n_i in the tree is a model restriction of the model of it's parent node n_{i-1}, and a constraint ϕ_i.

Definition 4. *Iterative Model Restriction. For a planner P, and a user H: Let $\mathbb{C}^P$ and Π^P be the planner's underlying capability and planning model and $\mathbb{C}_0^H$ and Π_0^H be the initial capability and planning model of H. Let ϕ_i be the set of user imposed constraints, which is initially empty, i.e. $\phi_0 = \emptyset$. Each stage, i (initially zero), of this process starts with the planner producing a plan $\pi_i^P = \mathbb{C}^P(\Pi_i^P)$ for the model $\Pi_i^P = \Pi^P \times \phi_i$.*

The user responds to this plan π_i^P by potentially updating their capability and model to $\mathbb{C}_{i+1}^H$ and Pi_{i+1}^H and then either terminating the interaction, or asking a question that imposes a new constraint ϕ_{i+1} on the problem. This results in the planner solving a new constrained problem $\Pi_{i+1}^P = \Pi^P \times \phi_{i+1}$ at the next step.

We have assumed here that the planner's underlying capability and planning model $\mathbb{C}^P$ and Π^P do not evolve during the process. While this is not strictly necessary, possible evolution or improvement of the planner capabilities and model based on the sequence of user questions and the resulting ϕ_i is an issue we do not consider here. In contrast, the user's capability and planning model $\mathbb{C}^H$ and Π^H are assumed to evolve, but in unknown ways. Again, we do not attempt to model the user's learning process.

The exploration process could end in a variety of different ways. One way that the exploration can end is that the plan produced for the final model yields a plan that is acceptable to the user, so that the user adopts this plan for the original model. Alternatively the user, having explored the plans for several models, is persuaded in this process that the first plan produced by the planner for the original model is actually the desired plan. The exploration can also result in the selection of a plan somewhere between these two extremes, in which the user decides to adopt a plan produced for some intermediate model in the exploration. Finally, the exploration can end when the user explores the space and then rejects all of the plans the planner offers. In this case, the user might modify their planning model and capability as a consequence of what they observe and they might or might not conclude the process with a satisfactory plan for the original model. Krarup et al. [21] explore the hypothesis that the user will usually find value in the exploration and conclude in one of the three cases in which a mutually agreed plan is identified.

2.3   Temporal, Numeric, and Probabilistic Model Restrictions

The Iterative model restriction process presents a natural method to explore a space of plans through dialogue with the system, but does not succinctly represent more complex constraints in the space of solutions that arise from the interaction between numeric and probabilistic parts of the model. For instance, the trade-offs between two different rewards that the human user wishes to capture in the model's metric could be iteratively refined so that the user can see the outcome of different weightings between those rewards - but this is not an efficient way to represent what could be visually presented immediately with a Pareto-optimal set of solutions - if such a thing is possible to produce given the automated planner's capability.

In addition to this, our process does not account for uncertainties that might alter the plan during execution, which is a natural occurrence when executing a plan in the real world. While comparing different plans allows the user to understand the space of solutions to the planning instance, it might not reveal differences in how those plans might be realised in an uncertain environment.

3   Optimisation Under Temporal Uncertainty

In many applications, the activities that need to be performed are already known, but there remains the problem of deciding when to perform those activities in order to meet constraints and optimise reward. As an example, consider the problem of 5G network slicing. Containerised components are hosted on pods in nodes within a data center (DC). Each pod is an allocation of a component's required share of resources. Multiple components can be linked to provide a service which satisfies the requirements defined in the service level agreement (SLA) reached between the provider and customer. However a number of events can occur which may result in the service configuration no longer being valid. Congestion at component input, for example, can result in packet drops such that the terms outlined in the SLA are no longer satisfied. Under such a scenario it may be necessary to reconfigure how the components are hosted within the DC. The decision of when to reroute traffic is influenced by two conflicting factors: the increased cost of migrating components early, and the risk associated with the probability distribution describing the SLA violation.

It is not known by the decision maker a-priori which combination of risk and cost is desired. The problem can be considered a bi-objective optimisation problem in which the solution is a Pareto optimal set of schedules optimising risk and cost. The relation to plan exploration is clear: the problem has many possible solutions with different characteristics, and the decision maker can benefit from exploring this space of solutions.

In this section we provide a background on the temporal network formalism and definitions of controllability. Then we discuss the Relaxable Chance Constrained Probabilistic Simple Temporal Network (r-cc-PSTN) which was introduced by Yu et al. [41]. We show that this can be expressed as a Joint Chance Constrained Optimisation Problem (JCCP) for which a rich suite of solution methods exist. Finally we discuss the potential for this to be incorporated within a bi-objective optimisation framework capable of generating the Pareto optimal set of schedules.

3.1 Temporal Networks and Controllability

Simple Temporal Networks (STN) [5] are used to represent temporal domains and reason about decisions under the influence of temporal constraints. An STN is a graph in which the nodes correspond to *time-points* and the edges (*links*) correspond to durations between the time-points. A solution to an STN is a schedule at which to execute a number of time-points such that the temporal constraints are satisfied. As such they are a natural formalism to represent scheduling problems such as 5G network slicing.

Simple Temporal Networks with Uncertainty (STNU) were introduced [39] to capture uncertainty in the problem through the inclusion of set-bounded *contingent links*, over which the operator has no control. In STNU semantics, a distinction is made between *contingent links*, for which the duration of the interval is uncertain and *requirement links* for which we can choose the duration.

Definition 5 (STNU). *A STNU is a tuple,* $S^U = \langle T_c, T_u, C, G \rangle$ *where* $b_1, b_2, ..., b_B \in T_c$ *is the set of controllable time-points and* $e_1, e_2, ..., e_E \in T_u$ *is the set of uncontrollable time-points, such that* $t_1, t_2, ..., t_n \in \{T_c \cup T_u\}$. *The set* C, *is the set of temporal requirement constraints between two time-points, normally written in the form* $c(t_j, t_i) = t_j - t_i \in [l_{ij}^c, u_{ij}^c]$. *The set* G *is the set of contingent links given in the form* $g(e_i, b_i) = e_i - b_i \in [l_i^g, u_i^g]$. *Here,* $l^{c \vee g}, u^{c \vee g}$ *denote the lower and upper limits for the constraint or contingent link respectively. Let* $s(b) \in \mathcal{R}^+$ *be the assignment of a value to the controllable time-point* b. *Let* $o(e) \in \mathcal{R}^+$ *be the value observed by an uncontrollable time-point* e. *A projection of a contingent link* g_i *is* $\omega_i := o(e_i) - s(b_i)$.

The challenge in scheduling STNUs lies in the fact that the set of contingent links may take any random value within their bounds, and therefore an effective execution strategy must consider all possible projections for each contingent link.

When dealing with uncertainty in temporal networks it is typical to classify the problem in terms of controllability [40], which can be considered as a way of classifying how much control the agent has over the outcome of the network [40]. Controllability of an STNU is typically separated into 3 categories (strong, dynamic, weak). In a strongly controllable network, there exists an assignment to all controllable time-points that can be determined a-priori and will satisfy all constraints no matter the outcome of the contingent links.

Definition 6 (Strong Controllability). *Denote* Ω, *the space of projections of the contingent links:* $\Omega = \times_{g \in G} [l^g, u^g]$. *Let the schedule* δ, *be the assignment* $s(b)$, $\forall b \in T_c$. *An STNU* S *is said to be strongly controllable if:* $\exists \delta \mid \forall \omega \in \Omega$, δ *satisfies all constraints.*

We denote: $C_u \subseteq C$, the set of *uncontrollable constraints* containing an uncontrollable time-point. One can substitute $e = b + \omega$ for the contingent link preceding/succeeding the uncontrollable constraint. To check whether an STNU, S_U is SC, it is sufficient to check that the uncontrollable constraints are satisfied for the worst possible projection of the contingent links. i.e. $\min\{c \mid \omega \in [l^g, u^g]\} \geq l^c$, $\max\{c \mid \omega \in [l^g, u^g]\} \leq u^c$ for every $c \in C_u$.

Where sufficient data is available, it is often more representative to model the space of possible projections of a contingent link by a probability density function [11,36], creating a Probabilistic Simple Temporal Network (PSTN). This allows the scheduling process to focus on the durations *most likely* to be realised at execution.

Definition 7 (PSTN). *A PSTN is a tuple, $S^P = \langle T_c, T_u, C, D \rangle$, where T_c, T_u and C are as per the STNU. The set of probabilistic constraints, D are in the form $d(e_i, b_i) = e_i - b_i = X_i$, where X_i is a random variable with a set of outcomes Ω_i, probability density function $f(\omega_i)$ and cumulative probability function $F(\omega_i)$.*

It should be noted that it is often impossible to find a SC schedule robust to all possible outcomes of an unbounded distribution. As a result, it is typical to squeeze the distribution by neglecting the extreme, unlikely outcomes in the tails of the distributions, i.e.: $\Omega_i^* = [l_i^d, u_i^d]$. We denote $d^*(e_i, b_i)$, the restricted probabilistic constraint, and performing this restriction transforms the probabilistic constraint to a contingent link, i.e. $d^*(e_i, b_i) = e_i - b_i = X_i^* \in [l_i^d, u_i^d] \equiv g(e_i, b_i)$. Applying this transformation to all $d \in D$ is equivalent to transforming the PSTN, S^P to an equivalent STNU, S^{U*}. However the schedule is now only robust to the outcomes considered in S^{U*}. The probability mass excluded by performing this transformation is the *risk* of S^P.

Definition 8 (Robustness and Risk). *We denote $\Omega_R \subseteq \Omega$ and $c(\omega)$ the value of each constraint $c \in C$ given an outcome ω. If $\omega \in \Omega$ and for every $c \in C$, $c(\omega) \in [l_{ij}^c, u_{ij}^c]$: then $\omega \in \Omega_R$. The robustness R, is $P(\Omega_R)$, while the risk Δ, is $P(\bar{\Omega}_R)$, where $\bar{\Omega}_R$ denotes the complement of the set Ω_R.*

Since the joint probability function $P(\bar{\Omega}_R)$ is non-trivial, it is typical to treat uncontrollable constraints independently and bound above the risk using Boole's inequality. The risk can of then be approximated through: $\Delta = \sum_i^{|C_u|} F(l_i^d) + (1 - F(l_i^d))$. The values of u_i^d and l_i^d are determined through the SC relationships outlined previously, through substituting l^g, u^g for l^d, u^d.

3.2 PSTN Strong Controllability and Risk in Literature

Tsamardinos [36] takes a risk minimisation approach to PSTN SC, and makes use of various assumptions to leverage Sequential Quadratic Programming. Likewise, Santana et al. [32] and Lund et al. [24] make varying assumptions to permit the use of LPs to allocate risk in PSTNs. Fang et al. [11] introduced the notion of chance constrained PSTNs (cc-PSTN); by enforcing an allowable tolerance on the risk as a constraint in the system, such as $\Delta \leq \alpha$, where $\alpha \in [0, 1]$. Some other objective function could then be optimised, while ensuring that the schedule risk does not exceed α.

In some instances the risk required to enforce SC can be deemed too high. Yu et al. [41] extended the chance-constrained framework to the *relaxable* chance constrained probabilistic simple temporal network (r-cc-PSTN) by permitting the use of soft constraints which can be relaxed. A cost is then paid relative to the amount of relaxation. This enables solutions to be found for over-constrained cc-PSTNs. The r-cc-PSTN is very general, and is solved by Yu et al. using a nonlinear solver, combined with a conflict detection mechanism based on identification of negative cycles in STNUs. Nonlinear optimization problems are solved to eliminate these cycles.

To the best of the authors' knowledge, all previous SC approaches for PSTNs either use Boole's inequality to bound above the risk [11, 24, 32, 41], or solve a generic non-linear optimisation problem [36]. Using Boole's inequality permits the use of Linear Programming solvers, however it can be overly conservative - particularly when the number of uncontrollable constraints is large. Whereas posing the problem in a generic non-linear setting can either be computationally expensive or offer no guarantee of global optimality.

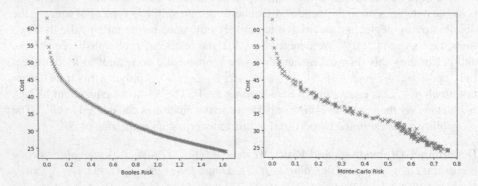

Fig. 2. Figure showing the Pareto optimal front generated using Boole's inequality (left) in comparison to the equivalent Monte-Carlo risk (right)

In Fig. 2, an example r-cc-PSTN was solved for strong controllability with Boole's inequality bounding the risk. Following this, the schedules obtained for each cost were simulated using a Monte-Carlo execution approach enabling the cost to be plotted against the true risk. As can be seen, the Pareto front obtained using Boole's inequality is not guaranteed to be the true Pareto optimal solution for cost and risk. Likewise as the number of uncontrollable constraints increases, the Boole's risk is not guaranteed to be bounded within $[0, 1]$. As such it is not interpretable and gives little useful information to the human required to reason over the Pareto front.

3.3   On Pareto Optimal Schedules to PSTNs

In this section we discuss in greater detail the r-cc-PSTN [41] and highlight how these can be solved as a Joint Chance Constrained Optimisation Problem (JCCP) enabling the evaluation of true Pareto optimal solutions.

Definition 9 (r-cc-PSTN). *A r-cc-PSTN is a tuple $S^R = \langle T_c, T_u, C_c, C_u, D, W, \alpha \rangle$, where T_c, T_u and D are as per the definition of PSTN. The set of requirement constraints C is partitioned into a set of controllable constraints C_c: $c(b_j, b_i) = b_j - b_i \in \{l_{ij}^c, u_{ij}^c\}$ and uncontrollable constraints C_u: $c(e_j, b_i) = e_j - b_i \in \{l_{ij}^c, u_{ij}^c\} \vee c(b_j, e_i) = b_j - e_i \in \{l_{ij}^c, u_{ij}^c\}$. There exists some subset $C_{c,s} \subseteq C_c$ and $C_{u,s} \subseteq C_u$ which are considered soft constraints. We introduce the lower and upper relaxation variables: $\breve{r}_{ij}, \hat{r}_{ij} \in \mathcal{R}^+$ for each constraint in $\{C_{c,s} \cup C_{u,s}\}$: $c(t_j, t_i) = t_j - t_i \in \{l_{ij}^c - \breve{r}_{ij}, u_{ij}^c + \hat{r}_{ij}\}$.*

The relaxation weight $w \in W$, associated with relaxing constraint $c \in \{C_{c,s} \cup C_{u,s}\}$ is the relative cost of relaxing the constraint by one time unit, such that the relaxation cost k is calculated as the linear sum: $k = w\check{r} + w\hat{r}$. Finally, $\alpha \in [0, 1]$ is the risk bound representing the maximum allowable probability of failure across all $c \in C_u$.

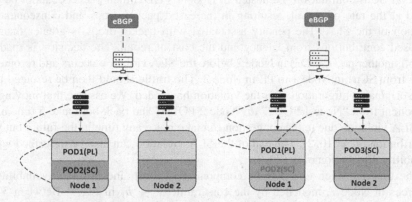

Fig. 3. Diagram showing data center configuration before (left) and after (right) migrating traffic.

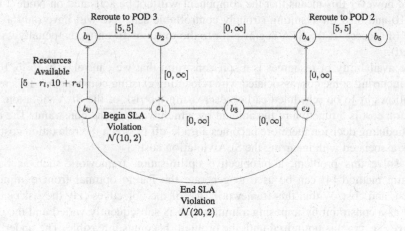

Fig. 4. Example PSTN showing data center problem.

To elucidate the key characteristics of such a problem, we return to the motivating example of 5G slicing. First we describe an example situation (Fig. 3), and then the example PSTN problem that results (Fig. 4). In Fig. 3, we consider two nodes. A service consisting of two components, payload (PL) and service controller (SCtrl), is hosted in the DC. Traffic is processed by PL and then by SCtrl before exiting through the exit gateway. We consider three conditions outlined in the SLA: latency of the path, the percentage of packet drops, and the cost of hosting the pods on the nodes. The rental of Node 2 is higher than that of Node 1, and the latency of the path POD1 → POD3 is larger than that of POD1 → POD2. Initially, PL and SCtrl are hosted in POD1 and POD2 of Node1 such that the terms in the SLA are met.

At some point in the day, increased traffic to the service requires a scaled up SCtrl for which there is insufficient resources available in the current configuration using POD2. If SCtrl continues to be hosted in Node 1 POD2, then packets cannot be processed at the rate of arrival, resulting in increased packet drops and consequently a violation of the SLA. The penalty associated with packet drops is greater than the increased contributions from latency and the cost of rental. The decision is made to spin off another pod (POD3) in Node 2 before the SLA violation occurs and reroute the traffic from SCtrl in Node 1 to PL in Node 2. The traffic should then be rerouted back to the original configuration after the violation has ended. We assume that moving the component from "Node 1 POD2" to "Node 2 POD3" and back both take 5 time units. The SLA violation due to the congestion can take place any time in the future but with a distribution of $\mathcal{N}(10, 2)$. The end of the SLA violation can also be described with a probability distribution of $\mathcal{N}(20, 2)$.

The time at which to move the component is constrained by the availability of resources in Node 2, modelled by the constraint $b_0 \rightarrow b_1$ in Fig. 4. Between 5 and 10 units after b_0, there exists sufficient resources for PL to be spun on Node 2. The ideal decision would be to move the component as early as possible to minimise the probability that the SLA violation penalty will be incurred. We can choose to schedule $b_1 = 5$, however this means that the component will not be activated on Node 2 until $b_2 = 10$ and thus the resulting strongly controllable schedule will have only a 50% chance of success (if the SLA begins prior to the mean of 10 units, the penalty will be incurred).

The availability of resources is a soft constraint that we can relax from $[5, 10]$ to $[0, 10]$ incurring some cost associated with relocating existing components. This relaxation allows b_1 to be scheduled earlier, decreasing the risk of the SLA violation. The relaxation cost is a function of the amount by which we relax the constraint. The optimal scheduling decision therefore becomes a trade-off between the relaxation cost and the risk associated with incurring the SLA violation cost.

To solve this problem, a bi-objective optimisation framework such as the ϵ-constraint method [4] can be used to generate the Pareto optimal front minimising both risk and cost. Within this framework, one of the objectives (i.e. the risk) can be treated as a constraint by imposing a limit which is subsequently varied and the other objective (i.e. cost) is optimised until the problem becomes infeasible. The underlying problem of minimising cost subject to the constraint on risk can be considered as a JCCP: $\min_x \{ c^T x \mid Ax \leq b, P(Tx + q \geq \xi) \geq 1 - \alpha \}$.

With some algebraic manipulation, r-cc-PSTNs can quite easily be expressed in this form. The decision vector $x \in \mathcal{R}^n$, would be the controllable time-points comprising the schedule, combined with the relaxation variables for each soft constraint. The controllable constraints can be encapsulated in the linear inequality: $Ax \leq b$, where $A \in \mathcal{R}^{m \times n}$ are the constraint coefficients and $b \in \mathcal{R}^m$ are the upper bounds. Similarly, the uncontrollable constraints can be captured in the joint chance constraint: $P(Tx + q \geq \xi) \geq 1 - \alpha$, where $T \in \mathcal{R}^{p \times n}$ is the matrix of coefficients and $q \in \mathcal{R}^p$ are the bounds. Here, ξ is a p dimensional random variable with mean vector, μ and covariance matrix, Σ and $\alpha \in [0, 1]$ is the joint bound on the probability of failure. Finally any linear objective can be implemented within the objective function $c^T x$, however we consider that we wish to minimise the relaxation cost and thus $c \in \mathcal{R}^n$, is the vector of relaxation weights w associated with each relaxation variable.

Prekopa [27,28] proved that if the probability distribution is log-concave, then the cumulative probability function $F(z) = P(\xi \leq z)$ is also log-concave and thus the set $\{z \mid -\log(F(z)) \leq -\log(1-\alpha)\}$ is convex. Many interesting distributions contain this characteristic [29]. The result is that r-cc-PSTN SC as JCCP is a convex optimisation problem with a tractable evaluation of the global optimal schedule. More detail can be found in a recent survey of solution methods [10,37] and overview on the topic [30].

4   Discussion and Conclusion

In this section we briefly discuss three possible directions for future work that could combine the approaches from Sects. 2 and 3. A naive approach would be to use iterative plan exploration to generate a plan $\pi = \langle a_1, a_2, \ldots, a_n \rangle$, whose *happenings* become the nodes of a PSTN. That PSTN could then be analysed for SC. The limitation of this naive approach is that the plan exploration would not benefit from the additional insight provided by the PSTN SC analysis. Below we describe three alternatives for closer integration of the approaches.

Constrastive Explanations of Strongly Controllable Plans. In iterative plan exploration, model restrictions are used to generate a hypothetical plan that embodies the "what if" question posed by the user. Plans are compared against one another as a form of explanation – the aim of which is to make explicit the impact of their suggestions. In the user study carried out by Krarup et al. [21], plan metrics were directly compared, assuming a single realisation of the plan's time-points that was selected by the planner. Instead, the approach presented in Sect. 3 could be used to provide a more in-depth comparison between the two plans by comparing Pareto-optimal schedules for their respective actions.

Iterative Restrictions to PSTNs. A direction for future work in explainable scheduling would be to apply the paradigm of iterative plan exploration to the problem of PSTN SC. Just as it is the case that the decision maker might have preferences that are not completely captured by the planner's model, it can also be the case that the Pareto optimal frontier does not actually represent the complete set of solutions of interest. By allowing the user to apply restrictions as new constraints in the PSTN the user will be able to see the impact of restrictions that iteratively force solutions away from the Pareto-optimal frontier. Just as in iterative plan exploration, this process could converge in a schedule that better adheres to the user's true preferences, or increase their trust in the original set of solutions.

Plan Exploration in Discrete and Continuous Spaces. Krarup et al. [21] showed that by using the most common restrictions requested by users – action inclusion, exclusion, ordering, and temporal constraints – iterative model restriction can combine these constraints to encapsulate more specific questions and eventually converge to any valid plan. However, using successive queries to explore a continuous space such as real-valued cost or risk would be very inefficient. This limitation could be tackled by embedding the analysis provided by the PSTN SC analysis into the plan exploration tools developed by Krarup et al. This would extend the common restrictions above to also include constraints on cost and risk that are drawn from observation of the Pareto-optimal set of solutions. Unlike the *iterative restrictions to PSTNs* described above, these constraints would be applied to a planning model in the current exploration tree and used to generate a new plan that could potentially have a different set of actions. The result would be that the user could efficiently explore the different trade-offs exhibited by a variety of possible plans, before converging upon a chosen plan and schedule.

References

1. Bercher, P., et al.: Plan, repair, execute, explain-how planning helps to assemble your home theater. In: ICAPS (2014)
2. Chakraborti, T., Sreedharan, S., Zhang, Y., Kambhampati, S.: Plan explanations as model reconciliation: moving beyond explanation as soliloquy. In: IJCAI (2017)
3. Chakraborti, T., Sreedharan, S., Kambhampati, S.: The emerging landscape of explainable AI planning and decision making. In: IJCAI, pp. 4803–4811 (2020)
4. Chircop, K., Zammit-Mangion, D.: On-constraint based methods for the generation of pareto frontiers. J. Mech. Eng. Autom. **3**(5), 279–289 (2013)
5. Dechter, R., Meiri, I., Pearl, J.: Temporal constraint networks. Artif. Intell. **49**(1–3), 61–95 (1991)
6. Edelkamp, S.: On the compilation of plan constraints and preferences. In: ICAPS, pp. 374–377 (2006)
7. Eifler, R., Cashmore, M., Hoffmann, J., Magazzeni, D., Steinmetz, M.: A new approach to plan-space explanation: analyzing plan-property dependencies in oversubscription planning. In: AAAI, pp. 9818–9826 (2020)
8. Eriksson, S., Helmert, M.: Certified unsolvability for SAT planning with property directed reachability. In: ICAPS, vol. 30, pp. 90–100 (2020)
9. Eriksson, S., Röger, G., Helmert, M.: Unsolvability certificates for classical planning. In: AAAI (2017)
10. Fábián, C.I., et al.: Probability maximization by inner approximation. Acta Polytech. Hung. **15**(1), 105–125 (2018)
11. Fang, C., Yu, P., Williams, B.C.: Chance-constrained probabilistic simple temporal problems. In: AAAI (2014)
12. Fox, M., Long, D.: Extending the exploitation of symmetries in planning. In: ICAPS, pp. 83–91 (2002)
13. Fox, M., Long, D.: PDDL2.1: an extension to PDDL for expressing temporal planning domains. JAIR **20**, 61–124 (2003)
14. Fox, M., Long, D., Magazzeni, D.: Explainable planning. In: IJCAI-2017 Workshop on Explainable AI (2017)
15. Gerevini, A., Long, D.: Plan constraints and preferences in PDDL3. Technical report, Department of Electronics for Automation (2005)
16. Ghallab, M., Nau, D., Traverso, P.: Automated Planning: Theory and Practice. Elsevier, Amsterdam (2004)
17. Göbeldecker, M., Keller, T., Eyerich, P., Brenner, M., Nebel, B.: Coming up with good excuses: what to do when no plan can be found. In: Dagstuhl Seminar Proceedings (2010)

18. Helmert, M.: Decidability and undecidability results for planning with numerical state variables. In: AIPS, pp. 44–53 (2002)
19. Kasenberg, D., Roque, A., Thielstrom, R., Chita-Tegmark, M., Scheutz, M.: Generating justifications for norm-related agent decisions. arXiv preprint arXiv:1911.00226 (2019)
20. Kim, J., Muise, C., Shah, A., Agarwal, S., Shah, J.: Bayesian inference of linear temporal logic specifications for contrastive explanations. In: IJCAI, pp. 5591–5598 (2019)
21. Krarup, B., Krivic, S., Lindner, F., Long, D.: Towards contrastive explanations for comparing the ethics of plans. In: ICRA-2020 Workshop on Against Robot Dystopias (2020)
22. Krarup, B., Krivic, S., Magazzeni, D., Long, D., Cashmore, M., Smith, D.E.: Contrastive explanations of plans through model restrictions. JAIR **72**, 533–612 (2021)
23. Kulkarni, A., Zha, Y., Chakraborti, T., Vadlamudi, S.G., Zhang, Y., Kambhampati, S.: Explicablility as minimizing distance from expected behavior. arXiv preprint arXiv:1611.05497 (2016)
24. Lund, K., Dietrich, S., Chow, S., Boerkoel, J.: Robust execution of probabilistic temporal plans. In: AAAI (2017)
25. McDermott, D.: The 1998 AI planning systems competition. AI Mag. **21**(2), 35–55 (1998)
26. Mueller, S.T., Hoffman, R.R., Clancey, W.J., Emrey, A., Klein, G.: Explanation in human-AI systems: a literature meta-review, synopsis of key ideas and publications, and bibliography for explainable AI. CoRR abs/1902.01876 (2019)
27. Prékopa, A.: Logarithmic concave measures with applications to stochastic programming. Acta Scientiarum Mathematicarum **32**, 301–316 (1971)
28. Prékopa, A.: On logarithmic concave measures and functions. Acta Scientiarum Mathematicarum **34**, 335–343 (1973)
29. Prékopa, A.: Probabilistic programming. Handb. Oper. Res. Manag. Sci. **10**, 267–351 (2003)
30. Prékopa, A.: Stochastic Programming, vol. 324. Springer, Dordrecht (2013)
31. Rudin, C.: Stop explaining black box machine learning models for high stakes decisions and use interpretable models instead. Nat. Mach. Intell. **1**(5), 206–215 (2019)
32. Santana, P., Vaquero, T., Toledo, C., Wang, A., Fang, C., Williams, B.: PARIS: a polynomial-time, risk-sensitive scheduling algorithm for probabilistic simple temporal networks with uncertainty. In: ICAPS (2016)
33. Smith, D.: Planning as an iterative process. In: AAAI (2012)
34. Sreedharan, S., Chakraborti, T., Kambhampati, S.: Handling model uncertainty and multiplicity in explanations via model reconciliation. In: ICAPS (2018)
35. Sreedharan, S., Srivastava, S., Smith, D., Kambhampati, S.: Why couldn't you do that? Explaining unsolvability of classical planning problems in the presence of plan advice. arXiv preprint arXiv:1903.08218 (2019)
36. Tsamardinos, I.: A probabilistic approach to robust execution of temporal plans with uncertainty. In: Vlahavas, I.P., Spyropoulos, C.D. (eds.) SETN 2002. LNCS (LNAI), vol. 2308, pp. 97–108. Springer, Heidelberg (2002). https://doi.org/10.1007/3-540-46014-4_10
37. Van Ackooij, W.: A discussion of probability functions and constraints from a variational perspective. Set-Valued Var. Anal. **28**(4), 585–609 (2020). https://doi.org/10.1007/s11228-020-00552-2
38. Van Melle, W.: MYCIN: a knowledge-based consultation program for infectious disease diagnosis. Int. J. Man Mach. Stud. **10**(3), 313–322 (1978)
39. Vidal, T., Ghallab, M.: Dealing with uncertain durations in temporal constraint networks dedicated to planning. In: ECAI (1996)
40. Vidal, T., Fargier, H.: Handling contingency in temporal constraint networks: from consistency to controllabilities. JAIR **11**, 23–45 (1999). https://doi.org/10.1080/095281399146607
41. Yu, P., Fang, C., Williams, B.: Resolving over-constrained probabilistic temporal problems through chance constraint relaxation. In: Proceedings of the AAAI Conference on Artificial Intelligence (2015)

The Impact of Synchronization in Parallel Stochastic Gradient Descent

Karl Bäckström[✉], Marina Papatriantafilou[✉], and Philippas Tsigas[✉]

Department of Computer Science and Engineering,
Chalmers University of Technology, Gothenburg, Sweden
{bakarl,ptrianta,tsigas}@chalmers.se

Abstract. In this paper, we discuss our and related work in the domain of efficient parallel optimization, using Stochastic Gradient Descent, for fast and stable convergence in prominent machine learning applications. We outline the results in the context of aspects and challenges regarding synchronization, consistency, staleness and parallel-aware adaptiveness, focusing on the impact on the overall convergence.

Keywords: Stochastic gradient descent · Lock-free · Machine Learning

1 Introduction

Among the most prominent methods used for common optimization problems in data analytics and Machine Learning (ML), especially for problems tackling large datasets using *Artificial Neural Networks* (ANN), is the widely used Stochastic Gradient Descent (SGD) optimization method, introduced by Augustin-Louis Cauchy back in 1847. By iteratively processing data, SGD enables Artificial Neural Network (ANN) training, Logistic Regression, Support Vector Machines, and other ML methods. Let us use ANNS as an example. ANNs build on the concept of biological neurons, where the model of a neuron is called a perceptron. Several perceptions can be used in connected layers, forming an ANN that can be trained on different ML tasks. A perceptron consists of a weight, a bias, and a non-linear activation function. The network will produce an output for a given input, and this output can be compared to an expected output through a loss function. From this point, the training process becomes a numerical optimization problem where the sets of weights and biases producing the lowest error are the target. On one hand large datasets generally allow for more complex tasks and better generalizing capabilities of the model; on the other hand they demand larger computational time. Parallelism is one of the major way for both speeding up model training and handling large datasets.

This work is supported by the Wallenberg AI, Autonomous Systems and Software Program (WASP), Knut and Alice Wallenberg Foundation, the SSF proj. "FiC" nr. GMT14-0032 and the VR proj. with nr. 2021-05443.

R. Bapi et al. (Eds.): ICDCIT 2022, LNCS 13145, pp. 60–75, 2022.
https://doi.org/10.1007/978-3-030-94876-4_4

Many algorithms for ML are far from trivial to parallelize. Taking SGD as the primary example, but any other iterative algorithm as well, usually every iteration requires the computation of the previous iteration to be completed, and available to be used in the next. As a consequence, parallelization would impose either that threads work in parallel only during each individual iteration and synchronize at the end in a lock-step manner, or relax the semantics of the original algorithm. These two main approaches to parallel SGD came to be known as *synchronous* and *asynchronous* parallel SGD, respectively, with fundamentally different properties in scalability, convergence and applicability.

It is easy to realize that synchronous parallelization suffers limitations in scalability due to the fact that each iteration is only as fast as the slowest contributing thread. Hence, slow threads, i.e. stragglers, present particularly in heterogeneous computing environments, can significantly impact the convergence time. Asynchronous approaches alleviate this limitation, showing improved scalability in some applications. However, the reduced inter-thread coordination that asynchrony entails breaks the semantics of the original SGD algorithm, and hence introduces several questions, among the most important is how the convergence time of SGD is affected. Moreover, the degree of synchronization that is still required, such as when accessing shared variables, becomes a focal point. For example, degradation in convergence due to lock-free inconsistent access is a risk, depending on the application. This can be avoided with consistency-enforcing mechanisms, one option being locking, however it is unclear whether or not it is worth the computational overhead it introduces in practice.

In this paper, we survey our work together with other recent related results in the domain of efficient parallel optimization with SGD for fast and stable convergence in prominent machine learning applications. We explore aspects of synchronization, consistency, staleness and parallel-aware adaptiveness, focusing on the impact on the overall convergence.

2   Preliminaries

2.1   SGD and Machine Learning

Machine learning with SGD is at its core an optimization problem:

$$\underset{\theta}{\text{minimize}} \quad f_D(\theta) \tag{1}$$

for a non-negative function $f : \mathbb{R}^d \rightarrow \mathbb{R}^+$. In machine learning (ML) applications, $\theta_t \in \mathbb{R}^d$ typically represents an encoding of the *learned knowledge*, and f_D quantifies the performance error of the model θ_t on the dataset D at iteration t. Solutions may be found using Stochastic Gradient Descent (SGD), defined as repeating the following with data mini-batches $B \in D$ sampled randomly:

$$\theta_{t+1} = \theta_t - \eta \widetilde{\nabla} f_B(\theta_t) \tag{2}$$

where $\widetilde{\nabla} f_B(\theta_t)$ and an unbiased estimate of the true gradient. The choice of the initialization point θ_0 is chosen at random according to some distribution, which as one might expect may significantly impact the convergence [32].

The negative gradient of a function constitutes the direction of *steepest descent*, resulting in a trajectory corresponding to the slope of the target function. The iteration (2) is repeated until a solution θ^* of sufficient quality is found, i.e. $f_D(\theta^*) < \epsilon$, referred to as ϵ-convergence.

The original deterministic counterpart Gradient Descent (GD) to SGD simply lets $B = D$, i.e. considers the entire dataset in every iteration. The stochastic element of random data subsampling in SGD entails two major benefits, namely that (i) sampling and processing only small mini-batches enables significantly faster iterations and (ii) the algorithm is effective on also non-convex target functions, as opposed to GD. However, SGD introduces a new hyper-parameter, the batch size b, which introduces *stochasticity* or *noise* in the convergence. While a certain degree of noise is necessary for enabling convergence in non-convex settings, it can be fatal when too high, causing endless sporadic oscillation about the initialization point θ_0. In practice, b consequently requires careful tuning. An established method for reducing such oscillation, while maintaining the stochasticity as necessary, is *Momentum-SGD* (MSGD), defined as follows:

$$\theta_{t+1} \leftarrow \theta_t + \mu(\theta_t - \theta_{t-1}) - \eta \widetilde{\nabla} f_B(\theta_t) \tag{3}$$

for some momentum parameter $\mu \in [0, 1]$. Momentum can accelerate the convergence of SGD in many practical settings, especially so for target functions which are irregular and asymmetric in shape, forming narrow valleys. Such irregularities are in particular known to arise in *deep learning* (DL) applications.

2.2 Performance Metrics

The implementation of any algorithm affects its performance and usefulness in practice. Considering SGD, or any iterative optimization algorithm, the performance is influenced by many implementation aspects and system features. As described in [22] a useful decomposition of the performance is to consider the *statistical* and *computational* efficiency, defined as follows.

1. *statistical efficiency* measures the number of SGD iterations required until reaching a solution of sufficient quality, ϵ-convergence
2. *computational efficiency* measures the number of iterations per time unit

The overall *convergence rate*, i.e. the wall-clock time until ϵ-convergence, is the most relevant in practice, and is essentially the product [22]:

$$\text{convergence rate} = \text{statistical efficiency} \times \text{computational efficiency}$$

Consequently, when proposing new algorithms (or altering existing ones) in this application domain that potentially change the *computational efficiency*, it is not sufficient to evaluate the invention by measuring only the *statistical efficiency*, i.e. counting the iterations until convergence. One must in general consider these metrics in conjunction, and measure the overall convergence rate. Ideally, they should also be measured separately, as this is the only way to truly understand from where potential improvements originate.

These metrics become particularly important in parallel algorithms for iterative optimization, since the parallelization method can have significant impact on the computational and statistical efficiency, as we shall see in the following.

3   Parallel SGD

While parallelism can improve computational efficiency, simply by managing to apply a greater number of updates in each unit of time, the impact on the statistical efficiency, and thereby the overall convergence rate, is unpredictable. Parallelization is consequently not trivial, and requires synchronization in every iteration (prior to applying an update) in order to not break the original sequential semantics of SGD. Alternatively, threads can execute the SGD algorithm, i.e. accessing and updating the shared state θ, asynchronously, although this might not conform to the sequential semantics.

These approaches correspond to two main directions of methods for parallel SGD, referred to as *synchronous* and *asynchronous*.

Most methods mentioned in this paper were originally introduced in the centralized shared-state context, either on a shared-memory parallel system or a distributed one with one node acting as a parameter server, which sequentializes updates. Most approaches can be naturally generalized to different computing infrastructure, and also to their decentralized counterpart. However, in this paper we retain the focus on asynchronous SGD in the context of shared-memory parallel systems, but keep in mind distributive and decentralizing generalizations, with occasional remarks on that topic.

3.1   Synchronous SGD

Synchronous SGD (SyncSGD) is a lock-step data-parallel version of SGD where threads or nodes access the shared θ_t at an iteration t, then compute gradients based on individual randomly sampled data-batches, see Fig. 1. The threads synchronize by averaging the resulting gradients before taking a global step according to (2) [37]. In the original version, *SyncSGD* is statistically equivalent to sequential SGD with larger mini-batch size [13], and can hence be considered a method for accelerated gradient computation. From this perspective, the *SyncSGD* approach does not break the semantics of the sequential SGD algorithm, and the vast empirical results and theoretical convergence guarantees in the literature entail predictable performance of *SyncSGD*. From a scalability perspective, since each SGD iteration is only as fast as the slowest contributing thread, the presence of slower threads, i.e. *stragglers*, becomes a bottleneck. A comprehensive overview of methods along this approach is provided in [8].

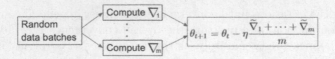

Fig. 1. In *SyncSGD* the threads' individual gradients are aggregated by averaging, after which a global iteration is performed. *SyncSGD* essentially corresponds to parallelization on the gradient computation level.

Stale-synchronous parallel (SSP) relaxes the strict synchronous semantics of *SyncSGD*, allowing faster threads to asynchronously compute a bounded number of SGD steps based on a local version of the state before synchronizing [14]. The method is useful in heterogeneous computing systems, where stragglers are kept in check. SSP has been proven useful for distributed DL applications, e.g. in [36] where a method for dynamically adjusting the *staleness* (the number of applied updates between the read vector and the one where the update is applied on) threshold is proposed, enabling improvements in computational efficiency.

From a progress perspective, note that the original *SyncSGD* as well as SSP provide weak progress guarantees, since in the presence of halting threads, the system as a whole will halt indefinitely in the synchronization step. This is partially addressed by *n-softsync* [35], a further relaxed variant of *SyncSGD* with partial synchronization, requiring only a fixed number n of threads to contribute a gradient at the synchronization point. Contrary to SSP, there is no bound on the maximum staleness. Introduced originally in the context of centralized distributed SGD with a parameter server [13,35], the recent work [18] implements similar semantics in a decentralized setting utilizing a `partial-allreduce` primitive which atomically applies the aggregated updates and redistributes the result.

3.2   Asynchronous Parallel SGD

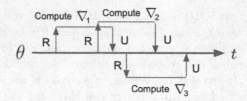

Fig. 2. *AsyncSGD* parallelizes the SGD iterations, allowing asynchronous read (R) and update (U) operations on the shared state.

Asynchronous parallel SGD (*AsyncSGD*) removes the gradient averaging synchronization step, allowing threads to access and update the shared state asynchronously. Consequently, while an update is being computed by one thread, there can be concurrent updates applied by other ones, i.e. *AsyncSGD* follows:

$$\theta_{t+1} \leftarrow \theta_t - \eta \widetilde{\nabla} f(v_t) \tag{4}$$

where $v_t = \theta_{t-\tau_t}$ is a thread's *view* of θ and τ_t is the number of concurrent updates, which defines the staleness. Updates are consequently generally computed based on states which are older than the ones on which the updates are applied (Fig. 2). The resulting impact on the convergence is referred to as *asynchrony-induced noise*, and affects, together with the overall distribution of the stalenesses τ_t, the statistical efficiency.

AsyncSGD enables increased computational efficiency with higher parallelism, up to a point where contention due to concurrent shared-memory access attempts becomes severe. We denote the corresponding number of threads by m_C^*; at this point the system stagnates and additional computing threads provide no additional speedup. In addition, the presence of staleness in *AsyncSGD* causes decay in statistical efficiency from the asynchrony-induced noise, which grows as more threads are introduced. Over-parallelization may thereby not only be redundant, but in fact harm the statistical efficiency, with potentially dire consequences on the overall convergence. There is hence a trade-off between computational and statistical efficiency, which in practice requires careful tuning of the level of parallelism (number of threads) m. The appropriate choice of m depends on the properties of the optimization problem itself, as well as the other hyper-parameters, e.g. the step size η and the batch size b.

AsyncSGD and Momentum. The research direction of asynchronous iterative optimization is not new, and sparked due to the works by Bertsekas and Tsitsiklis [9] in 1989. More recently, Chaturapruek et al. [11] show that, under several analytical assumptions such as convexity (linear and logistic regression), the convergence of *AsyncSGD* is not significantly affected by asynchrony and that the noise introduced by staleness is asymptotically negligible compared to the noise from the stochastic gradients. In [19] Lian et al. show that these assumptions can be partially relaxed, and it is shown that convergence is possible for non-convex problems, however with a bounded number of threads, and assuming bounded staleness. Several works have followed, aiming at understanding the impact of asynchrony on the convergence. In [26] Mitliagkas et al. show that under certain stochastic staleness models, asynchronous parallelism has an effect on convergence similar to momentum. This work is extended in parts of [6], which introduces models which capture the dynamics of the system more accurately, leading to alternate conclusions, as well as means to improve the statistical efficiency by asynchrony-awareness. In [23] Mania et al. model the algorithmic effect of asynchrony in *AsyncSGD* by perturbing the stochastic iterates with bounded noise. Their framework yields convergence bounds which, as described in the paper, are not tight, and rely on strong convexity of the target function. In the recent [2] Alistarh et al. introduced the concept of bounded divergence between the parameter vector and the threads' view of it, proving convergence bounds for convex and non-convex problems.

AsyncSGD and Lock-Freedom. HOGWILD! [28], introduced by Niu et al., implements *AsyncSGD* with *lock-free* accesses to the shared state θ. This is achieved in a straightforward manner by allowing uncoordinated, component-wise atomic access to the shared state θ_t, as opposed to traditional consistency-preserving access implemented with locks. This significantly reduced the computational synchronization overhead, and was shown to achieve near-optimal convergence rates, however assuming sparse updates. *AsyncSGD* with sparse or component-wise updates has since been a popular target of study due to the performance benefits of lock-freedom [27,29]. De Sa et al. [12] introduced a framework for analysis of HOGWILD!-style algorithms for sparse problems. The analysis was extended in [3], showing that due to the lack of θ-*consistency* (shared state consistency for shared state θ) of HOGWILD! (i.e. read operation includes partial updates) the convergence bound increases with a magnitude of $\sqrt{d}$ when relaxing the sparsity assumption. This indicates in particular higher statistical penalty for high-dimensional problems and motivates development of algorithms which, while enjoying the computational benefits of lock-freedom, also ensure consistency, in particular for high-dimensional problems such as DL. This is the main focus of [10], where a consistency-preserving lock-free implementation of *AsyncSGD* for DL is introduced. In [22] a detailed study of parallel SGD focusing on HOGWILD! and a new, GPU-implementation, is conducted, focusing on convex functions, with dense and sparse data sets and a comparison of different computing architectures.

AsyncSGD for DL. In [33] the focus is the fundamental limitation of data parallelism in ML. They observe that the limitations are due to concurrent SGD parameter accesses, during ML training, usually diminishing or even negating the parallelization benefits provided by additional parallel compute resources. To alleviate this, they propose the use of static analysis for identification of data that do not cause dependencies, for parallelizing their access. They do this as part of a system that uses Julia, a script language that performs just-in-time compilation. Their approach is effective and works well for e.g. Matrix factorization SGD. For DNNs, as they explain, their work is not directly applicable, since in DNNs permitting "good" dependence violation is the common parallelization approach. Asynchronous SGD approaches for DNNs are scarce in the current literature. In the recent work [21], Lopez et al. propose a semi-asynchronous SGD variant for DNN training, however requiring a master thread synchronizing the updates through gradient averaging, and relying on atomic updates of the entire parameter vector, resembling more a shared-memory implementation of parameter server. In [31] theoretical convergence analysis is presented for *SyncSGD* with *once-in-a-while* synchronization. They mention the analysis can guide in applying *SyncSGD* for DL, however the analysis requires strong convexity of the target function. [15] proposes a consensus-based SGD algorithm for distributed DL. They provide theoretical convergence guarantees, also in the non-convex case, however the empirical evaluation is limited to iteration counting as opposed to wall-clock time measurements, with mixed performance positioning relative to the baselines. In [20] a topology for decentralized parallel SGD is proposed, using pair-wise averaging synchronization.

Asynchrony-Adaptive SGD. Delayed optimization in asynchronous first-order optimization algorithms was analyzed initially in [1], where Agarwal et al. introduce step sizes which diminish over the progression of SGD, depending on the maximum staleness allowed in the system, but not adaptive to the actual delays observed. Adaptiveness to delayed updates during execution was proposed and analyzed in [24] under assumptions of gradient sparsity and *read* and *write* operations having the same relative ordering. A similar approach was used in [35], however for synchronous SGD with the *softsync* protocol. In [35] statistical speedup is observed in some cases for a limited number of worker nodes, however by using *momentum SGD*, which is not the case in their theoretical analysis, and step size decaying schedules on top of the staleness-adaptive step size. In [30], AdaDelay is proposed, which addresses a particular constrained convex optimization problem, namely training a logistic classifier with projected gradient descent. It utilizes a network of worker nodes computing gradients in parallel which are aggregated at a central parameter server with a step size that is scaled proportionally to the inverse staleness, τ^{-1} (τ denotes staleness defined as the number of applied concurrent updates). The staleness model in [30] is a uniform stochastic distribution, which implies a strict upper bound on the delays, making the system model partially asynchronous. [6] extends this line of research, exploring further the idea of adapting updates based on staleness, and studies in particular analytical foundations to motivate how.

4 Problems and Challenges with Parallel SGD

4.1 Scalability

Growing Batch Size. In *SyncSGD*, stragglers become a bottleneck, making every iteration only as fast as the slowest thread. This issue can however partially be reduced through relaxed semantics, such as SSP and the n-softsync protocol (see Sect. 3). Moreover, the convergence of *SyncSGD* under increasing parallelism is statistically equivalent to sequential SGD with a larger *mini-batch size b* [13], also shown in [6], which is a hyper-parameter that requires careful tuning depending on the problem. In particular, the convergence can be slower if b is too large [16, 25]. As discussed in Sect. 3.1, this indicates limited scalability, as over-parallization will impose large-batch properties, which in some cases slows down the convergence [13]. This motivates further exploration of asynchronous parallelism for scalability.

Staleness. *AsyncSGD* eliminates many scalability bottlenecks of *SyncSGD* due to reduced inter-thread coordination, however this also introduces other challenges related to asynchrony. As discussed in Sect. 3.2, asynchronous access to and update of the shared state leads to staleness due to the fact that updates may occur by threads concurrently to the gradient computation. The updates that are applied are in fact rarely in practice based on the latest shared state, as described by (4). For problems satisfying assumptions on convexity, smoothness and bounded gradients, staleness has little impact on the convergence of *Async-SGD* [11]. However, for a wider class of problems, staleness can have significant impact. In particular for problems not conforming to e.g. convexity assumptions, such as the recently relevant DL applications. Crucial steps toward understanding how convergence is affected in *AsyncSGD* due to staleness were taken by Mitliagkas et al. [26], explicitly quantifying the impact of concurrency, under a certain statistical staleness model. The results indicate that the influence of asynchrony has an effect similar to momentum in SGD, and a reduced step size. This analysis is extended in [6], proposing models better capturing the staleness dynamics, and showing that the momentum effect grows and the step size reduces monotonically as the parallelism is increased. This indicates a scalability limitation in convergence, which however can be partially alleviated by using a staleness-adaptive step size.

Progress and Consistency Guarantees. As previously mentioned, read and update operations on the shared state θ become focal in *AsyncSGD*, since they constitute the remaining synchronization steps in the otherwise asynchronous algorithm. There must be primitives in place to handle concurrent attempts to read and update by several threads, and these become bottlenecks for scalability at sufficiently high levels of parallelism. Traditionally, a separate thread or node acting as a parameter server is responsible for providing the latest parameter state to workers, as well as processing contributing gradients, sequentializing the updates [17]. To efficiently utilize multi-core systems, this was extended to shared-memory implementations [19,28,29]. The access to the shared state is then scheduled by the operating system, and regulated by some synchronization method, such as locking, to ensure consistency in case of concurrent read and update attempts. However, locks can be relatively computationally expensive, in particular when the gradient computation step itself incurs little latency. In addition, the total time spent on waiting for locks grows as more threads are introduced to the system, potentially making it scalability bottleneck. By allowing completely uncoordinated component-wise atomic read and update operations, i.e. HOGWILD! [28], such contention is eliminated, allowing significant speedup for sparse optimization problems in particular. However, for other problems, HOGWILD! introduces inconsistency when read and update operations occur concurrently, with unpredictable impact on the convergence. There is currently a lack of methods providing a middle-ground solutions in the literature in the realm in between these two endpoints of the synchronization spectrum, i.e. the consistency-enforcing lock-based *AsyncSGD* and the lock-free inconsistency-prone HOGWILD!. This spectrum is explored further in [10], and *Leashed-SGD* is proposed as a middle-ground solution. *Leashed-SGD* ensures consistency in arbitrarily dense problems, while enjoying the benefits of lock-freedom, reducing computational synchronization bottlenecks (see Sect. 5.1).

Memory Consumption. An additional aspect of scalability to consider is memory consumption; standard *AsyncSGD* implementations in the literature require each thread to copy the entire shared state θ prior to its individual gradient computation. The result of the computation, i.e. the stochastic gradient, is of the same dimension d as θ, and is stored locally until applied to the shared state in an SGD iteration. The magnitude of d varies, however in DL applications it is often in the magnitude of hundreds of thousands, sometimes millions, which is why the memory consumption of the *AsyncSGD* implementation needs to be carefully considered. This aspect is discussed further in [10], and possible improvements are explored.

4.2 Convergence Under Asynchrony

Staleness. The staleness that arises in *AsyncSGD* due to parallelism significantly impacts the statistical efficiency of the convergence; it has been shown analytically that the number of SGD iterations to ϵ-convergence increases linearly in the maximum staleness [3,12]. Hence, only if the gains in computational efficiency from parallelism are sufficiently great, will there be an overall improvement in wall-clock time until ϵ-convergence. In addition, inconsistent synchronization as in HOGWILD! potentially incurs further statistical penalty; the expected number of iterations required increases linearly in $\sqrt{d}$ [3]. Subsequently, there are challenges in understanding whether it is worth the computational overhead to ensure consistency for a given problem, and which synchronization primitives are appropriate to utilize.

Synchronization. As a consequence of Amdahl's law [5], when there is a synchronization overhead, the achievable speedup is bounded. In the context of *AsyncSGD*, this applies in particular for the computational efficiency, i.e. how many SGD updates can be applied in a given time unit. This implies that there is a *computational saturation point* m_C^*, for which additional threads will not provide additional significant computational speedup. For this statement, as well as the ones to follow in this paragraph, empirical evidence is provided in [10]. Moreover, due to the presence of staleness there is a degradation of statistical efficiency coupled to parallelism in *AsyncSGD* [23,33]. Hence, as more threads are introduced to the system, more iterations are required until reaching ϵ-convergence. At some level of parallelism, which we refer to as the *system saturation point* m_S^*, additional threads will no longer reduce the wall-clock time to ϵ-convergence, and might instead even increase it. It can be concluded that $m_S^* \leq m_C^*$ from a simple argument of contradiction, assuming that statistical efficiency degrades with higher parallelism. This assumption is in accordance with results in previous literature [3,12], and explored further in [6,10] There are substantial challenges in understanding the appropriate range of the number m of threads in order to (i) fully utilize the parallel computation ability of the system and (ii) avoid over-parallelization, potentially harming or completely obstructing convergence. Ideally an implementation of *AsyncSGD* feature resilience to tuning, providing reliable and fast convergence over a broad spectrum of parallelism, towards which [10] takes significant steps (see Sect. 5.2).

4.3   Benchmarking and Evaluation

Standardization. There are significant challenges in conducting empirical evaluations and comparisons which are useful and fair within the domain of parallel SGD, for several reasons: Firstly, there are several metrics of interest related to convergence of SGD, the measurements of which must be effectively aggregated as to show the overall performance. Traditionally, in ML the statistical efficiency is the metric most used, i.e. the number of SGD iterations until reaching sufficient performance, i.e. ϵ-convergence. However, when improvements in statistical efficiency is achieved by altering the underlying algorithm, this potentially alters the computational efficiency, i.e. the number of SGD iterations per time unit. In such cases, it is hence necessary that evaluations take this into consideration, and ideally provide measurements of the overall convergence rate, i.e. the wall-clock time until converging to a solution of sufficient quality. Secondly, the domain of shared-memory parallel SGD lacks established universal procedures for benchmarking, leaving the task of setting up an appropriate test environment to the individual authors. The domain contains a wide spectrum of questions, ranging from efficient communication protocols [4] in wide distributed DL networks to exploring the impact of progress guarantees and synchronization in shared data structures [3,28]. This renders the task of designing a universal benchmarking platform for parallel SGD including such universal procedures immensely difficult, if not impossible. The Deep500 framework [7] takes important steps in providing such an environment, although it focuses primarily on higher-level distributed SGD. For instance, the framework provides a Python interface for development, which does not facilitate exploration of for instance efficient shared data structures for fine-grained synchronization and mechanisms for memory management.

Hyper-parameter Dependencies. Another key issue in benchmarking parallel SGD for machine learning is the inherent dependency between parallelism and various hyper-parameters crucial for achieving convergence [13,26], some of the most important being the step size η and the mini-batch size b. As mentioned above, it is known that higher parallelism in *SyncSGD* exhibits similar convergence properties as sequential SGD with a larger batch size. As more threads or nodes are introduced to the system, the scalability of *SyncSGD* can hence appear to be limited due to the statistical penalty from a too large value of b. This can be avoided by choosing a sufficiently small initial b for each thread or node, which will then instead give the appearance of high scalability, but only until a certain level of parallelism [13]. It is hence of interest in such evaluations to provide empirical evidence from test scenarios that indicate the general ability of the proposed method to scale independently of hyper-parameter choices. Analogously, for *AsyncSGD*, there is delicate interplay between the step size η and the staleness distribution, stemming from the fact that stale updates correspond to gradients based on old views of the state, and are applied with a coarsity proportional to η [24,34]. A smaller η implies less impact on the convergence per update, hence tends to tolerate updates with higher staleness, and subsequently higher levels of parallelism. This can give the appearance of good scalability, showing speedup for a larger number of threads. It is in this case also of interest to provide empirical results that indicate scalability independently of hyper-parameters, such as η, for instance by testing for several choices of η.

In summary, there are challenges in establishing evaluation methodologies, making fair and useful comparisons between methods difficult. This is mainly due to the wide span of research questions in the domain. A collective strive towards standardized benchmarking platform for various methodological aspects is imperative. In addition, the dependence of the performance and scalability of parallel SGD algorithms on various hyper-parameters, such as step size η and batch size b, complicate empirical evaluations.

5 Our Work on Parallelizing SGD

5.1 Convergence of Staleness-Adaptive SGD

The scalability limitations of traditional synchronous parallel SGD highlighted in Sect. 4.1 motivates further exploration of asynchronous parallelization, i.e. *AsyncSGD* which has shown promising improvements in ability to scale for many applications. The degradation of statistical efficiency due to staleness is however a limiting factor, forcing the user to carefully tune the level of parallelism in order to maintain an actual overall speedup in convergence rate, as also highlighted in Sect. 4.1. In order to address this issue, we first propose methods to statistically model the behaviour of staleness in *AsyncSGD*. The models, which are proposed based on reasoning of the dynamics of the algorithm and its dependency on scheduling, capture the staleness distribution in practice to a high degree of precision, and more accurately than models previously proposed in the literature.

Based on the proposed staleness models, we provide analytical results that quantify the side-effect of asynchrony on the statistical efficiency. Moreover, our approach enables derivation of a staleness-adaptive step size, referred to as *MindTheStep-AsyncSGD*, which provably reduces this side-effect, and in expectation can, depending on the rate of adaptiveness, alter it into the more desired behaviour of momentum. We prove also that the staleness-adaptive step size is efficiently computable, ensuring minimal additional synchronization overhead for maximal scalability capability, as described in Sect. 4.2. We provide an empirical evaluation of the proposed staleness models and the adaptive step size for a relevant use case, namely DL for image classification. The empirical results show in particular: (i) significantly improved accuracy in modelling the staleness with our proposed models, (ii) reduced penalty from asynchrony-induced noise, leading to up to a ×1.5 speedup in convergence compared to baseline (standard *AsyncSGD* with constant step size) under high parallelism.

5.2 A Framework for Lock-Freedom and Consistency

Asynchronous parallelization of SGD, i.e. *AsyncSGD*, significantly reduces waiting compared to *SyncSGD*, as explained in the previous sections. However, the remaining synchronization that is needed, in particular access to the shared state, becomes focal and constitute a possible bottleneck. Motivated by analytical results in previous literature that indicate great computational benefits of lock-freedom, however a statistical penalty from inconsistency and staleness, we propose *Leashed-SGD* (lock-free consistent asynchronous shared-memory SGD), which is an extensible framework supporting algorithmic lock-free implementations of *AsyncSGD* and diverse mechanisms for consistency, and for regulating contention. It utilizes an efficient on-demand dynamic memory allocation and recycling mechanism, which reduces the overall memory footprint. We provide an analysis of the proposed framework in terms of safety, memory consumption, and model the progression of parallel threads in the execution of SGD, which we use for estimating contention over time and confirming the potential of the built-in contention regulation mechanism to reduce the overall staleness distribution.

Among the analytical results for *Leashed-SGD*, we provide guarantees on lock-freedom and atomicity, safety and exhaustiveness and bounds on the memory consumption. Moreover, we model the progression of the algorithm over time, finding in particular fixed points in the system useful for estimating potential contention and the effect of the built-in contention-regulating mechanism.

We conduct an extensive empirical study of *Leashed-SGD* for Multi-Layer Perceptron (MLP) and Convolutional Neural Network (CNN) training for image classification. The empirical study focuses on scalability, dependence on hyperparameters, distribution of the staleness, and benchmarks the proposed framework compared to established baselines, namely lock-based *AsyncSGD* and HOGWILD!. We draw the following main conclusions:

1. *Leashed-SGD* provides significantly higher tolerance towards the level of parallelism, with fast and stable convergence for a wide spectrum, taking significant steps towards addressing the scalability challenges highlighted in Sect. 4.1. The baselines however require careful tuning of the number of threads in order to avoid tediously slow convergence and are more prone to completely failing or crashing executions.
2. The lock-free nature of *Leashed-SGD* entails a self-regulating balancing effect between latency and throughput, leading to an overall reduced staleness distribution, which in many instances is crucial for achieving convergence.
3. For MLP training we observe up to 27% reduced median running time for ϵ-convergence for *Leashed-SGD* compared to baselines, with similar memory footprint. For CNN training, we observe a $\times 4$ speedup for ϵ-convergence, with a memory footprint reduction with 17% on average.

For the empirical study, a modular and extensible C++ framework is developed with the purpose of facilitating development of shared-memory parallel SGD with varying synchronization mechanisms (https://github.com/dcs-chalmers/shared-memory-sgd). Hence, we take steps towards addressing the challenges (highlighted in Sect. 4.3) that the community faces regarding a general platform for further exploration of aspects of fine-grained synchronization in this domain.

6   Conclusions

There are significant challenges for asynchronous parallel SGD methods for machine learning to scale, due to (i) staleness and reduced update freshness and (ii) computational overhead from synchronization for shared-memory operations.

While higher parallelism in *AsyncSGD* enables more iterations per second, its inherent staleness and asynchrony-induced noise leads to an deteriorating statistical efficiency, requiring a growing number of iterations to achieve sufficient convergence. Understanding and modelling the dynamics of the staleness enables explicitly quantifying its side-effect on the convergence, towards which important steps were taken in [26], however under simplifying assumptions. Under a more practical system model, this analysis was extended in [6], and used to show how adaptiveness to staleness reduces asynchrony-induced noise, and thereby improves convergence. In addition, it allows derivation of the proposed staleness-adaptive *MindTheStep-AsyncSGD* which provably reduces this side-effect. The analytical results are confirmed in practice in [6], showing increased statistical efficiency in ANN training for image classification.

Relaxed inter-thread synchronization, with weak consistency requirements as in HOGWILD! [28], enables a straightforward way for achieving lock-freedom without consistency guarantees in shared state. The reduced computational overhead allows overall speedup for sparse problems, where inconsistency might have little impact [28] and asymptotic convergence bounds can be established. However, the inconsistency has implications on the statistical efficiency, as observed theoretically in [3] and confirmed in [6,10]. In [10] an interface is introduced, providing abstractions of operations on the shared state θ, utilized in the proposed lock-free *Leashed-SGD* framework, which includes an implementation that guarantees consistency and which is extensible to provide configurable consistency. The lock-free nature of *Leashed-SGD* has a self-regulating effect which avoids congestion under high parallelism, which by reducing the overall staleness distribution enables fast and stable convergence in contexts where the baselines fail. In this context, the dynamic memory allocation featured in *Leashed-SGD* allows for significantly reduced memory footprint, which is critical in particular for DL applications where the problems dimension can be in the order of millions.

References

1. Agarwal, A., Duchi, J.C.: Distributed delayed stochastic optimization. In: Advances in Neural Information Processing Systems, pp. 873–881 (2011)
2. Alistarh, D., Chatterjee, B., Kungurtsev, V.: Elastic consistency: a general consistency model for distributed stochastic gradient descent. arXiv preprint arXiv:2001.05918 (2020)
3. Alistarh, D., De Sa, C., Konstantinov, N.: The convergence of stochastic gradient descent in asynchronous shared memory. In: ACM Symposium on Principles of Distributed Computing, PODC 2018, pp. 169–178. ACM, New York (2018). https://doi.org/10.1145/3212734.3212763
4. Alistarh, D., Grubic, D., Li, J., Tomioka, R., Vojnovic, M.: QSGD: communication-efficient SGD via gradient quantization and encoding. In: Advances in Neural Information Processing Systems, pp. 1709–1720 (2017)

5. Amdahl, G.M.: Validity of the single processor approach to achieving large scale computing capabilities. In: Proceedings of the April 18–20, 1967, Spring Joint Computer Conference, pp. 483–485 (1967)
6. Bäckström, K., Papatriantafilou, M., Tsigas, P.: MindTheStep-AsyncPSGD: adaptive asynchronous parallel stochastic gradient descent. In: 2019 IEEE International Conference on Big Data (Big Data), pp. 16–25. IEEE (2019)
7. Ben-Nun, T., Besta, M., Huber, S., Ziogas, A.N., Peter, D., Hoefler, T.: A modular benchmarking infrastructure for high-performance and reproducible deep learning. In: 2019 IEEE International Parallel and Distributed Processing Symposium (IPDPS), pp. 66–77. IEEE (2019)
8. Ben-Nun, T., Hoefler, T.: Demystifying parallel and distributed deep learning: an in-depth concurrency analysis. ACM Comput. Surv. (CSUR) **52**(4), 1–43 (2019)
9. Bertsekas, D.P., Tsitsiklis, J.N.: Parallel and Distributed Computation: Numerical Methods, vol. 23. Prentice Hall, Upper Saddle River (1989)
10. Bäckström, K., Walulya, I., Papatriantafilou, M., Tsigas, P.: Consistent lock-free parallel stochastic gradient descent for fast and stable convergence. In: 2021 IEEE International Parallel and Distributed Processing Symposium (IPDPS), pp. 423–432 (2021). https://doi.org/10.1109/IPDPS49936.2021.00051
11. Chaturapruek, S., Duchi, J.C., Ré, C.: Asynchronous stochastic convex optimization: the noise is in the noise and SGD don't care. In: Advances in Neural Information Processing Systems, pp. 1531–1539 (2015)
12. De Sa, C.M., Zhang, C., Olukotun, K., Ré, C., Ré, C.: Taming the wild: a unified analysis of Hogwild-style algorithms. In: Advances in Neural Information Processing Systems, vol. 28, pp. 2674–2682. Curran Associates, Inc. (2015). http://papers.nips.cc/paper/5717-taming-the-wild-a-unified-analysis-of-hogwild-style-algorithms.pdf
13. Gupta, S., Zhang, W., Wang, F.: Model accuracy and runtime tradeoff in distributed deep learning: a systematic study. In: 2016 IEEE 16th International Conference on Data Mining (ICDM), pp. 171–180. IEEE (2016)
14. Ho, Q., et al.: More effective distributed ml via a stale synchronous parallel parameter server. In: Advances in Neural Information Processing Systems, pp. 1223–1231 (2013)
15. Jiang, Z., Balu, A., Hegde, C., Sarkar, S.: Collaborative deep learning in fixed topology networks. In: Advances in Neural Information Processing Systems, pp. 5904–5914 (2017)
16. Keskar, N.S., Mudigere, D., Nocedal, J., Smelyanskiy, M., Tang, P.T.P.: On large-batch training for deep learning: generalization gap and sharp minima. arXiv:1609.04836 (2016)
17. Li, M., et al.: Scaling distributed machine learning with the parameter server. In: 11th Symposium on Operating Systems Design and Implementation, pp. 583–598 (2014)
18. Li, S., Ben-Nun, T., Girolamo, S.D., Alistarh, D., Hoefler, T.: Taming unbalanced training workloads in deep learning with partial collective operations. In: 25th ACM SIGPLAN Symposium on Principles and Practice of Parallel Programming, pp. 45–61 (2020)
19. Lian, X., Huang, Y., Li, Y., Liu, J.: Asynchronous parallel stochastic gradient for nonconvex optimization. In: Advances in Neural Information Processing Systems, pp. 2737–2745 (2015)
20. Lian, X., Zhang, W., Zhang, C., Liu, J.: Asynchronous decentralized parallel stochastic gradient descent. In: International Conference on Machine Learning, pp. 3043–3052. PMLR (2018)

21. Lopez, F., Chow, E., Tomov, S., Dongarra, J.: Asynchronous SGD for DNN training on shared-memory parallel architectures. In: International Parallel and Distributed Processing Symposium Workshops (IPDPSW), pp. 1–4. IEEE (2020)
22. Ma, Y., Rusu, F., Torres, M.: Stochastic gradient descent on modern hardware: multi-core CPU or GPU? Synchronous or asynchronous? In: 2019 IEEE International Parallel and Distributed Processing Symposium (IPDPS), pp. 1063–1072. IEEE (2019)
23. Mania, H., Pan, X., Papailiopoulos, D., Recht, B., Ramchandran, K., Jordan, M.I.: Perturbed iterate analysis for asynchronous stochastic optimization. SIAM J. Optim. **27**(4), 2202–2229 (2017)
24. McMahan, B., Streeter, M.: Delay-tolerant algorithms for asynchronous distributed online learning. In: Advances in Neural Information Processing Systems, vol. 27, pp. 2915–2923. Curran Associates, Inc. (2014). http://papers.nips.cc/paper/5242-delay-tolerant-algorithms-for-asynchronous-distributed-online-learning.pdf
25. Mishkin, D., Sergievskiy, N., Matas, J.: Systematic evaluation of convolution neural network advances on the ImageNet. Comput. Vis. Image Underst. **161**, 11–19 (2017)
26. Mitliagkas, I., Zhang, C., Hadjis, S., Ré, C.: Asynchrony begets momentum, with an application to deep learning. In: 54th Annual Allerton Conference on Communication, Control, and Computing, pp. 997–1004. IEEE (2016)
27. Nguyen, L.M., Nguyen, P.H., van Dijk, M., Richtárik, P., Scheinberg, K., Takáč, M.: SGD and Hogwild! convergence without the bounded gradients assumption. arXiv preprint arXiv:1802.03801 (2018)
28. Recht, B., Re, C., Wright, S., Niu, F.: Hogwild: a lock-free approach to parallelizing stochastic gradient descent. In: Advances in Neural Information Processing Systems (NIPS), vol. 24, pp. 693–701. Curran Associates, Inc. (2011)
29. Sallinen, S., Satish, N., Smelyanskiy, M., Sury, S.S., Ré, C.: High performance parallel stochastic gradient descent in shared memory. In: IEEE International Parallel and Distributed Processing Symposium, pp. 873–882. IEEE (2016)
30. Sra, S., Yu, A.W., Li, M., Smola, A.J.: AdaDelay: delay adaptive distributed stochastic convex optimization. arXiv preprint arXiv:1508.05003 (2015)
31. Stich, S.U.: Local SGD converges fast and communicates little. In: International Conference on Learning Representations (ICLR) (2019)
32. Sutskever, I., Martens, J., Dahl, G., Hinton, G.: On the importance of initialization and momentum in deep learning. In: International Conference on Machine Learning, pp. 1139–1147 (2013)
33. Wei, J., Gibson, G.A., Gibbons, P.B., Xing, E.P.: Automating dependence-aware parallelization of machine learning training on distributed shared memory. In: 14th EuroSys Conference 2019, pp. 1–17 (2019)
34. Zhang, W., Gupta, S., Lian, X., Liu, J.: Staleness-aware Async-SGD for distributed deep learning. arXiv preprint arXiv:1511.05950 (2015)
35. Zhang, W., Gupta, S., Lian, X., Liu, J.: Staleness-aware Async-SGD for distributed deep learning. In: Proceedings of the Twenty-Fifth International Joint Conference on Artificial Intelligence, IJCAI 2016, pp. 2350–2356. AAAI Press (2016)
36. Zhao, X., An, A., Liu, J., Chen, B.X.: Dynamic stale synchronous parallel distributed training for deep learning. In: 2019 IEEE 39th International Conference on Distributed Computing Systems (ICDCS), pp. 1507–1517, July 2019. https://doi.org/10.1109/ICDCS.2019.00150
37. Zinkevich, M., Weimer, M., Li, L., Smola, A.J.: Parallelized stochastic gradient descent. In: Advances in Neural Information Processing Systems, pp. 2595–2603 (2010)

Distributed Computing

A Distributed Algorithm for Constructing an Independent Dominating Set

Suman Banerjee[✉], Abhishek Dogra, Anurag Kumar Singh,
and Subhasis Bhattacharjee

Department of Computer Science and Engineering, Indian Institute of Technology
Jammu, Jammu 181201, Jammu and Kashmir, India
{suman.banerjee,2018ucs0070,2018ucs0069,
subhasis.bhattacharjee}@iitjammu.ac.in

Abstract. Given a simple finite undirected graph, finding a minimum INDEPENDENT DOMINATING SET is a fundamental graph algorithmic problem. In this paper, we propose a distributed algorithm for constructing an independent dominating set (IDS) in the CONGEST model of distributed computing. Our algorithm requires only 2-hop partial information at each node for computations, and hence each node takes various decisions without having any global knowledge of the graph. The algorithm consists of mainly three steps. First, we construct a dominating set using a node estimation and voting mechanism. Then each dominating node finds out a vertex cover of its 2-hop graph by an incremental greedy algorithm along with a few optimizations and tie breaking. We prove that the union of the vertex covers computed by each dominating node is a vertex cover of the original graph. Finally, we construct an independent set by complementing the vertex cover. Considering this independent set as an IDS (of the induced graph by the closed neighborhood of the independent set), its closed neighborhood is deleted from the original graph to construct the reduced graph. We repeat the above three-step process until the reduced graph is null.

To the best of our knowledge, this is the first distributed algorithm for constructing an IDS. We experimented on eight real-world networks and synthetic networks from well-known Erdos-Renyi graph generators. We observe that in most of the cases our algorithm takes only a few (approx 5) iterations and returns an IDS whose size is fractionally higher than the size of IDS computed by a sequential greedy algorithm.

Keywords: Distributed algorithm · Vertex cover · Voting ·
Independent Dominating Set

1 Introduction

Given a graph, a subset of its vertices is said to be an *independent set* if between every pair of vertices there is no edge [5]. Similarly, a subset of the vertices of an undirected graph is said to be a *dominating set* if every vertex which is not in

© Springer Nature Switzerland AG 2022
R. Bapi et al. (Eds.): ICDCIT 2022, LNCS 13145, pp. 79–95, 2022.
https://doi.org/10.1007/978-3-030-94876-4_5

the subset has at least one neighbor in the subset. Combining these two, a subset of the vertices is said to be an IDS if it is both independent and dominating. Finding a maximum size independent set, minimum size dominating set and also the minimum size IDS are popular NP-Complete problems. Given an undirected graph finding a minimum size IDS is a graph algorithmic problem having applications in *wireless networks*, social networks [10], etc. Next, we report relevant studies on the independent dominating set problem.

Related Work. Haraguchi [9] proposed a local search technique for this problem which uses k-swap as the neighborhood operation. For $k = 2$ and 3, their algorithm runs in $\mathcal{O}(n \cdot \Delta)$ and $\mathcal{O}(n \cdot \Delta^3)$ time, respectively where n and Δ denote the number of nodes and maximum degree of the graph. Hurink and Nieberg [10] first proposed a polynomial time approximation scheme for this problem for the graphs with polynomially bounded growth. Gaspers and Liedloff [7] proposed a branch-and-reduce algorithm for this problem having the running time $\mathcal{O}(1.3575^n)$. Subsequently, Bourgeois et al. [4] proposed a branching algorithm with running time $\mathcal{O}^*(2^{0.424n})$. Subsequently, this has been improved by Bourgeois et al. [3] to $\mathcal{O}^*(2^{0.417n})$. Liu et al. [12] showed that this problem is NP-Complete even on cubic bipartite graphs. Several soft computing-based approaches have also been proposed [18,19]. Goddard et al. [8] presented a comprehensive survey on different combinatorial results on this problem. Loverov et al. [13] showed that the IDS problem in NP-Complete even on cubic planner graph. Most of the studies are either complexity theoretic or combinatorial in nature, not algorithmic. Also, to the best of our knowledge, there does not exist any distributed algorithm for this problem.

Our Contributions. In this paper, we study the Independent Dominating Set problem and propose a purely distributed algorithm. Our algorithm requires only two hop connectivity information from every node and the message passing is from any node to its immediate neighbors only. Our algorithm is broadly divided into three steps. First, we extract out a dominating set where dominating nodes are elected based on estimates and voting. These dominating nodes construct a vertex cover of the graph. Finally, we construct an independent set by complementing the vertex cover and reduce the graph by deleting the closed neighborhood of the independent set. The algorithm repeats the above three-step process until the vertex set of the graph is exhausted. The most important feature of our algorithm is that all the above three steps are computed in $\mathcal{O}(1)$ rounds of message communications among the immediate neighbors of each node. Moreover, a node does not need to know the size, the diameter or the maximum degree of a node in the graph. A node stops itself when it is either marked itself as an Independent Dominating Node (namely, IDN) or it is a neighbor of an Independent Dominating Node (namely, NIDN). The algorithm finishes when all nodes are marked. We have experimented with our proposed approach with real-world as well as synthetic datasets.

Organization of the Paper. Section 2 contains some preliminary concepts and states the problem. Section 3 contains the proposed solution approach. Section 4 contains the experimental evaluation of the proposed approach. Finally, Sect. 5 concludes our study.

2 Preliminaries and Problem Definition

Graphs considered in this paper are finite, simple, and undirected [5]. A graph is denoted by $G(V, E)$ where $V(G)$ and $E(G)$ denotes the vertex and edge set of the graph. We denote the number of vertices and edges of G by n and m, respectively. For any vertex $v \in V(G)$, its open k-hop neighbor is denoted as $N^k(v)$ and defined as $N^k(v) = \{u : dist(u, v) \le k\}$. Here, $dist(u, v)$ denotes the shortest path distance from u to v. Similarly, closed k-hop neighbor of v is defined as $N^k[v] = N^k(v) \cup \{v\}$. When $k = 1$, we call this as the open and closed neighborhood of v and denoted by $N(v)$ and $N[v]$, respectively. Instead of a single vertex for a subset of vertices S, $N^k(S)$ is defined as $N^k(S) = \{u : u \in V(G) \setminus S$ and $\exists v \in S$ such that $dist(uv) \le k\}$, and $N^k[S]$ as $N^k[S] = S \cup N^k(S)$. The cardinality of the open neighborhood is defined as *degree*. A vertex is said to be a *pendent vertex* and *isolated vertex* if its degree is one and zero, respectively.

A subset of the vertices $\mathcal{D} \subseteq V(G)$ is said to be a dominating set of G if every vertex which is not in the subset has at least one neighbor in $\mathcal{D}$, i.e., $N[\mathcal{D}] = V(G)$. The nodes in $\mathcal{D}$ are called 'dominating' nodes and the remaining nodes are called non-dominating nodes. Finding a dominating set of minimum size is a well known NP-Complete problem [5]. A subset of vertices $S \subseteq V(G)$ is said to be an *independent set* if for every $u, v \in S$ and $(u, v) \notin E(G)$. Finding an independent set of minimum size is a well known NP-Complete problem [5]. Given a subset of the vertices $\mathcal{C}$ it is called as the IDS if it is both independent set and dominating set. Given a graph $G(V, E)$ and a positive integer k, the decision version of this problem asks to determine whether G contains an IDS of size at most k. The size of a minimum IDS is known as the *'independent domination number'* of G and denoted as $id(G)$.

INDEPENDENT DOMINATING SET PROBLEM (Decision Version)

Input: A Simple Undirected Graph $G(V, E)$, $k \in \mathbb{Z}^+$.
Question: Does G contain an independent dominating set of size of at most k or is $id(G) \le k$?

The IDS Problem is also NP-Complete. Next, we proceed to describe our distributed algorithm.

3 The Proposed Algorithm

Our algorithm is broadly divided into three steps. Given the graph, first we construct a dominating set. Next, using this dominating set, we construct a vertex cover of the graph. We know the complement of the vertex cover of a graph is independent set. Subsequently, We delete the close neighborhood of the independent set from the graph. Now on the reduced graph, we repeat this process until the whole graph is exhausted. Algorithm 1 describes this procedure.

Algorithm 1: Proposed algorithm for independent dominating set construction

---

Data: A simple undirected graph $G(V, E)$
Result: An independent dominating set Φ of G
1 $\Phi \leftarrow \emptyset$;
2 **Initialization for** $All\ u \in V(G)$ **do**
3 $\quad$ State(u) = null, Comment: State$(u) \in \{\text{null}, \text{IDN}, \text{NIDN}\}$;
4 **while** $\exists v \in V(G)$ and $State(v) = null$ $Comment$: $V(G) \neq \emptyset$ **do**
5 $\quad$ **Step 1:** Construct a dominating set of the graph;
6 $\quad$ **Step 2:** From the dominating set information construct a vertex
$\quad\quad$ cover (say $\mathcal{B}$);
7 $\quad$ **Step 3:** Construct the independent set, $\mathcal{S} \leftarrow V(G) \setminus \mathcal{B}$;
8 $\quad$ **for** $All\ u \in \mathcal{S}$ **do**
9 $\quad\quad$ State(u) = IDN;
10 $\quad$ **for** $All\ u \in N(\mathcal{S})$ and $All\ u \notin \mathcal{S}$ **do**
11 $\quad\quad$ State(u) = NIDN;
12 $\quad$ $\Phi \leftarrow \Phi \cup \mathcal{S}$;
13 $\quad$ $V(G) \leftarrow V(G) \setminus N[\mathcal{S}]$
14 **return** Φ

Now, we describe each steps involved in the algorithm in details. Along with the description, we also explain our with an example. For this purpose, we use the graph shown in Fig. 1.

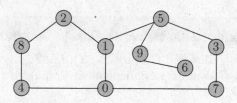

Fig. 1. Graph considered for running example in this study.

3.1 Construction of the Dominating Set (Step 1)

For any node $v \in V(G)$, first we define its k-hop partial graph. Let $G[V']$ denotes the subgraph induced by the vertex set V' in G.

Definition 1 (k-hop Partial Graph). *For a given graph G, the k-hop partial graph for a node v is denoted as $PG^k(v)$ whose vertex set is $V(PG^k(v)) = \{u : dist(u,v) \leq k\}$ and the edge set is $E(PG^k(v)) = E(G[V(PG^k(v))]) \setminus \{u, w \in V(PG^k(v)) : dist(u,v) = dist(w,v) = k$ and $(u,w) \in E(G)\}$.*

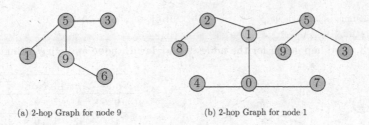

(a) 2-hop Graph for node 9   (b) 2-hop Graph for node 1

Fig. 2. Two hop graph for the nodes 9 and 1.

Figure 2 shows the 2-hop partial graphs for the nodes 1 and 9. *We will prove that knowing only the 2-hop partial graph at each node is sufficient to construct the IDS in a fully distributed manner.* At the start of algorithm, we assume that each node is aware of its neighbors (i.e., 1-hop neighbors). Then, each node collects 1-hop neighbor information from each of its neighbor to get the knowledge of 2-hop partial graph. This can be done in just one round of message exchange with a total of n messages. So, it can be safely accepted that we describe the proposed distributed algorithm at each node with only the local knowledge of the 2-hop partial graph.

In our method, each node checks its suitability to be included in the dominating set. Hence, it calculates an estimate which is stated in Definition 2.

Definition 2 (Node and Edge Estimate). *For an edge $(uv) \in E(G)$, we denote its estimate $\mu(uv)$ and defined as the nodes that are at least neighbor of at least one of these two nodes, i.e., $\mu(uv) = |N(u) \cup N(v)|$. The estimate of a node v is the maximum among all the edges that are incident with the node v, i.e., $\mu(u) = max\{\mu(uv) : v \in N(u)\}$.*

After calculating the node estimate, each node $v \in V(G)$ informs its estimate to its neighbor. After hearing the estimates every node recommends exactly one node to be included in the dominating set with the highest estimate value. We break ties based on the node id. Now, we illustrate this with an example. Observe the 2-hop partial graphs as shown in Fig. 3. Consider the $(5,9)$ edge of the graph shown in Fig. 3(a). We observe that $N(5) = \{1, 9, 3\}$ and $N(9) = \{5, 6\}$. As per Definition 2, the estimation of the edge $(5,6)$ is $\mu(5,6) = |N(6) \cup N(5)| = 5$.

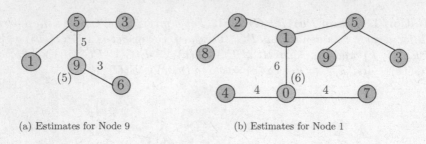

(a) Estimates for Node 9   (b) Estimates for Node 1

Fig. 3. Two hop graph for the nodes 9 and 1 with node and edge estimates

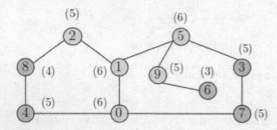

Node	Voted	Node	Voted
0	1	5	1
1	0	6	9
2	1	7	0
3	5	8	2
4	0	9	5

Fig. 4. Example graph with node estimates. The table contains node id with their corresponding voted node id.

Similarly, the estimation of edge $(9,6)$ is 3. These are the only two edges incident with the vertex 9. The node estimate for the node 9 is the maximum of 5 and 3 which is 5. Similarly, if we work out in the 2-hop partial graph of the node 0 as shown in Fig. 3(b), the estimate for the node 0 is 6.

Figure 4 shows our example graph along with its node estimates (shown inside bracket). We can observe that the node 0 has the neighbors 1, 4, and 7. Their respective nodes estimates are 6, 5, and 5. Every node votes a neighbor node with the highest estimate. So, node 0 will vote 1. For the example graph, nodes with their respective voted nodes are shown in Fig. 4.

Algorithm 2 describes this process in the form of psudocode. This kind of estimation technique has been previously used to find out the connected (and smaller) dominating set of a topology graph of a wireless sensor network [1,2].

Algorithm 2: Dominating set construction Algorithm

   Data: A simple undirected graph $G(V, E)$
   Result: A dominating set $\mathcal{D}$ of G
1 $\mathcal{D} \leftarrow \emptyset$;
2 **Initialization for** $All\ u \in V(G)$ **do**
3   **for** $All\ v \in N(u)$ **do**
4   Calculate $\mu(uv)$;
5   Calculate $\mu(u)$;
6 **First Round for** $All\ v \in V(G)$ **do**
7   Exchange $\mu(v)$ among the nodes in $N(v)$;
8 **Second Round for** $Each\ v \in V(G)$ **do**
9   Let $\mu(u) > \mu(w)\ \forall w \in N(v)$;
10 **Final for** $Each\ v \in V(G)$ **do**
11   **if** v *is recommended by some* $u \in N(v)$ **then**
12        $\mathcal{D} \leftarrow \mathcal{D} \cup \{v\}$;

Now, we show a few theoretical results related to our dominating set construction (Algorithm 2). For the purpose of determining the computational complexity, let us assume that the maximum degree of a node in the graph is Δ where is $\Delta << n$ for large graphs in general. By computational complexity, we denote the amount of computation that a node does for a decision or message exchange. Our distributed algorithm however does not need any global knowledge of n and Δ. It is easy to note that the total number of nodes in a 2-hop partial graph $(PG^2(v))$ of any node v is $\mathcal{O}(\Delta^2)$. Also, as the degree of each node of $N^2(v)$ is 1 in $PG^2(v)$, the total number of edges in a $PG^2(v)$ is $\mathcal{O}(\Delta^2)$.

Lemma 1. *Let,* $v \in \mathcal{D}$ *and* $|\mathcal{D}| > 1$ *then there exists a node* $u \in N(v)$ *such that* $u \in \mathcal{D}$.

Proof. It is clear the algorithm that each node $v \in V(G)$ recommends exactly one node $u \in N(v)$ to be included in the dominating set. So, for any node $v \in \mathcal{D}$ there exists one node $u \in N(v)$ which is in $\mathcal{D}$.

Lemma 2. *The computation complexity, message complexity and time complexity of our dominating set construction procedure are* $\mathcal{O}(\Delta^2)$ $\mathcal{O}(n)$ *and* $\mathcal{O}(1)$, *respectively.*

Proof. For edge estimate, each node v computes the size of union of v's neighbor with all of its Δ (at most) neighbors. Each node has to do at most 2Δ operations for one set union operation. And there are at most Δ set unions operations to be computed by each node. For node estimate, each node has to find the node with the maximum edge estimate in Δ operations. So, the computation complexity is $\mathcal{O}(\Delta^2)$. Each node $v \in V(G)$ sends exactly one recommend message to its direct neighbors and at most one declared dominating message in the second round. Hence, for each node the number of messages are 2 and total number of messages are $2n$ (which is of $\mathcal{O}(n)$). Also, this clearly shows that two rounds are sufficient for generating the dominating set leading to the time complexity of $\mathcal{O}(1)$.

Theorem 1. *The selected nodes in $\mathcal{D}$ by Algorithm 2 is a dominating set of G.*

Proof. To prove that $\mathcal{D}$ is the dominating set we need to show $N[\mathcal{D}] = V(G)$. Now, each node $v \in V(G)$ recommends exactly one node of its neighbors and all such recommended nodes are included in the dominating set. So, irrespective of whether $v \in \mathcal{D}$ or $v \notin \mathcal{D}$ there is at least one neighbor $u \in N(v)$ (Here, node u is recommended by v.). Thus according to the definition of dominating set $\mathcal{D}$ is a dominating set of G.

Lemma 3. *The union of all the 2-hop graphs of the dominating nodes constitute the whole graph, i.e., $\bigcup_{v \in \mathcal{D}} PG^2(v) = V(G)$.*

Proof. We prove this statement by showing two cases:

Case 1 (Nodes are Preserved): Here, we need to show that for all $u \in V(G)$, there exists at least one $w \in \mathcal{D}$ such that $u \in PG^2(w)$. u can be either a dominating or a non-dominating node. If u is a dominating node then certainly it belongs to $PG^2(u)$. So, in this case $u \equiv w$. On the other hand, if u is not a dominating node then there must exist a $v \in \mathcal{D}$ such that $v \in N(u)$. So, u contained in $V(PG^2(v))$. This proves that the node set of the original graph is preserved.

Case 2 (Edges are Preserved): Here, we need to show that for all $(u, v) \in E(G)$, there exists at least one $w \in \mathcal{D}$ such that $(u, v) \in E(PG^2(w))$. Now, any one of the following cases may happen. Both, u and v are dominating nodes. In that case, the edge (u, v) belongs to both $PG^2(u)$ and $PG^2(v)$. So, the union of the $PG^2(w)$ for all $w \in \mathcal{D}$ contains the edge (u, v). Now, assume that one of them is dominating and the other one is non-dominating node. Without loss of generality, assume that u is dominating and v is non-dominating. Certainly, the edge (u, v) belongs to $E(PG^2(u))$. Hence, in this case also the edge (u, v) is preserved. The remaining case is that both u and v are non-dominating nodes. As $\mathcal{D}$ is a dominating set of G, there must exists a node $w \in \mathcal{D}$ such that $w \in N(u)$. We can easily follow that the edge (u, v) belongs to $PG^2(w)$. So, in this case also the edge is preserved. This completes the proof.

3.2   Construction of Vertex Cover (Step 2)

Once we have the dominating set, the next step is to construct the vertex cover. The construction algorithm is as follows. However, before stating the procedure, we highlight that this step will be carried out by the dominating nodes only. Other nodes will safely skip this step. For every dominating node $v \in V(G)$, we construct its two hop graph denoted as $PG^2(v)$. Now, in each partial graph, we construct their respective vertex covers in the following way. We calculate the degree of all the non-dominating nodes present in the partial graph, short them in the decreasing order and greedily picks up one with the highest degree and delete the edges incident on this to obtain a reduced graph. This process is repeated until all the dominating nodes are checked. However, we can observe that there may be some edges which can not be covered by non-dominating nodes. To cover such edges between the two end vertices (both of them are dominating one), we pick one with the lowest node id. For a dominating node v, we denote the vertex cover of the 2-hop partial graph of v as $VC(PG^2(v))$. This procedure has been described in the form of psudocode in Algorithm 3.

Algorithm 3: Vertex cover construction algorithm

Data: A simple undirected graph $G(V, E)$. and its dominating set $\mathcal{D}$
Result: A Vertex cover $\mathcal{C}$ of G

1 $\mathcal{C} \leftarrow \emptyset$;
2 **Computation for** *All $u \in \mathcal{D}$* **do**
3      $\mathcal{C}(u) \leftarrow \emptyset, \mathcal{C}^1(u) \leftarrow \emptyset, \mathcal{C}^2(u) \leftarrow \emptyset$;
4   **while** *$\exists v \in V(PG^2(u))$ and $v \notin \mathcal{D}$* **do**
5   Let $w \in V(PG^2(u))$ is highest degree;
6          $\mathcal{C}^1 \leftarrow \mathcal{C}^1 \cup \{w\}$;
7   Remove all edges from $PG^2(u)$ incident to w;
8   Remove all isolated nodes from $PG^2(u)$;
9   **while** *$\exists v \in V(PG^2(u))$ Comment: all $v \in \mathcal{D}$* **do**
10   Let $w \in V(PG^2(u))$ is lowest id;
11         $\mathcal{C}^2 \leftarrow \mathcal{C}^2 \cup \{w\}$;
12   Remove all edges from $PG^2(u)$ incident to w;
13   Remove all isolated nodes from $PG^2(u)$;
14      $\mathcal{C}(u) \leftarrow \mathcal{C}^1(u) \cup \mathcal{C}^2(u)$
15 **First Round for** *All $u \in \mathcal{D}$* **do**
16   Inform each $v \in \mathcal{C}(u)$ as a VC node;
17 **Final for** *Each $v \in V(G)$* **do**
18   **if** *v is infomred as a VC node by some $u \in N(v)$* **then**
19         $\mathcal{C} \leftarrow \mathcal{C} \cup \{v\}$;

Now, we illustrate the execution of Algorithm 3 with an example. Figure 5(a) shows the 2-hop partial graphs of node 1 where the dominating nodes are marked in yellow. In the 2-hop partial graph of the node 1 contains all the dominating nodes, namely, 0, 1, 2, 5, and 9. Now, all the non-dominating nodes have the degree 1 and there is a tie among these four nodes. As in our methodology, we are braking the tie by picking up the node with lowest id, hence, in this case node 3 is picked up. Subsequently, the edge $(3, 5)$ is deleted and this leads to the isolated node 3, which has also been deleted. This reduced graph has been shown in Fig. 5(b). If we repeat this process all the remaining non-dominating nodes will be deleted from the graph and the remaining graph is shown in Fig. 5(c). Now, the graph is left with only dominating nodes, and hence, the procedure mentioned in Line 11 to 15 will be applied. So, in the remaining graph the lowest node id is 0. So, this node is taken as a vertex cover node and the edge $(0,1)$ is deleted. This leads to the isolated node 0 and this is deleted from the graph. This reduced graph is shown in Fig. 5(d). In the remaining graph, the node with the lowest id is 5, so it is taken as a vertex cover node and both the incident edges to it $(1,2)$ and $(1,5)$ are deleted. This leads to the isolated node 2 and deleted from the graph. Now, the remaining graph consist of only one edge $(5,9)$ where the lowest node id is 5. After taking this as a vertex cover node and deleting the edge $(5,9)$ the isolated node 9 is remaining and this has also been deleted. Now, the remaining graph is an empty graph and the execution stops. The vertex cover returned by Algorithm 2 of the 2-hop partial graph of node 2 is $\{0,1,3,4,5,7,8\}$ which has been shown in Fig. 5(e) marked in pink color.

Lemma 4. *The vertex set C returned by Algorithm 3 is a vertex cover of G.*

Proof. Proof by Contradiction: So assume that the final vertex set returned by Algorithm 3 is not a vertex cover of G. So, there must be an edge say (u,v) such that none of u and v are in the final vertex set returned by Algorithm 3. However, in Lemma 3, we have already shown that the union of partial graphs cover the entire graph. This implies that there must be some $w \in \mathcal{D}$ whose $PG^2(w)$ covers the edge (u,v). Now, in Algorithm 3, we have computed the vertex cover for every partial graph and each of the vertex cover of the partial graphs together constitute the final vertex set. So, either u or v or both must be in the final vertex set. This holds for every edge (u,v) of G. So, the final vertex set returned by Algorithm 3 is a vertex cover of G.

It is important to observe that entire vertex set of a graph is also a vertex cover of the graph. If in Step 2 we find the entire vertex set as a vertex cover, then it leads to an empty set as an independent set. In that case we can not reduce our input graph, and hence, the `while loop` of Algorithm 1 will be an infinite loop. So, it is important that in our methodology Step 2 should find out a vertex cover which is a proper subset of the vertex set of the graph. In Lemma 5, we show that the vertex cover chosen by Algorithm 3 is a proper subset of the vertex set.

Lemma 5. *The size of the vertex cover returned by Algorithm 3 is a proper subset of the vertex set of the original graph G.*

Proof. We need to show that at least one node in G is not present in the union of the vertex cover returned by all the dominating nodes. Let us assume that v be a dominating node with the highest node id. Our claim is that v can not be present in the vertex cover returned by any of the dominating nodes. We prove this claim by two cases. Case 1, Let all neighbors of v are non-dominating. Then from step 6 to 10 of algorithm, it is clear that once all neightbors of v are taken in VC, node v is removed from $PG^2(v)$. So, v can not in the VC returned by v or any other dominating node whose two hop partial graph contains v. Case 2, Let $\exists u \in N(v)$ and u is also a dominating node. Note that $id(u) < id(v)$ by assumption that v is a dominating node with the highest node id. Then from

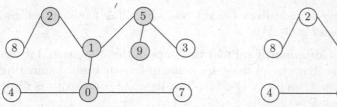

(a) 2-hop Partial Graph of Node 2.
Dominating Nodes are marked in yellow.

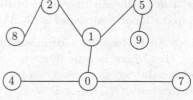

(b) 2-hop Partial Graph of the Node 2 after
processing the non-dominating node with lowest id.

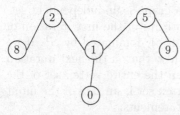

(c) 2-hop Partial Graph of the Node 2 after
processing all the non-dominating nodes.

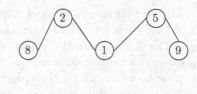

(d) 2-hop Partial Graph of the Node 2 after
processing the dominating node with lowest id.

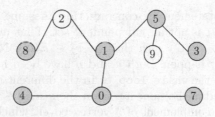

(e) 2-hop Partial Graph of Node 2.
Vertex Cover Nodes are marked in pink.

Fig. 5. Demonstration of our vertex cover selection algorithm (Color figure online)

step 11 to 15 of algorithm, it is clear that node u must have been taken in VC to cover the edge (u, v). So, again v is not in VC returned by v or any other dominating node whose two hop partial graph contains v. However, in practice, there will be many nodes which will not be in the union of the vertex cover returned by all the dominating nodes.

Lemma 6. *The computational complexity, message complexity and time complexity of Algorithm 3 are* $\mathcal{O}(\Delta^4)$, $\mathcal{O}(n)$ *and* $\mathcal{O}(1)$, *respectively.*

Proof. **Computational Complexity at Each Node:** As this step is skipped by the non-dominating nodes hence computational complexity of these nodes will be of $\mathcal{O}(1)$. Now, we analyze the computational complexity for each dominating node. There are $\mathcal{O}(\Delta^2)$ edges in a $PG^2(v)$ of a dominating node v. The while loop in the **Computation** can run at most $\mathcal{O}(\Delta^2)$ iterations as at least one edge is removed in each iteration. And during each iteration, a node needs to find the maximum degree node from $\mathcal{O}(\Delta^2)$ nodes in $\mathcal{O}(\Delta^2)$ operations. So, computational complexity is $\mathcal{O}(\Delta^4)$.

Time and Message Complexities: From the steps of the Algorithm 3 it can seen that there is only 1 round of massage communication from dominating nodes only. So, the time complexity is $\mathcal{O}(1)$. The message complexity is $\mathcal{O}(n)$ (viz., exactly $\mathcal{O}(\mathcal{D})$, but $\mathcal{D} = \mathcal{O}(n)$)

3.3   Independent Set Construction and Graph Shrinking (Step 3)

It is known that complement of a vertex cover of a graph is an independent set. Let, $\mathcal{S}^1$ be an independent set chosen by our algorithm in the first iteration of the while loop. Then the nodes are in $N(\mathcal{S}^1)$ will be dominated by $\mathcal{S}^1$. If we can safely delete the nodes in $N[\mathcal{S}^1]$ from the graph so that in the next iteration this process will work on the reduced graph. When the entire vertex set of the graph is exhausted we will show the generated vertex set is an IDS of the input graph. However, before that we prove few other statements.

Lemma 7. *The final vertex set returned by Algorithm 1 is an independent set of the input graph.*

Proof. We prove this statement by contradiction. Assume that the vertex set returned by Algorithm 1 is not an independent set. That means there exists at least two vertices $u, v \in V(G)$ such that $(u, v) \in E(G)$. Now, any one of the following two cases may happen. Both u and v have been included in the set Φ in the same iteration of the while loop, or in the different iterations. If both of them have been included in the same iteration then $(u, v) \notin E(G)$, because both of them belongs to the complement of a vertex cover, which is an independent set. Now, consider the other case where u and v has been included in two different iterations of the while loop. Without loss of generality, let us assume that u has been included before v. As per the working principle of our algorithm, once u is included its closed neighborhood is deleted. Hence, if $(u, v) \in E(G)$ then v belongs to the closed neighborhood of u. So, when u is included then v must be deleted and there is no question of inclusion of v in Φ. So, our assumption that Φ is not an independent set is false. So, this implies the lemma statement.

Lemma 8. *The final vertex set returned by Algorithm 1 is a dominating set of the input graph.*

Proof. Proof by contradiction: Assume that the vertex set returned by our algorithm is not a dominating set. This means that $N[\Phi] \neq V(G)$, or in other words, there exists at least one vertex v which is not in $N[\Phi]$. Here, we need to show that for any $v \in V(G)$, if $v \notin \Phi$ then at least one of its neighbors must be in Φ. Without loss of generality, assume that the while loop of Algorithm 1 takes ℓ many iterations to exhaust the whole graph, and in each iteration the vertex set returned by our algorithm is $\Phi_1, \Phi_2, \ldots, \Phi_\ell$. Hence, $\bigcup\limits_{i \in [\ell]} \Phi_i = \Phi$, and also $\bigcup\limits_{i \in [\ell]} (\Phi_i \cup N(\Phi_i)) = V(G)$. Now, consider any vertex $v \in V(G)$. If $v \in \Phi_i$ for some

$i \in [\ell]$ then $v \in \Phi$. Now, consider the other case $v \in N(\Phi_i)$ for some $i \in [\ell]$. By definition of the neighborhood, there exists some $u \in \Phi_i$ such that $(u, v) \in E(G)$. As per the working principle of our algorithm $\Phi_i \subseteq \Phi$ for all $i \in [\ell]$, and hence $u \in \Phi$. This proves that for every $v \in V(G)$, either $v \in \Phi$ or if $v \notin \Phi$ there exist at least one $u \in N(v)$ such that $(u, v) \in E(G)$. This means that Φ is a dominating set of G.

Combining Lemma 7 and 8, we have the correctness statement described in Theorem 2.

Theorem 2. *The vertex set returned by Algorithm 1 is an independent dominating set of the input graph.*

4   Experimental Evaluation

Datasets. In our experiments, we use eight real-world as well as syntactic datasets. Among the eight real-world datasets, four of them are social networks, namely, **Facebook**[1] [14], **LastFM**[2] [17], **Facebook Pages Politician**, **Facebook Public Figure**[3]. [15,16]; next two are collaboration networks, namely, **General Relativity and Quantum Cosmology collaboration network (GR-QC Colla)**[4] [11], **High Energy Physics - Theory collaboration network (HEPT Colla)**[5] [11]; and the remaining two are pear to pear network, namely, **Gnutella peer-to-peer network 1**[6] and **2**[7].

Now, we describe the generation of synthetic datasets, which are basically Erdős-Rényi random graphs [6]. A random graph of n vertices with connection probability p will have $p \cdot \frac{n(n-1)}{2}$ number of edges in expectation. We have used the Erdős-Rényi random graph generator of NetworkX[8].

Experimental Setup. First, we fix the connection probability and increase the number of nodes and secondly, we fix the number of nodes and increase the connection probability. For the first case, we experimented with two different probability values, 0.002 and 0.01. For each probability value, we start with the number of nodes value as 2000 continued upto 20000 with an increment of 2000 each time. For the second case, we experimented with two different number of nodes value 10000 and 20000. For each of these values, we start with the connection probability value 0.002 continued till 0.01 with an increment of 0.002 each time.

Goals of the Experiments. For the benchmark datasets, we compare the performance of the proposed approach with the incremental greedy algorithm

---

[1] http://snap.stanford.edu/data/ego-Facebook.html.
[2] http://snap.stanford.edu/data/feather-lastfm-social.html.
[3] http://networkrepository.com/fb-pages-public-figure.php.
[4] http://snap.stanford.edu/data/ca-GrQc.html.
[5] http://snap.stanford.edu/data/ca-HepTh.html.
[6] http://snap.stanford.edu/data/p2p-Gnutella04.html.
[7] http://snap.stanford.edu/data/p2p-Gnutella05.html.
[8] https://networkx.org/documentation/stable/reference/generators.html.

which is a sequential. This works in the following way: it computes the degree of the nodes pick the highest degree node as an independent dominating node and delete the closed neighborhood. This process is repeated until the whole graph is exhausted. We report the size of the independent dominating set returned by this algorithm. Next, we report the size of the IDS returned by the proposed distributed algorithm, the difference between the size of the IDS returned by the incremental greedy algorithm and the proposed algorithm. Certainly, lesser the value of the difference, better is the algorithm. Next important thing is how many iterations the `while loop` takes to finish. Finally, the last one is the portion (and correspondingly the percentage) of the independent dominating nodes obtained after the first iteration itself.

For the synthetic datasets, our experimental goals are two folded. One way, we want to study how the sizes of the IDS by our algorithm and the incremental greedy approach, the portion of the IDS obtained after the first iteration, and the number of passes taken by our algorithm increases with the increase of network size for a fixed connection probability. In the similar way, we also study the change of this matrices with the increase of the connection probability for a fixed number of nodes. Next, we proceed to describe the experimental results with detailed observations and discussions.

Experimental Results with Discussion. Table 1 shows the results of the benchmark datasets. Here, we observe that the proposed distributed algorithm can find an IDS within 2 to 6 passes of the while loop and the difference between the cardinality of the independent dominating set found by the incremental greedy approach and the proposed distributed algorithm varies from 2.42 to 8.23% with respect to the number of nodes of the graph. In most of the datasets, 10 to 40% of the nodes of the final independent dominating set is obtained in the first pass itself. It is important to notice that once our algorithm chooses a node to be included as an independent dominating node it never goes out. That means once the independent dominating nodes after first pass is obtained, they immediately start serving their purpose. Naturally, it is better to have more number of independent dominating nodes after the first pass itself. We observe that for HEPT Colla and GR-QC Colla datasets this size is 32% and 40% which is significantly high. We also observe that for most of the datasets, the size of the independent dominating set returned by our proposed distributed algorithm is upto 38% of the number of nodes of the graph.

Table 1. Results for the benchmark datasets.

Benchmark name	Nodes	Edges	Greedy IDS size	Proposed distributed algorithm					
				IDS size	Diff	% of extra nodes	# of passes	% of nodes in 1st pass	% of nodes in IDS
CA-HepTh.txt_Hashed.txt	9877	51971	3170	3409	239	2.42	6	32.70	34.51
CA-GrQc_Hashed.txt	5242	28980	1558	1708	150	2.86	5	40.40	32.58
fb-pages-politician.edges	5908	41729	1381	1867	486	8.23	5	10.07	31.60
facebook_combined.txt	4039	88234	261	319	58	1.44	6	1.88	7.90
fb-pages-public-figure.edges	11565	67114	3747	4401	654	5.65	6	12.22	38.05
lastfm_asia_target.txt	7624	27806	4327	4899	572	7.50	2	0.12	64.25
p2p-Gnutella04.txt	10879	39994	3867	3913	46	0.4	7	13.08	35.97
p2p-Gnutella05.txt	8846	31839	3017	3212	195	2.20	6	12.80	36.31

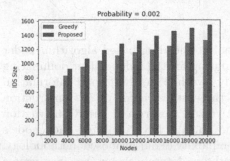
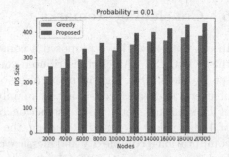

Fig. 6. Number of nodes Vs. IDS size plots for probability values 0.002 and 0.01

Figure 6 shows the plots for the IDS Size Vs. Number of Nodes for two different probability values 0.002 and 0.01. From the figure, we can observe that for a fixed probability value if we increase the number of nodes then for both the methodologies the size of the IDS is also increasing. It is natural that for a larger graph, the size of the independent set is bigger. Also, in this case as the probability is kept fixed so the density of the graph is also not changing.

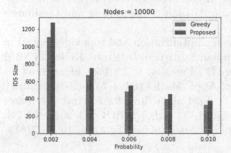
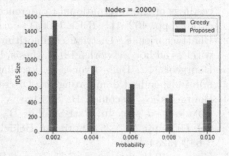

Fig. 7. Probability Vs. IDS size plots for the number of nodes 10000 and 20000

Figure 7 shows the plots for the IDS Size Vs. Probability for two different fixed values of n (namely, 10000 and 20000). From the figure we observe that, for a fixed number of nodes if we increase the probability value for both the methodologies the IDS Size is gradually decreasing.

However, we observe that the fractional difference in the size of IDS returned by our algorithm against the greedy sequential algorithm (i.e., $\frac{\text{IDS}_{Proposed} - \text{IDS}_{Greedy}}{n}$) decreases as n increases for a fixed probability. We observer the similar behavior when probability value is increased keeping the n fixed. This implies that our algorithm converges towards the greedy sequential algorithm as n increases with fixed probability or, as probability increases with fixed n.

5   Concluding Remarks

In this paper, we have proposed a constant round distributed algorithm under the CONGEST Model of distributed computing for the independent dominating set problem. Our algorithm requires only two-hop neighborhood information of every node and consisting of mainly three steps, namely (i) Construction of Dominating Set, (ii) Construction of Vertex Cover, and (iii) Construction of Independent Set and Reducing the graph. We have analyzed each node's computational complexity and message complexity of our proposed methodology. Experimentation with benchmark and synthetic datasets shows the effectiveness of our methodology. More importantly, in some cases a significant portion (up to 40%) of the final result is obtained after the first pass itself. The immediate question is to extend our algorithm for other models of distributed computing. There are many variations of the domination in a graph. Hence, our algorithm can be extended to solve those kinds of domination problems.

References

1. Bhattacharjee, S., Dattagupta, J., Srimani, P.K.: An efficient coordinated scheme of constructing connected dominating set in adhoc and sensor networks. In: Proceedings of the International Conference on Advanced Computing and Communications, pp. 402–411. IEEE (2004)
2. Bhattacharjee, S.: Distributed algorithms for initialization and topology control in wireless ad hoc networks. Ph.D. thesis, Indian Statistical Institute, Kolkata (2010)
3. Bourgeois, N., Della Croce, F., Escoffier, B., Paschos, V.T.: Fast algorithms for min independent dominating set. Discret. Appl. Math. 161(4–5), 558–572 (2013)
4. Bourgeois, N., Escoffier, B., Paschos, V.T.: Fast algorithms for MIN INDEPENDENT DOMINATING SET. In: Patt-Shamir, B., Ekim, T. (eds.) SIROCCO 2010. LNCS, vol. 6058, pp. 247–261. Springer, Heidelberg (2010). https://doi.org/10.1007/978-3-642-13284-1_20
5. Cormen, T.H., Leiserson, C.E., Rivest, R.L., Stein, C.: Introduction to Algorithms. MIT Press, Cambridge (2009)
6. Frieze, A., Karoński, M.: Introduction to Random Graphs. Cambridge University Press, Cambridge (2016)
7. Gaspers, S., Liedloff, M.: A branch-and-reduce algorithm for finding a minimum independent dominating set in graphs. In: Fomin, F.V. (ed.) WG 2006. LNCS, vol. 4271, pp. 78–89. Springer, Heidelberg (2006). https://doi.org/10.1007/11917496_8
8. Goddard, W., Henning, M.A.: Independent domination in graphs: a survey and recent results. Discret. Math. 313(7), 839–854 (2013)
9. Haraguchi, K.: An efficient local search for the minimum independent dominating set problem. arXiv preprint arXiv:1802.06478 (2018)
10. Hurink, J.L., Nieberg, T.: Approximating minimum independent dominating sets in wireless networks. Inf. Process. Lett. 109(2), 155–160 (2008)
11. Leskovec, J., Kleinberg, J., Faloutsos, C.: Graph evolution: densification and shrinking diameters. ACM Trans. Knowl. Discov. Data (TKDD) 1(1), 2-es (2007)
12. Liu, C.H., Poon, S.H., Lin, J.Y.: Independent dominating set problem revisited. Theoret. Comput. Sci. 562, 1–22 (2015)

13. Loverov, Y.A., Orlovich, Y.L.: NP-completeness of the independent dominating set problem in the class of cubic planar bipartite graphs. J. Appl. Ind. Math. **14**(2), 353–368 (2020)
14. McAuley, J.J., Leskovec, J.: Learning to discover social circles in ego networks. In: NIPS, vol. 2012, pp. 548–56. Citeseer (2012)
15. Rossi, R.A., Ahmed, N.K.: The network data repository with interactive graph analytics and visualization. In: AAAI (2015). http://networkrepository.com
16. Rozemberczki, B., Davies, R., Sarkar, R., Sutton, C.: GEMSEC: graph embedding with self clustering. In: Proceedings of the 2019 IEEE/ACM International Conference on Advances in Social Networks Analysis and Mining 2019, pp. 65–72. ACM (2019)
17. Rozemberczki, B., Sarkar, R.: Characteristic functions on graphs: birds of a feather, from statistical descriptors to parametric models. In: Proceedings of the 29th ACM International Conference on Information and Knowledge Management (CIKM 2020), pp. 1325–1334. ACM (2020)
18. Wang, Y., Chen, J., Sun, H., Yin, M.: A memetic algorithm for minimum independent dominating set problem. Neural Comput. Appl. **30**(8), 2519–2529 (2018)
19. Wang, Y., Li, C., Yin, M.: A two phase removing algorithm for minimum independent dominating set problem. Appl. Soft Comput. **88**, 105949 (2020)

An Approach to Cost Minimization with EC2 Spot Instances Using VM Based Migration Policy

Sharmistha Mandal[1], Sk Shahryar Saify[1(✉)], Anurita Ghosh[1], Giridhar Maji[2], Sunirmal Khatua[1], and Rajib K. Das[1]

[1] Department of Computer Science and Engineering, University of Calcutta, Kolkata, India
[2] Department of Electrical Engineering, Asansol Polytechnic, Asansol, India

Abstract. Amazon provides several different options for deploying workloads to AWS in the form of *on-demand, reserved* and *spot* instances. Spot instances come with steep discount offers but are susceptible to revocation and hence are not reliable. Using spot instances to run Workloads dramatically lowers computational cost, but we cannot guarantee the SLA requirements. In this paper, we have developed a novel technique that uses spot instances to minimize cost. It can also scale itself based on the workload and maintain SLA even during bulk preemption. Our system employs the following strategies. (i) Allocation of workloads based on a measure of *spot score* (represents the general trend of spot prices of a particular VM type over a predetermined duration of time), rather than just checking the spot price at a particular instant which may be high due to a temporary spike in traffic and may lead to an inefficient allocation. (ii) Migration of workloads triggered by certain resource utilization threshold conditions and spot price fluctuations over time. The proposed scheme is implemented and simulated on AWS spot instances with real demand traces from Google. The cost in our proposed method is significantly lower compared to the case when workloads run purely on on-demand instances or spot instances without VM migration. The results indicate that the proposed technique can reduce the cost of running large enterprise applications and compute-intensive workloads to a great extent.

Keywords: AWS spot instances · Cost minimization · Spot score · VM migration

1 Introduction

Cloud computing delivers through the internet computing services such as storage, network, servers, etc. Cloud computing has gained immense popularity these days due to its ease of use and cost benefits. Nowadays, Cloud service providers (CSPs) offer several types of virtual machines (VMs) that differ in performance and cost models.

© Springer Nature Switzerland AG 2022
R. Bapi et al. (Eds.): ICDCIT 2022, LNCS 13145, pp. 96–110, 2022.
https://doi.org/10.1007/978-3-030-94876-4_6

Amazon EC2 [2] provides scalable cloud computing capacity in the form of Amazon Web Services (AWS). Amazon EC2 gives three types of purchasing options for different VM instances: *on-demand*, *reserved*, and *spot*. With On-demand instances, users, depending on the instance type, pay for computing capacity by the hour or the second. No long-term commitments or upfront payments are needed. On the other hand, reserved instances provide a significant discount compared to on-demand instances but require an upfront reservation charge. Spot instances let users take advantage of unused EC2 capacity in the AWS cloud through a bidding mechanism. Spot instances are available at up to a 90% discount compared to on-demand prices and do not need upfront payments.

Amazon allocates spot instances on spare EC2 capacity at a much lower price than the on-demand instances. The hourly price of a spot instance is known as the spot price, and it depends on its demand and availability. Before requesting a spot instance, the user specifies a maximum price per hour (aka bid). By default, it is the on-demand price. The requested instance is launched if the user's bid exceeds the current spot price of that instance and capacity is available. In case of non-availability of capacity or current spot price exceeding the maximum price, Amazon revokes the spot instance after a 2 min warning period.

Most of the prior work focuses on selecting an optimal VM based on expected resource usage and future spot prices. SpotOn [12] and Tributary [6] have introduced several fault-tolerant mechanisms like checkpointing to reduce the amount of work lost during revocation. HotSpot [11] has proposed proactive migration based on the current spot prices. Earlier, users had to bid for the spot instance, and the spot price was equal to the highest unfulfilled bid. This spot instance pricing policy was updated in 2017 by Amazon. Now, the spot prices are solely dependent on the supply and demand of that instance. With this policy change, revocation rates have gone down by a big margin. Thus, the overhead incurred by the fault-tolerant mechanisms exceeds the benefits.

In this paper, we have introduced a flexible migration technique that allows workloads to self-migrate to new VMs responding to changes in spot price or resource utilization. We have introduced *buckets* - a new categorization system for the spot instances, based on resource parameters of the VM instances such as RAM, bandwidth, etc. Our technique monitors the change in the spot price and the resource utilization of the workload and places the workload in the appropriate *bucket*. Thus, it ensures a minimal number of migrations, cost reduction, and no significant degradation in performance.

This paper is arranged in the following way - First, we have discussed significant prior works in this field and why they are inadequate considering the current spot pricing scenario in Sect. 2. Next, we have described our proposed model in Sect. 4, followed by the implementation details in Sect. 5. The data preparation is outlined in Sect. 6. Experimental results are discussed and compared to other strategies in Sect. 7. Section 8 points out the limitations of the present work and envisages the future direction of work. Finally, Sect. 9 concludes the paper.

2   Related Work

The prior works on this topic focus on reducing the cost by choosing the optimal VM after revocation and reducing the work lost due to migration. SpotOn [12] deals with revocations as faults and introduces several fault-tolerant mechanisms like checkpoints and replication. HotSpot [11] uses proactive migration to reduce cost and optimize performance. Tributary [6] and SpotCheck [10] aim at improving performance by mixing batch and interactive jobs.

Tributary [6] is a new elastic control system that uses multiple preemptible resource pools to reduce cost and chances of bulk preemption. *SpotCheck* [10] uses a combination of on-demand and spot VMs to offer always-available VMs on demand for a cost near that of spot servers, and support all types of applications, including interactive ones. *Cumulon* [7] is another approach that optimizes the cost of executing mixed interactive and batch workloads on cloud platforms using transient VMs. *SpotOn* [12] is a model that calculates the cost for all the spot markets across all available zones and chooses the market with the least cost and the fault-tolerant mechanism with the least overhead.

Bid Selection for Deadline Constrained Jobs [8] is a greedy approach for bidding where, with effective use of checkpointing, the total cost of using spot instances is reduced further without violating the deadline constraint. They have compared the cost of their solutions with the optimal given by an ILP. *HotSpot* [11] uses a pro-active migration policy to migrate whenever it can find a VM with a lower spot price. Thus, HotSpot effectively decreases the cost and is capable of dealing with pre-emption. But the cloud spot markets suffer from bulk pre-emptions frequently.

We observe from the above discussion that most of the existing literature is based on Amazon's old spot instance pricing policy. As a result of Amazon's 2017 policy update, the revocation rates have decreased to about less than 5% on an average [1]. Thus, the prior works like [10,12] that use the fault-tolerant mechanisms incur more overhead in this new pricing model. Our proposed algorithm does not have any fault-tolerant mechanism. Instead, its migration decision is based on the current spot price and thus eliminates overheads otherwise required for checkpointing or replication. Also, most of the prior work like [6,11,12] considers the spot price as the sole parameter for migration. However, without adequate resources, a job's execution time can increase, leading to higher costs. Our proposed algorithm considers resource utilization and migrates to a new VM when the resource utilization exceeds a certain threshold value. Thus, our proposed algorithm aims at reducing the cost by proposing a new migration policy based on spot price and resource utilization.

3   Problem Statement

Let a job run for N_k hours on a virtual machine v_k. Let $S_{v_k}^i$, $i = 1, 2, \cdots N_k$, be the spot price for v_k at the ith hour. Also, assume o^k is the on-demand instance price of the same VM. The maximum price (or bid) is the on-demand price, so the cost of provisioning a VM will be the minimum of spot price and on-demand price. Then the total cost incurred for executing the job on VM v_k for N_k hours is:

$$C_{v_k} = \sum_{t=1}^{N_k} min(S_{v_k}^t, o^k) \qquad (1)$$

Now, the job is migrated based on certain conditions among a set of VMs. Let $V = \{v_1, v_2, v_3 \ldots v_p\}$ be the sequence of VMs, such that the job executes for N_i hours on VM v_i, where C_{v_i} is the cost of execution in VM v_i. Then the total cost of executing the job to completion will be:

$$C = \sum_{i=1}^{p} C_{v_i}$$

Our objective is to *minimize C* through the optimum use of migration based on *resource utilization* and *spot price trends*, such that the total cost of computation is reduced without significant loss in performance.

4   Proposed Algorithmic Modelling

The spot prices of AWS spot instances are continuously changing, based on the free capacity in the AWS cloud at that time. However, the spot price at a particular instant in time may accurately reflect the general trend of the spot price of that instance. Thus, to get a general representation of the spot price trend, we adopt a metric *"Spot Score"* calculated as follows:

$$SpotScore - \frac{1}{w} \sum_{t=1}^{w} min(s_t, o) \qquad (2)$$

where s_t = spot price at instant t and o = on-demand price for the concerned VM instance type.

Here w indicates a predetermined past duration of time based on which to observe the trend. From the above definition, we can express the cost of Eq. 1, as $N_k * SpotScore$ where the $SpotScore$ is computed over those N_k hours. That means, if we have to choose between several instances, the one with a lower $SpotScore$ will lead to lower costs (assuming total execution time remains the same).

Also, a categorization system is adopted for the VM types available, hereafter referred to as **buckets**. Each bucket contains VMs conforming to a certain range of RAM, CPU, and bandwidth. The exact ranges of parameters of the buckets are dependent on the dataset under consideration, as explained later in Sect. 5.

Based on this measure of *spot score* and the bucket system, we formulate our strategy to minimize the cost of computation of jobs. As during Cloudsim [9] simulation, we map the jobs to cloudlets, so henceforth we refer to jobs as **cloudlets**.

We migrate cloudlets from one VM to another, triggered by certain "EVENTS". The following events may occur during the execution of the job on a VM. *REVO-CATION* event occurs when cloud service provider reclaims its spot instances with a two-minute warning; Another event *SPOT_SCORE* occurs when spot price exceeds the on-demand price. The other two events occur due to a change in resource utilization. The third event occurs when resource requirements become so high that resource utilization crosses a pre-fixed *UPPER_THRESHOLD*. Similarly, the fourth event occurs on utilization going below *LOWER_THRESHOLD*. We stop monitoring when *JOB_COMPLETED* event occurs. Algorithm 1 outlines the process step-by-step.

Let us now explain the proposed algorithm with some concrete details. We are concerned about RAM as a primary VM resource. The RAM demanded by each cloudlet varies with time. When the demand exceeds a certain threshold, say x% of the total RAM available, for more than y% of the time, in the past z minutes, we assume that the average RAM requirement of the cloudlet exceeds the threshold. Suppose we observe last (z=) 100 min/h of RAM utilization by the job and find that RAM usage remains below (x=) 80% for (y=) 90 observations. In this case, the job keeps running on the same VM. In other words, in the chosen VM the job is expected to run without throttling on memory/cpu. In case we observe that RAM usage crosses 80% of allotted RAM for more than 90% of the time, we decide to migrate to a bucket with more memory. Then we migrate the cloudlet to another VM belonging to a bucket with more memory and having the minimum *spot score*. During experiments, we need to fine-tune the values for x, y, and z. Here z is the preceding time-window length (henceforth called sliding window) in consideration during the above computations.

Migrating to a VM in the next bucket ensures a lower frequency of migrations as we can expect that the RAM requirement of the cloudlet will not exceed the RAM threshold in a higher bucket. Even if it does, the overall migration frequency will be low as we tend to counter a sudden momentary spike in resource usage using a window of size z. This is important since frequent migrations will decrease the cloudlet's performance, which translates to a poor experience for the cloud service consumer and may even violate SLAs.

In case the cloudlet is already assigned to a VM in the highest bucket available, the cloudlet is migrated to another VM in the same bucket based on *spot score* if amazon revokes a running instance. The VM is selected based on the least spot score among the VMs available in the bucket.

The RAM demanded by a cloudlet may also decrease and stay below the x% threshold of the lower bucket for an extended amount of time. When the frequency of RAM under-utilization reaches y%, the cloudlet is migrated to a lower bucket. If it is in the lowest bucket, we migrate it to another VM in the same bucket but with a lower RAM (if such a VM exists).

The spot price of each instance varies with time. If the spot price exceeds the on-demand price at some point of time,

1. If the spot price of some VM within the same bucket at that time is lower than the on-demand price, the cloudlet is migrated to that VM.

Algorithm 1: VM migration based on resource utilization

    input   : J: Incoming Job, $\mathbb{V}_a$: Set of available VMs

    output   : $\mathbb{V}_s$: Sequence of VMs the job runs on until completion

1 $\mathbb{V}_a$ is divided into k-buckets $\mathbb{B} = B^1, B^2, \ldots B^k$ based on the available resources. Each bucket consists of a few number of VMs such that:

2 $B^1 \cup B^2 \cup \ldots \cup B^k = \mathbb{V}_a$

3 Effectively each VM belongs to any one bucket only i.e., $\forall i, j B^i \cap B^j = \Phi$

4 Initially J is assigned to a VM from the nearest matched bucket (B^j) based on expected resource requirement of the job.

5 The *spot score* values of all the VMs of the chosen bucket is computed following eqn. (2)

6 Let the VM $V_{B^j}^i \in \mathbb{B}^j$ is the chosen one with the minimum *spot score*

7 We call this as the first VM in the sequence $\mathbb{V}_s$, i.e., $\mathbb{V}_s^1 = V_{B^j}^i$

8 **while** *(OnEvent)* **do**

9   **if** *(Revocation Event with 2 min warning)* **then**

10   Migrate to another VM from the same bucket, $V_{B^j}^x \in \mathbb{B}^j$

11   Add $V_{B^j}^x$ to the List: $\mathbb{V}_s$

12   **end**

13   **if** *(spot price exceeds on-demand price)* **then**

14   Compute the *spot score* $\forall$ VMs in the corresponding bucket $\mathbb{B}^j$

15   List them in ascending order of *spot score*

16   Loop through the list of VMs and stop when spot price is less than on-demand price of the current VM

17   Migrate to the chosen VM from the same bucket

18   If the minimum spot price of all VMs in the bucket is more than on-demand price of the current VM

19   Migrate to the on-demand instance of the same VM

20   Add $V_{B^j}^y$ to the List: $\mathbb{V}_s$

21   **end**

22   **if** *(Resource utilization exceeds upper$_t$hreshold)* **then**

23   Choose the best matched bucket based on current resource utilization

24   Migrate to another VM from the chosen bucket, $V_{B^k}^y \in \mathbb{B}^k$

25   Add $V_{B^k}^y$ to the List: $\mathbb{V}_s$

26   **end**

27   **if** *(Resource utilization goes below lower$_t$hreshold)* **then**

28   Choose the best matched bucket based on current resource utilization

29   Migrate to another VM from the chosen bucket, $V_{B^k}^y \in \mathbb{B}^k$

30   Add $V_{B^k}^y$ to the List: $\mathbb{V}_s$

31   **end**

32   **if** *(Job Completed execution)* **then**

33   Break

34   **end**

35   Return $\mathbb{V}_s$

36 **end**

---

2. If the spot prices of all the other VMs are higher than the on-demand price, the cloudlet is migrated to an on-demand instance of the same VM type.

5 Implementation

The above algorithm has been implemented in Python v3.5.

We use Cloudsim [9] to simulate the architecture of AWS cloud with the following details:

- The jobs run on a datacenter with characteristics such as CPU architecture, OS, VMM, time zone, etc.
- The host machines in the datacenter with features such as RAM, CPU, bandwidth, storage, and MIPS.
- A datacenter broker provisions VMs on appropriate hosts and assigns cloudlets to VMs based upon the given allocation policy.
- A set of cloudlets submitted to the datacenter broker for assigning VMs and initiating execution.

The flowchart in Fig. 1 gives an overview of the program flow, followed by a detailed description of the programming logic and the code used to arrive at the results (Table 1).

Table 1. Bucket boundaries

RAM usage	Bucket
0–8	1
9–32	2
33–64	3
64 and above	4

The boundaries of the buckets are completely determined by the dataset under consideration, and may need to be changed if another dataset is considered.

6 Data Aggregation and Preprocessing

The prototype is evaluated using a production Google workload trace [5] for the month of May 2019, and publicly-available EC2 spot price traces [2]. The Google workload trace is downloaded in a JSON format through Google BigQuery API. It describes every job submission, scheduling decision, and resource usage data for the jobs that ran in those clusters. The normalized value of average RAM usage, highest RAM usage, and cycles-per-Instruction (CPI) for every 5 min are described by the workload trace as can be seen in Table 2.

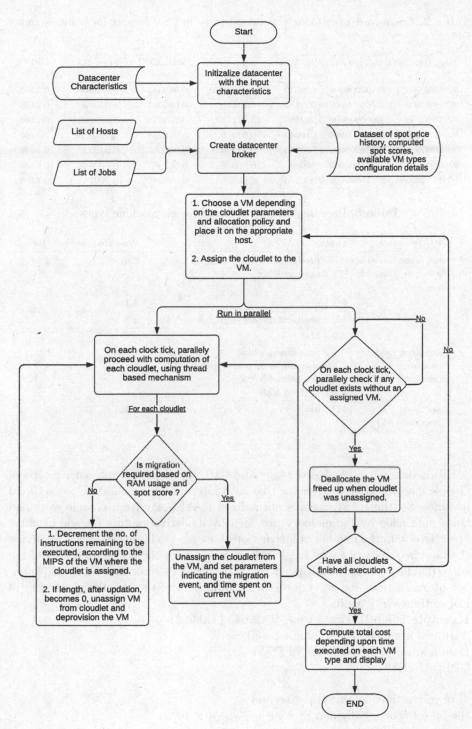

Fig. 1. Basic overview of the implementation

Table 2. One record from Google workload trace in CSV format for instance index 645

Start time μs	End time μs	Avg. CPU usage	Avg. RAM usage	Max. CPU usage	Max. RAM usage	CPI
928800000000	929100000000	0.029510	0.015899	0.089355	0.019866	0.7406
929100000000	929400000000	0.022583	0.011154	0.055297	0.019866	0.7406
929700000000	930000000000	0.022186	0.011367	0.085815	0.0198974	0.7406
929400000000	929700000000	0.0190429	0.0101928	0.088256	0.020050	0.7406
928500000000	928800000000	0.030975	0.016265	0.090087	0.019927	0.7406
930000000000	930133000000	0.00046	0.000883	0.007492	0.002048	0.7406
930133000000	930150000000	0.000365	0.000654	0.003299	0.000741	0.7406

Table 3. Base frequency of different Google machine types

CPU processor	Supported VMs	Base frequency (GHz)
Intel Xeon Scalable Processor (Cascade Lake)	– N2 predefined VMs – N2 custom VMs	2.8
	C2 VMs	3.1
	M2 ultramem memory-optimized VMs	2.5
	A2 VMs	2.2
Intel Xeon Scalable Processor (Skylake)	– E2 predefined VMs – M1 megamem memory-optimized VMs – N1 predefined VMs – N1 custom VMs	2.0
Intel Xeon E7 (Broadwell E7)	M1 ultramem memory-optimized VMs	2.2

To de-normalize the RAM usage and CPI, we map each job with a type of Google machine [3, 4]. We assume that each job runs on a separate Google Cloud instance. So, the RAM usage is normalized RAM usage from Google workload trace multiplied by the memory provided by its corresponding Google machine type. To obtain the number of instructions for each job for every 5 min, we divide the base frequency of each Google instance type with the normalized CPI of the corresponding job and multiply it by 300 (5 min in seconds). The total number of instructions for every job is the summation of the calculated number of instructions every 5 min.

Example 1: job ID (instance index): 645 (Table 2)

Assumed instance type: n2-highcpu-80.

Base frequency: 2.8 GHz for N2 (Table 3).

CPI = .740588

# of instructions executed per second =
the base frequency divided by CPI = $\frac{2.8}{0.740588} \times 10^6$.

# of instructions executed in 5 min = $\frac{2.8}{0.740588} \times 10^6 \times 300 = 1134234125$.

Table 4. Memory of different Google machine type

Machine name	vCPUs	Memory (GB)	Machine name	vCPUs	Memory (GB)
n2-standard-2	2	8	n2-standard-32	32	128
n2-standard-4	4	16	n2-standard-48	48	192
n2-standard-8	8	32	n2-standard-64	64	265
n2-standard-16	16	64	n2-highcpu-80	80	80

Table 5. A job (job id 645) mapped to a Google instance type. It has RAM 80 GB, Clock Speed of 2.8 GHz and CPI as 0.740588.

Instance type	CPI	No. of instructions	Avg. RAM normal	Max. RAM normal	Average RAM denormal	Max. RAM denormal
N2-highcpu-80	0.740588	1,13,42,3412	0.0159	0.019867	1.272	1.589
N2-highcpu-80	0.740588	1,13,42,34,125	0.01115	0.019867	0.892	1.589
N2-highcpu-80	0.740588	1,13,42,34,125	0.01136	0.019897	0.908	1.591
N2-highcpu-80	0.740588	1,13,42,34,125	0.01626	0.019928	1.3008	1.59
N2-highcpu-80	0.740588	1,13,42,34,125	0.0159	0.019867	1.272	1.589
N2-highcp-80	0.740588	1,13,42,34,12	0.00088	0.002048	0.0704	0.16
N2-highcpu-80	0.740588	1,13,42,34,125	0.00065	0.000741	0.052	0.059

The denormalized value of the average/maximum RAM is derived by multiplying the normalized value of the average/maximum RAM with the memory of the mapped instance type.

Example 2: Normalized maximum RAM = 0.019867 (Table 5, first row)
Normalized average RAM = 0.0159 (Table 5)
Memory of N2-highcpu-80 − 80 GB (Table 1).
  Thus,

$$De - normalised\ max\ RAM = 0.019867 \times 80\ \text{GB} = 1.589\ \text{GB} \tag{3}$$

$$De - normalised\ avg\ RAM = 0.015900 \times 80\ \text{GB} = 1.272\ \text{GB} \tag{4}$$

The total number of instructions for the job id 645 is calculated by taking the summation of number of instructions for each 5 min.
Thus,

$$Total\ number\ of\ instructions = 1, 13, 42, 34, 125$$
$$+ 1, 13, 42, 34, 125 + 1, 13, 42, 34, 125 + 1, 13, 42, 34, 125$$
$$+ 1, 13, 42, 34, 125 + 1, 13, 42, 34, 125 + 1, 13, 42, 34, 125$$
$$= 7, 93, 96, 38, 875$$

Similarly, avg. RAM usage is taken as the maximum of the avg. RAM usage for every 5 min.

$$Avg\ RAM = max(1.589, 1.589, 1.5911, 1.604,$$
$$1.59, 0.16, 0.059)\ GB = 1.604\ \text{GB}$$

The number of instructions obtained for each job was not sufficient to observe migration in our prototype. So, we have clubbed similar jobs based on the clock speed and highest RAM usage. The final set of data obtained after merging the data is as shown in the Table 6. The last column is the RAM distribution. To get a time-based RAM usage of each job, we have obtained 1000 RAM usage values following the normal distribution whose mean is the average RAM usage and the standard deviation is 10% of the average RAM usage.

Table 6. Final dataset after merging jobs

Cloudlet ID	Clock speed (Hz)	No. of instructions	Avg. RAM usage	Max. RAM usage	RAM distribution (GB)
0	2	103957692413	9.98715	11.00610352	12.157, 12.776 ...
1	2.2	105291126524	19.45987	20.09859848	21.614, 18.329 ...
2	2.3	78306432526	2.5649	4.317475586	4.030, 5.287 ...
3	2.5	85644903258	55.5486	58.51168213	60.100, 63.086 ...
4	2.6	50542997136	4.8789354	6.324296874	6.511, 6.033 ...
5	2.8	60117559682	3.12056	6.800415039	5.776, 7.552 ...
6	2.8	13109861479	7.587	7.890	7.981, 6.940 ...

7   Results and Analysis

The Table 7 shows the results obtained on execution of the above algorithm on the dataset in Table 6. All costs are in USD. Here, L_RAM indicates migration due to under-utilization of RAM of the currently allocated VM, and H_RAM, migration due to over-utilization of RAM.

The costs of execution of a policy of no-migration on the same dataset appear in Table 8. Here, the job runs on the initially chosen VM based on ram or spot score until completion.

7.1   Cost Analysis

We compare the costs obtained using *no migration strategy*, *lowest spot score strategy* and running cloudlets on *on-demand instances only*, and see, in Fig. 2, that there is a significant cost reduction when we follow the lowest spot score based allocation and migration approach.

7.2   Sliding Window Duration Analysis

We ran our migration algorithm using sliding windows of different time durations. The time durations selected for testing are - 10 min, 30 min, and 60 min. The results are as shown in Fig. 3:

Table 7. Costs for lowest spot score first algorithm

Cloudlet ID	VM type	End time (in sec)	Instance type	Migration event	Cost
0	a1.2xlarge	45198	Spot	COMPLETED	0.494 667
1	a1.4xlarge	45778	Spot	COMPLETED	1.002 030
2	a1.xlarge	34046	Spot	COMPLETED	0.186 307
3	m5n.4xlarge	3660	Spot	H_RAM	0.164 395
	m5zn.6xlarge	7500	Spot	L_RAM	0.419 862
	m5n.4xlarge	11220	Spot	H_RAM	0.586 952
	m5zn.6xlarge	15000	Spot	L_RAM	0.838 427
	m5n.4xlarge	18660	Spot	H_RAM	1.002 822
	m5zn.6xlarge	22471	Spot	COMPLETED	1.256 359
4	a1.xlarge	20220	Spot	H_RAM	0.110 648
	a1.2xlarge	21976	Spot	COMPLETED	0.129 867
5	a1.xlarge	4020	Spot	H_RAM	0.021 998
	a1.2xlarge	7740	Spot	L_RAM	0.062 712
	a1.xlarge	11700	Spot	H_RAM	0.084 382
	a1.2xlarge	15420	Spot	L_RAM	0.125 095
	a1.xlarge	19140	Spot	H_RAM	0.145 452
	a1.2xlarge	22800	Spot	L_RAM	0.185 508
	a1.xlarge	26144	Spot	COMPLETED	0.203 807
6	a1.xlarge	3600	Spot	H_RAM	0.019 700
	a1.2xlarge	5700	Spot	COMPLETED	0.042 683

Table 8. Costs for no migration Policy Algorithm

Cloudlet ID	VM type	End time (in sec)	Instance type	Migration event	Cost
0	a1.2xlarge	45198	Spot	COMPLETED	0.494 667
1	a1.4xlarge	45778	Spot	COMPLETED	1.002 030
2	a1.2xlarge	34046	Spot	COMPLETED	0.372 615
3	m4.10xlarge	35685	Spot	COMPLETED	4.196 379
4	a1.2xlarge	21975	Spot	COMPLETED	0.240 504
5	a1.2xlarge	26138	Spot	COMPLETED	0.286 066
6	a1.2xlarge	5699	Spot	COMPLETED	0.062 372

In the above figures (Fig. 3), we see, for a 60-min sliding window duration, the number of migrations is minimum. Since a cloudlet migrates only if the spot price increases or there is a *sustained* increase/decrease in its resource requirement, a longer window leads to less migration. Reducing migration decreases the cost of computation and also helps to maintain SLA requirements.

In some cases, the cost increases with an increase in the duration of the sliding window (job 4 and job 5). If the job was running on a VM with a higher spot price and migration to a lower-priced bucket is delayed by a longer window, the cost may increase.

7.3 SLA Violation Analysis

We have measured the number of SLA violations by executing the program using both no-migration and Lowest Spot Score strategies. As shown in Fig. 4, the number of SLA violations is significantly less when we follow the Lowest Spot Score strategy.

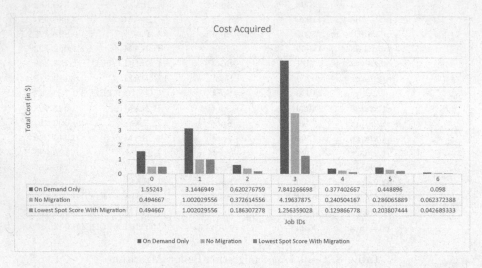

Fig. 2. Comparison of cost when using on-demand instance, spot instance with *no migration* based algorithm and spot instance with lowest spot score algorithm

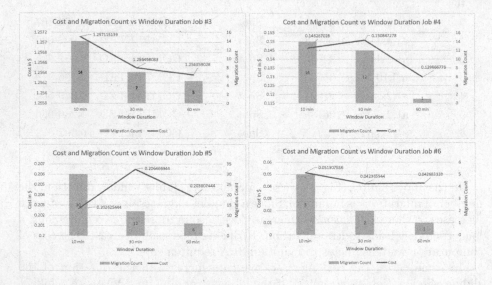

Fig. 3. Comparison of no. of migrations and computation cost for job IDs 3, 4, 5 and 6 when the sliding window is 10 min, 30 min and 60 min

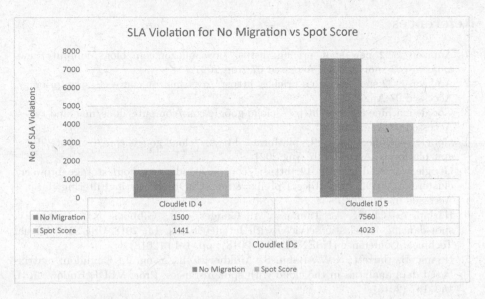

Fig. 4. Comparison of number of SLA violations when executing jobs using *no migration* strategy vs using Spot Score Strategy

8 Limitations and Future Work

Computation of the running time of a job by dividing its number of instructions by the MIPS (millions of instructions per second) does not always hold. If the job requires more RAM than is available, its running time may be affected. Thus, future studies can explore the impact on the execution time by the over-utilization of RAM.

9 Conclusion

This paper presents an efficient algorithm for cost optimization in the spot market. The prototype automatically selects and migrates cloudlets to a new VM when the spot price exceeds the on-demand price or the VM is over-utilized (the RAM usage of the job exceeds 90% of the VM's available memory). We categorize the VMs into buckets based on the RAM available. A job never migrates to a VM with memory capacity lower than its RAM usage, and so there is no degradation in performance. We demonstrate the benefits of switching VMs in EC2's spot market in terms of cost and performance. We implement a prototype on EC2 and evaluate it using job traces from a production Google cluster. We compare our prototype with the other approaches (on-demand or no-migration) and show that it can significantly lower cost with minimal change in performance.

References

1. Amazon EC2 new spot pricing. https://aws.amazon.com/blogs/compute/new-amazon-ec2-spot-pricing. Accessed 07 Aug 2021
2. Amazon EC2 spot instances pricing. https://aws.amazon.com/ec2/spot/pricing/. Accessed 07 Aug 2021
3. Google machine families. https://cloud.google.com/compute/docs/machine-types. Accessed 07 Aug 2021
4. Google machine type CPU platforms. https://cloud.google.com/compute/docs/cpu-platforms. Accessed 07 Aug 2021
5. Google workload trace 2019. https://console.cloud.google.com/storage/browser/clusterdata_2019_a;tab=objects?prefix=&forceOnObjectsSortingFiltering=false. Accessed 07 Aug 2021
6. Harlap, A., Chung, A., Tumanov, A., Ganger, G.R., Gibbons, P.B.: Tributary: spot-dancing for elastic services with latency SLOs. In: 2018 USENIX Annual Technical Conference (USENIX ATC 2018), pp. 1–14 (2018)
7. Huang, B., Jarrett, N.W., Babu, S., Mukherjee, S., Yang, J.: Cümülön: matrix-based data analytics in the cloud with spot instances. Proc. VLDB Endow. **9**(3), 156–167 (2015)
8. Mandal, S., Khatua, S., Das, R.K.: Bid selection for deadline constrained jobs over spot VMs in computational cloud. In: Krishnan, P., Radha Krishna, P., Parida, L. (eds.) ICDCIT 2017. LNCS, vol. 10109, pp. 118–128. Springer, Cham (2017). https://doi.org/10.1007/978-3-319-50472-8_10
9. Rodrigo, N., Rajiv, R., César, R., Rajkumar, B.: CloudSim: a novel framework for modeling and simulation of cloud computing infrastructures and services. CloudSim ICCP **1**, 1–9 (2009)
10. Sharma, P., Lee, S., Guo, T., Irwin, D., Shenoy, P.: SpotCheck: designing a derivative IaaS cloud on the spot market. In: Proceedings of the Tenth European Conference on Computer Systems, pp. 1–15 (2015). https://doi.org/10.1145/2741948.2741953
11. Shastri, S., Irwin, D.: Hotspot: automated server hopping in cloud spot markets. In: Proceedings of the 2017 Symposium on Cloud Computing, pp. 493–505 (2017)
12. Subramanya, S., Guo, T., Sharma, P., Irwin, D., Shenoy, P.: SpotOn: a batch computing service for the spot market. In: Proceedings of the Sixth ACM Symposium on Cloud Computing, pp. 329–341 (2015)

Transforming Medical Resource Utilization Process to Verifiable Timed Automata Models in Cyber-Physical Systems

Rizwan Parveen[✉][iD] and Neena Goveas[iD]

Birla Institute of Technology and Science Pilani, Pilani, Goa, India
`rizwanp@goa.bits-pilani.ac.in`

Abstract. Effective resource utilization in healthcare related systems is the prime objective to ensure patient care. However, to effectively utilize the treatment time, for example such as transporting patients to diagnostics centres, and providing timely medication, requires efficient optimization of the resources. These resources are hospital staff such as caregivers, nurses, physicians, etc. and other diagnostic resources such as MRI machines, X-Ray machines and other general-purpose resources such as hospital beds, wheelchairs, etc. To model the behaviour of a system with time constraints, timed automata are useful and also helpful in representing system dynamic properties (i.e., requirements). However, the health-care applications such as utilizing healthcare resources require formal verification to ensure the system's correctness. The paper presents an approach to model the resource allocation process as Timed Automata and further verifies the system's properties using a model checking tool, UPPAAL. The applicability of our approach is demonstrated using a hospital situation where the combination of patient and caregiver is used. A few example healthcare resource utilization scenarios are derived to use as a case study to validate the proposed approach. We show how an individual patient is efficiently assigned to the available caregiver in a clinical setup.

Keywords: Healthcare · Resources · Timed automata · UPPAAL

1 Introduction

The timely availability of healthcare resources (i.e. treatment timing) plays an important role in patient care. The complex task of managing and allocating multiple resources to patients is mostly done manually by the staff. Automation of resource management is one way to reduce the burden on the staff and provide a decision support system for the hospital staff. However, automating a clinical process requires domain knowledge, often the output that is produced can go wrong (i.e., can lead to deadlock) if the results are not validated and verified. Over the last few years, efforts have been made to automate the process of correctly allocating clinical resources [1–3]. various approaches and tools have been used for transforming processes based on medical requirements to computerized systems for easy operations. For example, Guo et al. present cardiac

© Springer Nature Switzerland AG 2022
R. Bapi et al. (Eds.): ICDCIT 2022, LNCS 13145, pp. 111–126, 2022.
https://doi.org/10.1007/978-3-030-94876-4_7

arrest treatment scenarios using Yakindu statecharts to show how medical practices are modelled as statecharts and then transformed into UPPAAL models for further verification [4]. However, for automating resource allocation, unexpected resource demand and unpredictable delays in resource availability are some of the properties that have to be factored in. The resultant multiparameter complex system is not easy to solve optimally and in some cases may lead to incorrect solutions being proposed. In a usual clinical process, resources vary from the hospital staff such as caregivers, nurses, physicians, etc., and other diagnostic resources such as MRI machines, X-Ray machines to the other general-purpose resources such as hospital beds, wheelchairs, etc. Healthcare resource availability being blocked (even temporarily) due to breakdown, human error or false updates in the computerized system, can violate the safety property of the system. Such violations of safety properties in healthcare systems can be severe and often, impact human life. Additionally, it is not easy to verify if safety requirements are met by human intervention without setting up a formal multilevel rule-based system.

To address these challenges, we present a formal approach to automate the resource allocation in a clinical setup. In this approach, we show how the medical resource allocation process is transformed to a verifiable timed automata model. In particular, we use UPPAAL to construct a model for our resource allocation problem. UPPAAL is then used for model checking and verification of the resulting solution to ensure all safety requirements are satisfied. These requirements are captured formally using temporal logic.

The paper is organized as follows. Section 2 briefly presents why Model-based design is appropriate for the design and development of medical applications and how UPPAAL is a helpful tool in this regard. Section 3 describes the case study of the hospital resource allocation process and model of patient and caregiver timed automata developed using UPPAAL. We show the execution of individual processes running in parallel and describe the essential properties in Subsect. 3.3. System's properties are verified using temporal logic in Sect. 3.4. Finally, we conclude in Sect. 4.

2   Background and Related Work

2.1   Usefulness of UPPAAL in Healthcare Applications

UPPAAL is an open-source model checking tool that is appropriate for the systems that can be modeled as a collection of non-deterministic processes with finite control structure [5]. With this ability, it has been used in multiple fields like complex automobiles [6] and medical applications [7, 8]. It is based on the concept of finite state machine (also known as timed automata) where various system's components or subprocesses are modelled as individual timed automata and communicate through synchronized channels. These individual timed automata form a network which is known as Networked Timed Automata [9]. It has a user-friendly editor, simulator and verifier window where various results can be observed and analysed. The output during the execution can be visualized in the form of Gantt charts. The UPPAAL interface can also help medical professionals, who are not familiar with the software, to visualize the overall system.

Clinical processes and resource sharing are complicated as every individual has a different set of requirements. These processes are typically multistage with well-defined criteria to be satisfied to go from one stage to another. These requirements are often interpreted as the system's safety requirements. To this end, UPPAAL provides a model checking capability to verify the system's safety requirement. These requirements are presented in the form of a system's properties and written formally in temporal logic. Using UPPAAL, we demonstrate component interactions in the form of a timed automata model. Each component is modelled as an individual timed automaton. These automata depict the internal dynamics of component communication and help to capture unexpected system behaviors when failure events occur. This particular feature is especially crucial in healthcare applications where many medical instruments and devices work in an integrated and interoperable environment, and often take inputs from the healthcare staff. Moreover, processes associated with medical personals and their interaction with healthcare instruments can be modelled as automata in UPPAAL. The formal model-based approaches have been widely used and applied to many safety-critical systems [10] because they provide a unified method for thorough analysis and provide the ability to resolve the risk at the model level itself. Model-based approach is a widely acceptable design choice that helps to abstract the complex behavior of the system. Models do not only help to predict the errors at the early design phase but also provide options to rectify the problem at the model level itself [11, 12]. In such context, UPPAAL provides a suitable simulation and verification environment to perform various safety checks at the model level of a healthcare process and medical software, which seems an efficient design choice in safety-critical healthcare systems as the testing of an instrument or a clinical process is expensive and life-critical.

2.2 Model-Based Development: Tools and Programming Languages

Model-based development tools and programming languages are widely used and accepted in various domains such as robotics, avionics, smart transportation, industrial automation, business process modeling, and so on. However, when it comes to model physical interaction in the Cyber-Physical Systems (CPS) application, current UML profilers and simulation tools either require significant extension or revision in order to exploit the full potential of the Model-based approach [13, 14]. To address CPS design concerns such as heterogeneity, dynamism in component interaction, modeling and validating system behavior under various scenarios and to address the design constraints many tools need to be combined and used in co-simulation [15]. Model checking tool UPPAAL for timed automata that has already been used in the industry successfully. It allows users to model the behavior of systems in the form of states and transitions, and to simulate and analyze the models for various system's properties. A preliminary case study that implements a scenario of a patient undergoing laser tracheotomy (medical CPS) was carried out via model checking UPPAAL tool [16]. Another example is the design of an implantable pacemaker with the help of UPPAAL is presented by [7]. With the help of UPPAAL, it is possible to find safety violations, development of patient-specific algorithms and prove the correctness of medical device algorithms.

2.3 Defining Formalism Using Temporal Logic

Typically, two kinds of inputs are required by a model checker: a model that characterizes the state-transition behaviors of a finite state concurrent system, and a temporal logic formula that specifies the property of the system to be verified and validated. The modeling formalism used in UPPAAL is timed automata and the temporal logic formulas are written in TCTL [17]. The temporal logic TCTL helps in formalizing a wide range of user requirements such as reachability, liveness, safety, and responsiveness [18]. Liveness is to guarantee that there exists a state where the specific condition will eventually be true, expressed as $A <> p$ and $\phi \rightarrow \psi$ (whenever ϕ is satisfied, then eventually ψ will be satisfied). Reachability is to check if the given query ϕ, possibly be satisfied by any reachable state, expressed as $E <> p$ which is interpreted as there is an execution path in which property p eventually (in some state of the path) holds. Safety is to guarantee that the system will never go into a bad state, or another way of stating this is: nothing bad will ever happen. It is expressed as $E[] p$ and $A[] p$, where it checks if there exists an execution path to hold the specific condition in all the states and property p holds for each (all) execution path in all the states, respectively. Deadlock properties to check if any deadlock is possible or not in the model, expressed as "$A[] not deadlock$".

A timed automaton T is a tuple $T = \{L, l_0, C, I, E, A\}$ where L is a set of states (also called locations), $l_0 \in L$ is the initial location, C is a set of real-valued clock variables, I is *invariant* which represents that time elapses in a location only as long as its invariant stays true, A is the action set (for example, in Fig. 1, $a!$ and $a?$ are actions on the two transitions in the given automaton, hence $A: \{a\}$). $E \subseteq L \times C(X) \times A \times 2^X \times L$ is a finite set of transitions which is defined as $e = (l, g, a, r, l') \in E$ represents a transition from l to l', g is the guard of transition e, $r \in R$ on an edge is the set of clocks that is reset by edge e when a transition involving the edge is fired, and $a \in A$ is the action of e. The transition is represented as $l \overset{g,a,r}{\rightarrow} l'$ for any $e \in E$. $C(X)$ is a set of clock constraints over X and 2^X is a power set of all possible sets build over x [19].

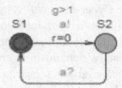

Fig. 1. Timed automata representation in UPPAAL

An example of timed automata in UPPAAL is shown in Fig. 1 where S1 and S2 are two states and transition between $S1 \rightarrow S2$ enabled when the guard $g > 1$ is true, then it sends action $a!$ ($a?$ represent the receive action from another timed automata) and update the variable r to zero.

UPPAAL provides an ability to trace back the property which fails. By checking the corresponding state transition, we are able to observe the behaviour of our resource allocation model. For example, we check whether a particular resource is occupied for longer than expected or a particular resource is not being used for a longer period. Moreover, by looking at the Gantt chart, it is easy to check if corresponding states are correct, which otherwise can be missed. The paper presents an approach to show the resource allocation of medical resources in a clinical setup. The aim of this paper is to present an approach to build a formal model for analyzing the resource utilization for a clinical process.

3   Design and Modeling of Medical Resource Utilization Process

The correct functioning of a Cyber-Physical system depends on the monitoring and control of complex physical processes where the targeted application runs on dedicated execution platforms in a resource constrained manner, which is often expected to follow the correct timing behavior. These CPS such as Healthcare applications are viewed as collections of various interdependent but atomic tasks where the timing guarantees depend on the coordination of the individual tasks in an orderly manner. The challenge here is to assure the timing guarantee for the individual tasks running in the system as well as for the overall system. We modelled a clinical process to enforce the correct execution sequence of allocating and deallocating the medical resources, which includes preconditions-postconditions validation, behaviour monitoring and expected responses checking. The following subsections explain the UPPAAL based model for the hospital resource allocation procedure. The model consists of two automata: Patient and Caregiver.

3.1   Case Study of Caregiver Assignment

This paper addresses the problem of organising and automating patients being assigned and transported in and out of a treatment facility (we named it as Diagnostic Centre) in a hospital, to a medical resource: caregiver. We design an automated system that allows a patient to be assigned to a caregiver. To demonstrate the simultaneous assignment of multiple patients (i.e., multiple processes running in parallel), we create n numbers of patient objects and m numbers of caregiver objects. The value of n and m can be modified to test various scenarios, for example, in our experiment we kept the number of patients $n = 4$ and number of caregivers $m = 2$. As stated in the earlier section, there are the pre-conditions and post-conditions validation. For instance, the pre-condition here is to check if a caregiver is available to take a patient request, else the patient request will be queued to be served based on the FIFO principle. After the patient is dropped at the diagnostic centre (DC), another pre-condition here is to check the patient's service time (i.e., the time required for a patient to complete the treatment at the diagnostic centre) is more or less than a predefined threshold time. This threshold time is introduced to decide whether the caregiver has to wait for the patient at the DC till the patient completes his treatment or to release the patient and leave without the patient. In the post-condition validation, the patient, if left at DC, should be taken back by another or the same caregiver in subsequent trips. Another queue (at DC) is maintained for the patients where the patients are picked up by caregivers in a FIFO manner. This way, it assures that all the patients at DC will be picked up certainly in an orderly manner and their waiting time at DC is not forever, but time-bound. In this resource allocation model, the property which must satisfy is to assure that one patient must be assigned to only one caregiver at a time and the same condition holds during the return of the patient from DC. Another way to state this is that two patients cannot be assigned to a single caregiver. The model must satisfy the property of avoiding clashes in the assignments of the resources. Another property that we check is that a patient cannot be in the waiting state forever as stated earlier. If a patient is taken to the diagnostic centre, he must return.

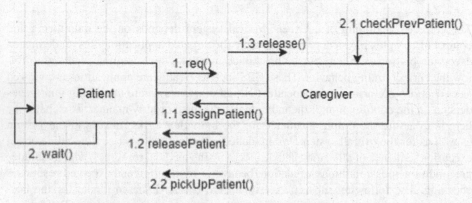

Fig. 2. Process of healthcare resource allocation to the patient.

Figure 2 shows a collaboration diagram to depict the process of resource (i.e., Caregivers) allocation to the patients in a clinical setup.

3.2 Model Implementation Using UPPAAL

We create a scenario where a patient arrives at the hospital, requests for a service, based on the request, a hospital resource such as caregiver (i.e., nurse or medical staff) is allocated to the patient. However, to make it more realistic, we made a few assumptions in our design. In our scenario, the number of caregivers is limited and less in number than the patients. Every patient who arrives at the hospital requests certain services and where each service has its own time of completion. For example, if there are three patients (*P0, P1, P2, … , Pn*). *P0* requires an x-ray which takes 10 time units, *P1* requires an MRI machine which takes 15 time units and *P2* requires a general checkup, which takes 5 time units. Hence, *P0's* service time is considered as 10, *P1's* 15 and *P2's* 5 time unit.

It is a hospital resource allocation system that controls how the resource is assigned and released. Figure 3 shows the model of patients and Fig. 4 shows the model of caregivers in the editor of UPPAAL. A caregiver is assigned to the patient to carry the patient to the diagnostic centre (DC). The patient request and caregiver assignment are represented by **ReqService** in the Patient automata and **Assigned** state in the caregiver automata, respectively, as shown in Fig. 3 and Fig. 4. The patients arrive in a random sequence, for instance, if there are *N* patients (*P0, P1, P2, ... , Pn*), then, *P2* can arrive before *P1* and *Pn* and arrive before *P(n − 1)*. The initial state of a patient is **Start** and then it transitions to request for a service (**ReqService**). From the **ReqService** state, the next state (**isTaken**) is reached when a patient's request is approved for the service. These requests are enqueued if none of the caregivers is free. To avoid the clashes in the request assignment, we check the '**id**' value of the patient associated with the caregiver id (*caregiver[0]* or *caregiver*[1]). The patient's request is approved only if a caregiver (with the particular **id** number) is available (**Available**) to transport the patient. Otherwise, the variable *isNotAvailable (i.e., isNotAvailable[m])* becomes true. For example, *isNotAvailable = {1, 0}* means *caregiver[0]* is busy and *caregiver[1]* is available. This shows the dependency of execution of one task (arrival of patient's request) on another task (checking if a caregiver is available). Once the caregiver is available, the patient's request will be dequeued. The enqueuing and dequeuing of a request is based on the queue's principle of First-in-First-Out (FIFO). Once the patient reaches the diagnostic centre (named as DC), the boolean variable *isSafe* sets to true and the patient state changes to **ReachedDC**. Similarly, in the caregiver process, as depicted in Fig. 4, the initial state of the caregiver is **Available** which changes to **Assigned** when a patient is assigned to the caregiver.

We keep a constant integer variable **threshold** value for the service time where we check if the patient's service time is more than the **threshold** value. This condition check can be seen as the two outgoing transitions from the **ReachedDC** state in the Patient automata where the condition **patientDelay[id]>threshold** enables the transition of **Wait_inDC** and the *patientDelay[id] <threshold* enable the transition which is leading back to the initial state of the patient (back to initial state shows that the system is continuous transition system and a patient reaching back to initial state means that the cycle of that previous patient object is complete and a new patient object will start the process again and this will go on). In other words, if the condition *patientDelay[id] <threshold* is true then the patient returns instantly with the caregiver, considering that the patient has completed the service. When the condition **patientDelay[id]>threshold** is true, then, the assigned caregiver will drop the patient at DC and will be released from that patient and that patient's treatment cycle is complete. Another way to interprets this is that the caregiver need not wait at the diagnostic centre for a patient to complete the service, this patient is picked up by any available caregiver once he finishes his service time. The waiting patients at the diagnostic centre are picked by the caregivers as and when a caregiver arrives at the diagnostic centre to drop another patient (this is the 'wait' state of caregiver where a caregiver waits and checks for the existing waiting patient before leaving from DC). Every patient is distinguished from another patient through their **id** numbers, passed as a value in synchronized channels and variables used on the transitions, for example, the **patientDelay[2] <threshold** means the service time of Patient no. 2 *(can be expressed as Patient[2]* or P2) is less than the threshold value, hence the P2 does not go in **Wait_inDC** state. To make the system more realistic, a randomized patient and caregiver selection is added on respective automaton's transitions. For example, **e:id_p** on transitions [9] (id_p is a type of id, see below code snippet) of the caregiver automaton show that patients are selected randomly from the given total number of the

patients and id of the patient helps to distinguish which patient request is accepted and which patient is to be picked from the DC.

```
const int P = 4; //total number of patients
const int C = 2; //total number of caregivers
typedef int[0,P-1] id_p;  //id number of patient
typedef int[0,C-1] id_c;  // id number of caregiver

Patient Parameters: const id_p id
Caregiver Parameters: const id_c id
```

The *CheckPrevPatient* state of the caregiver automata is the state where the caregiver checks if there is any earlier patient waiting at DC (using a boolean variable *prevPatient*) to be picked up after he releases his current patient at DC; caregiver picks up that previous patient and returns with him (see the outgoing transition no. 2 of *CheckPrevPatient* state in caregiver automata). If the *prevPatient* is false, meaning there is no patient to be picked from DC, then the caregiver returns without any patient (see the outgoing transition no. 1 of *CheckPrevPatient* state in caregiver automata). Otherwise, if the patient's service time is less than or equal to the threshold time value, then the caregiver returns with the same patient (see the outgoing transition no. 3 of *Wait* state in caregiver automata).

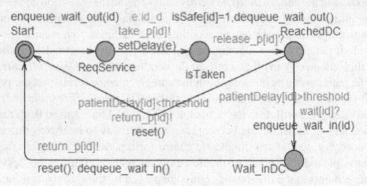

Fig. 3. Patient automata

In a scenario, when there is no new patient request arrived, but there are patients who were earlier dropped at DC and now waiting for return, then, the caregiver's state *GoToCollectPatient* becomes enabled, provided that the caregiver is free (i.e., in *Available* state). The following guard condition must be true to take the transition of *GoToCollectPatient* state.

$$lenOfWQueueO==0 \ \&\& \ lenOfWQueueI>0$$

Here, the variable *lenOfWQueueO* corresponds to the length of the waiting queue outside (i.e., patient's request queue) and *lenOfWQueueI* corresponds to the length of the waiting queue inside DC.

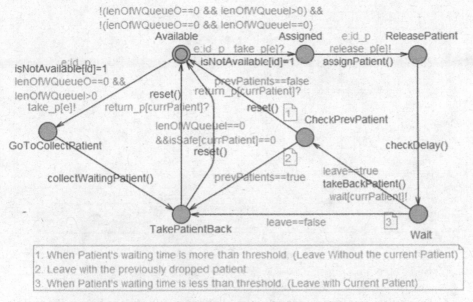

Fig. 4. Caregiver automata

There are two outgoing transitions from the state *TakePatientBack*. The left-most transition enables after a caregiver collects the waiting patient and returns. However, there may be a situation when more than one caregiver (in our case, both caregivers) are free and also there is no new patient request to serve, in that case, state *GoToCollectPatient* becomes enables for both the caregivers which leads to the possibilities of getting stuck at the *TakePatientBack* state and eventually leads to the deadlock situation. To avoid such conflict, another transition from *TakePatientBack* is designed (right-most transition) where it is checked if the patient is picked up; this check is done through the *isSafe* (is true) variable and *lenOfWQueueI* (is zero).

3.3   Concurrent Execution of Patient and Caregiver Processes in UPPAAL

We run the execution with four patients and two caregiver automata and observe the behaviour of individual tasks running in parallel. The time each individual automaton spends in a particular state is depicted via Gantt chart in different color coding as shown in the bottom window of Fig. 5. Figure 5 shows that all four patients are in different states. It is interpreted as *Patient(0)* is arrived first, since *Patient(0)'s* service time (modelled as *patientDelay*) is more than the *threshold*, hence *Patient(0)* goes in **Wait_inDC** state.

The subsequent state of the caregiver automata would be the *Wait* state. While hovering the mouse over the Gantt chart, it shows the time duration of start and end of a state; as an example, a small box shows the *Patient(0)'s* total waiting time and time interval.

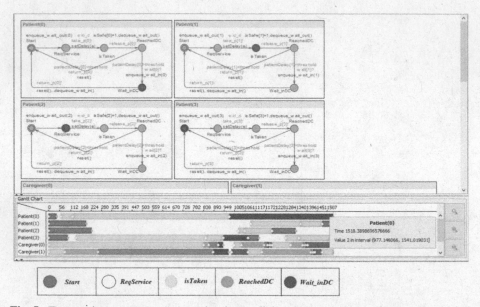

Fig. 5. Four patient processes are running in parallel and a gantt chart at bottom shows their corresponding state during the execution. (Color figure online)

Figure 6 shows two caregiver processes simultaneously running along with the patient automata, where *Caregiver(0)* is seen in *Wait* state and *Caregiver(1)* is in *GoTo-CollectPatient* state. The same can be seen in the Gantt chart at bottom of the image where *Caregiver(1)* goes from *TakePatientBack* (light blue color) to *Available* state (green color), then almost immediately goes to *GoToCollectPatient* state (yellow color). The execution shows that it satisfies the expected behaviour as one of the patients is in *Wait_inDC* state and there is no new patient request at the time when the caregiver was in the *Available* state. However, it is quite possible that soon after *Caregiver(1)* reaches *GoToCollectPatient* state, a new patient might arrive, which will be enqueued to be served whenever the caregiver is in *Available* state again.

3.4   Model Verification

Timed automata are useful for representing systems, however, to represent the properties of a system (such as nondeterministic properties) temporal logics with timed constraints are necessary [19]. Using model checking, it can be assured that there are no safety violations, which further assures that there will be no violation during the execution. In

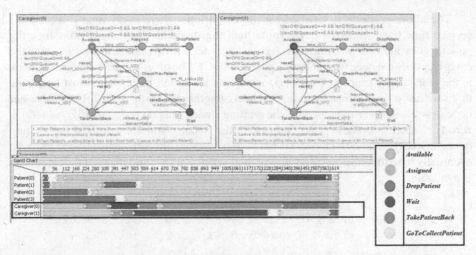

Fig. 6. Two caregiver processes are running in parallel and a gantt chart at bottom shows their corresponding state during the execution. (Color figure online)

UPPAAL, the individual processes (in our case, these processes are Patients and Caregivers), the interdependencies between the tasks these automata run, and their timing constraints, are modeled as timed automata and UPPAAL verifies the properties using model checking. A timed automaton is a finite-state machine extended with clock variables and TCTL is an extended version of CTL which is specially introduced for checking the timed constrained logics [17]. Using TCTL, we checked our model's reachability, safety, and liveness properties as stated in earlier sections. There are certain conditions that must be true every time a particular event occurs. For example, if a patient is taken to the diagnostics centre and is in waiting state, it is expected that the patient eventually must return from the diagnostics centre (i.e., a patient must not wait forever in a diagnostic centre). We defined the following property check to assure the given scenarios:

```
forall (i : id_p) Patient(i).Wait_inDC --> forall
            (i : id_p) Patient(i).Start
```

The above query represents 'Always eventually', if a patient is waiting, will eventually always return. This property is known as the "leads-to" property (i.e., Liveness property) which specifies that whenever P is reached then for all subsequent paths where Q is reached also satisfies, for $(P \rightarrow Q)$. The "**leads-to**" property pattern $(\phi \rightarrow \psi)$ which is a shorthand for $A[](\phi \Rightarrow A <> \psi)$, stating that whenever ϕ is satisfied, then eventually ψ will be satisfied [9, 19]. Another property which we check is the following:

```
A[] forall (i: id_p) (Patient(i).Wait_inDC imply
            patientDelay[i]>threshold)
```

The above property is satisfied for the conditions where every time if a patient's service time (i.e., *patientDelay*) is more than the predefined *threshold* time, then the patient goes into the waiting state (i.e., a treatment which takes more time and the caregiver does not need to wait for the patient at DC). The other property which we check is the reachability property *(A <> ϕ)* which means for all paths there must be a state that satisfies *ϕ*. In our case, we want to check whether the state of ***GoToCollectPatient*** is achieved whenever the length of the waiting queue outside (i.e., *lenOfWQueueO*) is zero (i.e., there is no new patient request in the queue), and the length of the waiting queue inside (i.e., *lenOfWQueueI*) is not zero (i.e., there are patients waiting at DC who eventually have to return after consuming their service at DC) and if any of the caregivers is available.

```
A<> forall (i: id_c) Caregiver(i).GoToCollectPatient
        imply (lenOfWQueueO==0 && lenOfWQueueI>0
                && isNotAvailable[i]==0)
```

Furthermore, we plot some of the query results to observe the behaviour of the model over the particular time units. For example, Fig. 7 shows the plot for the length of the queues (*lenOfWQueueO* in red marking and *lenOfWQueueI* in blue marking) over fifty time units (Fig. 7(a)) and over hundred time units (Fig. 7(b)). These queues represent the number of patients requesting the service (*lenOfWQueueO*) and the number of patients waiting at DC (*lenOfWQueueI*). Figure 7(a) shows one patient is in the request queue towards the end. However, the waiting queue is constantly getting empty. The query which plots the graph is following where we kept the *bound* value as fifty:

```
simulate[<=bound]{lenOfWQueueO,lenOfWQueueI}
```

The *bound* is the time bound on the simulations. Similarly, in Fig. 7(b), the plot shows the results of the simulation for hundred time units (bound value is hundred). It is observed that as time progresses length of the request queue (*lenOfWQueueO*) decreases and the waiting queue at DC becomes zero which is interpreted as all patient requests are served and no patient is waiting at DC.

Using the following query, we assure that the patient is returned from the DC within some time interval:

```
Pr[#<=20](<> forall (i : id_c) (Caregiver(i).prevPatients
  == true) imply Caregiver(i).TakePatientBack)>= 0.98
```

The above query checks that within 20 discrete transitions the probability of taking the patient back (if there is any previous patient waiting in DC) is larger than 98%. It means the possibility of picking up the waiting patient from DC is highly likely. The result of this query is shown in Fig. 8.

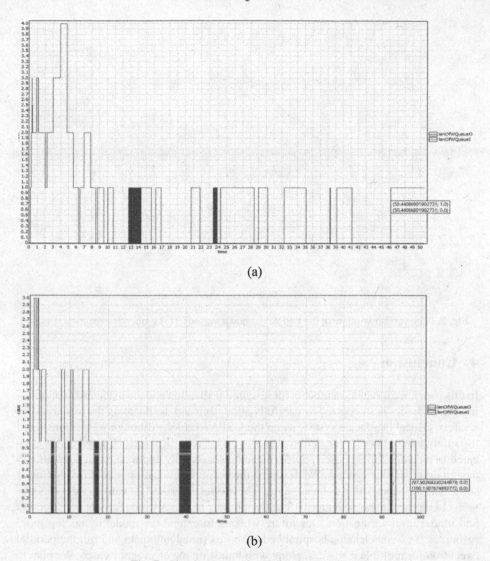

(a)

(b)

Fig. 7. Simulation results (Color figure online)

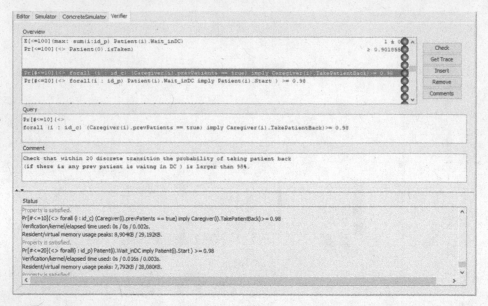

Fig. 8. The verifier window of the UPPAAL shows various TCTL queries execution results.

4   Conclusion

In this paper, we modelled a process for resource utilization and the mechanism of utilizing the resources is strategized by carefully allocating and deallocating the resources for a safety-critical healthcare system using the UPPAAL tool. Although we demonstrated the safety assured design for a clinical process where medical staff (Caregivers) is allocated to patients, the proposed approach can be reasonably applicable and adaptable to design other similar systems. We designed the resource allocation model by looking at some real-life scenarios in a clinical setup. The model is verified for various safety checks to avoid clashes in the assignment. The design part includes formal model construction and model level verification. Our future work is to extend the model by adding more resources (i.e., wheelchairs, hospital beds, etc.) as timed automata and run the parallel execution for multiple resources, along with handling the emergency cases. We plan to develop a code and test case generation for the network of timed automata.

References

1. Porres, I., Domínguez, E., Pérez, B., Rodríguez, Á., Zapata, M.A.: A model driven approach to automate the implementation of clinical guidelines in decision support systems. In: 15th Annual IEEE International Conference and Workshop on the Engineering of Computer Based Systems (ECBS 2008), pp. 210–218 (2008). https://doi.org/10.1109/ECBS.2008.35
2. Bernardi, S., Colom, J., Albareda, J., Mahulea, C.: A model-based approach for the specification and verification of clinical guidelines. In: Proceedings of the 2014 IEEE Emerging Technology and Factory Automation (ETFA), pp. 1–8 (2014). https://doi.org/10.1109/ETFA.2014.7005058

3. Heiden, K.: Model-based integration of clinical practice guidelines in clinical pathways. In: CAiSE (2012)
4. Guo, C., Fu, Z., Ren, S., Jiang, Y., Rahmaniheris, M., Sha, L.: Pattern-based statechart modeling approach for medical best practice guidelines - a case study. In: 2017 IEEE 30th International Symposium on Computer-Based Medical Systems (CBMS), pp. 117–122 (2017). https://doi.org/10.1109/CBMS.2017.14
5. UPPAAL Homepage. https://uppaal.org/. Accessed 21 May 2021
6. Kim, J.H., Larsen, K.G., Nielsen, B., Mikučionis, M., Olsen, P.: Formal analysis and testing of real-time automotive systems using UPPAAL tools. In: Núñez, M., Güdemann, M. (eds.) FMICS 2015. LNCS, vol. 9128, pp. 47–61. Springer, Cham (2015). https://doi.org/10.1007/978-3-319-19458-5_4
7. Jiang, Z., Pajic, M., Moarref, S., Alur, R., Mangharam, R.: Modeling and verification of a dual chamber implantable pacemaker. In: Flanagan, C., König, B. (eds.) TACAS 2012. LNCS, vol. 7214, pp. 188–203. Springer, Heidelberg (2012). https://doi.org/10.1007/978-3-642-28756-5_14
8. Wetselaar, P., Lobbezoo, F., de Jong, P., Choudry, U., van Rooijen, J., Langerak, R.: A methodology for evaluating tooth wear monitoring using timed automata modelling. J. Oral Rehabil. **47**(3), 353–360 (2020). https://doi.org/10.1111/joor.12908. Epub 5 Dec 2019. PMID: 31721264; PMCID: PMC7027495
9. Behrmann, G., David, A., Larsen, K.G.: A tutorial on UPPAAL 4.0 (Updated November 28, 2006). Extended version of 'A Tutorial on Uppaal'. In: Bernardo, M., Corradini, F. (eds.) Formal Methods for the Design of Real-Time Systems. SFM-RT 2004. LNCS, vol. 3185. Springer, Heidelberg (2004). https://www.it.uu.se/research/group/darts/papers/texts/new-tutorial.pdf
10. Larsen, K.G., Lorber, F., Nielsen, B.: 20 Years of UPPAAL enabled industrial model-based validation and beyond. In: Margaria, T., Steffen, B. (eds.) ISoLA 2018. LNCS, vol. 11247, pp. 212–229. Springer, Cham (2018). https://doi.org/10.1007/978-3-030-03427-6_18
11. Lee, E.A.: Cyber physical systems: design challenges. In: 11th IEEE International Symposium on Object and Component-Oriented Real-Time Distributed Computing (ISORC), pp. 363–369 (2008). https://doi.org/10.1109/ISORC.2008.25
12. Lee, I., et al.: Challenges and research directions in medical cyber–physical systems. In: Proceedings of the IEEE, vol. 100, no. 1, pp. 75–90, January 2012. https://doi.org/10.1109/JPROC.2011.2165270
13. Derler, P., Lee, E.A., Sangiovanni Vincentelli, A.: Modeling cyber–physical systems. In: Proceedings of the IEEE, vol. 100, no. 1, pp. 13–28, January 2012. https://doi.org/10.1109/JPROC.2011.2160929
14. Quadri, I., Bagnato, A., Brosse, E., Sadovykh, A.: Modeling methodologies for cyber-physical systems: research field study on inherent and future challenges. Ada User J. **36**, 246–253 (2016)
15. Espinoza, H., Cancila, D., Selic, B., Gérard, S.: Challenges in combining SysML and MARTE for model-based design of embedded systems. In: Paige, R.F., Hartman, A., Rensink, A. (eds.) ECMDA-FA 2009. LNCS, vol. 5562, pp. 98–113. Springer, Heidelberg (2009). https://doi.org/10.1007/978-3-642-02674-4_8
16. Ma, X., Rinast, J., Schupp, S., Gollmann, D.: Evaluating on-line model checking in UPPAAL-SMC using a laser tracheotomy case study. OpenAccess Ser. Inform. **36**, 100–112 (2014). https://doi.org/10.4230/OASIcs.MCPS.2014.100
17. Bouyer, P.: Model-checking timed temporal logics. Electron. Notes Theor. Comput. Sci. **231**, 323–341 (2009). ISSN 1571-0661

18. Shuhao, L., Balaguer, S., David, A., Larsen, K., Nielsen, B., Pusinskas, S.: Scenario-based verification of real-time systems using UPPAAL. Formal Methods Syst. Des. **37**, 200–264. (2010). https://doi.org/10.1007/s10703-010-0103-z

19. Bouyer, P., Laroussinie, F.: Model checking timed automata. In: Merz, S., Navet, N. (eds.) Modeling and Verification of Real-Time Systems, Chap. 4 (2008). https://doi.org/10.1002/9780470611012

An SDN Implemented Adaptive Load Balancing Scheme for Mobile Networks

Madhukrishna Priyadarsini[1]([✉]) [iD] and Padmalochan Bera[2]

[1] KIIT Deemed to be University, Bhubaneswar, India
mdhu.priyadarsinifcs@kiit.ac.in
[2] Indian Institute of Technology, Bhubaneswar, India
plb@iitbbs.ac.in

Abstract. In the last decade, mobile networks face challenges in providing reliable communication with enhanced performance and quality of service for handling the large volume of heterogeneous traffic. Software-defined networking (SDN) has gained significant attention as an effective deployment platform for the Internet and enterprise networks. In SDN, the separation between the controller (program), and forwarding switches (data) allows configuring network parameters, routing policies on the fly based on changes in application requirements and topologies. Moreover, it allows distributing the traffic load to the controllers that may help users and service providers to run applications with heterogeneous requirements as a pay-per-use basis. In this work, we modeled an SDN integrated adaptive load balancing scheme for mobile networks that efficiently process traffic from multiple nodes simultaneously. The experimentation results indicate that our scheme experiences a less number of packet drops, which is less than 1.3% of the total number of message exchanges among the base stations during the load balancing process

Keywords: SDN · MANET · Load balancing · OpenFlow · Node migration

1 Introduction

Today, the necessary use of mobile devices and applications has triggered an explosion in cellular data traffic [1]. The mobile networks are largely driven by the demand to serve heterogeneous content requirements from various servers [2]. However, satisfying the requirements from a large number of users while enhancing performance, reliability, QoS is a major challenge. There are mainly two lines of effort to address this. Firstly, the content requirements can be served within the single mobile network using existing load balancing approaches. Second, the traffic of highly loaded base stations can be migrated to lightly loaded stations. The former does not provide efficient load distribution; and the later undergoes inter-network communication issues [3,4].

Software-defined networking (SDN) is capable of serving heterogeneous traffic simultaneously by an effective distribution of traffic load in the network. In

© Springer Nature Switzerland AG 2022
R. Bapi et al. (Eds.): ICDCIT 2022, LNCS 13145, pp. 127–139, 2022.
https://doi.org/10.1007/978-3-030-94876-4_8

SDN, the separation of control programs (controller) and data plane (OpenFlow switches) makes it flexible to handle multiple content requests with less number of flow rules (less intervention to the controller). The controller generates flow rules for the packets and the switches forward the packets as per the flow rules. This effectively reduces the load in the network. Also, SDN contributes to bandwidth savings, which in turn reduces the cost for the Mobile Network Operators (MNOs) in terms of both Capital Expenditures (CAPEX) and Operational Expenditures (OPEX). Therefore, SDN architecture has the potential to greatly improve mobility support in the network with enhanced performance [5]. In addition, SDN provides inter-network communication which is essential for mobile networks. A generic architecture of SDN is shown in Fig. 1 comprises three controllers, seven OpenFlow switches.

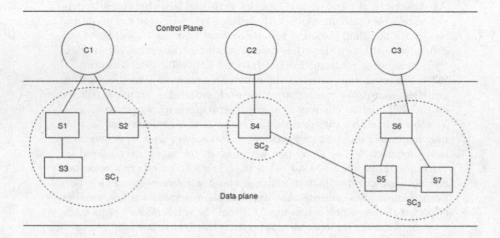

Fig. 1. A generic architecture of SDN

Current research on load balancing in mobile networks covers two classes of spectrum efficiency analysis, namely spatial and temporal efficiency [3]. Temporal efficiency serves cellular traffic by exploring additional spectrum, including offloading cellular traffic to WiFi and the recent 60 GHz millimeter-wave communication endeavor. However, in the case of spatial efficiency reducing cell size, operators can accommodate more (low-power) base stations in an area and reuse radio frequencies more efficiently to increase network capacity. Both approaches are based on spectrum analysis and they do not scale well for large systems and are not robust and reliable [4]. In addition, these processes increase the time of the load balancing process. The completion time of load balancing can be reduced using multiple controllers, however, it requires higher bandwidth. It has been studied that the load balancing problems are NP-complete in nature [6]. Therefore, the key challenges in mobile networks are as follows:

1. How to migrate mobile nodes from one base station to others under high load conditions?

2. How to dynamically adjust the threshold of base stations when no suitable lightly loaded base stations are found?

In this paper, we modeled a heuristic approach, named as *self-adaptive load balancing (SALB)* scheme for MANET, to effectively distribute the load on the base stations. The key features of this scheme are listed as follows:

1. The impact of the radio range has been considered while migrating mobile nodes from one base station to another.
2. Dynamic adjustment of base threshold in the base stations has been implemented depending on the traffic load variations on them.
3. Our modeled SALB scheme for MANET implements simultaneous migration of nodes from a set of highly loaded base stations to a set of lightly loaded stations.

The basic idea of SALB is presented in our work of SDN load balancing [6]. In this work, we model a SALB scheme for load balancing in MANET considering its environmental constraints. In the next subsection, we describe the overview of the software-defined network which is the basis of our work.

1.1 SDN Overview

SDN is a network design and implementation platform that mainly rely on separation of data (data plane) from control programs (control plane) to enable dynamic configuration of network parameters for easier traffic management and monitoring. The control plane (i.e., controller) that generates rules for traffic routing based on heterogeneous policies for different applications. On the other hand, the data plane (i.e., OpenFlow switches) is responsible for only forwarding the traffic according to the flow rules generated by the controller.

The OpenFlow architecture [7] with a defined set of protocols enables the communication between the controller and switches to determine the path for network packets. An OpenFlow switch forwards the data packet from any of its hosts according to the flow rules in its flow table. The flow table consists of mainly three fields, namely; header, actions, and counter (expiration timer) [7]. A packet is processed with necessary actions if its header matches one or more rules in the flow table. If there is no match between the packet header and the flow table, then the corresponding packet header information is forwarded to the controller as a *Packet-IN* event. Subsequently, the controller generates flow rules for this *Packet-IN* request using all running network control functions. Finally, this flow rule is forwarded to the underlying switch that stores the rule in its flow table for further processing. The examples of widely used open-source controllers are NOX, POX, Beacon, Floodlight, OpenDayLight, Ryu [8]. We have used the Floodlight controller for the implementation and evaluation of our proposed load balancing solution. However, it can also be used in integration with other controllers.

The rest of the paper is organized as follows. The problem is formulated formally in Sect. 2. The SALB scheme for MANET is described in Sect. 3. Detailed simulation results are presented and analyzed in Sect. 4. Finally, we conclude the paper in Sect. 5.

2   Problem Formulation

We have first proposed mapping between elements of the mobile network and that of SDN. The satellites are the major signal transmission elements for heterogeneous traffic in mobile networks. We integrate the functions of satellites to the application plane of SDN as the application plane pushes heterogeneous traffic requirements to the control plane. The end mobile nodes are implemented as switches in SDN which forward the traffic in the network. Finally, the traffic requirements of mobile nodes are served by base stations which are realized as a distributed set of logically centralized SDN controllers. Therefore, in our load balancing problem, our objective is to effectively distribute the traffic load of base stations with changes in network dynamics to satisfy QoS and performance requirements of the network. Another reason of using SDN in mobile networks is that, SDN provides high data rate, better connectivity and coverage to the network. Figure 2 shows the integration between SDN and Mobile networks.

Let a mobile network $G = \langle V = N \cup B, I \rangle$, where $N = \{N_1, N_2, \ldots, N_m\}$ is the set of m mobile nodes, $B = \{B_1, B_2, \ldots, B_n\}$ is the set of n base stations (controllers), and $I \subseteq V \times V$ is the set of interconnections among mobile nodes and base stations. Each base station B_i manages a potential mobile node set NB_i, and B_i can only process the requests from those mobile nodes. Each mobile node $N_i \in N$ sends some requests to the base station, and is termed as load of the

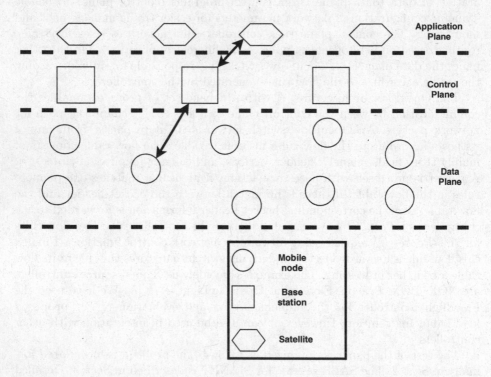

Fig. 2. Mobile network and software-defined network integration framework

node, NL_i. The current load BL_i of ith base station is the sum of the requests from the connected mobile nodes, i.e., $BL_i = \sum_{j \in NB_i} NL_j$. Each base station B_i has a base threshold BT_i that signifies the capacity of B_i. The value of B_i varies between BT_i^{min} and BT_i^{max}, which depend on the hardware specification of the base station (controller). For example, different controllers have different base thresholds. However, the value may vary in a certain limit. A mobile network is *overloaded* if $\exists B_i \in B, BL_i > BT_i^{min}$. We define HLB as the set of base stations for which the current loads are greater than their respective base thresholds, i.e. $HLB = \{B_i | BL_i > BT_i\}$. Similarly, $LLB = B \backslash HLB$ denotes the set of lightly loaded base stations. In other words, a mobile network is *not overloaded* if $HLB = \phi$. In general, the load balancing process in the mobile network selects a subset of nodes from NB_i of $B_i \in HLB$, and migrate them to LLB. This migration continues until the mobile network is not overloaded.

We consider *distance* of a node N_k to a base station B_i, as d_{ik}, is the radio range length from the node N_k to the base station B_i. Here, we introduce a parameter D, that defines the upper bound of distance d_{jk} from a migrating node $N_k \in NB_i$ to a target base station B_j.

It may so happen that a base station $B_i \in HLB$ could not find a suitable $B_j \in LLB$ for migrating an overloaded node N_k. This can happen due to one of the two following reasons. Firstly, the distance constraint for node migration, i.e., $d_{jk} \leq D$ may be violated. Secondly, the association of a node N_k to a base station B_j makes B_j overloaded, i.e., $BL_j + NL_k > BT_j$. If a base station $B_i \in HLB$ could not find a suitable $B_j \in LLB$ for migrating a node N_k, BT_j will increase. However, depending upon the hardware limit of the base station (controller) B_j, BT_j can be increased up to BT_j^{max}. In this paper, we present a *Self-Adaptive Load Balancing (SALB)* scheme for MANET that objectively solves the following problem:

SALB Problem for MANET. *Given a mobile network $G = \langle V = N \cup B, I \rangle$, with an initial load $BL^{init} = \{BL_1, BL_2, \ldots, BL_n\}$ $(BL_i \in Z^+)$ and base threshold $\{BT_1, BT_2, \ldots, BT_n\}$ $(BT_i \in Z^+)$, the objective is to derive an association of the mobile nodes to base stations $f : N \rightarrow B$ with final load $BL^{fin} = \{BL_1', BL_2', \ldots, BL_n'\}$ $(BL_i' \in Z^+)$ such that following constraints hold:*

1. *Network association constraint: $NB_1 \cup NB_2 \cup \ldots \cup NB_n = N$ and $NB_i \cap NB_j = \phi$ for $i \neq j$,*
2. *Load balancing constraint: $\forall B_i \in B, BL_i' \leq BT_i$, and*
3. *Distance constraint: $\forall B_i \in B \; \forall N_k \in N \quad f(N_k) = B_i \Rightarrow d_{ik} \leq D$.*   □

3   Self-adaptive Load Balancing Scheme for MANET

Here, we present our modeled self-adaptive load balancing (SALB) scheme for MANET in detail. Due to the heterogeneous content requirements of the mobile nodes such as traffic, weather, vehicle information etc., the load on multiple base stations increase simultaneously, which needs load balancing. Balancing load in MANET signifies the assignment of mobile nodes to base stations appropriately and satisfying their demand for requirements. Our scheme runs on each base station present in the network, and whenever there is a requirement of load balancing, it transfers control of nodes from highly loaded base stations (source) to the lightly loaded stations (target). In the first step, highly loaded stations find suitable station-node pairs for load balancing, and in the second step, they migrate the selected nodes to the target stations considering the distance constraint. In due course, if the highly loaded stations do not find any suitable target for load migration, the threshold of base stations are adjusted dynamically.

The SALB scheme has four modules, namely, *Load measurement module* monitors the load on every station; *Load broadcast module* is responsible for broadcasting the load to other stations in the network; *Load balancing module* checks load balancing constraints under variable load in the network; *Load migration module* migrates the load of highly loaded source stations to lightly loaded stations identified by the load balancing module.

3.1 Description of *SALB* Scheme

The working procedure of our SALB scheme is described in the next subsections.

Load Measurement. In this module, the base station B_i measures its load BL_i by summing up the number of received requests from the mobile nodes NB_i that are connected to it, i.e., $BL_i = \sum_{j \in NB_i} NL_j$.

Load Broadcast. Here, initially BT_i is set to BT_i^{min}, and BL_i is set to zero. Each station B_i stores its previously informed load in a local variable PL_i, which is initialized to zero. In this phase, the station B_i sends the message $\langle LOAD, B_i, BL_i \rangle$ to other stations, when $|BL_i - PL_i| > BT_i/10$, and then sets PL_i as BL_i. The reason behind selecting such a broadcasting condition is as follows. Frequent broadcast of load information among the stations consumes large bandwidth of the network. However, if the time difference between two successive broadcasts is large, then BL_i of B_i may differ significantly from PL_i, and in that case, the load information of other stations may hardly be of any use.

Load Balancing. After the load broadcast phase is over, each station B_i has load information from other stations. A station is included in the list of highly loaded stations, HLB if the load BL_i is higher than BT_i. Otherwise, B_i is included in the list of lightly loaded stations, LLB. We consider the load distribution as *non-uniform distribution*, if there exists a station $B_j \in LLB$ such that $BL_j + NL_k < BT_j$, where $N_k \in NB_i$. Otherwise it is considered as *uniform distribution*.

In the case of *non-uniform distribution*, $B_i \in HLB$ will invoke node migration, which is clearly explained in the load migration module. For uniform load distribution, $B_i \in HLB$ won't find a suitable B_j for load migration, i.e.,

---

Algorithm 1. Load Balancing Algorithm for Station B_i

1: **procedure** ACTIVATELOADBALANCING(BL, BT_i^{min})
2:     **if** $BL_i > BT_i^{min}$ **then**
3:         $g\_loadBalancingActivated \leftarrow TRUE$
4:         BALANCELOAD()
5:     **else**
6:         $g\_loadBalancingActivated \leftarrow FALSE$
7:     **end if**
8: **end procedure**
9:
10: **procedure** BALANCELOAD(BL, NL, BT^{min})
11:     **for** k $\in$ NB, j $\in$ LLB **do**
12:         **if** $(BL_j + NL_k < BT_j^{min})$ **then**
13:             $ctrlNode \leftarrow$ STATIONNODEPAIR()
14:             MIGRATELOAD($ctrlNode$)
15:         **else**
16:             send ($\langle INCREASE, B_i, 0.1 \times BT_j \rangle$)
17:         **end if**
18:     **end for**
19: **end procedure**
20:
21: **procedure** UPDATETHRESHOLD(BT)
22:     **while** true **do**
23:         **if** $g\_loadBalancingActivated == TRUE$ **then**
24:             **for** $j \in LLB$ **do**
25:                 Receive ($<INCREASE, B_i, 0.1 \times BT_j>$)
26:                 $BT_j = BT_j + 0.1 \times BT_j$
27:                 **if** $BT_j \geq BT_j^{max}$ **then**
28:                     send ($\langle NACK, B_j, B_i \rangle$)
29:                 **else**
30:                     send ($\langle ACK, B_j, B_i \rangle$)
31:                 **end if**
32:                 **if** $BL_j < BT_j$ **then**
33:                     **while** $BL_j > BT_j^{min}$ **do**
34:                         $BT_j = BT_j - 0.1 \times BT_j$
35:                     **end while**
36:                 **end if**
37:             **end for**
38:             $g\_loadBalancingActivated \leftarrow FALSE$
39:         **end if**
40:     **end while**
41: **end procedure**

$\forall B_j \in LLB$, $BL_j + NL_k \geq BT_j$, where $N_k \in NB_i$. In such scenario, B_i sends $\langle INCREASE, B_i, 0.1 \times BT_j \rangle$ message to all B_j. After receiving this message, B_j updates its BT_j and acknowledges B_i with $\langle ACK, B_j, BT_j \rangle$ message. Station B_i again checks node migration condition, and if possible, then migrates its node to B_j. Otherwise, B_i sends $\langle INCREASE, B_i, 0.1 \times BT_j \rangle$ message to B_j until BT_j reaches to BT^{max}.

Similarly, other stations of HLB may send $\langle INCREASE, B_i, 0.1 \times BT_j \rangle$ message to B_j. Here, B_j calculates its BT_j for any one of the $B_i \in HLB$ arbitrarily, and sends $\langle ACK, B_j, B_i \rangle$ message. After sending $\langle ACK, B_j, B_i \rangle$ message to one of the stations, if B_j can accommodate another station's load (i.e., $BL_j + NL_k < BT_j$ holds), then it sends $\langle ACK, B_j, B_i \rangle$ to that station, otherwise, it sends $\langle NACK, B_j, B_i \rangle$ message.

However, if the load on B_j decreases below BT_j (i.e., $BL_j < BT_j$), then B_j reduces its BT_j to $0.1 \times BT_j$. In light load scenario, B_j continuously compares its BL_j and BT_j and reduces its BT_j upto BT_j^{min}. In the load reduction process, it may so happen that B_i sends a $\langle INCREASE, B_i, 0.1 \times BT_j \rangle$ message, and in that case, B_j may increase its BT_j. This increment and decrement of BT_j happen until the network is balanced (i.e., $\forall i \in B$, $BL_i < BT_i^{min}$).

Our scheme is self-adaptive in the sense that the base threshold is modified (in the range of BT^{min} and BT^{max}) depending on the load on various stations. The load balancing procedure is shown in Algorithm 1.

Load Migration. In this phase, a highly loaded station $B_i \in HLB$ first selects a subset $NB_{i'}$ of nodes from NB_i, and then each node $N_k \in NB_{i'}$ is migrated to a lightly loaded station $B_j \in LLB$. While migrating a node $N_k \in NB_{i'}$ from $B_i \in HLB$ to $B_j \in LLB$, our scheme takes care of the following issues:

(a) The migration of N_k from B_i to B_j should not overload B_j. We ensure this by the following equation.

$$BL_j + NL_k + BT_i/10 < BL_i \tag{1}$$

After migration of node N_k, the new load of station B_j will be $BL_j + NL_k$. However, in Eq. 1, we consider an extra load of $BT_i/10$. The reason behind considering the extra load is that the informed load BL_i of B_i may increase in due course while B_i calculates the new load of B_j.

(b) Considering (a), B_i may migrate the node N_k to other station. In this scenario, our scheme selects the station B_j that is inside the radio range of N_k. We consider the upper bound of distance (radio range) between B_j and N_k is D (i.e., $d_{jk} \leq D$). The parameter D is the maximum allowable distance for node migration in any mobile network. If the distance from N_k is the same for more than one station, then we choose the station B_j with minimum load. Again, if more than one station has the same minimum load, then our scheme selects arbitrarily any one of them.

The migration procedure of node N_k from station B_i to station B_j is described in Algorithm 2. The steps are as follows:

Algorithm 2. Station-node Pair Selection Algorithm for Station B_i

---

1: **procedure** STATIONNODEPAIR()
2:     **if** $LLB == \emptyset$ **then**
3:         return -1;
4:     **end if**
5:     **for** $k \in NB$ **do**
6:         **for** $j \in LLB$ **do**
7:             **if** $(BL_j + NL_k + BT_i/10) < BL_i$ && $(d_{jk} \leq D)$ **then**
8:                 send $(\langle MIGRATE, B_i, B_j, N_k \rangle)$
9:             **end if**
10:        **end for**
11:    **end for**
12:    **if** B_i Receives $\langle REJECT, B_j, B_i, N_k \rangle$ **then**
13:        STATIONNODEPAIR()
14:    **else**
15:        Send $(\langle Terminate, B_i, B_j, N_k \rangle)$
16:    **end if**
17: **end procedure**
18:
19: **procedure** ONRECEIPT($\langle MIGRATE, B_j, B_i, N_k \rangle$)
20:    $migreq \leftarrow false$
21:    **if** $migreq == false$ **then**
22:        Set $migreq \leftarrow true$
23:        Send $(\langle ACCEPT, B_j, B_i, N_k \rangle)$
24:    **else**
25:        Send $(\langle REJECT, B_j, B_i, N_k \rangle)$
26:    **end if**
27: **end procedure**

(a) B_i sends a message $\langle MIGRATE, B_i, B_j, N_k \rangle$ to B_j.

(b) On receiving $\langle MIGRATE, B_i, B_j, N_k \rangle$ by B_j, B_j may allow to accept the load migration from B_i for the node N_k, and in such scenario, B_j sends a message $\langle ACCEPT, B_j, B_i, N_k \rangle$ to B_i. However, if B_j is not able to accept the load migration from B_i for the node N_k, then B_j sends $\langle REJECT, B_j, B_i, N_k \rangle$ message to B_i. In that case, B_i tries to find another lightly loaded station from LLB after receiving the REJECT message from B_j and continues the same process.

(c) Station B_j do not get control over node N_k by sending ACCEPT message, since there may be some unfinished requests of N_k at B_i. After getting a $\langle Terminate, B_i, B_j, N_k \rangle$ message from B_i, both B_i and B_j update their status of node mapping.

Node migration does not impose an extra cost on the load balancing process rather than message transfer time. Also, multiple node migrations do not increase network traffic as well as do not affect bandwidth utilization of the network.

4 Experimental Evaluation

We evaluated the SALB scheme for MANET in two stages. Firstly, we analyzed the performance of the scheme, and then, we verified its accuracy using real-world traffic applications in the designed testbed.

Table 1. Performance analysis results of SALB scheme in MANET

	Control overhead	Load balancing time	Throughput	Packet drops
SALB	3.8% of # M	1.42 s	9.72 Mbps	.0182% of # M

4.1 Methodology

We implemented our modeled self-adaptive load balancing scheme in Java and used Floodlight controllers [9] as base stations. Then, we perform a simulation with real Internet service topology, Geant from the Internet Topology Zoo [10] to make our evaluation more similar to the real-time network scenario. We considered five controllers as base stations and 140 mobile nodes. The nodes are assigned to the five stations for their service requirements and content requests. More requests are generated by the nodes using the mininet platform to create a high load on the base stations. We considered the range of BT is from 75–90% of hardware capacity (i.e., BT^{min} and BT^{max}).

4.2 Performance Evaluation

We evaluated the performance of our scheme in terms of packet loss, control overhead, load balancing time, and throughput. Table 1 shows control overhead, load balancing time, throughput, packet drops on an average for the SALB scheme. In the table, M denotes the total number of messages exchanged (broadcast, migration) among base stations during the execution of the respective modules on an average. The average load balancing time for SALB is approximately 1.42 s, which is reasonably good for serving heterogeneous content requests of the mobile nodes. Also, we analyzed the computational complexity of our SALB scheme for MANET. The major computation is involved in the selection of suitable station-node pair, which is linearly dependent on the number of base stations present in the network. This shows the computational efficacy of our scheme.

We have compared the load of each base station by sending a large number of requests to them without load balancing and with the SALB scheme. Figure 3 presents the load comparison results of five base stations used in our simulation. The load of each station lies below BT^{min} after the execution of the SALB scheme. This comparison clearly indicates the efficacy of our load-balancing scheme in the MANET environment.

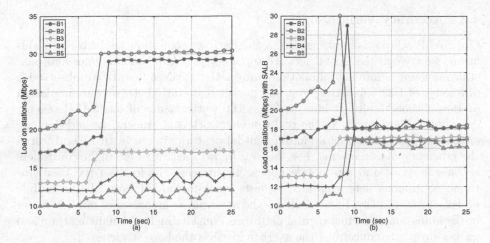

Fig. 3. Load distribution in different base stations (a) Without any load balancing scheme, (b) With SALB scheme

We have also tested the performance of the proposed scheme in comparison to the state-of-the-art mobile network load balancing methodologies [3,4]. Figure 4 represents the performance comparison of the existing load balancing techniques along with the proposed scheme in terms of throughput and packet drops. We have chosen Geant network topology for the simulation of the results. Here, the results show that our proposed load balancing scheme provides significantly higher throughput (approx. 6.71 Mbps) and less packet drops (approx. 2 4 packets/s) than the existing approaches.

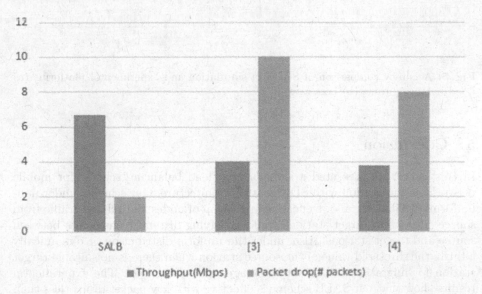

Fig. 4. Throughput comparison of proposed SALB with the existing load balancing schemes in [3] and [4]

4.3   Accuracy Verification

Our SALB scheme is implemented in the EstiNet-emulation testbed. For evaluation, we created the Geant network topology [10] with mobile nodes and base stations using a mininet simulation run on the EstiNet board. We observed a difference of 1.32% in throughput and packet drop ratio between our simulation and emulation results. It indicates that the performance of our SALB scheme does not deviate largely in the real-time network environment. In addition, we created large hardware set up in different laboratories in our institute and tested the efficiency of our scheme. For this setup, we used two Floodlight controllers as base stations and ten mobile nodes. To increase the load on the base stations, continuous heterogeneous requests were forwarded from all the mobile nodes simultaneously. Figure 5 shows the accuracy comparison of our scheme in both simulation and experimental platforms considering load balancing time and packet drop rate concerning the average load on the base stations.

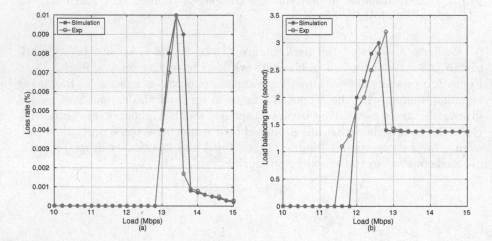

Fig. 5. Accuracy comparison of SALB in simulation and experimental platforms (a) Load balancing time, (b) Loss rate

5   Conclusion

In this paper, we presented a self-adaptive load balancing scheme for mobile networks in integration with SDN control architecture. Our scheme, under non-uniform distribution, allows effective migration of nodes and related traffic from source stations to target stations while satisfying distance constraints between source and target stations. Also, under the uniform distribution, it dynamically adjusts the threshold value of the source station when there is no suitable target station for migration and thereby manages the traffic load. The experimental results show that our SALB scheme is effective with low packet drops (less than 1.3% of the total number of message exchange) and high throughput (approx

9.72 Mbps). Thus, our scheme is suitable for any mobile application (LTE or VoLTE).

References

1. Sharma, A., Roy, A., Ghoshal, S., Chaki, R., Bhattacharya, U.: Load balancing in cellular network: a review. In: IEEE Conference on Computing and Networking Technology (2012)
2. Borst, S., Saniee, I., Whiting, P.: Distributed dynamic load balancing in wireless networks. In: Mason, L., Drwiega, T., Yan, J. (eds.) ITC 2007. LNCS, vol. 4516, pp. 1024–1037. Springer, Heidelberg (2007). https://doi.org/10.1007/978-3-540-72990-7_88
3. Gomes, A., Braun, T.: Load balancing in LTE mobile networks with information-centric networking. In: IEEE workshop on Cloud Computing Systems, Networks, and Applications (2015)
4. Deng, L., et al.: Device-to-Device load balancing for cellular networks. IEEE Trans. Commun. **67**(4), 3040–3054 (2019)
5. Priyadarsini, M., Bera, P., Bampal, R.: Performance analysis of software-defined network controller architecture-A simulation-based survey. In: IEEE International Conference on Wireless Communications, Signal Processing and Networking (2017)
6. Priyadarsini, M., Mukherjee, J., Bera, P., Kumar, S., Jakaria, A.H.M., Rahman, M.A.: An adaptive load balancing scheme for software-defined network controllers. Comput. Networks **164**, 106928 (2019)
7. Open Networking Foundation, OpenFlow Switch Specification, 1.4.0 ed., July 2017
8. Priyadarsini, M., Bera, P.: A new approach for SDN performance enhancement. In: IEEE International Conference on Computer Networks (CN) (2018)
9. Floodlight project. http://www.projectfloodlight.org/floodlight/
10. Knight, S., Nguyen, H.X., Falkner, N., Bowden, R.A., Roughan, M.: The internet topology zoo. IEEE J. Sel. Areas Commun. **29**(9), 1765–1775 (2011)

Rewriting Logic and Petri Nets: A Natural Model for Reconfigurable Distributed Systems

Lorenzo Capra[✉][iD]

Dipartimento di Informatica, Università Degli Studi di Milano, Milan, Italy
capra@di.unimi.it

Abstract. Petri Nets (PN) are a central model for concurrent or distributed systems, but not expressive enough to represent dynamically reconfigurable systems. On the other side, Rewriting Logic has proved to be a natural framework for several formal models of distributed systems. We propose an efficient `Maude` formalization of dynamically reconfigurable PT nets (with inhibitor arcs), using as a running example a fault-tolerant manufacturing system. We discuss the advantages of such a hybrid approach, as well as some concerns that are raised.

Keywords: Maude · PT nets · Reconfigurable distributed systems

1 Introduction

Modern distributed systems operate in highly dynamic environments and have to manage varying operational conditions. System components may become temporarily or permanently unavailable, may appear/disappear, e.g., due to failures or dynamic load balancing. Self-adaptation is increasingly used to face such complexity. Self-adaptive systems (and many other distributed systems, e.g., automated systems) rely on dynamic-reconfiguration policies that overlap with the base system functionality.

To validate early design choices and/or verify the system behaviour at runtime, there is an impelling need for formal methods modelling both the system's base architecture and the reconfiguration procedures.

Petri nets (PNs) are a central model of concurrent or distributed systems, but not expressive enough to specify dynamic structural changes. Several PN extensions have been proposed in which an enhanced expressivity is not adequately supported by analysis techniques. A representative is the "nets within nets" paradigm, introduced by Valk [19], that gave rise to special High-Level PNs such as [10]. As for PNs with indistinguishable tokens, we have to mention Reconfigurable PN, a family of PN-based formalisms composed of a marked net and a separated set of net-transformation rules specified consistently with algebraic Graph Transformations Systems, as (double) pushouts [7–9,11,16]. Most research has focused on trying to formulate these models as $\mathcal{M}$-adhesive categories. See [14] for a survey of dynamic PN extensions.

© Springer Nature Switzerland AG 2022
R. Bapi et al. (Eds.): ICDCIT 2022, LNCS 13145, pp. 140–156, 2022.
https://doi.org/10.1007/978-3-030-94876-4_9

This paper provides a formalization of "rewritable" PT nets with inhibitor arcs (a Turing-complete PN class) in rewriting-logic [3,13], using Maude as a specification language [6]. We focus on operational aspects, by proposing a Maude-based framework for the specification/analysis of rewritable PT systems. Compared to [1,15], in which a class of reconfigurable PNs are converted in Maude modules to exploit the model-checking tools of Maude, our encoding provides more data abstraction to ease the modeller task, is more compact and efficient, and promotes the definition of rewrite rules with a higher level of flexibility. Throughout the paper, we use a simple yet tricky benchmark, the model of a fault-tolerant Manufacturing System. We conduct some experiments of formal verification of properties and briefly discuss the advantages of using a somehow hybrid modelling approach like that we propose.

The presented work should be deemed as a preliminary, however, encouraging, step towards a Maude-based tool-set for the specification and the analysis of dynamically reconfigurable PT systems.

2   PT Nets

2.1   Multisets

A *multiset (bag)* b on D is $b : D \to \mathbb{N}$, where $b(d)$ is the *multiplicity* of d. $d \in b$ if and only if $b(d) > 0$. Let $Bag[D]$ be the set of bags over D, and $b_1, b_2 \in Bag[D]$. $b_1 + b_2$ and $b_1 - b_2$ are $Bag[D]$ elements such that $\forall d \in D$: $b_1 + b_2(d) = b_1(d) + b_2(d)$; $b_1 - b_2(d) = b_1(d) - b_2(d)$ if $b_1(d) \geq b_2(d)$, 0 otherwise. Also relational operators are component-wise: $b_1 < b_2$ if and only if $\forall d \in D\ b_1(d) < b_2(d)$. With $b_1\ rop'\ b_2$ we mean the *restriction* of rop to $\{d | d \in b_1\}$.

2.2   Place/Transition (PT) Nets with Inhibitor Arcs

A PT *net* [17] is a 5-tuple (P, T, I, O, H), where: P, T are non-empty, finite sets such that $P \cap T = \emptyset$. $I, O, H : T \to Bag[P]$ such that $\forall t \in T : I(t) \neq O(t)$.

P and T hold the net *places* and *transitions*. The former, drawn as circles, represent system state variables, whereas the latter, drawn as bars, represent events causing local state changes. A distributed state of a PT net, called *marking*, is a bag $m \in Bag[P]$. A net is a kind of directed, bipartite multi-graph whose nodes are $P \cup T$. Maps I, O, H describe the *input*, *output*, and *inhibitor* edges, respectively ($\bigcirc\!\!-\!\!\rightarrow\!\!\square$ $\square\!\!-\!\!\rightarrow\!\!\bigcirc$ $\bigcirc\!\!-\!\!\square$). Let $f \in \{I, O, H\}$: if $k = f(t)(p) > 0$, then a weight-k edge of corresponding type links p to t.

The behavior of a PT net is specified by the *firing rule*. A transition $t \in T$ is *enabled* in m if and only if: $I(t) \leq m \wedge H(t) >' m$.

If t is enabled in m it may fire, leading to m' (we denote this $m[t\rangle m'$), where:

$$m' = m + O(t) - I(t)$$

A PT-*system* is a pair (N, m), where N is a net and m is a marking of N. The interleaving semantics of (N, m_0), where m_0 denotes the PT system's initial state, is specified by the *reachability graph* (RG), an edge-labelled, directed graph (V, E) whose nodes are reachable markings. The RG is defined inductively: $m_0 \in V$; if $m \in V$ and $m[t\rangle m'$ then $m' \in V$, $m \xrightarrow{t} m' \in E$.

3   Rewriting Logic and the Maude system

Maude [6] is an expressive, strictly declarative language with a sound semantics in rewriting logic [3, 13]. Maude's statements are (possibly conditional) *equations* (keyword eq) and *rules* (keyword rl). Both sides of a rule/equation are terms of a given *kind* and may contain typed variables. Both rules and equations have a simple rewriting semantics in which instances of the lefthand side pattern are replaced by corresponding instances of the righthand side.

A Maude *functional* module (keyword fmod) contains only equations and is a functional program defining one or more operations through equations, used as simplifications. A Maude *system module* (keyword mod) contains rules and possibly equations. Rules are also computed by rewriting terms from left to right, but represent local transitions in a (concurrent) system. Although declarative in style and with a clear logical semantics, system modules are non-functional. In Maude, a distributed system's state is usually represented as a kind of associative "multiset". Rules apply *concurrently* to different portions of a system, leading to a new state. There is no assumption on the confluence of rewrites.

Maude features expressivity, simplicity and performance. A wide range of systems is naturally expressible with Maude, which may be used as a formal specification language, as a programming language and as a meta-language (in which other formalisms, languages and logics can be expressed). Maude's expressivity is achieved through: equational pattern matching modulo operator equational attributes; user-definable operator syntax/evaluation strategy; sub-typing(sorting) and partiality (kinds); generic types; reflection. A Maude program is a logical theory, and a computation is a deduction according to the theory's axioms. Under certain executability conditions, the mathematical and the operational semantics coincide. We refer to [2] and [20] for functional and system modules, respectively.

A functional module specifies an *equational theory* in membership equational logic [2, 12]. Formally, such a theory is a pair $(\Sigma, E \cup A)$, where Σ is the signature, that is, the specification of all the sort, subsort, kind[1], and (overloaded) operator declarations (considering also the imported functional modules); E is the collection of (conditional) equations and memberships declared in the module(s), and A is the collection of equational attributes (assoc, comm, and so on) of operators (treated as predefined equations). The models of functional modules are algebras, i.e., sets of data with related operations. The family of Σ-ground terms T_Σ defines a model called Σ-algebra ($T_{\Sigma(X)}$ denotes the whole set of terms). According to [4], the best model of $(\Sigma, E \cup A)$ is one that satisfies $E \cup A$ and is both

---

[1] A *kind* is an implicit equivalence class gathering all sorts connected by the subsort relation; terms having a kind but not a sort may be considered as *undefined* or *errors*.

junk-free (all elements can be denoted by T_Σ terms) and confusion-free (only elements that are forced to be equal by $E \cup A$ are identified). This model, called the *initial algebra* of $E \cup A$ and denoted $T_{\Sigma/E\cup A}$, does exist [2] and provides the denotational semantics of the Maude functional module specifying $(\Sigma, E \cup A)$. $T_{\Sigma/E\cup A}$ is the quotient of T_Σ in which the equivalence classes hold terms that prove equal using $E \cup A$.

If the axioms E are Church-Rosser and terminating modulo A (each ground term is thus simplified in a unique way regardless of the order in which equations apply) there is an intuitive, equivalent description for $T_{\Sigma/E\cup A}$. The final values (*canonical* forms) of all ground terms form an algebra called the *canonical term algebra*, denoted $CAN_{\Sigma/E\cup A}$. By definition, the reduce command of Maude interpreter reduces operators to their values in this algebra. The coincidence of the denotational and operational semantics is expressed by $T_{\Sigma/E\cup A} \cong CAN_{\Sigma/E\cup A}$.

A Maude's system module, with the imported submodules, specifies a generalized *rewrite theory* [3,13], that is, a four-tuple $\mathcal{R} = (\Sigma, E \cup A, \phi, R)$ where $(\Sigma, E \cup A)$ is the membership equational theory specified by the signature, equational attributes, and equation statements in the module; ϕ is a map specifying, for each operator in Σ, its frozen arguments; and R is a set of rewrite rules[2]. Intuitively, a rewrite theory specifies a concurrent system. The equational part $(\Sigma, E \cup A)$ specifies the algebraic structure of the states, formalized by the initial algebra $T_{\Sigma/E\cup A}$. The rules R (and ϕ) specify the system's dynamics, that is, the possible concurrent transitions of the system. In this context, they represent structural changes to a PT system. In rewriting logic, concurrent transitions become rewrite proofs; since several proofs may correspond to the same computation (because of equivalent interleavings), rewriting logic has an equational theory of proof equivalence [3,13]. The initial model $\mathcal{T}_\mathcal{R}$ of $\mathcal{R}$ associates to each kind k a labeled transition system (a category) whose states are $T_{\Sigma/E\cup A,k}$, and whose transitions take the form: $[t] \overset{[\alpha]}{\to} [t']$, with $[t],[t'] \in T_{\Sigma/E\cup A,k}$, and $[\alpha]$ an equivalence class of rewrites modulo the equational theory of proof-equivalence. Different $[\alpha]$ represent different "truly concurrent" computations.

The executability conditions for system modules match the notion of ground *coherence* between rules and equations [20]. Assuming that $E \cup A$ is Church-Rosser and terminating, an efficient strategy (adopted by Maude's rewrite command) is to first apply the equations to get a canonical form, then apply a rewrite rule in R. Coherence ensures that this strategy is complete, i.e., any rewrite of $t \in T_\Sigma$ with R is also possible with t's canonical form. Coherence is crucial because rewriting modulo an equational theory is in general undecidable. It reduces rewriting with R modulo $E \cup A$ to rewriting with E and R modulo A, which is decidable given an A-matching algorithm.

Checking the confluence, termination and coherence of Maude modules is under the user's responsibility. It is often possible to prove them using the Maude Formal Environment (MFE), available at https://github.com/maude-team/MFE, most

---

[2] R rules don't apply to frozen arguments; in the paper we do not use frozen arguments.

of which is currently integrated with the Maude's interpreter. The modules listed in this paper have been proven to be executable. Their functional part also meets two other desirable properties: i) each (equivalence class of a) ground term has a least sort (kind); ii) the canonical form of a well-defined ground term is only built of constructors (characterized by the ctor operator attribute). A syntactical condition (called term pre-regularity) and Maude's Sufficient Completeness Checker (SCC) have been used to verify properties i) and ii), respectively.

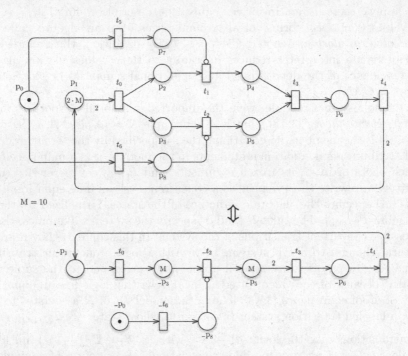

Fig. 1. The MS and its adaptation upon a fault on line 1.

4   Running Example: A Fault-Tolerant MS

We model a manufacturing system (MS) able to self-reconfigure to manage failures. Despite its simplicity, it is a benchmark for any formalism intended to specify highly dynamic systems. We use a variant of the model introduced in [5].

The MS (Fig. 1, top) is composed of two symmetric lines that work an even number of raw pieces. Pairs of worked pieces are assembled to get the final artefacts. Either line gets broken occasionally. In that case, the system adapts itself in order to work using one line. This involves significant changes to the topology and the transfer of raw pieces left on the faulty line to the other one (Fig. 1, bottom). If another fault then affects the left line, the MS goes back to its nominal configuration after a global repair (not represented). The parameter $M \in \mathbb{N}^+$ defines the number of raw pieces $(2 \cdot M)$ worked during an entire production cycle. Each artefact is immediately replaced by a pair of raw pieces, what makes the system's behaviour cyclic.

Tokens represent (raw or worked) pieces. The two production lines are modelled by the subnets $\{p_2, t_1 \ p_4\}$ (line 1) and $\{p_3, t_2, p_5\}$ (line 2). Transition t_3 models he assembly of raw pieces. Transition t_0 models the loader component, that (initially) picks up two raw pieces from a storage (place p_1) putting them onto the lines. Transition t_4 models the immediate reload of the MS. The fault occurrence is sketched by transitions t_5 (line 1) and t_6 (line 2). A fault causes the immediate block of a line, which is modelled by the inhibitor arc linking p_7 to t_1. We assume that the simultaneous failure of both the lines is not possible. For this reason, the transitions t_5 and t_6 are in symmetric structural conflict.

The PT net at the bottom of Fig. 1 illustrates the changes to the MS layout that allow it to operate in a degraded way, preserving the expected behaviour. The marking of the PT system at the top represents the system's initial state, whereas that of the PT system at the bottom shows the situation immediately after a fault: the (M) raw pieces left on line 1 (place p_2) have been moved to line 2 (place p_3). Two major concerns, addressed in the next section, are how to formally specify the MS reconfiguration(s) described in Fig. 1 and the condition(s) under which it may occur. The bounded expressivity of PT nets with inhibitor arcs (despite their Turing-completeness) makes it nearly impossible to specify scenarios like that described.

5 Formalization of Rewritable PT Systems with Maude

In this section, we describe the Maude formalization of rewritable PT systems. The sources are available at github.com/lgcapra/rewpt. A (system) module refers to a particular model, all the others are reusable: some functional modules specify the PT signature (the main is PT-SYS), a system module (PT-EMU) specifies the PT firing rule. The main modules are listed at the end of the section.

The formalization relies on two generic functional modules, BAG{X} and MAP+{X,Y}, whose type-parameters (satisfying the built-in elementary theory TRIV[3]) correspond to the bag's support and to the map's arity. Differently from [15,18], bags on a set are not merely represented as the free commutative monoid on that set. More data abstraction is provided by the $\_\cdot\_$, $\_+\_$, $\_[\_]$ $\_-\_$, $\_<=\_$, $\_>'\_$, set operators (the first two *constructors*). The commutative/associative $\_+\_$ makes it possible to intuitively represent a bag as a weighted sum, e.g., 3 . a + 1 . b. The module MAP+ defines a map as a "set" of entries, built with the associative/commutative operator $\_,\_$. Sort Entry, whose only constructor is the operator $\_|->\_$, is a subsort of Map. With respect to the Maude's built-in MAP module, MAP+ has a significant improvement: given that the constructor $\_,\_$ cannot ensure (for efficiency) the uniqueness of map keys ($\_,\_$ is a partial function), a conditional membership equation characterizes correct maps by assigning a term of kind [Map] the sort Map only if no duplicates are present.

---

[3] Maude uses views to instantiate the type-parameters (theories) of a generic module to concrete modules. In this context, theories and views are very intuitive.

PT Signature. The `Maude` PT signature complies with the definition in Sect. 2, thus passing from a formalization to the other is straightforward. The nodes of a PT net are indexed terms, e.g., `t(1)` (see module `TRAN`). The module `IMATRIX` provides a compact representation of a transition's incidence matrix as a triplet (as the edge types) of place bags (`[_,_,_]` constructor). `IMATRIX` imports `BAG` by preserving its initial semantics and renaming sorts/operators. Two extra operators are defined, to `remove` a place and to check the presence of a place (`in`).

The module `PT-SYS` builds on `MAP+` and `IMATRIX`, both imported in a protected way and with some renaming (in particular, the sort `MapTran,Imatrix` is renamed `Net`). That is, a PT net is syntactically expressed as a set of entries `t(i) |-> [I,O,H]`. This formalization allows us to specify system structural changes easily and consistently. A PT system term is the juxtaposition (the constructor `__`) of a `Net` term and a `BagP` term (representing a marking). The module provides three operators corresponding to the maps I, O, H of the formal definition, and three predicates: `enabled` encodes the transition enabling; `dead` (which builds on `enabled`) encodes a deadlock state; `in` tests the existence of a place. The co-domains of `__`, `enabled`, and `In`, `Out`, `Inh` are *kinds* i.e., these are *partial* functions. As for `__`, the reason is that the net of a PT system must not be empty (constant `emptyN`): a membership axiom specifies the correct `System` terms. The others make sense for `Tran` arguments belonging to the given net.

The module `PT-SYS` includes two equations specifying structural equivalences. One eliminates transitions having a null effect, according to the definition in Sect. 2. The other eliminates transitions structurally dead, as linked to a place by an input edge and by an inhibitor edge of non lesser weight.

PT System Dynamics. The generic (system) module `PT-EMU` specifies the PT system operational semantics. The module's type-parameter has to satisfy the theory `PTSYSTH`, that requires two constant operators describing a marking and a net. A conditional rewrite rule specifies the PT system firing rule (Sect. 2). Notice the use (in the rule's condition) of the associative connective `/\` and of a matching equation (`t := t'`) that makes the rule compact and efficient to apply. The rule's free variables `I, O, H, N'` are instantiated by matching the left-hand side of the matching equation against the canonical ground term bound to variable `N` (occurring on the rule's left-hand side).

Rewritable PT Systems. The model-dependent part consists of a `Maude` system module importing `PT-SYS` and satisfying the theory `PTSYSTH`, which is (in part) mechanically derived from a PT system (N, m_0). The module `RWPT-FMS`, e.g., comes from the PT system in Fig. 1-top. Two equations assign terms `net`, `m0` the expressions encoding N and m_0, respectively. These expressions are obtained by defining any two bijections $\phi_P : P \to \{0, \dots, |P| - 1\}$, $\phi_T : T \to \{0, \dots, |T| - 1\}$ (in our example, implicitly defined by subscripts of PT nodes). For the rest, the encoding of N is straightforward. The constant operator `M` makes the module syntactically parametric in the initial marking of place p_1.

The remaining part of the module contains a (possibly empty) set R of rewrite rules specifying structural changes that may occur during the evolution of the system initially represented by the term `net m0`. With respect to related approaches [15], where rewrite rules rigorously meet the model of algebraic GTS (based on pushout) and need to verify *glueing* conditions, our formalization fosters a flexible, though rigorous, modelling of dynamically reconfigurable systems.

We can classify rewrite rules based on the kind of $T_{\Sigma(X),k}$ terms in left- and right-hand sides: `Place`, `Tran`, `BagP`, `Imatrix`, `Net`, `System`. Except for rules of `System` type, all the other rules are local, that is, act on portions of the term describing a PT system. This ensures a lot of flexibility and is coherent with the intrinsically distributed operational semantics of rewriting logic, but may have uncontrolled effects. A rule of `BagP` type, e.g., may touch both the marking and some local incidence matrices of a `System`.

The system module `RWPT-FMS` specifies two (conditional) `System`-level rules that model the reconfiguration described in Fig. 1. Both `r1` (nominal=>faulty) and `r2` (faulty=>nominal) are *symbolic*, i.e., may refer to any of the two lines. That means a rule folds two cases. In rule `r1`, this is achieved by matching the rule's left-hand pattern, which contains some variables denoted by capital letters: variable `P3` may be instantiated to either ground term `p(2)` or `p(3)`, depending on which line gets faulty, then `P2` is consequently instantiated. In rule `r2`, the two matching equations in the rule's condition make the free variables `P2`, `P3` be instantiated one to `p(2)` and the other to `p(3)`, depending on which line is broken. The condition of rule `r1` ensures that the transformation nominal=>faulty may take place if there are no "worked" pieces left on the faulty line. These residual pieces are contextually moved to the working line (the marking of place bound to `P3` is cleared and that of the place bound to `P2` increased correspondingly). The last clause of `r2`'s conditions the back-transformation faulty=>nominal to the fact that the system (operating in a degraded way) has entererd a deadlock, upon another fault breaking the line left: this happens when in that line there is at most one "worked" piece and all the others are raw (the total is $2 \cdot M$). In order for the system to safely restart (after a global repair), M raw pieces are moved from that line to the other one (M tokens are withdrawn from the place bound to `P2` and added to the place bound to `P3`).

A Library of Net-Transformations. In the example, we use two monolithic rules, each implementing a system transformation as a whole. Besides being complex, such an approach is unrealistic when dealing with *adaptive* systems, where changes are local and meet a strategy. Using our model, we can define rewrite rules of varying granularity and locality, with a high degree of flexibility. To ease the modeller task, we also provide a minimal set of net transformations in the form of net operators. The functional module `PT-RWLIB` provides two such operators (the others are implicitly provided by modules `BAG`, `MAP+`, `IMATRIX`). `setw` allows us to set the weight of any edge, whose type is passed as an argument. Edges/nodes may be added to a net using `setw`. Edges may be removed using a zero-weight. This may cause the erasure of nodes that removed edges are incident to. The operator `remove` withdraws a place from a net. The homonym operator of `MAP+` may remove a transition. Using `BAG` operators (e.g., `set`) we may modify the marking of a PT system and its local incidence matrices, add/remove places. Module `PT-RWLIB` also defines an operator `w` reading the edge weight.

```
fmod TRAN is
 protecting NAT .
 sort Tran .
 op t : Nat -> Tran [ctor] .
 op subscript : Tran -> Nat .
 vars N : Nat .
 eq subscript (t(N)) = N .
endfm

fmod IMATRIX is
 pr BAG{Place} * (sort Bag{Place} to BagP, sort NeBag{Place} to NeBagP, op nil to nilP) .
 pr EXT-BOOL .
 sort Imatrix .
 op [_,_,_] : BagP BagP BagP -> Imatrix [ctor] .
 op remove : Imatrix Place -> Imatrix .
 op in : Imatrix Place -> Bool .
 vars X Y Z : BagP .
 var P : Place .
 eq remove([X,Y,Z], P) = [set(X,P,0),set(Y,P,0),set(Z,P,0)] .
 eq in([X,Y,Z], P) = X[P] =/= 0 or-else Y[P] =/= 0 or-else Z[P] =/= 0 .
endfm

fmod PT-SYS is
 pr MAP+{Tran, Imatrix} * (sort Map{Tran, Imatrix} to Net, op empty to emptyN) .
 sort System .
 op __ : Net BagP -> [System] [ctor] .
 ops In Out Inh : Net Tran -> [BagP] .
 op enabled : System Tran -> [Bool] .
 op dead : System -> Bool .
 op in : Net Place -> Bool . *** test the existence of a place
 var N : Net .
 var T : Tran .
 var P : Place .
 var I O H S : BagP .
 var Q : Imatrix .
 var K K' : NzNat .
 eq In((T |-> [I,O,H], N), T) = I .
 eq Out((T |-> [I,O,H], N), T) = O .
 eq Inh((T |-> [I,O,H], N), T) = H .
 eq in((T |-> Q, N), P) = in(Q, P) or-else in(N, P).
 eq in(emptyN, P) = false .
 eq T |-> [I,I,H] = emptyN [metadata "null t"] .
 ceq T |-> [K . P + I, O, K' . P + H] = emptyN if K >= K' [metadata "dead t"] .
 eq enabled( (T |-> [I,O,H], N) S, T) = I <= S and-then H >' S .
 ceq dead((T |-> Q, N) S) = false if enabled( (T |-> Q, N) S, T) .
 eq dead(N S) = true [owise] .
 cmb N S : System if N =/= emptyN . *** the net cannot be "empty"
endfm

fth PTSYSTH is
 protecting PT-SYS .
 op m0 : -> BagP .
 op net : -> Net .
endfth

mod PT-EMU{X :: PTSYSTH} is
 var T : Tran .
```

```
var I O H S : BagP .
var N N' : Net .
crl [firing] : N S => N S + O - I if T |-> [I,O,H], N' := N /\ I <= S /\ H >' S .
endm


mod RWPT-FMS is
protecting PT-RWLIB .
op net : -> Net .
op m0 : -> BagP .
op M : -> Nat . *** model's parameter
vars N N' : Net .
vars TL TF : Tran .
vars P2 P3 P4 P5 PF : Place .
var S : BagP .
var K : NzNat .
eq M = 50 .
eq net = t(0) |-> [2 . p(1), 1 . p(2) + 1 . p(3), nilP], t(1) |-> [1 . p(2), 1 . p(4),
  1 . p(7)], t(2) |-> [1 . p(3), 1 . p(5), 1 . p(8)], t(3) |-> [1 . p(4) + 1 . p(5),
  1 . p(6), nilP], t(4) |-> [1 . p(6), 2 . p(1), nilP],t(5) |-> [1 . p(0), 1 . p(7), nilP],
  t(6) |-> [1 . p(0), 1 . p(8), nilP].
eq m0 = 2 * M . p(1) + 1 . p(0) .
crl [r1] : (N, t(0) |-> [2 . p(1), 1 . P2 + 1 . P3, nilP] , t(3) |-> [1 . P4 + 1 . P5,
  1 . p(6), nilP],TF |-> [1 . p(0),1 . PF,nilP],TL |-> [1 . P3,1 . P5, 1 . PF]) S + 1 . PF
 => (N, t(0) |-> [1 . p(1), 1 . P2, nilP], t(3) |-> [2 . P4, 1 . p(6), nilP]) set(S, P3, 0)
    + S[P3] . P2 + 1 . p(0) if S[P5] = 0 .
crl [r2] : N S => net S + 1 . p(0) + M . P3 - M . P2 - 1 . p(7) - 1 . p(8) if 1 . P2 :=
    Out(N, t(0)) /\ 1 . P2 + 1 . P3 := Out(net, t(0)) /\ dead(N S) .
endm


view Fms from PTSYSTH to RWPT-FMS is
op m0 to m0 .
op net to net .
endv


mod FMS-EMU is
including PT-EMU{Fms} .
endm


fmod PT-RWLIB is
protecting PT-SYS .
sort Atype . *** arc type
ops i o h : -> Atype [ctor] .
op w : Net Tran Place Atype -> [Nat] . ***get an arc's weight
op setw : Net Tran Place Atype Nat -> Net . ***set an arc
op setwS : Net Tran Place Atype Nat -> Net . ***set an arc in a safe way
ops remove : Place Net -> Net .
var N N' : Net .
var T : Tran .
var P : Place .
var I O H M : BagP .
var Q : Imatrix .
var K K' : NzNat .
var Y : Nat .
var A : Atype .
eq w(N, T, P, i) = In(N,T)[P] .
eq w(N, T, P, o) = Out(N,T)[P] .
eq w(N, T, P, h) = Inh(N,T)[P] .
```

```
ceq setw(N, T, P, i, Y) = N, T |-> [Y . P, nilP, nilP] if N[T] = undefined .
 eq setw((N, T |-> [I,O,H]), T, P, i, Y) = N, T |-> [set(I, P, Y), O, H] .
ceq setw(N, T, P, o, Y) = N, T |-> [nilP, Y . P, nilP] if N[T] = undefined .
 eq setw((N, T |-> [I,O,H]), T, P, o, Y) = N, T |-> [I, set(O, P, Y), H] .
ceq setw(N, T, P, h, Y) = N if N[T] = undefined .
 eq setw((N, T |-> [I,O,H]), T, P, h, Y) = N, T |-> [I, O, set(H, P, Y)] .
 eq remove(P, (T |-> Q, N) ) = T |-> remove(Q, P), remove(P, N) .
 eq remove(P, emptyN) = emptyN .
ceq setwS(N, T, P, A, Y) = N' if N' := setw(N, T, P, A, Y) /\ N' =/= emptyN .
 eq setwS(N, T, P, A, Y) = N [owise] .
endfm
```

5.1   Base Notions and Properties of Rewritable PT Systems

In this section, we provide a theoretical basis for the Maude formalization of rewritable PT systems through a few intuitive notions and properties. We refer to the *canonical* form of ground terms, that does exist if a term is well-defined (i.e., has an associated least *sort*) and is built of constructors since all modules satisfy the executability conditions (end of Sect. 2).

Property 1 (correspondence between PT systems and well-defined terms). A PT system $S = (N, m)$ has an associated ground term of sort System, vice-versa, a ground term of sort System represents a PT system (up to isomorphism[4]).

We have described how to get a System term from $S = (N, m)$. Vice versa, we observe that a canonical term of sort System is built (by definition of PT-SYS and MAP+) of (n m), with n being a non-empty set of entries T:Tran -> Q:Imatrix (without duplicate-keys) with the first two components (in, out) of each local incidence matrix unequal, and m a bag of places. By the way, the property above sets a bijection, denoted ψ (a pair ψ_P, ψ_T), between (classes of isomorphic) PT systems and well-defined System terms.

Let r be a rewrite rule, t, t' two ground terms of kind k. The notation $t \xrightarrow{r(\sigma)} t'$ means that 1) the rule's lefthand side $u \in T_{\Sigma(X),k}$ matches t (i.e., there is a ground substitution σ such that $\sigma(u) = t$)[5], 2) t is rewritten to t' using r, σ.

Given a PT system $S = (N, m_0)$, let RWPT-S represent a system module (satisfying PTSYSTH) in which the term (net m0) encodes S, R be the set of rewrite rules defined in RWPT-S, and S-EMU the module PT-EMU whose parameter is instantiated (via an obvious view) to RWPT-S.

The interleaving semantics of a rewritable PT system specified by module RWPT-S is expressed naturally by the labelled transition system, denoted $RWLT_S$, which is built from the initial term/state (net m0).

---

[4] S and S' are isomorphic iff there are a two bijections $\phi_p : P \to P'$, $\phi_t : T \to T'$, preserving the edges and the initial markings.

[5] σ nay be empty is u is a ground term; if r is a conditional rule σ may involve free variables introduced by matching equations used in the rule's condition.

Definition 1 (State-transition system of RWPT-S**).** *Let* $R' = R \cup \{\texttt{firing}\}$. $RWLT_S$ *is an edge-labelled, directed graph* (V_{RW_S}, E_{RW_S}) *inductively defined:* $(\texttt{net m0}) \in V_{RW_S}$; *if* $s \in V_{RW_S}$ *and* $s \overset{r(\sigma)}{\to} s'$ *then:* $s' \in V_{RW_S}$, $s \overset{r(\sigma)}{\to} s' \in E_{RW_S}$.

By default, the Maude interpreter's search command explores the state-space associated with an initial term by executing one-step rewrite rules in a fair, breadth-first way, therefore, coherent with the definition above.

By the way, RWPT-S includes the ordinary behaviour of the PT system S.

Property 2 (RG inclusion). $RWLT_S$ contains a sub-graph isomorphic to RG_S.

It directly follows from the fact that, by definition, for any transition t and for any marking m of S: $m[t\rangle m'$ if and only if $\psi_P(m) \overset{\texttt{firing}(\sigma)}{\to} \psi_P(m')$, with $\sigma(\texttt{T}) = \psi_T(t)$ (T is the variable used in rule firing of module PT-EMU).

Notice that, in the event of badly defined/used rules, we may reach undefined (error) states, despite (net m0) well-definiteness. For example, the rule
```
crl  : (N, T |-> [I, 1 . P, nilP], T' |-> [1 . P, O, nilP]) S =>
    (N, T |-> [ I, O, nilP]) S if I[P] = 0 /\ O[P] = 0 /\ S[P] = 0 .
```
that aggregates two transitions connected by an intermediate empty place not linked to any other transitions, rewrites the System ground term
```
(t(1) |-> [1 . p(1),1 . p(2),nilP], t(2) |-> [1 . p(2),1 . p(1),nilP]) nilP
```
into: (emptyN nilP), an undefined term of kind [System] (due to the equations of functional module PT-SYS).

Definition 2 (Well-defined RWPT-S**).** RWPT-S *specifies a well-defined rewritable PT system if and only if all reachable states in* V_{RW_S} *are terms of sort* System.

Rule Validation. The module RWPT-FMS is well-defined. In general, however, ensuring the well-definiteness of Maude system modules specifying rewritable systems may not be simple. There are two approaches, shortly discussed in the following, each with different possible implementations.

One consists of defining (structurally) valid rewrite rules, and works also in the event the system state-space is infinite.

Definition 3 (Valid rewrite rule). $r \in R$ *is valid if and only if, for any ground term* s *of sort* System, *if* $s \overset{r(\sigma)}{\to} s'$ *then* s' *is of sort* System.

Each Maude rewrite rule crl [r] : s => s' if cond, where cond is the (possibly empty) rule's condition and s, s' $\in T_{\Sigma(X),\texttt{System}}$, may be rephrased as a valid rule using the built-in *sort predicate*

$$\texttt{crl [vr] s => s' if cond /\textbackslash\ s' :: System}$$

The weak spot of this elegant and efficient solution is that it may shadow bad design choices. As an alternative, we might define rewrite rules exclusively composed of *safe* net-operators. For example, the operator setw, defined in module PT-RWLIB, always results in a term of sort Net, possibly emptyN (for the sake of flexibility). The operator setwS, which builds on setw, also guarantees that the resulting term is a non-empty PT net (note the use of owise equation attribute mixed with a matching equation).

6   Examples of Formal Verification

In this section, we briefly discuss on the tools that are available to formally verify the properties of a Maude-based specification of rewritble PT systems, and we present a few experimental data.

A system module (which specifies a rewrite theory) provides an executable formal model of a distributed system. Under appropriate conditions, we can check that this model satisfies some properties, or obtain counterexamples. This kind of model-checking analysis is quite general and builds on the search command, which allows one to explore (following a breadth-first strategy) the reachable state-space in different ways. For example, using bounded model-checking, if the system state-space is huge (or even infinite), or model-checking of infinite-state systems through abstractions. Under finite reachability assumptions, we can efficiently model check any linear time temporal logic (LTL) property of a system module. We here focus on a simple, yet very useful, model-checking capability, namely, the model checking of invariants using the search command.

One invariant we might like to verify about a rewritable PT system is dead-lock freedom. A straightforward way to check this property is to issue the search command below, which searches for all *final* states of our running example, starting from the PT system's nominal configuration.

search in FMS-EMU : net m0 =>! X:System .

It gives no solution, meaning that the self-adaptive MS is deadlock-free[6]. Table 1 reports some data about the performance of this command, as the system size varies. The data refer to a Intel Core i7-6700 equipped with 32 GB of RAM.

Another interesting search concerns the existence of dead states inside the different configurations (the nominal one and the two symmetric, faulty ones) that the system enters during its evolution. The command to issue is (* means "in zero or more steps", dead is the predicate defined in module PT-SYS):

search net m0 =>* X:System such that dead(X:System) .

There are six solutions (for any M), two for each configuration of the system. For example, for $M = 50$, we get (for readability, in the following excerpt of the command's output, we use the terms net, faulty1, faulty2 to denote the system's nominal and faulty configurations instead of the longer canonical forms)

Table 1. Performance of search command as M varies

M	# states	# rewrites	time (ms)
3	350	35730	44
5	1232	130539	153
10	8932	995724	1192
20	84007	9737494	36090
50	2186132	261564504	862536

---

[6] Using the LTL modules we can even check that the initial marking is a home-state.

```
Solution 1 (state 133541) rewrites: 16647633 in 65130ms cpu
X:System --> faulty1 1 . p(8) + 100 . p(3)
Solution 2 (state 133542) rewrites: 16647811 in 65140ms cpu
X:System --> faulty2 1 . p(7) + 100 . p(2)
Solution 3 (state 142860) rewrites: 17841539 in 68140ms cpu
X:System --> faulty2 1 . p(4) + 1 . p(7) + 99 . p(2)
Solution 4 (state 142865) rewrites: 17842109 in 68140ms cpu
X:System --> faulty1 1 . p(5) + 1 . p(8) + 99 . p(3)
Solution 5 (state 1083022) rewrites: 143322169 in 781220ms cpu
X:System --> net 1 . p(8) + 50 . p(3) + 50 . p(4)
Solution 6 (state 1084477) rewrites: 143524908 in 782130ms cpu
X:System --> net 1 . p(7) + 50 . p(2) + 50 . p(5)
```

We may suppose a generic form for the six states above in which expressions $M, 2 \cdot M, 2 \cdot M - 1$ should be used in place of values 50, 100, 99, respectively.

As a last example of use of **search**, we check whether the system correctly evolves from an inner deadlock: the command below lists the **system** states reachable in one-step from a dead state which refers to the system's nominal configuration after line 2 gets faulty (for $M = 10$).

```
search net  1 . p(8) + 10 . p(3) + 10 . p(4) =>1 X:System .
```

```
Solution 1 (state 1) rewrites: 23 in 0ms cpu
X:System --> faulty2 1 . p(0) + 10 . p(2) + 10 . p(4)
```

As you can see, the system enters a state in which only line 1 is working and the raw pieces left on the faulty line (a half of the total) have been moved on line 1.

6.1 Exploiting PT Net Structural Analysis

In a somehow hybrid modelling framework like that proposed, we can benefit from the tools/techniques available for both formalisms. For example, structural analysis of Petri nets may be an interesting, really efficient alternative/complement to state-space inspection techniques, when the system state-space is huge and performances degrade (as shown in Table 1). Not only that. Structural analysis doesn't depend on the initial marking of a PT system, so we may use it to get some parametric outcomes. Let us show an application of semiflows on this direction to our running example.

Table 2. P- and T-semiflows of the PT nets specifying the MS (Fig. 1)

Nominal behavior		Faulty behavior	
pin_1	$p_1 + 2\,{}^{*}p_6 + 2\,{}^{*}p_2 + 2\,{}^{*}p_4$	pin_1'	$p_1 + 2\,{}^{*}p_6 + p_3 + p_5$
pin_2	$p_1 + 2\,{}^{*}p_6 + 2\,{}^{*}p_3 + 2\,{}^{*}p_5$	pin_2'	$p_0 + p_8$
pin_3	$p_0 + p_7 + p_8$		
tin_1	$t_0 + t_1 + t_2 + t_3 + t_4$	tin_1'	$2\,{}^{*}t_0 + 2\,{}^{*}t_2 + t_3 + t_4$

Let $\mathbf{Q}$ be the $|P| \cdot |T|$ matrix such that is $\mathbf{Q}_{[p,t]} = O(t)(p) - I(t)(p) \in \mathbb{Z}$. Any P-vector $\mathbf{p}$ which is a non-null, positive integer solution of the product $\mathbf{p} \cdot \mathbf{Q} = \mathbf{0}$, called P-semiflow, expresses a conservative law for the marking of places corresponding to non-zero entries of $\mathbf{p}$. Any T-vector $\mathbf{t}$ which is a non-null, positive integer solution of the product $\mathbf{Q} \cdot \mathbf{t} = \mathbf{0}$, called T-semiflow, expresses a cyclicality effect for firing sequences matching the semiflow. By inspecting the module RWPT-FMS one can (formally) check that the system's layout may only be one of those described in Fig. 1, more a symmetrical faulty one.

Table 2 shows the semiflows[7] of the PT nets in Fig. 1 (there are symmetric semiflows for the other faulty configuration). The PT nets are covered by P-semiflows, therefore, the whole system is structurally bounded. The T-semiflows represent a base production cycle in the nominal and faulty configurations of the MS. Consider the two P-semiflows of the faulty configuration, and the initial marking immediately after a system switch. We derive these invariant marking-expressions: $\forall m : m(p_0) + m(p_8) = 1$, $m(p_1) + 2 \cdot m(p_6) + m(p_3) + m(p_5) = 2 \cdot M$. With simple arguments we can show that if $m(p_8) = 1$ then we *eventually* reach either of the two dead states: $m' = 1 * p_8 + 2 \cdot M * p_3$, $m'' = 1 * p_8 + 1 * p_5 + (2 \cdot M - 1) * p_3$, corresponding to matches 1,4 found with the search command (for $M = 50$). We have used this parametric outcome in rule r2 of module RWPT-FMS.

Even if, in general, a static prediction of all the possible structural changes of a rewritable PT system specified with Maude may be more complex, or even impossible, the opportunity to exploit the structural analysis capabilities of Petri nets together with the formal analysis tools of Maude looks promising.

7   Conclusion

We have presented a Maude formalization of "rewritable" PT nets, a framework for the specification/analysis of automated distributed system with reconfiguration capabilities. With respect to similar approaches, the proposed encoding provides much more data abstraction, to ease the modeller task, is more compact and efficient, and fosters the definition of rewrite rules with the maximum degree of flexibility. We have used as a (simple but tricky) running example throughout the paper a self-healing MS. We have reported some experiments of formal verification of properties and discussed about the possible advantages of such a hybrid modelling approach.

Ongoing Work and Open Issues. We plan to enrich the modular and intuitive Maude specification presented in the paper with structural extensions (e.g., test/flush arcs, transition priorities) that further enhance the model expressivity. The idea is to use "decorated" terms representing PT nodes (e,g, t(1,"line",0), where 0 denotes the priority) and to update the firing rule

---

[7] Computed with the GreatSPN tool (github.com/greatspn/SOURCES).

in module PT-EMU accordingly. A more interesting extension would be the formalization of rewritable *High-Level* PN possibly using the Maude meta-level and unification modules.

The Labelled Transition System of a Maude specification of rewritable PT nets should be defined up to isomorphism of PT systems (the running example's statespace would be reduced by half). A possible solution is to define a normal form for PT systems using equations. This is generally complex, but some heuristics could help dramatically reduce the inefficiency in most practical cases, e.g., by defining classes of "symmetrical" PT nodes (using labels) so that an isomorphism preserves these classes.

Non-deterministic, rule-based transformations are simple to specify, but sometimes they are shown to be flawed and ill-equipped for representing realistic situations. Passing to more sophisticated and suitable forms should be possible and convenient using Maude's reflection and/or Maude's strategy language.

References

1. Barbosa, P., et al.: SysVeritas: a framework for verifying IOPT nets and execution semantics within embedded systems design. In: Camarinha-Matos, L.M. (ed.) DoCEIS 2011. IAICT, vol. 349, pp. 256–265. Springer, Heidelberg (2011). https://doi.org/10.1007/978-3-642-19170-1_28
2. Bouhoula, A., Jouannaud, J.P., Meseguer, J.: Specification and proof in membership equational logic. Theor. Comput. Sci. **236**(1), 35–132 (2000). https://doi.org/10.1016/S0304-3975(99)00206-6
3. Bruni, R., Meseguer, J.: Generalized rewrite theories. In: Baeten, J.C.M., Lenstra, J.K., Parrow, J., Woeginger, G.J. (eds.) ICALP 2003. LNCS, vol. 2719, pp. 252–266. Springer, Heidelberg (2003). https://doi.org/10.1007/3-540-45061-0_22
4. Burstall, R.M., Goguen, J.A.: Algebras, theories and freeness: an introduction for computer scientists. In: Broy, M., Schmidt, G. (eds.) Theoretical Foundations of Programming Methodology: Lecture Notes of an International Summer School, directed by F. L. Bauer, E. W. Dijkstra and C. A. R. Hoare, pp. 329–349. Springer, Dordrecht (1982). https://doi.org/10.1007/978-94-009-7893-5_11
5. Camilli, M., Capra, L.: Formal specification and verification of decentralized self-adaptive systems using symmetric nets. Discrete Event Dyn. Syst. **31**(4), 609–657 (2021). https://doi.org/10.1007/s10626-021-00343-3
6. Clavel, M., et al.: All About Maude - A High-Performance Logical Framework: How to Specify, Program and Verify Systems in Rewriting Logic. LNCS, vol. 4350. Springer, Heidelberg (2007). https://doi.org/10.1007/978-3-540-71999-1
7. Ehrig, H., Hoffmann, K., Padberg, J., Prange, U., Ermel, C.: Independence of net transformations and token firing in reconfigurable place/transition systems. In: Kleijn, J., Yakovlev, A. (eds.) ICATPN 2007. LNCS, vol. 4546, pp. 104–123. Springer, Heidelberg (2007). https://doi.org/10.1007/978-3-540-73094-1_9
8. Ehrig, H., Padberg, J.: Graph grammars and petri net transformations. In: Desel, J., Reisig, W., Rozenberg, G. (eds.) ACPN 2003. LNCS, vol. 3098, pp. 496–536. Springer, Heidelberg (2004). https://doi.org/10.1007/978-3-540-27755-2_14
9. Kahloul, L., Chaoui, A., Djouani, K.: Modeling and analysis of reconfigurable systems using flexible petri nets. In: Zavoral, F., Yaghob, J., Pichappan, P., El-Qawasmeh, E. (eds.) Networked Digital Technologies, pp. 343–357. Springer, Heidelberg (2010). https://doi.org/10.1109/TASE.2010.28

10. Köhler-Bußmeier, M.: Hornets: nets within nets combined with net algebra. In: Franceschinis, G., Wolf, K. (eds.) PETRI NETS 2009. LNCS, vol. 5606, pp. 243–262. Springer, Heidelberg (2009). https://doi.org/10.1007/978-3-642-02424-5_15

11. Llorens, M., Oliver, J.: Structural and dynamic changes in concurrent systems: reconfigurable petri nets. IEEE Trans. Comput. **53**(9), 1147–1158 (2004). https://doi.org/10.1109/TC.2004.66

12. Meseguer, J.: Membership algebra as a logical framework for equational specification. In: Presicce, F.P. (ed.) WADT 1997. LNCS, vol. 1376, pp. 18–61. Springer, Heidelberg (1998). https://doi.org/10.1007/3-540-64299-4_26

13. Meseguer, J.: Conditional rewriting logic as a unified model of concurrency. Theor. Comput. Sci. **96**(1), 73–155 (1992). https://doi.org/10.1016/0304-3975(92)90182-F

14. Padberg, J., Kahloul, L.: Overview of reconfigurable petri nets. In: Heckel, R., Taentzer, G. (eds.) Graph Transformation, Specifications, and Nets. LNCS, vol. 10800, pp. 201–222. Springer, Cham (2018). https://doi.org/10.1007/978-3-319-75396-6_11

15. Padberg, J., Schulz, A.: Model checking reconfigurable petri nets with Maude. In: Echahed, R., Minas, M. (eds.) ICGT 2016. LNCS, vol. 9761, pp. 54–70. Springer, Cham (2016). https://doi.org/10.1007/978-3-319-40530-8_4

16. Prange, U., Ehrig, H., Hoffmann, K., Padberg, J.: Transformations in reconfigurable place/transition systems. In: Degano, P., De Nicola, R., Meseguer, J. (eds.) Concurrency, Graphs and Models: Essays Dedicated to Ugo Montanari on the Occasion of His 65th Birthday. LNCS, vol. 5065, pp. 96–113. Springer, Heidelberg (2008). https://doi.org/10.1007/978-3-540-68679-8_7

17. Reisig, W.: Petri Nets: An Introduction. Springer-Verlag, New York Inc., New York (1985). https://doi.org/10.1007/978-3-642-69968-9

18. Stehr, M.-O., Meseguer, J., Ölveczky, P.C.: Rewriting logic as a unifying framework for petri nets. In: Ehrig, H., Padberg, J., Juhás, G., Rozenberg, G. (eds.) Unifying Petri Nets. LNCS, vol. 2128, pp. 250–303. Springer, Heidelberg (2001). https://doi.org/10.1007/3-540-45541-8_9

19. Valk, R.: Object petri nets. In: Desel, J., Reisig, W., Rozenberg, G. (eds.) ACPN 2003. LNCS, vol. 3098, pp. 819–848. Springer, Heidelberg (2004). https://doi.org/10.1007/978-3-540-27755-2_23

20. Viola, E.: E-unifiability via narrowing. In: ICTCS 2001. LNCS, vol. 2202, pp. 426–438. Springer, Heidelberg (2001). https://doi.org/10.1007/3-540-45446-2_27

MCDPS: An Improved Global Scheduling Algorithm for Multiprocessor Mixed-Criticality Systems

Lalatendu Behera[✉]

Department of CSE, NIT Jalandhar, Jalandhar, India
beheral@nitj.ac.in

Abstract. Real-time systems are increasingly involved in mixed-criticality tasks with different criticality levels. However, the focus is increasing on the multiprocessor systems that can help in reducing the cost, space, weight, time, and power consumption. There is significantly less work done in the literature to design a global scheduling algorithm for multiprocessor mixed-criticality systems. In this paper, we propose a global scheduling algorithm based on the DP-Fair scheduling algorithm for multiprocessor mixed-criticality systems. We also show that our proposed algorithm dominates the existing global scheduling algorithm in terms of the number of successful scheduling instances.

Keywords: Real-time systems · Dp-fair algorithm · Mixed-criticality systems · Global scheduling · GMCS · EDF

1 Introduction

In recent years, there is an increasing trend towards integrating applications at different importance/criticality levels and implementing them onto a single computation platform. Such an integrated system, often referred to as a mixed-criticality system, helps to reduce cost, energy consumption and resource under-utilization. For example, let us consider a UAV whose primary mission is to capture ground images. The functionalities (tasks) of such a UAV can be easily classified into two criticality-based categories: (i) safety-critical – functionalities related to safe flight operation of the UAV; higher in criticality (HI-criticality) and (ii) mission-critical – functionalities related to image capturing; relatively lower in criticality (LO-criticality). Satisfying the timing specifications of the HI-criticality functionalities even under the worst-case scenarios is very important as they are related to safe flight operation and are typically certified by Certification Authorities (CAs) who use very conservative tools to predict worst-case execution time (WCET). On the other hand, the general goal of the System Designers (SDs) is to satisfactorily execute both HI-criticality and LO-criticality functionalities. As only SDs are concerned about the timely execution of LO-criticality tasks and hence they are assumed to have only a single WCET (referred to as LO-criticality WCETs of LO-criticality tasks). The CAs are not concerned about the execution of LO-criticality tasks.

R. Bapi et al. (Eds.): ICDCIT 2022, LNCS 13145, pp. 157–162, 2022.
https://doi.org/10.1007/978-3-030-94876-4_10

Here we investigate for a new algorithm based on DP-Fair [9] which can schedule more number of task sets (a super set of task sets) and properly utilize the system resources. Here we plan to find an algorithm similar to the DP-fair algorithm which can be used to find a schedule for a task set and can be scheduled on a multiprocessor mixed-criticality systems. Since the execution time assumptions of CAs are very pessimistic, there is a fair chance that all the HI-criticality jobs will not execute their extra execution time. So we investigate the situation where at least K HI-criticality jobs execute their extra execution time in the HI-criticality scenario.

2   System Model

A mixed-criticality (MC) periodic task system $\mathcal{T}$ consists of a number of tasks $\tau_1, \ldots, \tau_n$. A task τ_i is characterized by a 4-tuple $(\chi_i, C_i(LO), C_i(LO), p_i)$, where $\chi_i \in \{LO, HI\}$, $C_i(LO) \in \mathbb{N}^+$, $C_i(HI) \in \mathbb{N}^+$, and $p_i \in \mathbb{N}^+$ denote the *criticality* level, the LO-criticality *WCET*, the HI-criticality *WCET* and *period*, respectively. We assume that $C_i(LO) \leq C_i(HI)$ for all tasks τ_i and the deadline of each task is the same as its period. Each of these tasks may generate an unbounded number of dual-criticality jobs, either of LO-criticality or HI-criticality. A job j_{ik} of task τ_i is characterized by a 5-tuple of parameters: $j_{ik} = (a_{ik}, d_{ik}, \chi_i, C_i(LO), C_i(HI))$, where $a_{ik} \in \mathbb{N}$ denotes the *arrival time*, $a_{ik} \geq 0$ and $d_{ik} \in \mathbb{N}^+$ denotes the *relative deadline*, $d_{ik} = p_i$.

Definition 1: A scheduling strategy is *feasible or correct* if and only if the following conditions are true:

1. If all the jobs finish their $C_i(LO)$ units of execution time on or before their deadlines.
2. If any job does not declare its completion after executing its $C_i(LO)$ units of execution time, then all the HI-criticality jobs must finish their $C_i(HI)$ units of execution time on or before their deadlines.

2.1   Literature Survey

In 2007, Vestal [10] introduced the mixed-criticality notion of the classical real-time systems to the research community. Since then a lot of work has been published on the various aspects of the mixed-criticality scheduling problem [1–6].

Here we plan to propose a method which will judiciously use the time-line to construct a schedule such that all the HI-criticality jobs will get their HI-criticality execution time and some of the LO-criticality jobs will still be guaranteed some execution in the HI-criticality scenario. In 2014, Baruah et al. [3] investigated the schedulability of the multiprocessor mixed-criticality systems namely Global mixed-criticality scheduling algorithm. Hereafter abbreviated as GMCS. We know that there are some task sets which are not scheduled by GMCS. Hence we show that the new proposed method not only schedules the task sets that are scheduled by the GMCS algorithm but also schedules some more task sets that are not scheduled by GMCS.

3   Our Algorithm

Here we present our mixed-Criticality DP-Fair Proportion Scheduling (MCDPS) problem. Our objective is to find a fairness schedule for the given task set $\mathcal{T}$ such as each job finishes its LO-criticality execution in the LO-criticality scenario and all HI-criticality job must execute their HI-criticality execution in the HI-criticality scenario.

In this section, we propose an algorithm which finds a fair schedule for the mixed-criticality task sets to be scheduled in a multiprocessor mixed-criticality system. Our main aim is to schedule the HI-criticality jobs as late as possible, so that more LO-criticality execution of all jobs can be executed before the change of scenario. Here we want to find a LO-scenario deadline (p_i^{Δ}) by which all the HI-criticality jobs must finish their LO-criticality execution. Since we follow the DP-fair paradigm, the time-line is demarcated using LO-scenario deadlines (only for HI-criticality jobs) and actual deadlines of all the jobs. If a HI-criticality job does not declare its completion on or before the LO-scenario deadline, then each HI-criticality job j_i must finish its $C_i(\text{HI}) - C_i(\text{LO})$ units of execution time before p_i as the scenario changes from LO-criticality to HI-criticality. In other words, each job j_i executes at $\frac{C_i(\text{LO})}{p_i^{\Delta}}$ rate in LO-criticality scenario, whereas each HI-criticality job j_k executes at $\frac{C_k(\text{HI})}{p_k - p_k^{\Delta}}$ rate in HI-criticality scenario. The LO-scenario deadline also indicates the time instant where a scenario change may be triggered. We know that each HI-criticality job requires at least $p_i - p_i^{\Delta}$ time to complete $C_i(\text{HI}) - C_i(\text{LO})$ units of execution time after scenario change. Suppose each HI-criticality job j_k requires $C_k(\text{HI}) - C_k(\text{LO})$ units of execution time on a scenario change at p_i^{Δ}, i.e., LO-scenario deadline of job j_i.

3.1   Special Case: At Least K HI-Criticality Tasks Meet Their Deadline in HI-Criticality Scenario

We know that the execution time estimations by the CAs are very pessimistic. There is a fair chance that all the HI-criticality tasks will not execute their $C_i(\text{HI}) - C_i(\text{LO})$ units of execution time in HI-criticality scenario. So reserving time in the scheduling time-line for these task sets enforces under-utilization of the system resources and deadline misses for other tasks as well. Therefore, we ensure at least K tasks which can execute their $C_i(\text{HI}) - C_i(\text{LO})$ units of execution time in HI-criticality scenario should meet their deadline. In this case, we compute the LO-scenario deadline for K HI-criticality tasks instead of n_H HI-criticality tasks. We can use the same algorithm given in Sect. 3 to find the mixed-criticality schedule for a task set.

4   Results and Discussion

In this section, we present the experiments conducted to evaluate MCDPS. The experiments show the impact of schedulability of a task set using MCDPS and the GMCS algorithm. We also verify the amount of execution of a LO-criticality

---

Algorithm 1. Mixed-Criticality DP-Fair Proportion Schedule (MCDPS)

Input : A task set $\mathcal{T} = \{\tau_1, \tau_2, ..., \tau_n\}$, where j_{ik} is a job of $\tau_i = < a_{ik}, d_i, \chi_i, C_i(\text{LO}), C_i(\text{HI}) >$.

Output : Fairness Schedule

1: Compute the LO-scenario deadline (p_i^Δ) of each job j_i as $p_i^\Delta = \lceil p_i - \frac{(C_i(\text{HI}) - C_i(\text{LO})) \times n_H}{m} \rceil$; //$n_H$ is the number of HI-criticality jobs
2: $\Gamma := \text{LO}$;
3: Divide the time line into different time slices (TS_l) based on p_i^Δ;
4: **for** each TS_l in TS **do**
5:   **for** each τ_i in τ **do**
6:     $sh_i^{\text{LO}} = \min(u_i^{\text{LO}} \times TSL, \overline{C_i(\text{LO})})$;
7:     $sh_i^{\text{HI}} = \min(u_i^{\text{HI}} \times TSL, \overline{C_i(\text{HI})})$;
8:     $\overline{C_i(\text{LO})} := \overline{C_i(\text{LO})} - sh_i^{\text{LO}}$;
9:     $\overline{C_i(\text{HI})} := \overline{C_i(\text{HI})} - sh_i^{\text{HI}}$;
10:   **end for**
11:   **for** (each active job j_i in TS_l) **do**
12:     **if** $(\Gamma = \text{HI})$ **then**
13:       Allocate sh_i^{HI} share of each job in EDF order considering p_i as the deadline;
14:     **else**
15:       Allocate sh_i^{LO} share of each job in EDF order considering p_i^Δ as the deadline;
16:       **if** (a HI-criticality job does not complete its execution after its $C_i(\text{LO})$ units of execution time) **then**
17:         $\Gamma := \text{HI}$;
18:         Allocate $sh_i^{\text{HI}} - sh_i^{\text{LO}}$ extra share of j_i in the available processors;
19:         Update the time-slices according to p_i;
20:       **end if**
21:     **end if**
22:     **if** SCAP > 0 **then**   //Any spare capacity in a time slice
23:       Update the final share sh_i^Γ of each incomplete job according to the EDF order based on p_i^Δ by assigning extra shares to fill up the spare capacity in the time slice TS_l its $\overline{C_i(\chi_i)}$;
24:     **end if**
25:     **if** $((\overline{C_i(\text{LO})} > 0$ or $\overline{C_i(\text{HI})} > 0)$ and $p_i^\Delta = TS_l^E)$ **then**
26:       Declare Failure;
27:     **end if**
28:     Use McNaughton's Wrap-around rule to arrange the final shares of time-slice TS_l in a scheduling table;
29:   **end for**
30: **end for**

---

job in HI-criticality scenario against the existing algorithms. The details of the task generation policy are as follows.

- The utilization (u_i) of the tasks of task set $\mathcal{T}$ are generated according to the Stafford's randfixedsum algorithm [8].

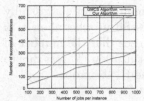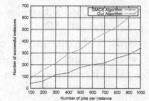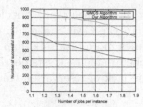

Fig. 1. Comparison of number of MC-schedulable task sets at a LO-criticality utilization of 1.5 and 2 processors

Fig. 2. Comparison of number of MC-schedulable task sets at a LO-criticality utilization of 3.5 and 4 processors

Fig. 3. Comparison of number of MC-schedulable task sets with different utilization and 2 processors

- We use the exponential distribution proposed by Davis *et al.* [7] to generate the period (p_i) of the tasks of task set $\mathscr{T}$.
- The $C_i(\text{LO})$ units of execution of the tasks are calculated by $u_i \times p_i$.
- The $C_i(\text{HI})$ units of execution of the tasks are calculated as $C_i(\text{HI}) = \text{CF} \times C_i(\text{LO})$ where CF is the criticality factor which varies between 2 and 6 for each HI-criticality task τ_i in our experiments.
- Each task set $\mathscr{T}$ contains at least one HI-criticality task and one LO-criticality task. We have generated random task sets for 2, 4, 8 and 16 processors, where each task set has at least $m+1$ number of tasks. Each task set is LO-scenario schedulable. We have used an intel core 2 duo processor machine with speed of 2.3 Ghz to conduct the experiments.

First we verify the schedulability of MCDPS and the GMCS algorithm. In the first experiment, we fix the utilization at LO-criticality level of each task set at 1.5 and let the period of the tasks vary between 1 and 2000. The number of tasks in each task set is set to 5. The number of processor is fixed to 2.

From the graph in Fig. 1, it is clear that MCDPS schedules more task sets successfully than the GMCS algorithm. As can be seen from Fig. 1, for a LO-criticality utilization of 1.5 more than 600 task sets out of 1000 task sets are successfully scheduled by MCDPS which is almost two times more than the GMCS algorithm. As the number of task sets increases, the success ratio is more or less stable. Next we vary the number of processors to 4 and LO-criticality utilization of each task set to 3.5. The results given in Fig. 2 are almost similar to the Fig. 1.

The next experiment checks the impact of the utilization on the schedulable task sets. Here the number of tasks in a task set is fixed to 10. The periods of the tasks in a task set range between 1 and 2000. The utilization at LO-criticality level of the task sets are varied over 1.1 to 1.9. The number of processors is fixed to 2. The graph in Fig. 3 shows the number of schedulable task sets from up to 1000 randomly generated task sets.

From the graph, it is clear that MCDPS schedules more task sets successfully than the GMCS algorithm. Typically MCDPS is successful in scheduling 1.75 times more task sets than the GMCS algorithm. We can see that the number of schedulable task sets decrease with the increase in the utilization. This is due to the lack of reservation time for HI-criticality tasks in the HI-scenarios.

5   Conclusion

In this paper, we propose a new algorithm which finds a fair schedule for multi-processor mixed-criticality systems. The proposed algorithm does not abandon every LO-criticality job in the HI-criticality scenario. We show that the MCDPS algorithm is better than the GMCS algorithm in terms of scheduling more number of task sets with various experiments. Then we discuss that at least K HI-criticality tasks can be scheduled in a HI-criticality scenario, if a task set failed to schedule due to the deadline miss of a HI-criticality task.

References

1. Baruah, S., et al.: Scheduling real-time mixed-criticality jobs. IEEE Trans. Comput. **61**(8), 1140–1152 (2012)
2. Baruah, S., et al.: The preemptive uniprocessor scheduling of mixed-criticality implicit-deadline sporadic task systems. In: 2012 24th Euromicro Conference on Real-Time Systems (ECRTS), pp. 145–154. IEEE (2012)
3. Baruah, S., Chattopadhyay, B., Li, H., Shin, I.: Mixed-criticality scheduling on multiprocessors. Real Time Syst. **50**(1), 142–177 (2014)
4. Baruah, S., Fohler, G.: Certification-cognizant time-triggered scheduling of mixed-criticality systems. In: 32nd IEEE Real-Time Systems Symposium (RTSS), pp. 3–12. IEEE (2011)
5. Behera, L., Bhaduri, P.: Time-triggered scheduling of mixed-criticality systems. ACM Trans. Des. Autom. Electron. Syst. (TODAES) **22**(4), 74 (2017)
6. Behera, L., Bhaduri, P.: Time-Triggered scheduling for multiprocessor mixed-criticality systems. In: Negi, A., Bhatnagar, R., Parida, L. (eds.) ICDCIT 2018. LNCS, vol. 10722, pp. 135–151. Springer, Cham (2018). https://doi.org/10.1007/978-3-319-72344-0_10
7. Davis, R.I., Zabos, A., Burns, A.: Efficient exact schedulability tests for fixed priority real-time systems. IEEE Trans. Comput. **57**(9), 1261–1276 (2008)
8. Emberson, P., Stafford, R., Davis, R.I.: Techniques for the synthesis of multiprocessor tasksets. In: Proceedings 1st International Workshop on Analysis Tools and Methodologies for Embedded and Real-time Systems (WATERS 2010), pp. 6–11 (2010)
9. Levin, G., Funk, S., Sadowski, C., Pye, I., Brandt, S.: DP-FAIR: a simple model for understanding optimal multiprocessor scheduling. In: 2010 22nd Euromicro Conference on Real-Time Systems, pp. 3–13, July 2010
10. Vestal, S.: Preemptive scheduling of multi-criticality systems with varying degrees of execution time assurance. In: 28th IEEE International Real-Time Systems Symposium. RTSS 2007, pp. 239–243, December 2007

Replication Based Fault Tolerance Approach for Cloud

Kamal K. Agarwal$^{(\boxtimes)}$ and Haribabu Kotakula$^{(\boxtimes)}$

Birla Institute of Technical Sciences, Pilani 333031, Rajasthan, India
{h20200286,khari}@pilani.bits-pilani.ac.in

Abstract. The usage of cloud computing has been increasing every-day and in almost every organization. It is now an integral part of the information technology market. And this rapidly growing need gives rise to consider two main criteria namely reliability and availability to sus-tain growing demand. To ensure SLAs, and gain customer confidence, cloud architectures use fault tolerant strategies. The work in the liter-ature towards fault tolerant cloud has not considered aspects such as using resource subsets to be fault tolerant. In this paper, we have used a replication based fault-tolerance strategy which considers cost and fault proneness of VMs. Simulation of the proposed algorithm has been car-ried out using CloudSim and the result shows an improvement in average total execution time and average delay time.

Keywords: Cloud computing · Fault-tolerance · Replication · CloudSim

1 Introduction

Cloud computing has become an integral part of the rapidly changing IT domain in recent years because of its multi-tenant based resource provisioning capabili-ties. Cloud computing has been characterized by its rapid elasticity, on-demand access, multi-tenancy and resource autonomy. Cloud computing infrastructure has a large number of components. Therefore it almost always has some fault proneness due to the interaction among those heterogeneous components. A fault is a defect or inability to perform its normal operations [11]. A fault in the system causes errors in the system leading to system failure, which further interrupts the normal delivery of services and degraded the performance of the system [7,11].

As the number of cloud users increases, the need for fault-tolerance also increases [9,12]. Fault tolerance is the ability of a system that enables systems to continue their anticipated operations regardless of faults [11,13,14].

Fault tolerance approaches in distributed systems such as Cloud discussed in the literature are [1] Reactive approaches such as checkpointing, Job-migration, Replication, Retry, Task Re-submission, Rescue overflow are primarily used

© Springer Nature Switzerland AG 2022
R. Bapi et al. (Eds.): ICDCIT 2022, LNCS 13145, pp. 163–169, 2022.
https://doi.org/10.1007/978-3-030-94876-4_11

to lower aftereffects of failures and proactive approaches such as self-healing, software rejuvenation, preemptive migration, load balancing are used to avoid failures.

2   Related Works

Some basic reactive approaches are RSVMP (Random selection VM placement) after creation VMs will be placed on randomly selected hosts but whenever there is VM failure data required by that request will be re-fetched from storage [2,16]. RLVMP improvement over RSVMP with some additional consideration on network resource consumption [but at the cost of restricting selection to a particular host], a copy of data will be kept on host node so whenever there is failure data can be reused at that same host but have to ensure that newly created VM will be placed in that particular host only [2]. OPVMP (Optimal redundant virtual machine placement) proposed by Wang et al. (2016) a replication based approach focused on FAT free topology works in 3 steps viz. selection of host server, optimal VM placement and recovery strategy.

Das and Khilar [14] proposed a replication-based method to increase the system availability and reduce the service time by using software variants and not schedulling tasks on fault prine VMs. Alhosban et al. [15] introduced a scheme that depends on prediction and planning. A recovery method out of two viz. replication and retry is selected based on failure history, user requirements and service weight and criticality. Saranya et al. [16] presented a method based on both re-submission of tasks and replication. It depends on the priority assigned to each task, task length, deadline and the out-degree of each task.

Most of the existing works based on replication consider a fixed number of replicas i.e. replication is done for all virtual machines, which is not a cost-effective or efficient approach.

In our work we consider replication as the main approach for fault tolerance to reduce storage and network resource consumption for fault tolerance.

3   Problem Description

As a replication strategy used for fault tolerance, if we replicate every VM for incoming requests it will increase the total number of VMs required as we are not considering any specific attributes of VMs. So replication should be applied to a subset of VMs.

Challenges exist in how to determine if a VM should be replicated or not. If we go by some intuitive reasoning that clients are assigned with VMs of different configuration, of which some have high configurations like the number of CPUs required, RAM and bandwidth required. So it would be better if we could consider this aspect in selecting a VM to be replicated as VMs with high configuration should be provided with better fault tolerance approach.

Also when a particular host has already experienced several faults it can be expected that VMs running or to be created on that host will be more prone to experience same kind of fault. So in our approach, we consider a combination of cost (as cost will be proportional to VM configuration requested) and the number of faults occurred on a host to select VMs to replicate. Also, to consider the faults for VMs which were not identified as fault prone would be resubmitted by the fault manager or broker to reduce overall turnaround time after a fault occurs.

4   Proposed Algorithm

The proposed algorithm provides fault-tolerance by way of replication, where fault prone VMs are identified and replicated based on rank of each VM. The Rank of each VM $(v_j)rank$ is determined by multiplying cost and number of faults in host. The proposed fault tolerant algorithm handles VM faults and host fault. Also, it will be able to handle failure of all VMs running on a host. Algorithm works in a way that for each cloudlet request (c_i), broker will select a VM (v_j) satisfying sufficient conditions such as RAM, CPU requirements etc. now for providing the fault tolerance, broker needs to identify if a given VM needs to be replicated. For this identification, VM rank (v_j) $rank$ is determined, if it is found to be greater than some predefined threshold broker will replicate the Cloudlet on one other VM (v_k) placed on other host to increase fault-tolerance. Both the VMs (orignal (v_j) and replicated VM (v_k)) will be executing the cloudlet request. The earliest result arrived from one of the VM will be accepted and other one will be discarded. Also, if at any point in time if it is found that both the VMs have failed, the broker will resubmit that cloudlet to be executed on some other VM.

5   Result

There are many cloud simulators such as CloudSim, CloudAnalyst, iCanCloud, GreenCloud, CloudSim Plus available to the research community. Among all, CloudSim [7] and CloudSim Plus [6] (an extension to CloudSim) is the most preferred one for simulating cloud environments.

The proposed algorithm has been implemented using CloudSim Plus. The fault injection part of the simulation has been done by destroying a random VM at a random instant of time. In the CloudSim user requests are generated as files that are processed with the help of an intermediary broker. The VMs are allocated to a particular host as per the VM allocation policy. In our setup, we have selected each host who satisfies the just sufficient requirements of a VM. For the part where we need to identify if we have to duplicate a request allocated on a VM, we need to rank VMs by calculating the product of cost and number of faults that occurred on the host of that VM. For the simulation experiment, we have assumed the cost of each VM as 1, as all the VMs created are of the same configuration. After ranking a VM the next step is to check if it is greater than some threshold defined. Here in this setup, we have assumed a threshold of 1 so it translates to a request to be duplicated if a host has faced at least

---

1: **procedure** $FT(C,V,flags)$ ▷ C list of Cloudlet requests, V list of Available VMs, $flags$ count of requests

2:     **for all** $Cloudlets$ $(c_i) \in C$ **do**

3:         **if** $(c_i) \in C$ not executed **then**

4:             get (c_i) parameters RAM, BW, Cost

5:             **for all** VMs $(v_j) \in V$ **do**

6:                 get (v_j) parameters VM size, Cost, number of faults in host

7:                 Calculate (v_j) rank as cost * faults in host

8:                 **if** $(v_j) = available$ and $(v_j)params \geq (c_j)params$ **then**

9:                     allocate $(v_j) \leftarrow (c_j)$

10:                     $(v_j) = BUSY$

11:                     **if** $(v_j)rank > Threshold$ **then**

12:                         get another VM (v_k) $from$ V

13:                         allocate $(v_k) \leftarrow (c_i)$

14:                         $(v_k) = BUSY$

15:                     break;

16:                 **if** (c_i) not $executed$ $successfully$ **then**

17:                     execute (c_i)

18:                     **if** $exe\ time\ (v_j) \leq exe\ time\ (v_k)$ **then**

19:                         $(c_i) \leftarrow executed$

20:                         $flag + +$

21:                         $(v_j) = available$

22:                     **else if** $exe\ time\ (v_j) > exe\ time\ (v_k)$ **then**

23:                         $(c_i) \leftarrow executed$

24:                         $flag + +$

25:                         $(v_j) = available$

26:                     **else**

27:                         $waiting\ list \leftarrow (c_i)$

28:

29:     **if** $flag == n$ **then**

30:         All cloudlets execute succesfully

31:     **else**

32:         Execute FT for waiting Cloudlets

33:

---

one fault. So in our setup, a cloudlet allocated to a particular VM (vm_1) will be replicated on one additional VM (vm_2) if the host of (vm_1) has faced at least one fault. Also, it is to be noted that the request assigned to (vm_2) will not be replicated again. The number of datacenter created is 1 and the ratio between total processing element of hosts to total processing elements required by all Vms has been kept to 75% to avoid resource contention. The execution results are shown in the Table 1 below.

The results obtained have been compared with the results of the algorithm presented in "Self-Healing fault tolerance Technique in cloud Data-center" [4]. Comparison between the two for average delay faced by each cloudlet over total execution time for the different number of VM failures has been displayed in Fig. 1. We can see that as the number of failures increases, the delay for the

Table 1. Simulation result.

No. of failed VMs	Total exec. time	No. of Cloudlet executed	Avg exec. time	Avg delay
1	15356.16	96	159.96	3.1365625
2	15356.16	96	159.96	3.1365625
3	16982.22	96	176.89	3.7638541
4	14573.32	92	158.40	3.6002173
5	21318.24	90	236.86	6.3567777
6	5600.46	72	77.78	2.0909722
7	4215.4	63	66.91	1.9117460
8	2770.12	48	57.71	2.5091666

proposed algorithm doesn't increase as rapidly as it is in Self-Healing. This is because the proposed algorithm considers the probability of failures beforehand and replicates cloudlets to reduce overall turnaround time. Also, the broker will be resubmitting a cloudlet request which was not replicated as a part of fault tolerance as soon as it identifies a VM fault, reducing overall turnaround time.

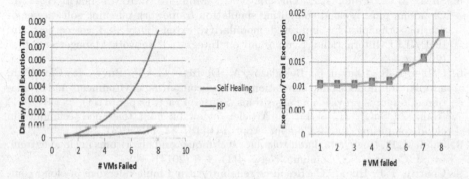

Fig. 1. (a) Average delay over total execution time. (b) Average execution time over total execution time.

Also, the comparison for the average execution time over total execution time for each Cloudlet has been displayed in Fig. 1. It can be seen that there is not much difference between the results produced by the proposed algorithm and self-healing. This is because of consideration of fault probability and resubmit to minimize total execution time for the request received.

6 Conclusion

The cloud computing environment is composed of heterogeneous components which make it obvious to have faults in the system and a challenging task well. The faults need to be handled to provide uninterrupted services to its users.

A replication based fault tolerance approach has been proposed which handles faults in VM and host failure due to failure of all the VMs running on that host. Results show the proposed method to be more efficient than many replication based approaches proposed earlier specifically in terms of reducing overall delay and average delay. In the future effort can be made to extend this idea to a real cloud environment to see if any further improvements are needed.

References

1. Kumari, P., Kaur, P.: A survey of fault tolerance in cloud computing. J. King Saud Univ. Comput. Inf. Sci. **33**, 1159–1176 (2018)
2. Zhou, A., et al.: Cloud service reliability enhancement via virtual machine placement optimization. IEEE Trans. Serv. Comput. **10**(6), 902–913 (2017). https://doi.org/10.1109/TSC.2016.2519898
3. Amoon, M.: Adaptive framework for reliable cloud computing environment. IEEE Access **4**, 9469–9478 (2016). https://doi.org/10.1109/ACCESS.2016.2623633
4. Devi, R.K., Muthukannan, M.: Self-healing fault tolerance technique in cloud datacenter. In: 2021 6th International Conference on Inventive Computation Technologies (ICICT), 2021, pp. 731–737, https://doi.org/10.1109/ICICT50816.2021.9358476
5. Silva, M.C., Filho, R.L. Oliveira, C.C., Monteiro, P.R.M., Inácio, F.M.M.: CloudSim plus: a cloud computing simulation framework pursuing software engineering principles for improved modularity, extensibility and correctness. In: IFIP/IEEE International Symposium on Integrated Network Management, p. 7 (2017)
6. Calheiros, R., Ranjan, R., Beloglazov, A., De Rose, C.A.F., Buyya, R.: CloudSim: a toolkit for modeling and simulation of cloud computing environments and evaluation of resource provisioning algorithms. Softw., Pract. Exper. **41**(1), 23–50 (2011)
7. Amin, Z., Singh, H., Sethi, N.: Article: review on fault tolerance techniques in cloud computing. Int. J. Comput. Appl. **116**(18), 11–17 (2015)
8. Saikia, L.P., Devi, Y.L.: Fault tolerance techniques and algorithms in cloud system. Int. J. Comput. Sci. Commun. Netw. **4**(1), 1–8 (2014)
9. Charity, T.J., Hua, G.C.: Resource reliability using fault tolerance in cloud computing. In: 2016 2nd International Conference on Next Generation Computing Technologies (NGCT), pp. 65–71. IEEE (2016)
10. Singh, G., Kinger, S.: A survey on fault tolerance techniques and methods in cloud computing. Int. J. Eng. Res. Technol. **2**(6), 1215–1217 (2013)
11. Nazari Cheraghlou, M., Khadem-Zadeh, A., Haghparast, M.: A survey of fault tolerance architecture in cloud computing. J. Netw. Comput. Appl. **61**, 81–92 (2016)
12. Machida, F., Kawato, M., Maeno, Y.: Redundant virtual machine placement for fault-tolerant consolidated server clusters. In: Proceedings of the IEEE Network Operations and Management Symposium, pp. 32–39, April (2010)
13. Engelmann, C., Vallée, G.R., Naughton, T., Scott, S.L.: Proactive fault tolerance using preemptive migration. In: Proceedings of the 17th Euromicro International Conference Parallel, Distribution Network-Based Process. PDP 2009, pp. 252–257 (2009)
14. Das, P., Khilar, P.M.: VFT: a virtualization and fault tolerance approach for cloud computing. In: 2013 IEEE Conference on Information & Communication Technologies, IEEE(ICT), pp. 473–478, April 2013

15. Alhosban, A., Hashmi, K., Malik, Z., Medjahed, B.: Self-healing framework for cloud-based services. In: 2013 ACS International Conference on Computer Systems and Applications (AICCSA), pp. 1–7, May 2013
16. Saranya, S.M., Srimathi, T., Ramanathan, C., Venkadesan, T.: Enhanced fault tolerance and cost reduction using task replication using spot instances in cloud. Int. J. Innov. Res. Sci., Eng. Technol. 4(6), 12–16 (2015)

Intelligent Technology

A Comparative Study on MFCC and Fundamental Frequency Based Speech Emotion Classification

Asfahan Shah[(✉)] and Tanmay Bhowmik

Bennett University, Greater Noida, Uttar Pradesh, India

Abstract. Speech emotion recognition and classification is one of the most important and emerging fields in artificial intelligence. It has various uses in different applications starting from medical science to smart home devices. Input feature selection is a very important part of speech processing. Mel Frequency Cepstral Coefficients is the most widely used features in the processing of audio data. In case of processing of emotion related data, the fundamental frequency also plays an important role. In this study a comparative analysis has been conducted to determine the better feature in the field of emotion classification. Emo-Db database was used for the study. For classification task the Support Vector Machine classifier with the radial basis and sigmoid function kernel has been used. The model was trained with both the audio features and the performances were compared. Better performance was observed with Mel Frequency Cepstral Coefficients which ensures the better performing speech features in emotion classification task.

Keywords: Speech emotion classification · MFCC · Fundamental frequency · SVM · Sigmoid kernel · RBF kernel

1 Introduction

Humans are emotional beings by nature. They have capability to express various kinds of emotions like anger, happiness etc. For human computer interaction, emotion detection and recognition by a computer becomes an important task. Mainly these emotions are expressed by facial expressions, but as human grows, an individual learns to control one's expressions thus, making emotion recognition a challenging task. Emotions can also be detected by using audio features of speech.

Speech emotional detection is one of the emerging domains in Artificial intelligence. Speech emotional recognition is a process of detecting an individual's emotions using the speech. This is effective as audio features like tone, pitch etc. changes according to the mood or emotion. A Speech emotion detection system mainly consists of two parts pre-processing and classification.

© Springer Nature Switzerland AG 2022
R. Bapi et al. (Eds.): ICDCIT 2022, LNCS 13145, pp. 173–184, 2022.
https://doi.org/10.1007/978-3-030-94876-4_12

Pre-processing part consists of extraction of audio features like pitch, Mel Frequency Cepstrum Coefficient (MFCC) etc. from the given audio. After extraction of features these are then normalized. Then comes the classification. Classification is done by various machine learning algorithms like Support Vector Machines, Decision Trees etc. One of the most important aspect of any classification algorithm is choice of features. Features should be chosen carefully before training the model.

Speech Emotion detection is important and has application in various fields. One of the applications is in the field of medical science, where it can used to evaluate emotional health of a person and can help in early detection of mental disorders like depression, post-traumatic stress disorder and suicidal tendencies. Speech Emotion detection can also be used to improve human computer interaction which in-turn improves various application like smart home appliances. Speech emotion detection can also be used to improve customer feedback systems.

The goal of this study is to compare and determine which Audio feature MFCC or Fundamental Frequency is better for emotion classification. In this study MFCC and Fundamental Frequency were extracted from various audio files and results were compared.

2   Literature Review

T. Seehapoch et al. in their study used SVM classifier with linear kernel function for emotion recognition [8]. They considered a combination of energy, fundamental frequency and MFCC for classification. The study was conducted on Japanese, Thai and German databases. The accuracy for classification was found as 98.00% for Thai, at 89.80% for German and 93.57% for Japanese. One of the main conclusions of the study is that speech recognition system that uses both prosodic and spectral features have high recognition rate.

P. P. Dahake et al. used a SVM classifier trained with feature vector of formants and cepstral features with MFCC for classification of emotions [3]. They compared various kernel functions of SVM classifier. Study concluded that RBF kernel function was best suitable for all emotion recognitions with an accuracy of 84%. Quadratic and Linear kernel functions showed high recognition rate for joy, sadness and fear. It was also found polynomial kernel didn't gave suitable results for speech emotion recognition.

Mohanta et al. in their study extracted acoustic parameters from speech signals for emotion classification [7]. Emotions that were classified were happy anger, sad and neutral. Fundamental frequency and formants were derived from signals using only vowels words of English language i.e., 'a', 'e', 'i', 'o', and 'u'. Now using these extracted features, emotions were classified using a Support Vector Machine (SVM) classifier.

T. Kathiresan et al. in their study extracted and used cepstral delta and cepstral double delta for emotion recognition [4]. They used Gaussian Mixture Model (GMM) classifier. Study concluded that these extracted features along with MFCC improved classification of specific emotions but not for all. It was also found that recognition pattern differs from language to language used in experiment.

T. Chaspari et al. used Emo-Db database and Athens Emotional States Inventory to show that instant amplitude and features derived from frequency can increase classification performance of widely used spectral and prosodic information [1].

Kuchibhotla et al. used a feature fusion which is a combination of energy pitch prosody features and MFCC for emotion classification [5]. They used these fused features to classify emotions using support vector machine (SVM), linear discriminant analysis (LDA), regularized discriminant analysis (RDA) and k nearest neighbour (KNN) individually. The results showed that RDA and SVM gave good recognition results as compared to other classifiers. It was also observed that use of fused features provided good results as compared to individual results.

3 Methodology

3.1 Database

Emo-Db database was used in this study. Emo-Db database is a German emotional database. This database was created by Institute of Communication Science, Technical University, Berlin Germany. The data base consists of 535 audio files and were recorded by a total of 10 speakers. The speakers were 5 females and 5 males with ages ranging from 21 years old to 35 years old. The audio was originally recorded at 48-KHz and is then sampled down to 16-KHz. This database consists of 7 emotions:

- Anger
- Anxiety
- Boredom
- Happiness
- Disgust
- Sadness
- Neutral

3.2 Features

In this study fundamental frequency and Mel-Frequency Cepstrum Coefficients (MFCC) were extracted from the audio files using Librosa library of Python 3.

Fundamental Frequency: Fundamental frequency in a complex signal can be defined as the lowest partial. For fundamental frequency estimation we use YIN estimator algorithm [2]. YIN estimator is a time-domain pitch detector algorithm and is based upon auto-correlation. Auto-correlation algorithm though simple in nature is prone to various errors. YIN algorithm tries to reduce these errors. YIN algorithm has a difference function. This can be defined over a window as:-

$$d_t(\tau) = \sum_{j=1}^{W}(x_j - x_{j+\tau})^2 \tag{1}$$

where x_j is the signal and $x_{j+\tau}$ is its duplicate which is delayed by τ. To reduce sub-harmonic errors, YIN uses a cumulative mean function:-

$$d_t'(\tau) = \begin{cases} 1 & \text{If } \tau = 0 \\ d_t(\tau)/\frac{1}{\tau}\sum_{j=1}^{\tau} d_t(j) & \text{Otherwise} \end{cases} \tag{2}$$

Other improvements in this estimator includes a Parabolic interpolation of local minimums.

Fundamental frequency carries information about linguistic characteristics like consonant voicing, prosodic features etc. [6]. Besides that, previous studies show that fundamental frequency changes depending upon the emotion of speaker [10]. The study [10] demonstrated that "anger" showed higher fundamental frequency than that of "neutral" emotion while average fundamental frequency of "sorrow" was lower than "neutral" emotion. The study also showed that average fundamental frequency of "fear" was less than "anger" and was close to fundamental frequency of "neutral" emotion.

Thus, keeping in view of above mentioned factors, fundamental frequency is taken into consideration in the study   .

Mel-Frequency Cepstrum Coefficients: Mel-Frequency Cepstrum Coefficients (MFCC) are audio features which are commonly used for speech recognition applications. MFCC is computed by [4] first taking fast Fourier transformation of the sound signal. After that a mel-filter bank is applied to this transformation. Further a logarithm is applied. The final process is to apply a discrete cosine transformation on the log-Mel-filter bank. This results in formation of a number of coefficients equal to number of filters in mel-filter bank. Process is illustrated in Fig. 1.

Generally, first 13 coefficients are used since they correspond to slow varying components in the spectrum, so n this study first 13 MFCC features were considered besides that, derivatives and double derivatives of these MFCC features are also considered. Therefore, when MFCC features is referred in this study, it is referring to these overall 39 features combined. After extraction of these features, SVM classifier was used to classify audio files into 7 different emotions.

3.3 Support Vector Machines

SVM is a nonlinear supervised learning classifier. It is used for binary as well as multiclass classification. This algorithm finds a hyperplane that correctly separates two classes with a maximum margin [9]. Suppose we have vector x_i with

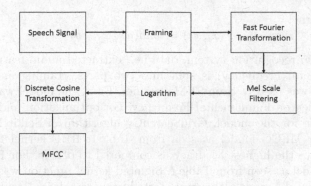

Fig. 1. Block diagram for extraction of MFCC.

$i = 1,2,3....N$. These vectors can correspond to $y \in \{-1,+1\}$. If these set of vectors is linearly separable then there exists b and w such that:-

$$y_i(w^T x_i + b) \geq 1 \tag{3}$$

The hyperplane is given in (4)

$$w^T x_i + b = 0 \tag{4}$$

To solve for w and b we consider equation below

$$\max_{\alpha} L_D = \sum_{i=1}^{N} \sum_{j=1}^{N} y_i y_j \alpha_i \alpha_j x_i^T x_j \tag{5}$$

$$\text{subject to } \sum_{i=1}^{N} \alpha_i y_i = 0 \tag{6}$$

For non-linear separable set of vectors, (5) can be rewritten as:-

$$\max_{\alpha} L_D = \sum_{i=1}^{N} \sum_{j=1}^{N} y_i y_j \alpha_i \alpha_j F(x_i, x_j) \tag{7}$$

where F represents kernel function.
Mostly commonly used kernel functions are:

– Linear kernel

$$F(x_i, x_j) = x_i^T x_j \tag{8}$$

– Radial basis function (RBF) kernel

$$F(x_i, x_j) = e^{-\gamma \|x_i - x_j\|} \tag{9}$$

– Polynomial kernel

$$F(x_i, x_j) = (1 + x_i^T x_j)^p \tag{10}$$

– Sigmoid kernel

$$F(x_i, x_j) = \tanh(a x_i^T x_j + b) \tag{11}$$

For emotion recognition system, data i.e., extracted audio features (MFCC and Fundamental Frequency) is split into two parts, training and test data. Training data was used to train SVM classifier. First, the model was trained on MFCC and then on Fundamental Frequency. For optimization and selection of kernel function for the model, GridSearchCv algorithm of Scikit learn library was used. For MFCC model as seen from Table 1, RBF kernel function was taken as it gave the highest accuracy as compared to others. For Fundamental Frequency model as seen from Table 1, Sigmoid kernel function was considered. After training of the models, they were tested using test data. Results from both the models were recoded and are shown in Table 2 and Table 3.

Table 1. Accuracy of various Kernel Functions of SVM model trained on MFCC and Fundamental Frequency.

Kernel function	Accuracy value	
	MFCC	Fundamental Frequency
Linear	69.6%	26.2%
Polynomial	71.3%	27.2%
RBF	72.1%	27.7%
Sigmoid	68.1%	28.2%

4   Results

The study was conducted according to methodology as proposed above. According to Table 2 and Table 3, it can clearly be observed that when emotions are taken collectively MFCC is a better parameter as compared to Fundamental Frequency.

Accuracy of model with MFCC is 74.6% while with Fundamental Frequency it is 27.6%. Besides the accuracy, the comparison of F1 scores for both models is given in Fig. 2. From Table 4 it can be observed that average weighted F1 score of MFCC is 74.3% and that of Fundamental Frequency it is 23.8%. On analysing the confusion matrix of both MFCC Fig. 3 and Fundamental Frequency Fig. 4, model trained with Fundamental Frequency has a lot of misclassifications as compared to model trained with MFCC.

Precision of a model can be defined as:

$$Precision = \frac{True\ Positives}{True\ Positives + False\ Positives} \tag{12}$$

While recall can be defined as:

$$Recall = \frac{True\ Positives}{True\ Positives + False\ Negatives} \tag{13}$$

Table 2. Metrics for MFCC trained model

Emotions	Metrics		
	Precision	Recall	F1-score
Anger	0.886	0.861	0.873
Boredom	0.667	0.857	0.750
Anxiety	0.611	0.647	0.629
Happiness	0.455	0.357	0.400
Sadness	0.778	0.824	0.800
Disgust	0.800	0.889	0.842
Neutral	0.867	0.650	0.743

Table 3. Metrics for Fundamental Frequency trained model

Emotions	Metrics		
	Precision	Recall	F1-score
Anger	0.300	0.333	0.316
Boredom	0.308	0.571	0.400
Anxiety	0.152	0.294	0.200
Happiness	0	0	0
Sadness	0.412	0.412	0.412
Disgust	0	0	0
Neutral	0.250	0.050	0.083

For a model when recall increases there is an increase in false positive rate (FPR). This increase in recall reduces precision of model. Similarly, if precision of a model is increased then there is a decrease in recall, FPR and TPR of model. When analysing a ROC curve, (a plot between TPR and FPR of model) if recall increases then both TPR and FPR increases which is obviously not good for the model and if precision is increased then FPR decrease but TPR also decrease which is again not ideal.

Hence just increasing recall or precision of model, doesn't guarantee good performance and a good ROC area value. For a good model both of the parameter's precision as well as recall should have sufficient high values. This maintains a balance between FPR and TPR which ensures a good ROC curve and area for the model. This can be observed from Fig. 5, Fig. 6, Table 2 and Table 3 where it can be seen emotion models which have high values for both precision and recall have high ROC area values, while those which don't have low ROC area values.

Looking at ROC curves of MFCC Fig. 5 and Fundamental Frequency Fig. 6, it can be seen that model trained with MFCC performed good when compared to model trained with Fundamental Frequency. MFCC Model had its ROC-area values in range from 0.807 to 0.996, while for model trained with Fundamental

Frequency, ROC area values where lying-in range from 0.411 to 0.802. With model trained with Fundamental Frequency, worst ROC area result was for happiness as its ROC area is 0.411 which is less than the baseline comparison value of 0.5, thus making this classification worse than a random guess. For model trained with MFCC, worst ROC area value was for happiness which is 0.807. Best ROC area value for MFCC model was 0.996 corresponding to disgust while for Fundamental Frequency model it was 0.802 corresponding to sadness.

Table 4. Weighted average metrics of MFCC and Fundamental Frequency

Parameter	Weighted average metrics		
	Precision	Recall	F1-score
MFCC	0.749	0.746	0.743
Fundamental Frequency	0.238	0.276	0.238

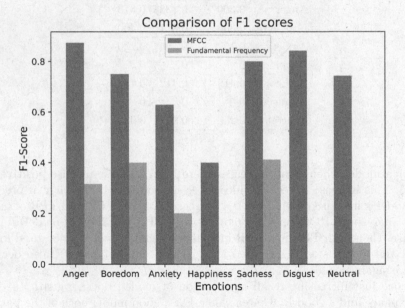

Fig. 2. Comparison of F1 scores of MFCC and Fundamental Frequency models

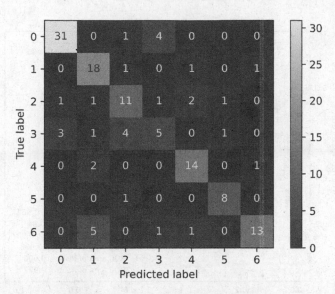

Fig. 3. Confusion matrix of model trained with MFCC. 0 = Anger, 1 = Boredom, 2 = Anxiety, 3 = Happiness, 4 = Sadness, 5 = Disgust, 6 = Neutral

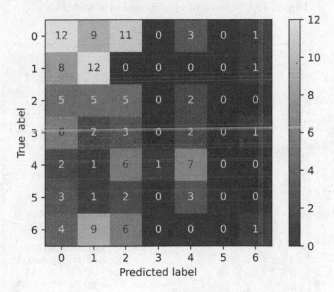

Fig. 4. Confusion matrix of model trained with Fundamental Frequency. 0 = Anger, 1 = Boredom, 2 = Anxiety, 3 = Happiness, 4 = Sadness, 5 = Disgust, 6 = Neutral

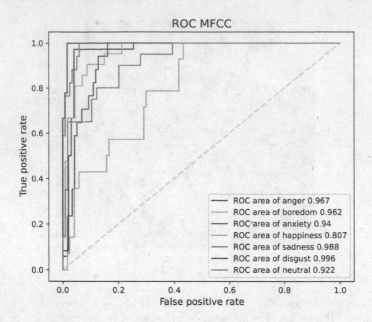

Fig. 5. ROC Curve of model trained with MFCC.

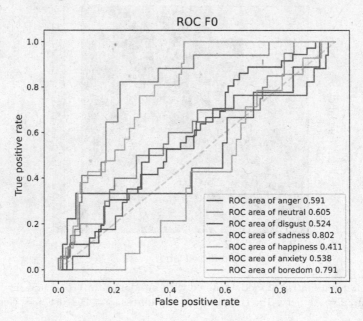

Fig. 6. ROC Curve of model trained with Fundamental Frequency.

5   Conclusion

The study was conducted on speech emotion classification using Emo-Db dataset. Support Vector Machine classifier with RBF and Sigmoid kernel function was used for classification. The model was trained on both MFCC and Fundamental Frequency. The study concluded that MFCC trained model (74.6% accuracy) was much better in classification as compared to Fundamental Frequency based model (27.6% accuracy). It was also seen that RBF kernel for MFCC and Sigmoid kernel function for Fundamental Frequency for SVM classifier gave good results for speech emotion classification.

Although ROC area values of emotions in MFCC model were more as compared to Fundamental Frequency, it was observed that ROC area values of boredom and sadness (0.791 and 0.802 respectively Fig. 6) of Fundamental Frequency model were also promising enough. Thus, consideration to fundamental frequency can be given when analyzing these two emotions. This can be useful (in analysis of the emotions) as the size of feature vector of fundamental frequency ($N \times 1$ where N is number of samples) is smaller than that of MFCC vector ($N \times 39$ where N is number of samples), thus taking less amount of time and computation.

In this study emotion were analysed and classified collectively rather than individually, further study needs to be done on efficacy of MFCC and Fundamental Frequency on each individual emotion rather than collectively. Another thing which was observed in the study was that for fundamental frequency model for emotions happiness and disgust, precision and recall had both values as 0. This needs to be analysed and studied further.

References

1. Chaspari, T., Dimitriadis, D., Maragos, P.: Emotion classification of speech using modulation features. In: 2014 22nd European Signal Processing Conference (EUSIPCO), pp. 1552–1556 (2014)
2. de Cheveigné, A., Kawahara, H.: Yin, a fundamental frequency estimator for speech and music. J. Acous. Soc Am. 111(4), 1917–1930 (2002). https://doi.org/10.1121/1.1458024
3. Dahake, P.P., Shaw, K., Malathi, P.: Speaker dependent speech emotion recognition using MFCC and support vector machine. In: 2016 International Conference on Automatic Control and Dynamic Optimization Techniques (ICACDOT), pp. 1080–1084 (2016). https://doi.org/10.1109/ICACDOT.2016.7877753
4. Kathiresan, T., Dellwo, V.: Cepstral derivatives in MFCCs for emotion recognition. In: 2019 IEEE 4th International Conference on Signal and Image Processing (ICSIP), pp. 56–60 (2019). https://doi.org/10.1109/SIPROCESS.2019.8868573
5. Kuchibhotla, S., Vankayalapati, H.D., Vaddi, R.S., Anne, K.R.: A comparative analysis of classifiers in emotion recognition through acoustic features. Int. J. Speech Technol. 17(4), 401–408 (2014). https://doi.org/10.1007/s10772-014-9239-3
6. McRoberts, G.W., Studdert-Kennedy, M., Shankweiler, D.P.: The role of fundamental frequency in signaling linguistic stress and affect: evidence for a dissociation. Percept. Psychophys. 57(2), 159–174 (1995)

7. Mohanta, A., Mittal, V.K.: Classifying emotional states using pitch and formants in vowel regions. In: 2016 International Conference on Signal Processing and Communication (ICSC), pp. 458–463 (2016). https://doi.org/10.1109/ICSPCom.2016.7980624

8. Seehapoch, T., Wongthanavasu, S.: Speech emotion recognition using support vector machines. In: 2013 5th International Conference on Knowledge and Smart Technology (KST), pp. 86–91 (2013). https://doi.org/10.1109/KST.2013.6512793

9. Solera-Ureña, R., Padrell-Sendra, J., Martín-Iglesias, D., Gallardo-Antolín, A., Peláez-Moreno, C., Díaz-de-María, F.: SVMs for automatic speech recognition: a survey. In: Stylianou, Y., Faundez-Zanuy, M., Esposito, A. (eds.) Progress in Nonlinear Speech Processing. LNCS, vol. 4391, pp. 190–216. Springer, Heidelberg (2007). https://doi.org/10.1007/978-3-540-71505-4_11

10. Williams, C.E., Stevens, K.N.: Emotions and speech: some acoustical correlates. J. Acous. Soc. Am. **52**(4B), 1238–1250 (1972)

Efficient Traffic Routing in Smart Cities to Minimize Evacuation Time During Disasters

Sayan Sen Sarma[1], Bhabani P. Sinha[2]([⊠]), and Koushik Sinha[3]

[1] Department of Computer Science and Engineering, University of Calcutta, Kolkata, West Bengal, India
[2] Department of Computer Science and Engineering, SOA University, Bhubaneswar, India
bhabaniprasadsinha@soa.ac.in
[3] School of Computer Science, Southern Illinois University, Carbondale, USA
koushik.sinha@cs.siu.edu

Abstract. Efficient traffic management during disaster evacuations is an essential component of intelligent transport systems in smart cities. In a natural disaster, a surge of vehicles from dense residential areas may simultaneously move towards the same nearest safe shelter following a shortest path for each individual vehicle, thereby often leading to congestion and resulting in increased evacuation time. In this paper, we consider time-optimal traffic distribution in such disastrous situations considering a Manhattan grid network of roads. Several research results on optimal-time traffic distribution in such a network exist in the literature, all of which consider a restricted scenario of a single safe destination at a corner point of the grid. In contrast, we describe a technique for minimizing average travel time of the vehicles assuming a general situation as experienced in real-life, where the destination node can be anywhere on a rectangular $m \times n$ grid network with multiple sources of traffic injection. Simulation results using SUMO on a road network of Manhattan borough of New York city show that our proposed technique outperforms the existing techniques on dynamic traffic assignment in terms of average travel time.

Keywords: Transportation network · Route planning · Intelligent transport system (ITS) · Queuing delay · Evacuation problem · Congestion control

1 Introduction

Route planning in urban areas during a natural disaster when many vehicles from dense residential areas start to simultaneously move towards the nearest safe shelter constitutes an important research problem in intelligent transport system design for smart cities [1]. A solution to such an evacuation problem [2] should provide a traffic distribution strategy so that, i) for every vehicle the maximum time to reach the final destination (sink) is minimized to keep it less than some specified upper limit, and ii) the average travel time to reach the sink is minimized.

An important aspect of the evacuation problem is that choosing the shortest route for every vehicle in such a disaster situation may not lead to the desired time-optimal solution due to creation of congestion, similar to that observed in wireless networks.

© Springer Nature Switzerland AG 2022
R. Bapi et al. (Eds.): ICDCIT 2022, LNCS 13145, pp. 185–197, 2022.
https://doi.org/10.1007/978-3-030-94876-4_13

Our aim in this paper is to provide a real-time navigation service for individual vehicles so as to reach the designated safe shelters with minimum travel-time, while avoiding congestion at intermediate links and intersection points.

In [3], authors addressed the evacuation problem in a dynamic network with several sources and sinks having fixed supply and specified demand, respectively and proposed a solution. However, their proposed solution is not practically applicable due to its high-order polynomial time complexity. A tractable and practically useful subclass of this problem was addressed by Kamiyama et al. [4] to propose a faster algorithm. If the given road network is a tree having n nodes and has a single sink then the evacuation problem can be solved in $O(n \log^2 n)$ time [5]. For the same tree structured network, Mamada et al. [6] proposed a solution with time complexity $O(n(C \log n)^{k+1})$, where n is the number of nodes, C is some constant and k is the number of sinks. Some dynamic traffic assignment (DTA) based approaches to solve evacuation problem have been proposed in [7–9]. Authors in [10] have proposed an optimal traffic distribution for such scenario, considering a rectangular $m \times n$ grid-structured network with multiple source points and a single destination. However, they assumed that the topmost-rightmost corner point of the grid will be considered as the single destination point, while in a real-life scenario the destination point can often be anywhere on the grid network instead of being a corner point of the grid. In [11], authors introduced the concept of non-corner destination point but no detailed formulation of the problem were given. In this paper, we propose a solution to remove the restriction on the position of the destination to match with the practical requirements, considering an $m \times n$ grid network with multiple source points. We derive the conditions to be satisfied for minimizing the average travel time of the vehicles and accordingly propose an algorithm for optimal traffic distribution. We simulate our proposed technique on a road network of Manhattan borough of New York city to show that it outperforms the existing best known solutions.

2   Basic Ideas

We assume a rectangular $m \times n$ grid network having m horizontal and n vertical roads intersecting each other at mn cross-points as shown in Fig. 1. We number the horizontal roads sequentially as $1, 2, \cdots, m$ with the bottommost one numbered as 1. Similarly, vertical roads are numbered sequentially as $1, 2, \cdots, n$ with the leftmost one numbered as 1. A cross-point (CP) at the intersection of qth horizontal and p^{th} vertical roads will be denoted by the coordinates (p, q). Let the cross-point S having the coordinates (t, l) be the safe shelter or the final destination point (sink) as shown in Fig. 1. By drawing dotted vertical and horizontal lines through this point $S(t, l)$, we divide the $m \times n$ grid in four rectangular sub-grids A, B, C and D of dimensions $l \times t$, $(m - l) \times t$, $(m - l) \times (n - t)$ and $l \times (n - t)$, respectively. Vehicles will be directed towards S along the shortest paths using up link (ul) and right link (rl) in sub-grid A, down link (dl) and right link in sub-grid B, down link and left link (ll) in sub-grid C, and up link and left link in sub-grid D. In each sub-grid, we draw diagonals as shown in Fig. 1 where a diagonal is the locus of all cross-points in the sub-grid at equal Manhattan distance from $S(t, l)$. We can visualize the traffic within each sub-grid flowing in a layer by layer

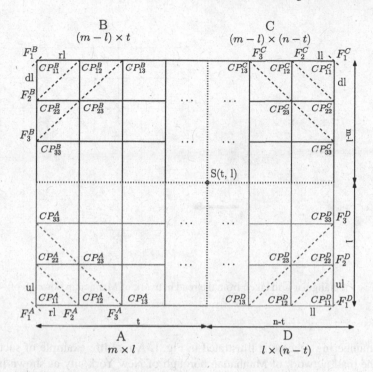

Fig. 1. Numbering of cross-points and flow-fronts in a $m \times n$ rectangular grid with destination at a non-corner point $S(t, l)$

fashion, from the farthest diagonal to the diagonal closest to $S(t, l)$. We term all these diagonals as flow-fronts which are numbered as $F_1^A, F_2^A, F_3^A, \cdots$ in sub-grid A. Flow-fronts in other sub-grids are also numbered likewise as shown in Fig. 1. In a sub-grid $r, r \in \{A, B, C, D\}$, of dimension $u \times v$, there will be $(u + v - 1)$ such flow-fronts $F_j^r, 1 \leq j \leq u + v - 1$. The number of cross-points C_j^r on flow-front F_j^r is given by,

$$C_j^r = \begin{cases} j, & \text{for } 1 \leq j < min(u, v) \\ min(u, v), & \text{for } min(u, v) \leq j \leq max(u, v) \\ u + v - j, & \text{for } max(u, v) < j \leq u + v - 1 \end{cases}$$

The ith cross-point on F_j^r is denoted by $CP_{ij}^r, 1 \leq i \leq C_j^r$. The cross-points on a particular flow-front F_j^r are numbered in the following manner:

- If there is a cross-point on the lower horizontal boundary of the main grid network of dimension $m \times n$, then we number that cross-point as CP_{1j}^r and continue to number the successive cross-points on that flow-front in increasing order.
- If there is no cross-point on the lower horizontal boundary of the main grid and there is a cross-point on the upper horizontal boundary of the main grid, then we number that cross-point as CP_{1j}^r and continue to number the successive cross-points on that flow-front in increasing order.

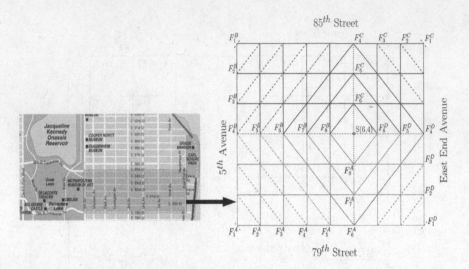

Fig. 2. A 7×9 rectangular grid taken from the road network of Manhattan borough of New York city

This numbering scheme is illustrated in Fig. 1. A real-life example of such a situation is the road network of Manhattan borough of New York city as shown in Fig. 2. From this road network, we consider a 7×9 rectangular grid as shown in Fig. 2, for our discussion. For simplicity, we consider that all the links of the grid are of equal length with equal vehicle velocity along all the links. We assume that the non-corner destination point S is located at the crossing of 82nd Street and 2nd Avenue. From Fig. 2, we can identify three types of traffic flow patterns as follows based on traffic in-flow to the cross-points on a flow-front from its neighboring flow-fronts:

- **Flow type 1:** This corresponds to the situation when all cross-points on a flow-front receive traffic from at most two incoming edges. Flow-fronts of a sub-grid having no common cross-point with any neighboring sub-grid(s), are having this type of traffic flow. Referring to Fig. 2, flow-fronts F_1^A, F_2^A, F_3^A, F_1^B, F_2^B, F_3^B, F_1^C, F_2^C, F_3^C, F_1^D, F_2^D, F_3^D, all have this flow type. Also, two flow-fronts in two different sub-grids having a common cross-point lying at one boundary of the main grid, e.g., F_4^A and F_4^B in Fig. 2, have such flow type. All these flow-fronts are shown as dashed line in Fig. 2.
- **Flow type 2:** This corresponds to the situation when there is at least one cross-point on a flow front receiving combined traffic flow along three incoming edges from two neighboring sub-grids and at least one of the intersecting flow-fronts is having one boundary cross-point that is not receiving combined traffic from any neighboring sub-grid. In Fig. 2, flow-fronts F_5^A and F_5^B have this type of traffic in-flow. All such flow-fronts having this type of traffic flow are shown as dash-dot lines in Fig. 2.

- **Flow type 3:** This corresponds to the situation when each of the two boundary cross-points of a flow-front receive combined traffic from both neighboring sub-grids. It can be checked that in this case the corresponding flow-fronts in four sub-grids form a square, as shown by solid lines in Fig. 2, e.g., flow-fronts F_6^A, F_6^B, F_4^C, F_4^D. The total traffic to be distributed from such a square formed by the four flow-fronts has contribution from all the four sub-grids.

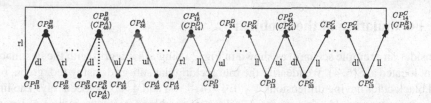

Fig. 3. Traffic flow graph showing traffic flow from flow-fronts F_5^B, F_5^A, F_3^D and F_3^C

Travel time of the vehicles has two components - link delay, i.e., the time taken by a vehicle to traverse a link connecting two consecutive cross-points, and queuing delay, which is defined as the waiting time of a vehicle in the queue generated at each intermediate cross-point. We assume that each link of the network is of same length and the average speed of each vehicle is same along any link which implies that link delay is a constant. Hence, optimizing only the queuing delay will lead to finding an optimal traffic distribution for our problem. We also assume that both traffic generation and service pattern follow Poisson distribution. We denote the mean rate of new traffic generation at CP_{ij}^r by λ_{ij}^r and the uniform service rate at each cross-point by μ. We would like to find an optimal traffic distribution so that queuing delay over each flow-front of a sub-grid is minimized. Using the results shown in [10], we express the total average queuing delay over a flow-front F_j^r as the sum of queuing delays at all cross-points on F_j^r.

$$W_j^r = \sum_{i=1}^{C_j^r} \left(\frac{A}{1 - \frac{x_{ij}^r}{\mu}} \times x_{ij}^r \right) / \sum_{i=1}^{C_j^r} x_{ij}^r, \tag{1}$$

where A is a constant, x_{ij}^r is the sum of the traffic received at CP_{ij}^r from the immediate previous flow-front and the new traffic generated at CP_{ij}^r itself. From any cross-point, traffic can flow in at most two possible directions - horizontally through left-link (ll)/right-link (rl), and vertically through up-link (ul)/down-link (dl). From an arbitrary cross-point CP_{ij}^r, the fraction of traffic going in the horizontal direction will be denoted by $f\_hor_{ij}^r$ and the remaining traffic diverted along the vertical direction will be denoted by $f\_ver_{ij}^r$. Clearly, $f\_hor_{ij}^r + f\_ver_{ij}^r = 1$.

Table 1. Traffic distribution factors for flow-fronts having independent traffic flow

Distribution at cross-point CP_{ij}^r		$r = A$			$r = B$			$r = C$			$r = D$		
		$i = 1$	$i = 2$	$i = 3$	$i = 1$	$i = 2$	$i = 3$	$i = 1$	$i = 2$	$i = 3$	$i = 1$	$i = 2$	$i = 3$
$j = 1$	$f\_hor_{ij}^r$	0.5000	-	-	0.5000	-	-	0.5000	-	-	0.1000	-	-
	$f\_ver_{ij}^r$	0.5000	-	-	0.5000	-	-	0.5000	-	-	0.9000	-	-
$j = 2$	$f\_hor_{ij}^r$	0.0000	0.0000	-	0.6667	0.3333	-	1.0000	0.0000	-	0.6667	0.3333	-
	$f\_ver_{ij}^r$	1.0000	1.0000	-	0.3333	0.6667	-	0.0000	1.0000	-	0.3333	0.6667	-

3   Formulation of the Problem

Consider an example scenario as shown in Fig. 2 using a 7×9 grid with the destination point located at $S(6, 4)$. We identify the four rectangular sub-grids using red, green, blue and black color having dimensions 4×6, 4×4, 4×4 and 4×6, respectively. The links common to two neighboring sub-grids will carry combined traffic from the corresponding neighboring sub-grids. We need to find the optimal traffic distribution fractions at all cross-points considering the three flow types as mentioned in the previous section. Depending on the computation, as given below, we can calculate $f\_ver_{ij}^r$ and $f\_hor_{ij}^r$ for all CP_{ij}^r.

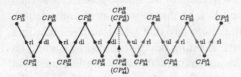

Fig. 4. Traffic flow graph showing traffic flow from flow-fronts F_4^B and F_4^A

Fig. 5. Combined traffic in-flow from level j to $j + 1$

3.1   Optimal Traffic Distribution for Flow Type 1

When a cross-point receives input traffic corresponding to flow type 1, it has no more than two incoming edges. As mentioned in Sect. 2, such a cross-point may belong to a flow-front of a sub-grid having no common cross-point with any neighboring sub-grid(s) or it can be a common cross-point on two intersecting flow-fronts in two different sub-grids and also lying at one boundary of the main grid. Authors in [10] have proposed an optimal solution for traffic distribution from a flow-front whose all cross-points receive input traffic from no more than two cross-points similar to this traffic flow type 1. Hence, we can directly apply the corresponding results from [10] to compute the optimal traffic distribution factors from all such cross-points.

3.2   Optimal Traffic Distribution for Flow Type 2

If a flow-front F_j^r has inputs of flow type 2, there must be a cross-point on it with three traffic incoming edges. Hence, the results from [10] are not directly applicable in this case. However, to calculate the optimal traffic flow from F_j^r in such a case, we proceed by converting every three-input junction (cross-point) on F_j^r to a two-input junction with a modified rate of new traffic generation at this cross-point. The method is best illustrated by the following example.

Example 1. Consider the flow-fronts F_5^B and F_5^A of Fig. 2 with the cross-point $CP_{45}^B (= CP_{45}^A)$ having three incoming edges from cross-points CP_{34}^B, $CP_{44}^B (= CP_{44}^A)$ and CP_{34}^A, respectively on previous flow-fronts F_4^B and F_4^A. Figure 4 is the traffic flow graph showing the parts of traffic flowing from the cross-points on F_4^B and F_4^A (shown in the lower row) into the cross-points on F_5^B and F_5^A (shown in the upper row). The arrows marked with ul, dl, rl represent parts of traffic flowing along up link, down link and right link, respectively from the respective cross-points. The traffic from CP_{44}^B is fully transferred to $CP_{45}^B (= CP_{45}^A)$ as shown by the dotted line arrow in Fig. 4. Let the total traffic at cross-points CP_{34}^B, $CP_{44}^B (= CP_{44}^A)$ and CP_{34}^A be x_{34}^B, $x_{44}^B (= x_{44}^A)$ and x_{34}^A, respectively.

Hence, assuming $\lambda_{45}^B (= \lambda_{45}^A)$ as the new traffic generated at $CP_{45}^B (= CP_{45}^A)$, the total traffic $x_{45}^B = x_{45}^A$ at cross-point $CP_{45}^B (= CP_{45}^A)$ is given by $f\_ver_{34}^B x_{34}^B + x_{44}^B + f\_ver_{34}^A x_{45}^B + \lambda_{45}^B = f\_ver_{34}^B x_{34}^B + f\_ver_{34}^A x_{34}^A + \lambda_{45}'^B$, where $\lambda_{45}'^B = \lambda_{45}^B + x_{44}^B$ may now be taken as the modified new traffic generation rate at $CP_{45}^B (CP_{45}^A)$ instead of just λ_{45}^B.

Thus, effectively a three-input cross-point on the intersecting flow-fronts of the neighboring sub-grids is converted to a two-input cross-point with this change and we can now apply the results of [10] to compute the optimal fractions of the combined traffic to be distributed from the respective flow-fronts, e.g., F_5^A and F_5^B in Example 2.

3.3 Optimal Traffic Distribution for Flow Type 3

In this case, four flow-fronts in the sub-grids A, B, C and D form a square having four corner vertices. If a corner vertex does not fall on a boundary of the main grid, it can have three incoming edges for traffic; otherwise if it falls on such a boundary, it will have only two incoming edges. Thus, the number of cross-points on such a square with three incoming edges may vary from 0 to 4. A square is assigned a level number j which increases successively from $j = 1$ for the outermost square to $j = d$ for the innermost square, if there are d such squares around the destination point. Let z be the number of three-input cross-points on a square. It follows that z can assume a value from 0 to 4 for the outermost square at level 1, while $z = 4$ for all squares other than the outermost square. Similar to the technique in Sect. 3.2, we convert all such three-input cross-points of a square at level $j + 1$, $0 \leq j \leq d - 1$, into two-input cross-points using a traffic flow graph described as in Sect. 3.2. The total number of cross-points on the square at level $j + 1$ is equal to $4(d - j) = \nu$ (say). Note that after converting all three-input cross-points on the square at level $j + 1$, the number of cross-points from which the cross-points on this square receive inputs becomes also equal to ν.

Example 2. Consider the square formed by the flow-fronts F_6^B, F_6^A, F_4^D and F_4^C of Fig. 2 which is at level 1 with respect to the destination $S(6, 4)$. Note that $d = 3$ for this example. Figure 3 represents the corresponding traffic flow graph where the cross-points on the upper row are those from F_6^B, F_6^A, F_4^D and F_4^C which receive input traffic from the cross-points on F_5^B, F_5^A, F_3^D and F_3^C. There will be $4 \times 3 = 12$ cross-points in the upper row of the traffic flow graph. The labels ul, dl, ll and rl on various edges of the graph represent up link, down link, left link and right link, respectively. In Fig. 3, the cross-point $CP_{46}^B (= CP_{46}^A)$ is a three-input junction receiving traffic from cross-points CP_{35}^A, $CP_{45}^B (= CP_{45}^A)$ and CP_{35}^B. The total traffic from cross-point $CP_{45}^B (= CP_{45}^A)$ is transferred to $CP_{46}^B (= CP_{46}^A)$ as shown by the dotted line arrow in Fig. 3. Assuming the total traffic at CP_{35}^B, CP_{35}^A and CP_{45}^B as x_{35}^B, x_{35}^A and x_{45}^B, respectively and λ_{46}^B as the new traffic generated at CP_{46}^B, we use the same technique as in Sect. 3.2 to convert this three-input cross-point $CP_{46}^B (= CP_{46}^A)$ to a two-input cross-point with total traffic as $f\_ver_{35}^B x_{35}^B + f\_ver_{35}^A x_{35}^A + \lambda_{46}'^B$, where $\lambda_{46}'^B = \lambda_{46}^B + x_{45}^B$ is the modified new traffic generated at CP_{46}^B.

Referring to Fig. 3, it is noted that the cross-points at level $j + 1$ located at the intersection of two neighboring sub-grids, has incoming edges which are either both horizontal (rl or ll) or both vertical (ul or dl). For example, in Fig. 3, cross-point $CP_{16}^A (= CP_{14}^D)$ has both incoming edges as horizontal, while $CP_{46}^A (= CP_{46}^B)$ has both incoming edges as vertical. Each of the remaining cross-points has one horizontal incoming edge (rl or ll) and one vertical incoming edge (ul or dl). For example, in Fig. 3, CP_{36}^A has a horizontal link (rl) and a vertical link (ul) as its two incoming edges.

Table 2. Traffic distribution factors for combined traffic flow from two neighboring sub-grids

		\multicolumn{4}{c}{Distribution at cross-point CP_{ij}^r}			

		\multicolumn{3}{c}{$r = A$}	$r = A/B$	\multicolumn{3}{c}{$r = B$}
		$i = 1$	$i = 2$	$i = 3$	$i = 4$	$i = 1$	$i = 2$	$i = 3$
$j = 3$	$f\_hor_{ij}^r$	1.0000	1.0000	1.0000	-	1.0000	1.0000	0.0000
	$f\_ver_{ij}^r$	0.0000	0.0000	0.0000	-	0.0000	0.0000	1.0000
$j = 4$	$f\_hor_{ij}^r$	1.0000	1.0000	1.0000	1.0000	1.0000	1.0000	1.0000
	$f\_ver_{ij}^r$	0.0000	0.0000	0.0000	-	0.0000	0.0000	0.0000

Consider a traffic flow graph in Fig. 5 describing the combined traffic flow from level j to $j + 1$ after converting all three-input cross-points at level $j + 1$ to two-input ones. Let the ith cross-point, $1 \le i \le \nu$ on level $j + 1$ in Fig. 5 have a total traffic of $\eta_{i,j+1}$ with a modified new traffic generation of $\xi_{i,j+1}$. Each cross-point at level j has two out-going links, a left-going link which may be horizontal or vertical, and a right-going link which may also be horizontal or vertical as explained above, for sending traffic to level $j + 1$. Let the fraction of total traffic at the ith cross-point on level j diverted to level $j+1$ through the right-going link be denoted by g_{ij}, $1 \le i \le \nu$, so that the remaining fraction $1 - g_{ij}$ of traffic is diverted along the left-going link. Therefore, the total traffic at level $j + 1$ can be calculated as,

$$\eta_{i,j+1} = (1 - g_{ij})\eta_{ij} + g_{i+1,j}\eta_{i+1,j} + \xi_{i,j+1}, \ 1 \le i < \nu \tag{2}$$

$$\eta_{\nu,j+1} = (1 - g_{\nu j})\eta_{\nu j} + g_{1j}\eta_{1j} + \xi_{\nu,j+1} \tag{3}$$

Queuing delay $W_{i,j+1}$ at each cross-point i, $1 \leq i \leq j+1$ of level $j+1$ is calculated as, $W_{i,j+1} = \frac{A}{1 - \frac{\eta_{i,j+1}}{\mu}}$. The average queuing delay (W_{j+1}^{av}) over the flow-front F_{j+1} can be calculated with the help of Eq. (1) by using the appropriate values of the total number of cross-points on F_{j+1} and also the total traffic at each of these cross-points as discussed above.

In our approach for finding the traffic distribution at different cross-points on a flow-front to get the minimum average travel time, we do not, however, look for globally optimizing the travel time by considering the total delay at all the flow-fronts taken together. This is because finding such a global optimum will be much more complex and time-consuming. On the other hand, we need a quick real-time solution to the traffic distribution problem. We therefore proceed to find the condition that will lead to the minimum queuing delay at every flow-front F_{j+1}, $j \geq 1$, considering the total traffic coming from the flow-front F_j as well as the new traffic generated at all the cross-points on F_{j+1}. Depending on that result for minimizing the queuing delay at each individual flow-front F_{j+1}, we will find out the required traffic distribution factors at all the cross-points on flow front F_j. Average queuing delay W_{j+1}^{av} over the flow front F_{j+1} can be minimized by properly adjusting the $\eta_{i,j+1}$ values. To simplify the notations, we denote $\eta_{i,j+1}$ by Y_i and $j + 1$ by N, so that W_{j+1}^{av} will be a function of the N variables $Y_1, Y_2, \cdots, Y_N$. Accordingly, we formulate the optimization problem as follows.

The Optimization Problem

$$\text{Minimize } F(Y_1, Y_2, \cdots, Y_N) = \frac{Y_1}{\mu - Y_1} + \frac{Y_2}{\mu - Y_2} + \cdots + \frac{Y_N}{\mu - Y_N} \qquad (4)$$

subject to the constraints:

$$Y_1 + Y_2 + \cdots + Y_N = T,$$
$$Y_1 \geq 0, Y_2 \geq 0, \cdots, Y_N \geq 0,$$
$$Y_1 < \mu, Y_2 < \mu, \cdots, Y_N < \mu$$

By simple algebric manipulations we can show that the KKT conditions for the above optimization problem exists when $Y_1 = Y_2 = \cdots = Y_N = T/N$, with the corresponding minimum of the objective function F as $\frac{NT}{\mu N - T}$.

In view of the above discussion, we get the following result.

Lemma 1. *The average queuing delay at any given unfolded representation of flow-fronts at level $j + 1$ will be minimum when the total traffic over level $j + 1$ is uniformly distributed over all the cross-points on that level.*

By virtue of Lemma 1, for having minimum queuing delay at level $j + 1$, we should have $\eta_{1,j+1} = \eta_{2,j+1} = \cdots = \eta_{\nu,j+1}$. Under such condition, the set of equations given in Eqs. (2) and (3) can be reorganized to have a set of simultaneous linear equations in g_{ij}'s, solving which we can compute the values of traffic distribution fractions that will optimize the total delay. The result is stated below.

Theorem 1. *The optimal values of the fractions g_{ij}, $1 \leq i \leq \nu$ of total traffic at the ith cross-point on level j diverted to level $j + 1$ through the right-going link, are computed from the given set of linear equations,*

$$\begin{bmatrix} -\eta_{1j} & 2\eta_{2j} & -\eta_{3j} & 0 & \cdots & 0 & 0 \\ 0 & -\eta_{2j} & 2\eta_{3j} & -\eta_{4j} & \cdots & 0 & 0 \\ \cdots & \cdots & \cdots & \cdots & \cdots & \cdots & \cdots \\ -\eta_{1,j} & 0 & 0 & \cdots & 0 & -\eta_{\nu-1,j} & 2\eta_{\nu,j} \\ 2\eta_{1,j} & -\eta_{2j} & 0 & \cdots & 0 & 0 & -\eta_{\nu,j} \end{bmatrix} \begin{bmatrix} g_{1j} \\ g_{2j} \\ \cdots \\ g_{\nu-1,j} \\ g_{\nu,j} \end{bmatrix}$$

$$= \begin{bmatrix} (\xi_{2,j+1} - \xi_{1,j+1}) - (\eta_{1,j} - \eta_{2,j}) \\ (\xi_{3,j+1} - \xi_{2,j+1}) - (\eta_{2,j} - \eta_{3,j}) \\ \cdots \\ (\xi_{\nu,j+1} - \xi_{\nu-1,j+1}) - (\eta_{\nu-1,j} - \eta_{\nu,j}) \\ (\xi_{1,j+1} - \xi_{\nu,j+1}) - (\eta_{\nu,j} - \eta_{1,j}) \end{bmatrix}$$

However, it is possible that the values of some of the g_{ij}'s as obtained from Theorem 1 may cross the allowed range [0,1]. In such cases, we first note that $W_{i,j+1}$ is a monotonically increasing function of $\eta_{i,j+1}$. Also, $\forall i, 1 \leq i \leq \nu$, $\xi_{i,j+1}$ is a linear monotonically increasing function of g_{ij} and for $2 \leq i \leq \nu$, $\eta_{i,j+1}$ is a linear monotonically decreasing function of $g_{i-1,j}$. Hence, in order to reach the condition of optimality, if any g_{ij} value needs to be negative, we assign its value to 0 (the limiting value on the left side of the interval [0,1]), and similarly when g_{ij} requires to be more than 1 for optimality, we assign its value to 1 so that we obtain the minimal possible queuing delay with the values of g_{ij} within its allowed range of [0,1] due to the monotonic property of $W_{i,j+1}$, although the exact condition of optimality, i.e., $\eta_{1,j+1} = \eta_{2,j+1} = \cdots = \eta_{\nu,j+1}$ cannot be achieved with such assignments.

After getting the values of g_{ij}'s as above, $f\_hor^r_{ij}$ can be calculated as g_{ij} or $1 - g_{ij}$, depending on the position of a cross-point CP^r_{ij} in the traffic flow graph. Next, $f\_ver^r_{ij}$ can be calculated as, $1 - f\_hor^r_{ij}$.

Table 3. Traffic distribution factors for combined traffic flow from four neighboring sub-grids

Distribution at cross-point CP^r_{ij}		$r = A/D$	$r = A$	$r = A$		$r = A/B$			$r = B$			$r = B/C$
		$i = 1$	$i = 1$	$i = 2$	$i = 3$	$i = 2$	$i = 3$	$i = 4$	$i = 1$	$i = 2$	$i = 3$	$i = 1$
$j = 5$	$f\_hor^r_{ij}$	-	0.0000	0.5000	0.5000	-	-	1.0000	0.0000	0.0000	0.5000	-
	$f\_ver^r_{ij}$	-	1.0000	0.5000	0.5000	-	-	0.0000	1.0000	1.0000	0.5000	-
$j = 6$	$f\_hor^r_{ij}$	0.0000	-	0.5000	1.0000	-	-	1.0000	-	0.5000	0.0000	0.0000
	$f\_ver^r_{ij}$	1.0000	-	0.5000	0.0000	-	-	0.0000	-	0.5000	1.0000	1.0000
$j = 7$	$f\_hor^r_{ij}$	0.0000	-	1.0000	-	-	1.0000	-	-	0.0000	-	0.0000
	$f\_ver^r_{ij}$	1.0000	-	0.0000	-	-	0.0000	-	-	1.0000	-	1.0000
$j = 8$	$f\_hor^r_{ij}$	0.0000	-	-	-	1.0000	-	-	-	-	-	0.0000
	$f\_ver^r_{ij}$	1.0000	-	-	-	0.0000	-	-	-	-	-	1.0000

		$r = C$			$r = C/D$			$r = D$				
		$i = 1$	$i = 2$	$i = 3$	$i = 2$	$i = 3$	$i = 4$	$i = 1$	$i = 2$	$i = 3$		
$j = 3$	$f\_hor^r_{ij}$	0.7500	0.5000	0.2500	-	-	-	1.0000	1.0000	1.0000		
	$f\_ver^r_{ij}$	0.2500	0.5000	0.7500	-	-	-	0.0000	0.0000	0.0000		
$j = 4$	$f\_hor^r_{ij}$	-	0.5000	1.0000	-	-	1.0000	-	1.0000	0.0000		
	$f\_ver^r_{ij}$	-	0.5000	0.0000	-	-	0.0000	-	0.0000	1.0000		
$j = 5$	$f\_hor^r_{ij}$	-	1.0000	-	-	1.0000	-	-	0.0000	-		
	$f\_ver^r_{ij}$	-	0.0000	-	-	0.0000	-	-	1.0000	-		
$j = 6$	$f\_hor^r_{ij}$	-	-	-	1.0000	-	-	-	-	-		
	$f\_ver^r_{ij}$	-	-	-	0.0000	-	-	-	-	-		

4 Algorithm

Based on the results obtained in Sect. 3, we now present an route recommendation algorithm (Algorithm 1). Our algorithm considers a $m \times n$ grid-structured road network and calculates the optimal traffic distribution fractions for each individual flow types using the method as described in Sect. 3. We assume that the location of the traffic generation points and their traffic generation rates along with the values of m, n are known *a priori*. For ease of notation in our following discussions, let us denote $min(m, n)$ by ρ. We use a two-dimensional array $lambda$ of size $\rho \times (m + n - 1)$ where $lambda(i, j)$ is denoting the rate of new traffic generation at each cross-point P_{ij}^r. Finally, at each cross-point vehicles are diverted to the horizontal or vertical link depending on the computed values of the optimal traffic distribution fractions as shown below in Algorithm *Route_Vehicle*.

Algorithm 1: *Route_Vehicle*

Input: $\rho \times (m + n - 1)$ array *lambda*.

Output: Routing of a vehicle along the horizontal or the vertical link from each cross-point P_{ij}^r .

At each cross-point P_{ij}^r, using the values of new traffic generation rate from array *lambda* compute $f\_ver_{ij}^r$ and $f\_hor_{ij}^r$ according to Section 3;

for *each vehicle at P_{ij}^r,* **do**

    if $f\_ver_{ij}^r = 1$ **then**

        Send the vehicle along vertical link;

    if $f\_hor_{ij}^r = 1$ **then**

        Send the vehicle along horizontal link;

    else

        Generate a uniform random number *rand* in $[0, 1]$;

        if $rand \le f\_ver_{ij}^r$ **then**

            Send the vehicle along vertical link;

        else

            Send the vehicle along horizontal link;

---

5 Simulation Results

We simulate our proposed approach using an example scenario as shown in Fig. 2. Figure 2 shows a 7×9 rectangular grid road network of Manhattan borough of New York city. We consider nine different traffic generating source points($y_{11}^A = 0.1$, $y_{13}^A = 0.05$, $y_{36}^A = 0.025$, $y_{11}^B = 0.15$, $y_{34}^B = 0.05$, $y_{24}^B = 0.025$, $y_{11}^C = 0.2$, $y_{23}^C = 0.1$, $y_{11}^D = 0.125$, $y_{12}^D = 0.1$) and a single destination point marked as $S(6, 4)$, to evaluate the performance of our proposed algorithm. We compute the optimal traffic distribution fractions at different flow-fronts which are shown in Tables 1, 2 and 3. r = A/B in column headings of Tables 2 and 3 implies the intersection of two flow-fronts in sub-grids A and B. Similarly, r = A/D, B/C and C/D refer to the intersections of

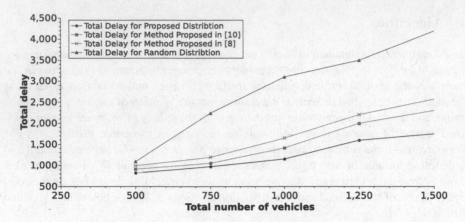

Fig. 6. Comparison of average delay using different techniques

sub-grids A and D, B and C, and C and D, respectively. For simulating our proposed algorithm, we use SUMO assuming a maximum vehicle speed of 13.9 m/s (equivalent to 50 Km/h along any link. Every link connecting two nodes in the network is assumed to be of length 500 m. We consider 750, 1000, 1250 and 1500 numbers of vehicles, respectively, to compare the average travel time of vehicles to reach the destination $S(6,4)$ using i) a random traffic distribution, ii) dynamic traffic assignment algorithm AR* [8] which is based on some heuristic, iii) traffic assignment algorithm as proposed in [10] and iv) our proposed approach. The algorithm given in [10] is applicable to the situation where the final destination point is located only at one corner of the grid network. Accordingly, to use the method in [10], we had to consider each individual sub-grid separately to compute the optimal traffic flow from the flow-fronts lying in that sub-grid only. The simulated values of average queuing delay with different methods as shown in Fig. 6 establish that our proposed method has the best performance of all.

6   Conclusion

We have considered the problem of route planning in case of a natural disaster when lot of vehicles from dense residential areas start to move simultaneously to the nearest safe-shelter. Authors in [10] proposed an optimal traffic distribution technique in a grid-structured road network under such scenarios. However, their approach was based on the assumption of a single destination point (safe shelter) located at the topmost-rightmost corner point of the grid which often cannot represent a real-life situation. In this paper, we have first analyzed the general traffic routing problem on a grid network with an arbitrary final destination point chosen anywhere on the grid, and then have proposed an optimal traffic routing strategy to minimize the average travel time of all the vehicles. Simulation results using SUMO on a road network of Manhattan borough of New York city show that our proposed technique outperforms the existing dynamic traffic assignment algorithms in terms of the average travel time of the vehicles from their respective source points to the final destination point. Future research work includes extending the ideas in the paper to non-grid networks.

References

1. Malik, F., Shah, M.A., Khattak, H.A.: Intelligent transport system: an important aspect of emergency management in smart cities. In: Proceedings of the 24th International Conference on Automation and Computing (ICAC), pp. 1–6 (2018)
2. Hoppe, B., Tardos, E.: Polynomial time algorithms for some evacuation problems. In: SODA 1994: Proceedings of the fifth Annual ACM-SIAM Symposium on Discrete Algorithms, vol. 94, pp. 433–441 (1994)
3. Hoppe, B., Tardos, É.: 'The quickest transshipment problem. Math. Oper. Res. **25**(1), 36–62 (2000)
4. Kamiyama, N., Katoh, N., Takizawa, A.: An efficient algorithm for evacuation problem in dynamic network flows with uniform arc capacity. IEICE Trans. Inf. Syst. **89**(8), 2372–2379 (2006)
5. Mamada, S., Uno, T., Makino, K., Fujishige, S.: An $O(n \log^2 n)$ algorithm for a sink location problem in dynamic tree networks. Explor. New Front. Theor. Inform. **155**, 251–264 (2004)
6. Mamada, S., Makino, K., Fujishige, S.: Evacuation problems and dynamic network flows. In: SICE 2004 Annual Conference, vol. 1, pp. 530–535. IEEE (2004)
7. Tong, C.O., Wong, S.C.: A predictive dynamic traffic assignment model in congested capacity-constrained road networks. Transp. Res. Part B Methodol. **34**(8), 625–644 (2000)
8. Pan, J., Popa, I.S., Zeitouni, K., Borcea, C.: Proactive vehicular traffic rerouting for lower travel time. IEEE Trans. Veh. Technol. **62**(8), 3551–3568 (2013)
9. Koh, S.S., Zhou, B., Yang, P., Yang, Z., Fang, H., Feng, J.: Reinforcement learning for vehicle route optimization in SUMO. In: IEEE 20th International Conference on High Performance Computing and Communications, Exeter, pp. 1468–1473 (2018)
10. Sarma, S.S., Sinha, K., Das, S.R., Sinha, B.P.: Fast transportation in a disaster situation along real-life grid-structured road networks. In: 2019 IEEE 90th Vehicular Technology Conference (VTC2019-Fall), pp. 1–5 (2019). https://doi.org/10.1109/VTCFall.2019.8891600
11. Sarma, S.S., Sinha, K., Sub-r-pa, C., Chakraborty, G., Sinha, B.P.: Optimal distribution of traffic in manhattan road networks for minimizing routing-time. IEEE Trans. Intell. Transp. Syst. **22**(11), 6799–6820 (2021). https://doi.org/10.1109/TITS.2020.2994836

Early Detection of Parkinson's Disease as a Pre-diagnosis Tool Using Various Classification Techniques on Vocal Features

Vaibhaw, Pratik Behera, Vaibhav Bal, and Jay Sarraf[✉]

School of Computer Engineering, KIIT - Deemed to be University,
Bhubaneswar 751024, Odisha, India

Abstract. Parkinson's disease is a non-curable progressive nervous system disorder affecting operations related to muscles movements. More than 1 million individuals are affected by Parkinson's disease in India per year. Due to the progressive nature of the disease, the symptoms generally start gradually and are barely noticeable; with symptoms that can start from normally unnoticeable shaking of a hand to noticeable speech and writing changes to even worse like loss of automatic movements. This project is concerned with contributing to the advancement of medical technologies and may help earlier detection of Parkinson's which will enable early treatment. In this paper, we have overviewed the current status of Parkinson's disease detection and studied the model for early detection of Parkinson's disease using various classifier approaches. The highest accuracy of about 96.61% was achieved using the XgBoost classifier.

Keywords: Parkinson's disease · Extreme Gradient Boosting (XgBoost) · Feature selection · Decision support systems · Medical diagnosis · Support Vector Machine · Artificial Neural Network

1 Introduction

Parkinson's disease is one of the non-curable progressive nervous system disorders which mostly occurs at older ages and mainly affects operations related to movements. It affects more than 1 million individuals in India per year. As it is a progressive disorder, the symptoms generally start gradually and are barely noticeable [1, 2]. The symptoms can start from normally unnoticeable shaking of a hand which can gradually progress to noticeable changes such as slowed movement, speech changes, writing changes, olfactory loss [3] to even worse like loss of automatic movements [4].

Most of the symptoms related to Parkinson's disease are caused because certain neurons in the area of the brain which is responsible for controlling muscles movement gradually get damaged which results in the death of the neuron cells. Generally, an important brain chemical is produced by these cells known as dopamine. When the neurons cells get impaired, it results in a decrease in the level of dopamine which is responsible for movement problems in Parkinson's disease [5, 6]. Also, the nerve endings in the

© Springer Nature Switzerland AG 2022
R. Bapi et al. (Eds.): ICDCIT 2022, LNCS 13145, pp. 198–209, 2022.
https://doi.org/10.1007/978-3-030-94876-4_14

brain get affected and the patients tend to lose the nerve endings which is responsible for producing the main chemical messenger of our sympathetic nervous system, nore-pinephrine [7, 8]. The sympathetic nervous system is responsible for controlling many functions of our body such as blood pressure and heart rate. This can explain the non-movement features of Parkinson's disease such as irregular blood pressure, sudden drop in blood pressure [9, 10], fatigue, decreased movement of foods from the digestive tract [11], etc.

The main cause of death of neuron cells that produce dopamine is still unknown but studies reflected that several factors such as genes due to hereditary which can be traced to some specific genetic mutations [12], environmental triggers (like environmental factor or like exposure to certain toxins) and presence of Lewy bodies within brain cells as it has been found that many brain cells of patients suffering from Parkinson disease contain Lewy bodies [13, 14].

Reduced speech intelligibility is a functional restriction of dysarthria and in the case of Parkinson's disease, it is related to phonatory impairment [15, 16]. This particular symptom of Parkinson's disease affects the articulatory component of the speech produc-tion mechanism of the human body. Voice abnormality tends to be the first indication of dysarthria and approximately 90% of the people with Parkinson's will develop it during the disease [17].

Although it is a chronic disease, studies suggest that early medication can be bene-ficial in controlling the symptoms [18]. As it is a progressive disease our project aims at early detection of the disease so that precautionary measures can be taken as early as possible to counter the effects of the disease.

This study is concerned with contributing to the advancement of medical tech-nologies, this project may help the patient as well as the medical assistance to detect Parkinson's earlier and along with early treatment, they may also get time to make advance directives and establish a durable attorney to ensure their healthcare wishes to be followed.

Interdisciplinarity includes medical science (knowledge about Parkinson's disease) and Computer science (knowledge about machine learning models to gain insight from medical data).

2 Related Works

There have been numerous studies conducted to obtain the possible biomarker in the case of Parkinson's disease based on various factors that influence patients suffering from Parkinson's disease like change in handwriting due to muscles impairment, olfactory loss, slow movements, voice impairment, etc.

Zayrit et al. [19] proposed a Parkinson's disease detection mechanism using support vector machine and other genetic algorithms. They use a publicly available dataset con-taining in total 34 voice recordings belonging to 20 patients suffering from Parkinson's disease and other 14 healthy controls. The data was sampled at 44.100 Hz and in total 21 feature vectors were extracted by decomposing the signal using discrete wavelet trans-form up to a3 approximation. Overall best accuracy obtained was 91.18% using SVM and the genetic algorithm.

Shivangi et al. [20] presented a Parkinson's disease detection mechanism using a dense artificial neural network for voice feature classification along with a convolution neural network for spectrogram image classification obtained by converting gait signal to spectrogram image. The voice impairment dataset used contains biomedical voice measurements of a total of 91 subjects out of which 43 were suffering from Parkinson's disease. The data were then normalized and inputted to a 3-layer perception network having 64, 32, and 16 neurons respectively. The overall accuracy obtained using the voice impairment dataset was around 89.15%.

Senturk et al. [21] presented an early Parkinson disease detection model using a machine learning method based on patient voice measurements. UCI Parkinson's dataset was used for the study and the data was collected from 31 subjects (23 patients suffering from Parkinson's diseases and 8 healthy control). Feature Importance technique was used for feature selection in Classification and Regression tree classification models and Recursive Feature Elimination was used with SVM and ANN. The highest accuracy of 93.84% was achieved using SVM.

Abdurrahman et al. [22] proposed an XgBoost Model for Parkinson's Disease detection. They use a publicly available dataset containing voice impairment data collected from 188 patients. The voice signals were sampled at 44.1 kHz gathering continuous phonation in three reparative times. By taking the whole feature set into account, an accuracy of 84.50% was achieved, they improved the model by ranking the feature set by its importance then important feature selection. The final accuracy of 85.60% was achieved.

Karabayir et al. [23] presented a Gradient boosting model for Parkinson's disease detection using voice impairment features. Replicated acoustic data was obtained from 80 subjects (40 patients with Parkinson's and 40 healthy subjects), containing 44 speech-test-based acoustic features, sampled at 44.1 kHz and 16 bits/sample. For each acoustic feature, three artificial variables were created for representing changes from one run to another, increasing the acoustic feature set to 264. Proper feature selection and reclassification have been performed resulting in 4-fold cross-validation. Overall accuracy of 88% was obtained.

Naranjo et al. [24] proposed a two-stage variable selection and classification approach is developed to match the replication-based experimental design. The statistical approach allows solving the computational problems with easy to implement Gibbs Sampling Algorithm. The results that were produced had an acceptable predictive capacity to differentiate between a PD patient and a non-PD patient. The accuracy, specificity and sensitivity 86.2%, 90%, 82.5% respectively. This approach had less computation time and better chain mixing as compared to the other approaches present at that time. This Bayesian approach fills the gap on variable selection and classification in the presence of the replicated data by properly matching the experimental design. This also proves that computer-assisted diagnostic systems had started playing important role in the diagnosis of Parkinson's Disease (PD).

Olanrewaju et al. [25] proposed a method in early detection and diagnosis of Parkinson's Disease that has been done using MLFNN (Multi-Layer Feed Forward) with Back Propagation algorithm. Here Back Propagation algorithm with a single hidden layer of MLFNN has been in which consists of 8 and 10 nodes of input and hidden layer respectively. There is only one output of the network which gives a value between 0 and 1. Log Sigmoid has been used as an activation layer in this research for both hidden and output layers with weight being chosen randomly. The output of the network is classified into two clusters which are Cluster One (for people with Parkinson's Disease) and Cluster Two (for healthy people). The output has a minimum and maximum value of 0.7394 and 0. 7221. Overall the whole study proves that it can be used due to good performance measured based on three parameters sensitivity, specificity, and accuracy which are 83.8%, 63.6%, and 80% respectively.

3   Methodology

This section discusses the methodology we have used for the study ranging from signal acquisition to signal pre-processing followed by discussing various classification models we have utilized for our study on Parkinson's disease classification (Fig. 1).

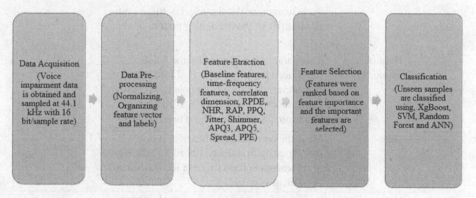

Fig. 1. Proposed methodology

3.1   Signal Acquisition

For our study, we used publicly available UCI Parkinson's dataset [26]. The dataset is composed of a range of biomedical voice measurements from 31 subjects, 23 with Parkinson's disease (PD) along with the remaining 8 healthy subjects. On average, six phonations ranging from one to thirty-six seconds in length were recorded from each of the subjects using a head-mounted microphone positioned 8 cm away from the source. The voice reading was sampled at 44.1 kHz with a 16-bit resolution. The dataset was created by the University of Oxford in collaboration with the National Center for Voice and Speech.

Table 1. Voice perturbation and nonlinear dynamic parameters measured

Attribute category	Attributes	Description	No of features
Feature vector	Vocal fundamental frequency	These are fundamental frequency parameters of vocal recording such as average, minimum, maximum values of frequency of vocal fold vibration, along with spread and frequency variation	5
	Jitter	Jitter is the extent of variation or alteration in the basic frequency from one vocal cycle to another vocal cycle. Useful in finding instabilities in the oscillating pattern of vocal folds	3
	Shimmer	Shimmer is the extent of variation or alteration in the amplitude from one vocal cycle to another vocal cycle. Useful in finding instabilities of the oscillating pattern of vocal folds	5
	Harmonic parameters	This parameter accounts for the noise introduced by the partial vocal fold closure that occurred in speech pathologies. HNR (Harmonics to noise ratio) and NHR (Noise to harmonics ratio) are those two features	2
	D2	D2 is the correlation dimension. It is calculated by first-delay embedding the signal to recreate the phase space of the nonlinear dynamical system	1
	RPDE	Recurrence period density entropy (RPDE) measures the distortion from the average vocal fundamental frequency. It is the measure of the extent to which vocal folds can sustain stable vocal fold oscillation	1
	DFA	Detrended Fluctuation Analysis (DFA). It is the measure of the stochastics self-similarity of the turbulent noise	1
	PPE	Pitch Period Entropy (PPE). It utilizes the logarithmic scale to measure the impaired control of average vocal fundamental frequency	1

(*continued*)

Table 1. (*continued*)

Attribute category	Attributes	Description	No of features
	PPQ	It is five-point period perturbation quotient (PPQ)	1
	RAP	It is relative amplitude perturbation (RAP)	1
	APQ 11	It is 11-point amplitude perturbation quotient (APQ)	1
Labels	Status	This parameter accounts for the status of the disease in a patient	1

3.2 Signal Pre-processing

Then, the voice impairment dataset is organized in an accurate format and separating the feature vectors and the labels for model training and then followed by pre-processing the dataset by normalizing the data by passing it through the min-max scaler to normalize it in the range from −1 to 1.

Normalization is a technique that is utilized as a part of data preparation for machine learning. It is mainly utilized for changing the numeric values involved in the dataset to a common scale without distorting the differences in the range of values involved [27]. As our dataset contains various features having different ranges, hence, we normalized it so that each feature is scaled to a particular range.

3.3 Feature Engineering

The next step involves feature selection based on feature importance. Feature importance refers to the techniques that assign a score to each feature based on how useful or important the feature is at predicting the output for a given feature vector [28, 29]. This technique allows us to analyze and interpret which features contribute to the accuracy of the model and which features can be ignored.

Ranking based feature selection technique has been implemented using XgBoost. The significance of each feature in the dataset is explicitly computed, allowing attributes to be graded and examined. The degree by which each feature split point improves the performance criteria, weighted by the set of observations the node is accountable for, is used to determine the importance of a single decision tree. The significance of each attribute is then averaged across all of the decision trees in the classification model.

Finally, map of feature importance is then plotted by analyzing and interpreting feature score (as in Fig. 2) and selecting the important feature in the feature selection phase a separate feature vector is created by ignoring the features such as Shimmer:DDA, Jitter:DDP, MDVP:Shimmer, HNR, and MDVP:Flo (Hz) whose feature score is nearly zero.

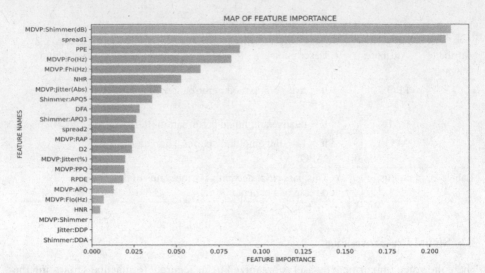

Fig. 2. Map of feature importance

3.4 Classification Algorithms

Various classification algorithms such as Support Vector Machine (SVM), Extreme Gradient Boosting (XgBoost) Classifier, Random Forest Classifier, and Artificial Neural Network.

3.4.1 Extreme Gradient Boosting (XgBoost) Classifier

Gradient boosting is a machine learning model which can be utilized for classification and regression problems. It worked by building an ensemble of weak learners a decision tree.

Boosting in gradient boosting model signifies the approach by which a weak learner such as a decision tree is converted or rather modified into a better learner by the means of fitting the weak learner into a modified version of the original dataset [30]. To make the model more robust a loss function is also defined mostly as a 14 logarithmic loss function in case of classification problem [31]. Our goal is to reduce the loss function so that the classification score increases hence the precision of the model.

$$F_{s-1}(x) = F_s(x) + f(x) \tag{1}$$

Where $F_s(x)$ is the function learned by the boosting model in 's^{th}' iteration. By this, we can fit the current iteration model $f(x)$ on residuals of the previous iteration.

We decided to utilize the XgBoost model as boosting is an ensemble method for primarily reducing bias, and also variance in supervised learning, and a family of machine learning algorithms that convert weak learners to strong ones. And also, it is computationally very efficient.

3.4.2 Support Vector Machine (SVM)

A support vector machine takes input data points and gives a hyperplane (which in this case (two-Dimensional space) it's simply a line) as an output that best separates the vectors. It is necessary to find the most optimal hyperplane to find the most accurate of the results [32]. This line is the decision boundary: anything that falls on the left side of it we will classify as an item belonging to first class, and anything that falls to the right as an item belonging to second class.

To find the best hyperplane in a linear SVM, linear algebra is used to transform the problem according to our needs. Here kernel plays a crucial role [33]. In linear kernel, the equation that is used to make the predictions for the new inputs using dot product between the input (x) and the support vectors is:

$$f(x) = B(0) + sum(ai * (x, x_i)) \tag{2}$$

This equation involves calculating the inner product of a new given input vector with all support vectors that are present in the data (data-set). The coefficients: 'B(0)' and 'ai' (for each input) must be estimated from the training data by the learning algorithm.

Similarly in our project SVM classifies between vectors in the same linear way, which helps us to classify, if someone is suffering from Parkinson's disease or not. Through this method the accuracy acquired is 91.52%.

3.4.3 Random Forest

Random forest is an ensemble learning technique that is used for regression and classification problems. It operates by constructing a forest of decision trees and then making the prediction by averaging the responses of each node which are individual decision trees [34]. A decision tree at its basics can be considered as a tree containing a condition or statement and two branches either yes or no; those branches can be further extended to fit a complex query. Formally, a decision tree is a non-parametric model which works on labeled data i.e., it is a supervised learning approach.

Further, extending the basic idea of a decision tree, a forest of multiple decision trees can be considered each having its predictions based on certain parameters. These parameters are chosen randomly for each of the decision trees at every split [35].

Bootstrap aggregating or bagging is utilized during the training phase in the random forest for drawing random samples from the training dataset with replacement. To output the prediction, the output from the individual decision tree is combined for input test point x'. Where bagging count is represented by B.

$$f = 1/B \sum_{B=1}^{B} f_b(x') \tag{3}$$

3.4.4 Artificial Neural Network (ANN)

An artificial Neural Network is a collection of connected units or nodes called artificial neurons. These neurons are typically aggregated into layers. Different transformations may be performed at different layers. These are trained by processing examples that contain a known input and result framing probability-weighted associations between the two. These are stored within the data net itself in the Data Structure. ANN (Artificial Neural Network) is composed of multiple nodes which are connected by lines and interact with each other [36]. The results of the tasks are passed to the neurons. The output at each node is called its activation value.

Each Link is associated with weight. ANNs (Artificial Neural Network) learn what happens by altering weight values. ANNs consist of layers that consist of an input layer, hidden layer, and output layer. Here backpropagation is the essence of neural net training [37]. It fine-tunes the weights of the neural net based on the error obtained from the epoch (iterations). So, it's all about feeding the loss backward in such a way that it helps in better predicting the neural network.

3.5 Training and Test Case Classification

Firstly, we have separated the feature vectors i.e., the voice features and the labels i.e., either suffering from Parkinson's disease or not, and then organized the data as per convenience to model it using the classification models. For our study, we have utilized 70% of the data for the training purpose and the remaining 30% for testing the classification model.

4 Results

Performance of various classification approaches was evaluated using the model precision, Recall, F1 score, support for both the class i.e., class 0 (not have Parkinson disease) or class 1 (have Parkinson disease) as mentioned in Table 2; and finally, the accuracy of the model as It has been mentioned in Table 1.

Table 2. Classification accuracy score

Algorithms	Accuracy
XgBoost	96.61%
Support Vector Machine	91.52%
Random Forest	84.74%
Artificial Neural Network	81.35%

Extreme gradient boosting (XgBoost) outperformed the other three algorithms and the highest accuracy of about 96.61% was achieved in our study. SVM was second on the list with achieved accuracy of about 91.52%. Random forest on third with an accuracy of 84.74% and finally ANN was last with achieved accuracy of about 81.35% (Table 3).

Table 3. Classification report for the different classification algorithm

Algorithm	Class 0				Class 1			
	Precision	Recall	F1 score	Support	Precision	Recall	F1 score	Support
XgBoost	1.00	0.89	0.94	19	0.95	1.00	0.98	40
SVM	1.00	0.55	0.71	11	0.91	1.00	0.95	48
Random Forest	0.57	0.73	0.64	11	0.93	0.88	0.90	48
ANN	0.83	0.53	0.65	19	0.81	0.95	0.87	40

5 Conclusion

A person showing stage one of Parkinson's may experience mild symptoms that generally do not interfere with daily activities, tremors, and changes in facial and walking expressions. Regardless of how long it takes to reach stage 4 of 5 a person with Parkinson's, the person will get symptoms that become debilitating if an early detection technique of Parkinson's can be made, it can become an empowering thing for patients as s the patients can start with the latest treatments before the harmful progression of the disease. Parkinson's disease can't be cured but medication and proper physiological therapies may help control the symptoms dramatically. With our machine learning model, the detection of PD can be made before it progresses to extreme stages. Contributing to the advancement of medical technologies, this project may help the patient as well as the medical assistance to detect Parkinson's earlier and along with early treatment, they may also get time to make advance directives and establish a durable attorney to ensure their healthcare wishes to be followed.

6 Application

An application can be deployed where the patient will be directed to record his voice signals according to given parameters in the application to form the feature set for the model, the formed dataset then can be sent over to a cloud for analysis, and the probable chance of having the Parkinson Disease is detected and the results are displayed to the patient, along with other important information and precautionary measures with mentioned other tests if required according to the results. This can help in remote diagnosis of the disease and the patients can consult their doctors at the early stages of this progressive neurological disease so that proper medication can be started as early as possible and can restrict Parkinson's disease from progressing further stages.

7 Future Work

The future scope of the project includes that in addition to voice frequency analysis and revelation, features to detect other symptoms like stationary tremors through computer vision can be achieved. So that a more robust model can be formed by considering various parameters into consideration related to the effects of Parkinson's Disease.

References

1. Khoo, T.K., et al.: The spectrum of nonmotor symptoms in early Parkinson disease. Neurology **80**(3), 276–281 (2013)
2. Verbaan, D., Marinus, J., Visser, M., van Rooden, S.M., Stiggelbout, A.M., van Hilten, J.J.: Patient-reported autonomic symptoms in Parkinson disease. Neurology **69**(4), 333–341 (2007)
3. Doty, R.L.: Olfactory dysfunction in Parkinson disease. Nat. Rev. Neurol. **8**(6), 329–339 (2012)
4. Pandya, M., Kubu, C.S., Giroux, M.L.: Parkinson disease: not just a movement disorder. Clevel. Clin. J. Med. **75**(12), 856–864 (2008)
5. Armstrong, M.J., Okun, M.S.: Diagnosis and treatment of Parkinson disease: a review. JAMA **323**(6), 548–560 (2020)
6. Charvin, D., Medori, R., Hauser, R.A., Rascol, O.: Therapeutic strategies for Parkinson disease: beyond dopaminergic drugs. Nat. Rev. Drug Discov. **17**(11), 804–822 (2018)
7. Rommelfanger, K.S., Weinshenker, D.: Norepinephrine: the redheaded stepchild of Parkinson's disease. Biochem. Pharmacol. **74**(2), 177–190 (2007)
8. Cash, R., Dennis, T., L'Heureux, R., Raisman, R., Javoy-Agid, F., Scatton, B.: Parkinson's disease and dementia: norepinephrine and dopamine in locus ceruleus. Neurology **37**(1), 42 (1987)
9. Goldstein, D.S., Holmes, C., Li, S.T., Bruce, S., Metman, L.V., Cannon III, R.O.: Cardiac sympathetic denervation in Parkinson disease. Ann. Intern. Med. **133**(5), 338–347 (2000)
10. Goldstein, D.S., Holmes, C., Lopez, G.J., Wu, T., Sharabi, Y.: Cardiac sympathetic denervation predicts PD in at-risk individuals. Parkinsonism Relat. Disord. **52**, 90–93 (2018)
11. Palma, J.A., Kaufmann, H.: Treatment of autonomic dysfunction in Parkinson disease and other synucleinopathies. Mov. Disord. **33**(3), 372–390 (2018)
12. Deng, H., Wang, P., Jankovic, J.: The genetics of Parkinson disease. Ageing Res. Rev. **42**, 72–85 (2018)
13. Ostojic, S.M.: Inadequate production of H2 by gut microbiota and Parkinson disease. Trends Endocrinol. Metab. **29**(5), 286–288 (2018)
14. Dickson, D.W.: Neuropathology of Parkinson disease. Parkinsonism Relat. Disord. **46**, S30–S33 (2018)
15. Poewe, W., et al.: Parkinson disease. Nat. Rev. Dis. Primers **3**(1), 1–21 (2017)
16. Moro-Velazquez, L., Gomez-Garcia, J.A., Arias-Londoño, J.D., Dehak, N., Godino-Llorente, J.I.: Advances in Parkinson's Disease detection and assessment using voice and speech: a review of the articulatory and phonatory aspects. Biomed. Sig. Process. Control **66**, 102418 (2021)
17. Zhang, T., Zhang, Y., Sun, H., Shan, H.: Parkinson disease detection using energy direction features based on EMD from voice signal. Biocybern. Biomed. Eng. **41**(1), 127–141 (2021)
18. Brabenec, L., Mekyska, J., Galaz, Z., Rektorova, I.: Speech disorders in Parkinson's disease: early diagnostics and effects of medication and brain stimulation. J. Neural Transm. **124**(3), 303–334 (2017). https://doi.org/10.1007/s00702-017-1676-0
19. Soumaya, Z., Taoufiq, B.D., Benayad, N., Yunus, K., Abdelkrim, A.: The detection of Parkinson disease using the genetic algorithm and SVM classifier. Appl. Acous. **171**, 107528 (2021)
20. Johri, A., Tripathi, A.: Parkinson disease detection using deep neural networks. In: 2019 Twelfth International Conference on Contemporary Computing (IC3), pp. 1–4. IEEE, August 2019
21. Senturk, Z.K.: Early diagnosis of Parkinson's disease using machine learning algorithms. Med. Hypotheses **138**, 109603 (2020)

22. Abdurrahman, G., Sintawati, M.: Implementation of xgboost for classification of Parkinson's disease. J. Phys. Conf. Ser. **1538**(1), 012024 (2020)
23. Karabayir, I., Goldman, S.M., Pappu, S., Akbilgic, O.: Gradient boosting for Parkinson's disease diagnosis from voice recordings. BMC Med. Inform. Decis. Mak. **20**(1), 1–7 (2020)
24. Naranjo, L., Perez, C.J., Martin, J., Campos-Roca, Y.: A two-stage variable selection and classification approach for Parkinson's disease detection by using voice recording replications. Comput. Methods Programs Biomed. **142**, 147–156 (2017)
25. Olanrewaju, R.F., Sahari, N.S., Musa, A.A., Hakiem, N.: Application of neural networks in early detection and diagnosis of Parkinson's disease. In: 2014 International Conference on Cyber and IT Service Management (CITSM), pp. 78–82. IEEE, November 2014
26. Little, M., McSharry, P., Hunter, E., Spielman, J., Ramig, L.: Suitability of dysphonia measurements for telemonitoring of Parkinson's disease. IEEE Trans. Biomed. Eng. **56**(4) (2008)
27. Patro, S., Sahu, K.K.: Normalization: a preprocessing stage (2015). arXiv preprint arXiv: 1503.06462
28. Saeys, Y., Inza, I., Larranaga, P.: A review of feature selection techniques in bioinformatics. Bioinformatics **23**(19), 2507–2517 (2007)
29. Guyon, I., Elisseeff, A.: An introduction to variable and feature selection. J. Mach. Learn. Res. **3**(March), 1157–1182 (2003)
30. Chen, T., He, T., Benesty, M., Khotilovich, V., Tang, Y., Cho, H.: Xgboost: extreme gradient boosting. R package version 0.4-2 **1**(4) (2015)
31. Chen, T., Guestrin, C.: XGBoost: a scalable tree boosting system. In: Proceedings of the 22nd ACM SIGKDD International Conference on Knowledge Discovery and Data Mining, pp. 785–794, August, 2016
32. Riesen, K., Neuhaus, M., Bunke, H.: Graph embedding in vector spaces by means of prototype selection. In: Escolano, F., Vento, M. (eds.) GbRPR 2007. LNCS, vol. 4538, pp. 383–393. Springer, Heidelberg (2007). https://doi.org/10.1007/978-3-540-72903-7_35
33. Noble, W.S.: What is a support vector machine? Nat. Biotechnol. **24**(12), 1565–1567 (2006)
34. Dollár, P., Zitnick, C.L.: Structured forests for fast edge detection. In: Proceedings of the IEEE International Conference on Computer Vision, pp. 1841–1848 (2013)
35. Breiman, L. Random forests. Mach. Learn. **45**(1), 5–32 (2001)
36. Cao, W., Wang, X., Ming, Z., Gao, J.: A review on neural networks with random weights. Neurocomputing **275**, 278–287 (2018)
37. Cilimkovic, M.: Neural Networks And Back Propagation Algorithm, vol. 15, pp. 1–12. Institute of Technology Blanchardstown, Dublin (2015)

Extracting Emotion Quotient of Viral Information Over Twitter

Pawan Kumar[1], Reiben Eappen Reji[1], and Vikram Singh[2]([✉])

[1] National Institute of Technology, Surathkal, India
{pawan.181ee133,reubeneappenreji.181ee136}@nitk.edu.in
[2] National Institute of Technology, Kurukshetra, India
viks@nitkkr.ac.in

Abstract. In social media platforms, a viral information or trending term draws attention, as it asserts potential user content towards topic/terms and sentiment flux. In real-time sentiment analysis, this viral information deliver potential insights, as encompass sentiment and co-located ranges of emotions be useful for the analysis and decision support. A traditional sentiment analysis tool generates the level of predefined sentiments over social media content for the defined duration and lacks in the extraction of emotional impact created by the same. In these settings, it is a multifaceted task to estimate precisely the emotional quotient viral information creates. The proposed novel algorithm aims, to (i) *extract the sentiment and co-located emotions quotient of viral information* and (ii) *utilities for comprehensive comparison on co-occurring viral informations*, and *sentiment analysis over Twitter text data*. The generated emotion quotients and micro-sentiment reveals several valuable insight of a viral topic and assists in decision support. A use-case analysis over real-time extracted data asserts significant insights, as generated sentiments and emotional effects reveals co-relations caused by viral/trending information. The algorithm delivers an efficient, robust, and adaptable solution for the sentiment analysis also.

Keywords: Big data · Emotion quotient · Sentiment analysis · Twitter

1 Introduction

The traditional social media platforms, e.g., Twitter, *Facebook*, etc. cater to the global users and list their personal information and media. The heterogeneous user data is often utilized for deriving common sentiments or trending information. The trending or viral information primarily harnesses the global content shared co-related to a particular topic and hash tag keywords [1].

A naive user or new user usually refers to this trending or viral list of information to see the most occurring or contributory piece of information [2, 3]. In this process, a user simply refers to the viral information and explores the related term over the Twitter API, without cognitive awareness of the emotional effect of viral information. A piece of viral information may have a list of information that may trigger the emotional effect on the user and lead to emotional splits or swings on the choice of information. User

© Springer Nature Switzerland AG 2022
R. Bapi et al. (Eds.): ICDCIT 2022, LNCS 13145, pp. 210–226, 2022.
https://doi.org/10.1007/978-3-030-94876-4_15

assistance is pivotal for the user, which may assist the user to showcase the emotional effects that viral information may carry. Though social media platforms offer limited or no functions or aspect-related views on the API for the generic user.

For example: Viral information related to '*Covid-2019*' may cause significant emotional effects on the citizens in current time. The cause-effect analysis over twitter may assist in administration (*Healthcare* offices) to track the sources/persons to take precautionary measures proactively. Similarly, for spectrum of applications where these estimated statistics may play a significant role:

- Sentiment analysis on social media is extensively used in the *Stock market* and *crypto market* to observe current trends and potential of *Panic sell*.
- Several sentiment models adapted on political elections recently, e.g. for US elections and Indian Elections. Similarly, a government office could utilize to track civil riot origins before they become uncontrollable, etc.

Typically, the designed algorithm for the sentiment analysis and emotion quotients (*EQ*) statistics could serve several pivotal objectives, as asserted by the experimental analysis also [7, 8]. The sentiment and *EQ* statistics generated could be utilized in several application areas: decision-making, advertising, public administrations, etc. Though, generating these statistics for real-time published data from the twitter data is a complex and multifaceted computing task [13, 14].

1.1   Motivation and Research Questions

The sentiment analysis is a complex computing task, mainly due to the semantic correlation that exists between the user-generated data and targeted sentiment level and created emotional quotients [14]. The task becomes multifaceted, primarily, when it is aimed for deriving the '*emotion effect*' co-located to a sentiment, as a micro-level. In these settings, a strategy could be the need of the hours that acquire the real-time twitter data and deliver the insights.

The research questions (RQs) are formalized to assist design of proposed adaptive strategy for the estimation of *sentiment level (SL)* and *emotion quotient (EQs)* of viral information on the real-time basis:

RQI: What are the key twitter data elements/features to extract the *SL* and *EQs*?
RQII: How to estimate the *SLs* and *EQs* and co-located overlap on both estimates?
RQIII: What *SL* and *EQ* statistics asserted for spectrum of application domains?

The designed *RQs* assist in conducting overall work and validate its feasibility for analytics and just-in-time decision-making over real-time published twitter data.

The key contribution is a robust and adaptive algorithm for sentiment and emotion evaluation, on just-in-time estimation for an interactive data play. Other contributions are as follows:

(i)   A portable and adaptive *UI*, to assist on generates the real-time statistics (*emotion and sentiment polarities*) for an emotion value 'as query' or viral information.

(ii) The strategy outlines pivotal features of text-based sentiment and emotion analysis on social media, e.g. *subjectivity, statement polarity, emotions expressed*, etc.

(iii) The experimental assessment asserts the overall accuracy upto 89% and 90%, respectively for *sentiment* and *EQs* estimation. The overall performance achieved is at significant-level in the view of real-time soft data analysis challenges.

The paper is organized as: *Sect. 2* lists the relevant research efforts to the sentiment and emotional statistics. *Section 3* elaborates the conceptual schema and internals of the designed strategy, with formulas and working example. *Section 4* describes the experimental assessment on the traditional metrics and advanced measures. Conclusion listed at last.

2   Related Work

In recent years, developing novel algorithms for sentiment and threaded emotional analytics estimation on soft data, particularly at micro-level on viral or trending information is area of interest. The located research areas fall under two heads:

2.1   Sentiment Analysis Over Soft Data (*Reviews/Posts/Viral Information*)

In recent years, the research efforts made on the accurate estimation of sentiment statistics, with a listed core task (i) *an automatic identification of relevant and text with opinion or documents* [15–20], (ii) *preparation of sentiment and threaded sentiment analysis*. Existing strategies and methods employed mainly *rule-based* and *statistical machine learning* approaches for these inherent tasks, e.g. opinion mining and sentiment analysis [22, 23].

A comprehensive survey is presented in [34] with two broad set of strategies (*opinion mining and sentiment analysis*). Whereas, Turney [38] asserts that an unsupervised algorithm, could be more suitable for the *lexicon-based* determination of *sentiment phrases* using function of opinion words over the word/sentences or document corpus, same is supported in [4, 36]. Another work in [5] highlighted the use of *SentiWordNet* as lexicon-based sentiment classifier over document and text segregation, as it may contains opinion strength for each term [22]. A prototype in [9], used the *SentiWordNet* Lexicon to classify reviews and [6] build a dictionary enabled sentiment classification over reviews with embedded adjectives.

Further, several work used Naïve-byes and SVM for sentiment analysis of movie reviews supported by inherent features, unigrams, bigrams, etc. These experimentations reveal that with feature a greater accuracy could be achieved sentiment polarity and statistics generation [23, 25].

In the recent potential work, a subsequence *kernel-based* voted *perceptron* prototype is created, and it is observed that the increase in the number of false positives is strongly co-related with the number of true positives. The designed models reveal its resiliency over intermediate star rating reviews classification, though five-star rating reviews is not utilized while training the model. Similar model is used for the sentiment analysis over the *microblog posts* using two phases: first phase involves partition of subjective and objective documents based on created and further for the generation of sentiment statistics (as *positive* and *negative*) in the second phase [10, 11, 34].

2.2 Emotion Quotients (EQs) Over Soft Data

The accurate detection of inherent '*Emotion*' over a text data using natural language processing and text analytics to discover people's feelings located subarea of research work. The usage of it could be tracking of disasters and social media monitoring.

Tracking user's opinions and inherent emotional quotients using posted soft data reveals interesting insights, e.g. tracking and analyzing Twitter data for election campaigns [6, 21, 22, 39, 41, 43]. There are several research studies asserts that sentiment topics and emotion topic/terms delivers promising outcomes for the generation of both polarities, such as for the tracking and monitoring '*earthquake disasters*' using '*Weibo*' a Chinese social media content is used to see the sentiments generated and sensitization [44]. In this, the proposed framework detected disasters related sentiment over massive data from a micro-blogging stream and to filter the negative messages to derive co-located event discovery in a post-disaster situation [23, 24, 37, 38].

The emergence of spectrum of social media platforms justified the need of social analytics for decision-making [38]. A system for tracking of sentiment on news entities over time [35, 39, 42], the socio-politics issues are detected over real-time streams. In this, sentiment-spike detection has been generated in [25–29, 40], Twitter data and analyzed the sentiment towards 70 entities from different domains. Similarly, in [30–33, 11, 15] a system to tracking health trends using microblogs data for the identification of province of several health related sentiment and co-located emotions are used. The authors introduced an open platform that uses crowd-sourced labeling of public social media content.

The key challenges in the accurate estimation sentiment and co-located *EQs* is the scalability of soft data and its rate of change for each inherent levels. Though, building an information system on the top of social media platform content could offer several useful takeaways to government's official and decision-makers. An end-to-end adaptive system is a focus of the system to generate these statistics to the spectrum of user, ranging from naïve to policy maker.

3   Proposed Strategy

The traditional social media platform, e.g. *Twitter, Facebook*, etc. caters global user's personal intents using posted media. The posted heterogeneous user data is pre-processed for acquiring generic sentiments and *EQs* of a viral information. The trending or viral information primarily harnesses the global content shared to a particular topic and key-word (e.g., *hashtag*). In this setting, a user simply refers to the viral information/hashtag or manually explores the related term over the twitter API, without cognitive awareness of the emotional effect of viral information. Though, social media platforms offer limited or no functions or aspect related views on the API for the generic user. The design system assists a naive user to understand its sentiment impact and further emotional quotients (EQs).

3.1 Conceptual Framework

A novel strategy for the real-time generation of emotional quotients of viral/trending information on twitter is designed. Figure 1 illustrates the internal computing blocks and their interactions for the intended objectives. The proposed framework begins with a traditional data collection over twitter API. The data extraction is driven by the user inputs, e.g. *keyword/hashtags, number of tweets, and duration.* The retrieved tweets from the *API*, are now to be stored in a temporary storage for later text-processing and feature extraction.

The local twitter data storage is also connected to the computing clock 'text pre-processing', each tweet extracted must go through local text processing and further supplied to the 'feature-extraction'. Further, a small computing thread is kept within the 'feature extraction' computing block for the estimation '*sentiment score (SC)*' and '*emotional quotient (EQ)*' co-located twitter data objects.

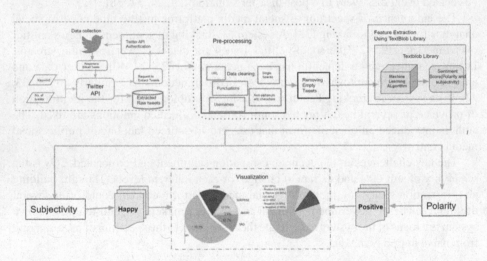

Fig. 1. Conceptual framework of proposed strategy

3.2   Generating Sentiment Level (SL) and Emotional Quotient (EQ)

The aim of the designed system is to generate the sentiments and emotion quotient. A prospective user (e.g., naïve, decision-maker, business analytics, admin, Govt. official, etc.) submit the data request over the user interface, using keywords, number of tweets of interest and name of emotional (optional). The designed system, evaluates the both statistics over a real-time.

The pre-processing stage, each extracted tweet is divided into tokens with estimated probability ($T_{prob} = Happy, Sad$, etc.). The python sentiment analysis is conducted using *NLTK* library [12]. The probability score (WGT_{Prob}.) is weighted a value, as to account of fewer negative tweets as there are positive and neutral ones. Additionally, token below a *threshold count* is truncated, since it is not significant and often little contributory. The latter is determined using the H_{10} entropy, formalized as *Eq. 1* as.

$$H_{10}(\text{token}) = -\sum\nolimits_{s \in \text{sentiment}} (p_{(s|\text{token})} \log_{10} p_{(s|\text{token})}) \tag{1}$$

The measures for *positive, neutral* and *negative* emojis are found. Finally, as given that a tweet is composed of several words; all the different features are aggregated/summed for each word, as to obtain an overall *tweet_value* (T_v), normalized by the *tweet_length* (T_{ct}).The *positive score (s^+)* and *negative scores(s^-)* for each tweet are determined as average of the both scores using *Eq. 2* and *Eq. 3* respectively. The overall *Sentiment Score* (SC) is estimated for the locating the topic proportion.

$$s^+ = \frac{\sum_{i \in t} \text{pos\_score}_i}{n} \tag{2}$$

$$s^- = \frac{\sum_{i \in t} \text{neg\_score}_i}{n} \tag{3}$$

$$\text{Overall Sentiment Score } (SC) = (s^+ - s^-) \tag{4}$$

To extract emotion from a tweet, the topical words (bigram) are taken from tweet content, based on '*item response theory*' [12] and further categorized using its unsupervised features. The proposed algorithm is based on '*Topic proportion*' that helps to identify related sentiment terms located to a topic sentiment lexicon.

Algorithm: Extracting *SL* and EQ of *Tweet_objects*

Input: Topic name (T_{kw}), No. of Tweets (*ToI*), and Emotion _name (*Emo*)
Output: *Tweet_list, EQ, SL*

Step 1: Cleaning up the tweets   /*denoising the ttweets such as links,@,#,etc.*/
    df['Tweet'] = df['Tweet'].apply(cleanUpTweets)
    all_tweets=df['Tweet'].tolist()
    df = df.drop(df[df['Tweet'] == ' '].index)

Step 2: Gathering and Storing Emotions   /*text2emotion EQ value generated for each tweet*/
    dict = te.get_emotion(text)
    for key in dict:
      if (key == "Happy"):
        *Happy.append(dict[key])/*Similartly also for "Sad","Fear" etc*/*

Step 3: Finding the dominating Emotion   /*For each tweet, store the dominating emotion values */
    for i in range(0,NoOfTweets):
    maxel=max(Happy[i],Sad[i],Angry[i],Fear[i])
      if((maxel==Happy[i])and(maxel!=0)):
        Happy2.append(all_tweets[i])   /*Similarly also for Sad2, Fear2 etc*/

Step 4: Finding the overall percentage of each emotion after analyzing each tweet on the topic
                */*All the values in each emotion are added and for each emotion percent is calculat-*
                ed by dividing summation of values for that emotion by the total sum/*
    happysum = sum(Happy)
    totalsum = zip(Happy, Sad, Angry, Surprise, Fear)
    for x in totalsum:
      f or y in x:
        total = total + y;
    happypercent = (happysum / total)   ** 100/*Similarly the percentage*
                of other emotions is calculated/*

Step5: Polarity analysis   /*For each tweet, polarity is analyzed& values are clas-
                sified into three groups */
    for tweet in self.tweets:
    analysis = TextBlob(tweet.text)
    polarity += analysis.sentiment.polarity
      if (analysis.sentiment.polarity== 0 neutral += 1;
      elif (analysis.sentiment.polarity> 0 and analysis.sentiment.polarity<0.3):wpositive += 1;
      elif (analysis.sentiment.polarity>0.3 and analysis.sentiment.polarity<=0.6): positive += 1;
      elif (analysis.sentiment.polarity> 0.6 and analysis.sentiment.polarity<= 1):spositive += 1;
      elif (analysis.sentiment.polarity> -0.3 and analysis.sentiment.polarity<= 0):wnegative += 1;
      elif (analysis.sentiment.polarity> -0.6 and analysis.sentiment.polarity<= -0.3): negative += 1;
      elif (analysis.sentiment.polarity> -1 and analysis.sentiment.polarity<= -0.6):snegative += 1;

The proposed algorithm is driven on the topic model, as extracted *tweet-object* is a mixture of one or more topics. A lexicon approach measures the sentiment of a group of documents '*corpus*', with the help of dictionary of words with associated polarity scores. A dictionary of lexicons elements is added externally to the corpus for the purpose of enhancing the embedded lexicons. The proposed *lexicon-based* sentiment estimation for *positive* and *negative* sentiment using *Eq. 5* and *Eq. 6* respectively, and formalized as following,

$$P(w\,|+) = \frac{M_w}{|N^+|} \tag{5}$$

$$P(w\,|-) = \frac{M_w}{|N^-|} \tag{6}$$

Here, M_w is the set of messages containing lexical token 'w'. Here, the estimated *positive* and *negative* sentiments of a message are coded as N^+, N^- respectively, for each implicit message (message) 'm'. The log likelihood ratio is calculated using the *Eq. 7* and utilized inherently during the estimation of place of sentiment and emotion quotient estimation:

$$S_m = \sum_{i=1}^{n} \log\left(\frac{P(w_i|-)}{P(w_i|+)}\right) \tag{7}$$

Here, *lexical unit* of the dictionary is presented by w and n is the number of words and collocations included in the dictionary, existences with the sentence m.

3.3   System Use-Cases of Sentiment and Emotional Analytics

The designed system is plugged with an interactive user interface (UI) for several types of users. The UI aimed is to offer estimated statistics and processed data for the different decision making and analytics purposes. There are several use-cases of designed system listed during the design phase, e.g. related viral information to an emotional value, comparing the emotional causes of more than one viral/trending information, etc.

The *first use-case* is coming from a naive user, as '*basic search on social media data for a sentiment and emotion value*', illustrated in Fig. 2. Here, two parts of UI steers user cognitive tasks, e.g. search, exploration, browse, etc., on the real-time analytics. For a user input '*keyword/hashtag/emotion name*', the system extracts the related tweets and prepares intermediate statistics to be shown in the graphical scheme.

Here, *Part 1* illustrates both information using pie chart with scores 'as % values', and within it tweets lists of the user interest is available. In *Part 2*, the feature of compares and explores offers a new dimension of the designed prototype. Here, a user may be interested to compare effects of pair of viral and trending information, for playing with the relevant social media data, further two trending or viral information or may delve into the deeper view of these statistics and values and related tweets.

The *second use-case* is robust exploration into the relevant viral/trending information for a user query. The designed system may be adapted for the social data exploration within emotion quotient, illustrated in Fig. 3. The matching viral information easily adapted for the analytics.

Further, *third use-case* is a capacity, to deliver a matching list of trending/viral information's for and matching viral the system for the exploration within the tweets data for an input, '*emotion quotient*'. The viral/trending topics may be extracted with the presence of the same emotional quotient values.

The *fourth use-case* is an inherent capability for systematic comparative view between more than one user inputs (*trending and viral information*) and its detailed view on the emotion quotients (EQs) and further exploration on the generated tweet text, also illustrated in Fig. 4.

3.4   Working Example

The *Olympic* is the world's biggest sporting event, as plethora of sentiments and emotion affect attached, as abundant amount of social media data is contributed globally on social

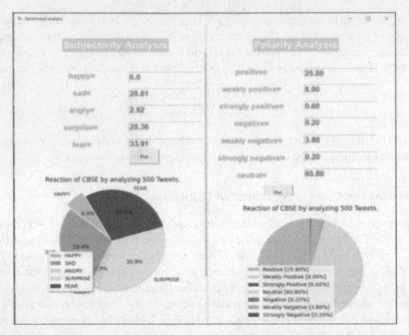

Fig. 2. User Interface (UI) for 1st use-case, for the sentiment and EQs explorations.

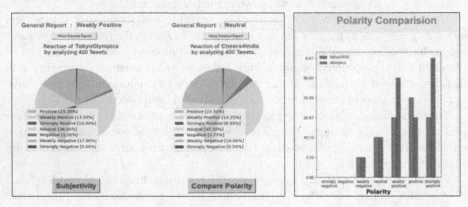

Fig. 3. User interface for comparing *SL* and *EQs* with *polarity* ('*tokyo2020*' & '*olympic*').

networking platforms. Similarly, the designed algorithm may be adapted for event, as it caters diverse user and their relevant content and Meta data, e.g. comments, share, tagging, repost, etc.

The designed prototype is configured over the twitter API and its settings. The data relevant data may extract on real-time basis and subsequently pre-processed, using traditional text processing. The interactive UI is designed to capture user cognitive actions support visualizations of derived analytics for the provided social media data.

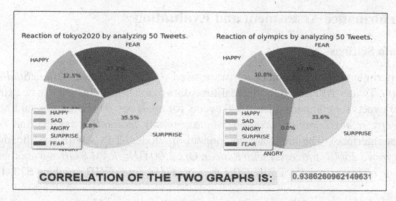

Fig. 4. User interface for ('*tokyo2020*' & '*olympic*' for 100 *IoT) sentiment* and *EQ* polarity.

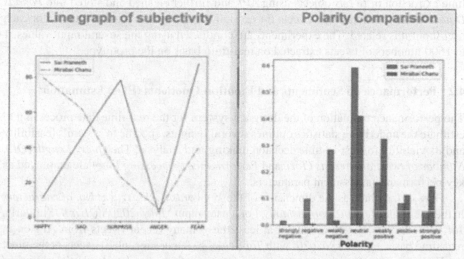

Fig. 5. Estimated *subjectivity* and *polarity* analysis

For instance, the men's single badminton player '*Sai Praneeth*', who lost both his initial matches and is out of the tournament, results to polarity positives (22.8%) is less than negative's (30.8%), here '*Fear*' and '*Surprise*' are dominating. Further, between '*Sai Praneeth*' and '*MirabaiChanu*' as trending pattern, polarity graph reveals interesting patterns, despite difference on sport zones, in Fig. 5 under Subjectivity graph. In subjectivity *Happiness* surrounds *Mirabai Chanu* with some sadness, for *Sai Praneeth* surprise, *Fear*, *Sadness* is mostly visible.

Next, *Sai Praneeth* and *KentoMomota* are compared to evolving polarity patterns. Subjectivity analysis appears similar, except to '*fear*' emotion, as higher fear is surrounded to '*KentoMomota*', illustrated in Fig. 5, under Polarity graph, while polarity graph reveals '*KentoMomota*' with higher positivity, while '*Sai Praneeth*' has trace of '*weak negativity*'.

4 Performance Assessment and Evaluation

4.1 Data Settings

The experimental setup includes software used *Jypter notebook*, *Visual Studio* and *PyCharm*. Twitter API isused for the real-time data extraction, at instance to be extracted 1 to 800 tweets for comparing 1 to 1600 tweets for analytics. There are several libraries, e.g. *tweepy, re, text2emotion, textblob, pandas, numpy, matplotlib, sys, csv* and *Tkinter* (for user interface). The hardware components includes, 2 PCs with specification as: *AMD Ryzen 5 2500U processer with Radeon Gfx 2.00 GHz, RAM 8 GB* and another with processor of *Intel Core i5(8250U)CPU @ 1.60 GHz, Intel UHD* graphics 620, 12 GB RAM).

The user interface (UI) is designed using *Python library Tkinter* and statistics are using *Python library Matplotlib* for extracted tweet objects for a user request. The real-time extraction of *tweets* objects using *API* and further cleaned and stored into *Pandas Data Frame*. The number of tweets for extraction is related to a user input, as for each user input it is related. The experiments are conducted using the several input values, 1 to 1600 numbers of tweets extracted on real-time basis on the prototype.

4.2 Performance on Sentiments and Emotion Quotients (EQs) Estimation

The performance evaluation of the designed system for the real-time data processing to estimate the underlying statistics outlines several insights, specific to system's feasibility and its viability for just-in-time decision making and analysis. The *Query Length (QL)*, *Number of tweet of interests (ToI)*, and *Performance (processing time)* are employed as key performance assessment parameters.

Here, *QL* defined as the dimension of the *keywords/hashtasg*, i.e. *No. of characters* in the user input *keywords or hashtags*. For a user input *'Tokyo2020'*, *QL is* 9. Similarly, *ToI* value directs system to extract at least these many recent tweets from API on in real-time basis, e.g. *'Tokyo2020'* with *ToI* value 20 fetches recent 20 tweets at the time.

Figure 6 illustrates the *overall processing time*, formalized as *'total time required for the preparation of both statistics on real-time'*, real-time appearing viral topics dated on *30 July 2021*. For each topic, relevant tweet set is extracted and subsequently ranked for implicit pre-processing. In this, at least *1000* tweets are fetched on co-located viral topics, based on priority based preference. A generic estimation of processing time usually increased with the higher no. of tweets, as higher *no. of tweets* harness increased coverage of sentiments and emotions.

Figure 7 depicts the *overall processing time* for the user submitted query or selected viral topics on real-time data. The different size of user input, as query length (QL) is adapted for the assessment, with an aim to highlight the fact that as *QL* increased to a level affects the overall computational time. In a generic settings, to different viral/trending topics appearing, as to ensure the *variable QL* and observed the processing time patterns for at least recent 1000 tweets on each viral or trending topics.

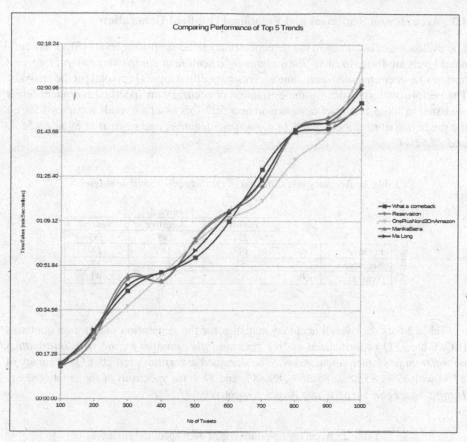

Fig. 6. Overall processing time for analyzing multiple *viral or trending* topics

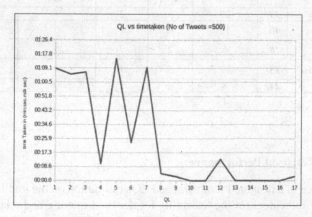

Fig. 7. Overall Query Response Time (QRT) for different size of user query, as '*QL*'

4.3 Accuracy on Sentiment and Emotional Quotient Generation

The evaluation of accuracy in the detection of accurate sentiment levels (SLs), as sentiment levels are formalized as '*the quantum of a sentiment contributes to viral information, w.r.t user contributed data*', and each user specified inputs is pivotal for the analysis. The performance statistics for the estimation of accuracy on specified *sentiment-levels* are listed in Table 1. A brief comparison over *500 ToIs* asserts overall accuracy 85% on the prediction of sentiment-levels (e.g. *positive, negative, and neutral* as 89%, 88.58%, and 77.62%).

Table 1. Accuracy on estimation of each specified *sentiment-levels*.

		Predicted		
		Positive	Negative	Neutral
		234	108	155
Actual	Positive 181	143	14	24
	Negative 177	54	86	37
	Neutral 139	37	8	94

Table 2 lists the overall accuracy statistics for the generation of emotion quotients (EQs), here EQ is formalized as '*the emotion influx created by the viral information on different fundamental emotions*'. The designed algorithm predicts EQs accuracy of 87%, with 89%, 85.88%, 85.66%, 89.88% and 88% for spectrum of the emotions, e.g. *Happy, Sad, Fear, Surprise and Anger* respectively.

Table 2. Accuracy on estimation of each specified emotion.

		Predicted				
		Happy	Sad	Fear	Surprise	Anger
		56	24	22	12	16
Actual	Happy 33	22	5	2	2	2
	Sad 40	15	6	8	6	5
	Fear 18	6	2	7	0	3
	Surprise 15	5	5	1	4	0
	Anger 24	8	6	4	0	6

4.4 Overall Retrieval Performance

The performance of a designed sentiment and EQs estimation on the traditional retrieval metrics are key indicators for the feasibility for decision making and related functions. The traditional metrics are adapted for the evaluation of the system performance, e.g. *Precision, recall and f-measure*. The precision is adapted in its fundamental notion, as a measure of 'precisely matched results to the user input', and recall as a measure '*closely relevant result to the user query*'. *F-measure* is a geometric mean of precision and recall.

Table 3 lists these indicators, when experimented with varying degree of user input (*Query length* and *ToI*).

Table 3. Traditional retrieval metrics for *sentiment level* and *emotion quotient estimation*

Sentiment type	Metric (scores)	
Positive	Precision	0.611
	Recall	0.389
	F-measure	0.475
Negative	Precision	0.796
	Recall	0.224
	F-measure	0.351
Neutral	Precision	0.606
	Recall	0.240
	F-measure	0.344

Emotion type	Metric (scores)	
Happy	Precision	0.393
	Recall	0.259
	F-measure	0.312
Sad	Precision	0.250
	Recall	0.113
	F-measure	0.156
Fear	Precision	0.318
	Recall	0.108
	F-measure	0.161
Surprise	Precision	0.333
	Recall	0.048
	F-measure	0.084
Anger	Precision	0.375
	Recall	0.063
	F-measure	0.107

5 Conclusion

The data generated over the various Social media platforms trigger significant changes on the public sentiment and emotional flux. A novel algorithm is designed to estimate the sentimental and emotional quotient of viral or trending information in real-time. The work is in line with current need to textual emoticons mining in several real-life application scenarios. The algorithm estimates sentiment and EQs of a user requested viral/trending information over the twitter on just-in-time basis over real-time twitter data. The approach builds a corpus of tweets and related fields where each tweet is classified with respective emotion based on lexicon approach. The systematic evaluation asserts the significance of delivered statistics for the user input '*viral information*', and its usability. The feasibility analysis of statistics for real-time analysis and decision-making is uncovered using 04 use-cases, also outlines the key features of social media data for the purpose.

The embedding interactive user interface is one of future scope of the current algorithm. An intent model for the estimating the user interest and its correlation with current trending or viral information in the social media platforms is another tentative direction.

References

1. Bikel, D.M., Sorensen, J.: If we want your opinion. In: International conference on semantic computing (ICSC 2007), pp. 493–500 (2007). https://doi.org/10.1109/ICSC.2007.81

2. Cambria, E., Schuller, B., Xia, Y., Havasi, C.: New avenues in opinion mining and sentiment analysis. IEEE Intell. Syst. **28**(2), 15–21 (2013). https://doi.org/10.1109/MIS.2013.30

3. Chen, R., Xu, W.: The determinants of online customer ratings: a combined domain ontology and topic text analytics approach. Electron. Commer. Res. **17**(1), 31–50 (2016). https://doi.org/10.1007/s10660-016-9243-6

4. Ding, X., Liu, B., Yu, P.S.: A holistic lexicon-based approach to opinion mining. In: Proceedings of the 2008 International Conference on Web Search and Data Mining, pp. 231–240 (2008). https://doi.org/10.1145/1341531.1341561

5. Esuli, A., Sebastiani, F.: Sentiwordnet: a publicly available lexical resource for opinion mining. In: Proceedings of 5th Language Resources and Evaluation, vol. 6, pp. 417–422 (2006)

6. Fei, G., Liu, B., Hsu, M., Castellanos, M., Ghosh, R.: A dictionary-based approach to identifying aspects implied by adjectives for opinion mining. In: Proceedings of 24th International Conference on Computational Linguistics, p. 309 (2012)

7. Feldman, R., Fresco, M., Goldenberg, J., Netzer, O., Ungar, L.: Extracting product comparisons from discussion boards. A model for senti-ment and emotion analysis of unstructured. In: Seventh IEEE International Conference on Data Mining (ICDM 2007), vol. 197, no. 123, pp. 469–474 (2007). https://doi.org/10.1109/ICDM.2007.27.

8. Godbole, N., Srinivasaiah, M., Skiena, S.: Large-scale sentiment analysis for news and blogs. In: Proceedings of the International Conference on Weblogs and Social Media (ICWSM), vol. 7, no. 21, pp. 219–222 (2007)

9. Hamouda, A., Rohaim, M.: Reviews classification using sentiwordnet lexicon. In: World Congress on Computer Science and Information Technology (2011)

10. Jindal, N., Liu, B.: Mining comparative sentences and relations. In: Proceedings of the 21st National Conference on Artificial Intelligence, vol. 2, pp. 1331–1336 (2006)

11. Van de Kauter, M., Breesch, D., Hoste, V.: Fine-grained analysis of explicit and implicit sentiment in financial news articles. Expert Syst. Appl. **42**(11), 4999–5010 (2015). https://doi.org/10.1016/j.eswa.2015.02.007

12. Loper, E., Bird, S.: Nltk: The natural language toolkit. arXiv preprint cs/0205028 (2002)

13. Li, Y., Qin, Z., Xu, W., Guo, J.: A holistic model of mining product aspects and associated sentiments from online reviews. Multimedia Tools Appl. **74**(23), 10177–10194 (2015). https://doi.org/10.1007/s11042-014-2158-0

14. Liu, B.: Sentiment analysis and subjectivity. Handb. Nat. Lang. Process. **2**, 627–666 (2010)

15. Liu, B.: Opinion mining and sentiment analysis. In: Web Data Mining: Exploring Hyperlinks, Contents, and Usage Data, pp. 459–526 (2011). https://doi.org/10.1007/978-3-642-19460-3_11

16. Liu, B.: Sentiment analysis and opinion mining. Synth. Lect. Hum. Lang. Technol. **5**(1), 1–167 (2012). https://doi.org/10.2200/S00416ED1V01Y201204HLT016

17. Liu, P., Gulla, J.A., Zhang, L.: Dynamic topic-based sentiment analysis of large-scale online news. In: Cellary, W., Mokbel, M.F., Wang, J., Wang, H., Zhou, R., Zhang, Y. (eds.) WISE 2016. LNCS, vol. 10042, pp. 3–18. Springer, Cham (2016). https://doi.org/10.1007/978-3-319-48743-4_1

18. Ma, Y., Chen, G., Wei, Q.: Finding users preferences from large-scale online reviews for personalized recommendation. Electron. Commer. Res. **17**(1), 3–29 (2017). https://doi.org/10.1007/s10660-016-9240-9

19. Mo, S.Y.K., Liu, A., Yang, S.Y.: News sentiment to market impact and its feedback effect. Environ. Syst. Decis. **36**(2), 158–166 (2016). https://doi.org/10.1007/s10669-016-9590-9

20. Montoyo, A., MartíNez-Barco, P., Balahur, A.: Subjectivity and sentiment analysis: an overview of the current state of the area and envisaged developments. Decis. Support Syst. **53**(4), 675–679 (2012). https://doi.org/10.1016/j.dss.2012.05.022

21. Nassirtoussi, A.K., Aghabozorgi, S., Wah, T.Y., Ngo, D.C.L.: Text mining of newsheadlines for forex market prediction: a multi-layer dimension reduction algorithm with semantics and sentiment. Expert Syst. Appl. **42**(1), 306–324 (2015). https://doi.org/10.1016/j.eswa.2014.08.004

22. Ohana, B.: Opinion mining with the sentwordnet lexical resource. M.Sc. Dissertation, Dublin Institute of Technology (2009)

23. Pang, B., Lee, L.: A sentimental education: sentiment analysis using subjectivity summarization based on minimum cuts. In: Proceedings of the 42nd Annual Meeting on Association for Computational Linguistics, p. 271 (2004). https://doi.org/10.3115/1218955.1218990

24. Pang, B., Lee, L.: Opinion mining and sentiment analysis. Found. Trends Inf. Retr. **2**(1–2), 1–135 (2008). https://doi.org/10.1561/1500000011

25. Pang, B., Lee, L., Vaithyanathan, S.: Thumbs up?: sentiment classification using machine learning techniques. In: Proceedings of the ACL-02 Conference on Empirical Methods in Natural Language Processing, vol. 10, pp. 79–86 (2002). https://doi.org/10.3115/1118693.1118704

26. Parkhe, V., Biswas, B.: Sentiment analysis of movie reviews: finding most important movie aspects using driving factors. Soft. Comput. **20**(9), 3373–3379 (2016). https://doi.org/10.1007/s00500-015-1779-1

27. Peng, J., Choo, K.K.R., Ashman, H.: Astroturfing detection in social media: using binary n-gram analysis for authorship attribution. In: Proceedings of the 15th IEEE International Conference on Trust, Security and Privacy in Computing and Communications (TrustCom 2016), pp. 121–1286 (2016)

28. Peng, J., Choo, K.K.R., Ashman, H.: Bit-level n-gram based forensic authorship analysis on social media: identifying individuals from linguistic profiles. J. Netw. Comput. Appl. **70**, 171–182 (2016). https://doi.org/10.1016/j.jnca.2016.04.001

29. Peng, J., Detchon, S., Choo, K.K.R., Ashman, H.: Astroturfing detection in social media: a binary n-gram-based approach. Concurrency Comput. Pract. Experience **29**(17), e4013 (2016). https://doi.org/10.1002/cpe.4013

30. Pröllochs, N., Feuerriegel, S., Neumann, D.: Enhancing sentiment analysis of financial news by detecting negation scopes. In: Proceedings of the 48th Hawaii International Conference on System Sciences (HICSS), pp. 959–968 (2015). https://doi.org/10.1109/HICSS.2015.119

31. Robinson, R., Goh, T.T., Zhang, R.: Textual factors in online product reviews: a foundation for a more influential approach to opinion mining. Electron. Commer. Res. **12**(3), 301–330 (2012). https://doi.org/10.1007/s10660-012-9095-7

32. Rout, J., Dalmia, A., Choo, K.K.R., Bakshi, S., Jena, S.: Revisiting semi-supervised learning for online deceptive review detection. IEEE Access **5**(1), 1319–1327 (2017). https://doi.org/10.1109/ACCESS.2017.2655032

33. Rout, J., Singh, S., Jena, S., Bakshi, S.: Deceptive review detection using labeled and unlabeled data. Multimedia Tools Appl. **76**(3), 3187–3211 (2017). https://doi.org/10.1007/s11042-016-3819-y

34. Sadegh, M., Ibrahim, R., Othman, Z.A.: Opinion mining and sentiment analysis: a survey. Int. J. Comput. Technol. **2**(3), 171–178 (2012)

35. Song, L., Lau, R.Y.K., Kwok, R.-W., Mirkovski, K., Dou, W.: Who are the spoilers in social media marketing? Incremental learning of latent semantics for social spam detection. Electron. Commer. Res. **17**(1), 51–81 (2016). https://doi.org/10.1007/s10660-016-9244-5

36. Taboada, M., Brooke, J., Tofiloski, M., Voll, K., Stede, M.: Lexicon-based methods for sentiment analysis. Comput. Linguist. **37**(2), 267–307 (2011). https://doi.org/10.1162/COLI_a_00049

37. Tang, H., Tan, S., Cheng, X.: A survey on sentiment detection of reviews. Expert Syst. Appl. **36**(7), 10760–10773 (2009). https://doi.org/10.1016/j.eswa.2009.02.063

38. Turney, P.D.: Thumbs up or thumbs down?: semantic orientation applied to unsupervised classification of reviews. In: Proceedings of the 40th Annual Meeting on Association for Computational Linguistics, pp. 417–424 (2002). https://doi.org/10.3115/1073083.1073153

39. Wang, D., Li, J., Xu, K., Wu, Y.: Sentiment community detection: exploring sentiments and relationships in social networks. Electron. Commer. Res. **17**(1), 103–132 (2017). https://doi.org/10.1007/s10660-016-9233-8

40. Zheng, L., Wang, H., Gao, S.: Sentimental feature selection for sentiment analysis of Chinese online reviews. Int. J. Mach. Learn. Cybern. **9**(1), 75–84 (2015). https://doi.org/10.1007/s13042-015-0347-4

41. Alves, A.L.F.: A spatial and temporal sentiment analysis approach applied to Twitter microtexts. J. Inf. Data Manag. **6**, 118 (2015)

42. Chaabani, Y., Toujani, R., Akaichi, J.: Sentiment analysis method for tracking touristics reviews in social media network. In: De Pietro, G., Gallo, L., Howlett, R.J., Jain, L.C. (eds.) KES-IIMSS 2017. SIST, vol. 76, pp. 299–310. Springer, Cham (2018). https://doi.org/10.1007/978-3-319-59480-4_30

43. Contractor, D.: Tracking political elections on social media: applications and experience. In: Proceedings of the Twenty-Fourth International Joint Conference on Artificial Intelligence, Buenos Aires, Argentina, 25–31 July 2015

44. Bai, H., Yu, G.: A Weibo-based approach to disaster informatics: incidents monitor in post-disaster situation via Weibo text negative sentiment analysis. Nat. Hazards **83**, 1177–1196 (2016)

45. Brynielsson, J., Johansson, F., Jonsson, C., Westling, A.: Emotion classification of social media posts for estimating people's reactions to communicated alert messages during crises. Secur. Inform. **3**(1), 1–11 (2014). https://doi.org/10.1186/s13388-014-0007-3

A Novel Modified Harmonic Mean Combined with Cohesion Score for Multi-document Summarization

Rajendra Kumar Roul[1(✉)] and Jajati Keshari Sahoo[2]

[1] Thapar Institute of Engineering and Technology, Patiala, Punjab, India
raj.roul@thapar.edu
[2] BITS-Pilani, K.K. Birla Goa Campus, Goa, India
jksahoo@goa.bits-pilani.ac.in

Abstract. The abundance of textual information that is generated on a daily basis on the web, social media, and other repositories makes it critical and difficult to extract important information from a large corpus. Automatic Text Summarization (ATS) works well in this direction, which can review many documents and pull out the relevant information from them. But the computational bottlenecks associated with ATS need to be removed by finding efficient workarounds. Although existing research works have focused on this direction for further improvements, there are still many limitations and challenges which need to be addressed. The current work proposes a semantic-based word similarity combined with sentence similarity to summarize a corpus of text documents. Finally, a relative entropy-based technique using KL-divergence is proposed, which arranges the sentences in the final summary as per their importance. Experimental results on DUC datasets are promising and show the potential of the proposed technique compared to the other state-of-the-art approaches.

Keywords: Cohesion · Extractive · Harmonic mean · Rouge · Semantic · Summarization

1 Introduction

Over the past few years, due to the growth of computational power and efficient deep learning models, there have been new approaches for presenting text corpus in a concise and human-cognizable manner. Automatic Text Summarization (ATS) is a process that distills the most important and silent information from a large collection of documents and generates a short-length text summary. It involves tasks like 'interpreting the text', 'extracting the relevant information', 'condensing extracted information', 'presenting summary representation to the reader in natural language' etc. [1]. The atomic stages of the summarization are *interpretation*, *transformation*, and *generation* [2,3]. The central challenges in ATS research include identifying silent parts of text correctly, avoiding redundancy efficiently, and combining chosen segments in a way that guarantees readability [4,5].

© Springer Nature Switzerland AG 2022
R. Bapi et al. (Eds.): ICDCIT 2022, LNCS 13145, pp. 227–244, 2022.
https://doi.org/10.1007/978-3-030-94876-4_16

ATS is either extractive or abstractive in nature. Extractive ATS concatenates the most important and silent sentences of a document without any modification. This mechanism can be put as mapping of a given input sequence of words contained in the source document to a target sequence known as the summary of the document. Abstractive ATS generates completely new sentences conveying the same meaning as the original document [6]. Generally, extractive summaries' major requirements include fluency, saliency, coherency, information correctness, and novelty. Technically, abstractive ATS is more challenging than the extractive one because it is more grammar coherent and involves higher-level techniques such as content organization, surface realization, and meaning representation. This indicates that the research on the extractive method is numerous, unlike abstractive ATS research. Although ATS has been a popular research topic since 1958 [7], it is still challenging to summarize text automatically using human-generated summary. This research area is still growing and needs much effort in trying new strategies to access the level of human-generated summaries. Based on the text data, the entire text summarization process is further categorized into two types- *single-text* and *multi-text* summarization. If the text is summarized from only one document, then we call it as single document text summarization. But if the system generates a coherent summary from multiple documents, then it is called multi-document text summarization.

1.1 Motivation

There have been surplus of research works already done on text summarization. Some of the existing techniques that have been proposed for text summarization include 'graph-based summarization [8]', 'clustering-based summarization [9]', 'machine learning based summarization [10]', 'summarization based on Fuzzy logic' [11], topic-modeling based summarization [12,13] etc. All these existing text summarization techniques have some common limitations as mentioned below:

– similar meaning can be inherited from two sentences composed out of entirely different words.
– surface matching methods generally exclude stop-word like 'a', 'an', 'the' 'of', etc., because they are very common to all the documents in the corpus. But for computing the sentence similarity, these words play major role because they carry structural information for interpreting the sentence meaning.
– meaning of the words in the context of the sentence is not taken into account.
– considering the equal weight to each word while computing the similarity among the sentences are still missing.

The main objective of the paper is to develop a novel multi-document extractive text summarization model which can take care of the above limitations in an efficient manner by using a combined approach of modified harmonic mean (based on word similarity) and cohesion score of each sentence (based on sentence similarity) and to evaluate its performance on DUC datasets.

1.2 Contribution

The contributions of the paper can be summarized as follows.

i. The proposed approach considered the document as a sequence of words and deals with all the words separately in a sentence according to their semantic structure. It also includes all the stop-words because these words contain syntactic information that cannot be ignored when either the sentence is very lengthy or the text is very concise.

ii. To rank all the sentences in the final summary while giving equal algebraic treatment to each word of a sentence, a modified harmonic mean score is calculated for every word.

iii. In order to ensure a more information-rich summary at the end, the semantic similarity between every pair of sentences of each document is computed.

iv. The task of organizing the extracted data and presenting them in a coherent manner has not yet received the importance that it should. To avoid redundancy, the proposed method computes the cohesion score of each sentence, and based on these scores, it selects top m% sentences and discards the remaining one from the final summary. This generates a coherent summary at the end.

v. To arrange the sentences in the final summary as per their importance, a relative entropy-based technique is proposed, which uses *KL-divergence* method to give the required weightage to each sentence.

Experimental results on DUC datasets show that the proposed approach is more efficient than the existing conventional extractive text summarization approaches.

The paper is organized on the following lines: A precise technique to generate a concise summary from a corpus of documents is discussed in Sect. 2. Experimental work is carried out in Sect. 3. The conclusion of the proposed work with some future enhancements is discussed in Sect. 4.

2 Proposed Approach

Consider a corpus C of documents $D = \{d_1, d_2, d_3, \cdots, d_x\}$. In the beginning, all the documents of C are merged into a set called D_{large}. This merging of documents does not follow any particular order. Then D_{large} is divided into n sentences, i.e., set $S = \{s_1, s_2, s_3, \cdots, s_n\} \in C$. The following steps are used to generate a coherent summary from the corpus C.

1. Word similarity calculation:
   A database using WordNet [1] is created to compute the semantical similarity between every pair of words w_p and w_q of the corpus C. In the semantic database, the words are arranged in a hierarchical structure where a set of similar words constitute a concept (also called synsets), and each concept is represented as a node in the hierarchy as shown in Fig. 1. The '$\cdots$' indicates some more synonym words of a node. The version of WordNet used

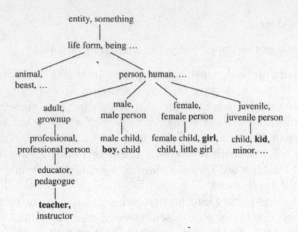

Fig. 1. Hierarchical semantic net

in the proposed work is WordNet 3.0, which has 206,941 words, organized into 117,659 synsets. A public .Net framework called WordNet.Net[1] is used to extract the information from WordNet. In order to find the similarity between a pair of words $sim(w_p, w_q)$, the minimum (or shortest) path length between the two synsets containing w_p and w_q is computed. For instance, the shortest path between the words 'girl' and 'kid' in Fig. 1 is 4, i.e., girl-female-person-juvenile-kid. The synset 'person' is called the subsumer (which is generally close to the root of the hierarchy) of the words 'girl' and 'kid'. But the minimum path length is not sufficient to find the similarity between two words. For example, the minimum path length between the words 'girl' and 'teacher' is 6, while it is 4 between 'girl' and 'animal'. This does not mean that 'girl' is more similar to 'animal' than 'teacher'. To handle such problem, in addition to 'minimum path length', 'depth of the concept' (or subsumer) in the hierarchical structure is also required to compute. Hence, $sim(w_p, w_q)$ can be a function of minimum path length (min_path) and depth of the subsumer ($depth\_sub$) in the hierarchy and is represented in Eq. 1.

$$sim(w_p, w_q) = function(f_1(min\_path), f_2(depth\_sub)) \qquad (1)$$

a. Computing minimum path length:
   While computing the minimum path length between a pair of words w_p and w_q, there can be three scenarios, and that can be handled on the following lines:
   i. w_p and w_q are in the same concept: in this case, a semantic path length of 0 is assigned between them because they have the same meaning.

---

[1] http://en.wikipedia.org/wiki/Brown_Corpus.

ii. w_p and w_q do not belong to the same concept, but their corresponding concepts consist of one or more common words: in this case, the similar words are partially shared by both the concepts and hence a semantic path length of 1 is assigned.

iii. w_p and w_q neither belong to the same concept nor their corresponding concept share any common words: in this case, the minimum path length between the two concepts containing each word is computed by 'max-similarity' algorithm [14] using Pywsd[2], which take care of 'word sense disambiguation' problem.

Considering the above three scenarios, the $f_1(min\_path)$ of Eq. 1 is set to be a monotonically decreasing function as shown in Eq. 2.

$$f_1(min\_path) = e^{-\alpha(min\_path)} \tag{2}$$

where α is a constant and $\alpha \in [0, 1]$, and it determines the contribution of the path to the overall similarity of the pair of words. As α increases, so does the contribution of path length.

b. Computing the depth of the subsumer:

The subsumer's depth is computed by counting the levels from the subsumer to the top of the hierarchical net. In the hierarchy, words at the upper layers have more general meaning and less semantic concepts compared to the words at the lower layers. This behavior needs to be taken into consideration while computing the similarity. Hence, it is required to scale up the $sim(w_p, w_q)$ for subsuming words at the lower layers and scale down the $sim(w_p, w_q)$ for subsuming words at the upper layers. This indicates $f_2(depth\_sub)$ of Eq. 1 should be monotonically increasing function with respect to the $depth\_sub$ and shown in Eq. 3.

$$f_2(depth\_sub) = \frac{e^{\beta.depth\_sub} - e^{-\beta.depth\_sub}}{e^{\beta.depth\_sub} + e^{-\beta.depth\_sub}} \tag{3}$$

where β is a smoothing factor and $\beta \in [0, 1]$, and it determines the contribution of subsumer depth. Comparing to α of Eq. 2, when β increases, the relative contribution of subsumer depth decreases. When $\beta > \infty$, the word's depth in the hierarchy is not considered, and it is an extension of Shepard's law [15]. The ideal values of α and β are set to 0.2 and 0.46 respectively [16].

c. Finally, the semantic similarity between w_p and w_q is computed using Eq. 4.

$$sim(w_p, w_q) = $$
$$e^{-\alpha.min\_path} * \frac{e^{\beta.depth\_sub} - e^{-\beta.depth\_sub}}{e^{\beta.depth\_sub} + e^{-\beta.depth\_sub}} \tag{4}$$

The value of $sim(w_p, w_q) \in [0, 1]$.

---

[2] https://github.com/alvations/pywsd.

2. *Modified Harmonic mean based word score*:
   Harmonic mean cannot be calculated ignoring any words of a corpus. It gives equal weight to each word, and useful for qualitative data. This is why harmonic mean has much uses in machine learning such as for prediction of true positive and false positive rate, computation of F-measure etc. A ranking score with respect to the entire corpus is calculated for each word based on the modified Harmonic Mean (HM) formula is shown in Eq. 5.

$$HM_q = \frac{n-1}{\sum\limits_{p,p\neq q} \frac{1}{sim(w_p,w_q)+k}} \tag{5}$$

Over here, n represents the total number of words in the corpus, $sim(w_p, w_q)$ represents the similarity score between the pair of words w_p and w_q as shown in Eq. 4. We have taken a summation over all the pairs of words except the reflexive pair. k is a factor that must be added to every similarity score in the formula so as to make sure that even in the cases when the similarity scores between two words are zero, the score, when divided by 1, does not give an exception.

3. *Selection of representative words*:
   After computing the modified harmonic score of each word of the corpus C, top l% words[3] are selected as the representative words of the corpus C and stored in a list $List_{rep}$. Now cosine-similarity ($cos\text{-}sim$) between every sentence $s \in C$ and the list $List_{rep}$ is computed as shown in Eq. 6.

$$cos\text{-}sim(s, List_{rep}) = \frac{s.List_{rep}}{||s|| * ||List_{rep}||} \tag{6}$$

Those sentences whose cosine similarity score is more than 0.75 (See Footnote 3) are considered, and the remaining sentences are discarded from C. This way now the corpus size gets reduced.

4. *Sentence similarity calculation*:
   Next, the similarity calculation between each pair of sentences of the reduced corpus C is done using the following steps:
   i. Constructing a joint word set:
      To compute the similarity between a pair of sentences s_1 and s_2, first a joint set of words $J_s = \{w_1, w_2, w_3, \cdots, w_n\}$ is constructed, where each $w_k, k \in [1, n]$ is a distinct word of s_1 and s_2. This indicates J_s does not contain any common words between s_1 and s_2. J_s also contain function words because they contain syntactic information. word form is maintained as they appear in the sentence. For example, 'dog', 'dogs', 'mouse', and 'mice' are four distinct words and are all included in J_s.
   ii. Semantic sentence similarity:
      Initially, lexical semantic vector ($lsv_i, i \in [1, 2]$) of both sentences s_1 and s_2 is calculated. Each entry of lsv_i correspond to a word in J_s. To calculate

---

[3] decided by the experiment.

the $lsv_i, i = 1$ for s_1 (denoted as lsv_1), the following steps are used for each word $w \in J_s$. Before the process starts, a semantic vector sv is considered whose all entries are initialize to 0.

case a. If $w \in s_1$, then the corresponding entry in the sv is set to 1. This value will multiply with the square of the value of w from corpus statistics (discussed in step iii) and is shown in Eq. 7.

$$lsv_1 = sv * I(w)^2 \tag{7}$$

case b. If $w \notin s_1$, then a most similar word (denoted as $\overline{w}$) is found out in s_1 by comparing the semantic similarity between w and each word of s_1 (semantic similarity computed using Eq. 4). If the similarity exceeds a per-determined threshold value (See Footnote 3), then the corresponding entry in the $(sv)_i$ is set to the calculated similarity, else it is set to zero. Next, the value is multiplied with the value of w and $\overline{w}$ from the corpus statistics as shown in the Eq. 8.

$$lsv_1 = sv * I(w) * I(\overline{w}) \tag{8}$$

Similarly, the lexical semantic vector lsv_2 is computed for the sentence s_2 by setting all the entries of sv to 0 initially, and repeating case a and case b.

- The final value of the semantic sentence similarity is the cosine coefficient between lsv_1 and lsv_2 as shown in the Eq. 9.

$$sim(lsv_1, lsv_2) = \frac{lsv_1.lsv_2}{||lsv_1|| * ||lsv_2||} \tag{9}$$

The value of $sim(lsv_1, lsv_2) \subset [0, 1]$.

iii. Statistics of the Corpus:

Using the corpus C statistics, we can weigh the importance of different words in a sentence. This is very important, as we have to include the stop-words which have less importance corresponding to other words in a sentence as shown in Eq. 10.

$$I(w) = 1 - \frac{log(n + 1)}{log(N + 1)} \tag{10}$$

Here, n represents frequency of word w in C, N is total number of words in C, To avoid zero, n and N are increased by 1. $I(w)$ value is within the interval $[0, 1]$.

5. *Computing the cohesion score of each sentence*:

The cohesion score of each sentence with respect to the corresponding document (i.e., $s_j \in d_i$) is computed by finding the Euclidean distance between the sentence s_j and the centroid of the document d_i and is shown in Eq. 11.

$$coh(s_j) = ||(sc_i - s_j)|| \tag{11}$$

where sc_i represents the centroid of the document d_i and is computed using Eq. 12.

$$sc_i = \frac{\sum_{i=1}^{n} s_i}{n} \tag{12}$$

where n is the total number of sentences in the document d_i.

6. *Final summary list generation*
   Based on the *cohesion score* of each sentence (shown in Eq. 11), top m% sentences are selected and stored in a new list NL which constitute the final summary.

7. *Arrangement of the sentences in the final summary as per their importance*
   To arrange all the sentences of NL as per their importance (i.e., weight), a relative entropy-based technique is proposed, which is discussed below:
   – Probability of the word $w \in NL$ in a sentence s is shown in Eq. 13.

$$P(w|s) = \frac{term\text{-}frequency(w, s)}{|s|} \tag{13}$$

   – Similarly, the probability of $w \in NL$ in a document d is shown in Eq. 14.

$$P(w|d) = \frac{term\text{-}frequency(w, d)}{|d|} \tag{14}$$

A sentence s is assigned a weight based on its comparison with the document d. Comparison is done using KL-divergence (KLD) [17] of s with d as shown in the Eq. 15.

$$KLD(s, d) = \sum_{w} P(w|s) log(\frac{P(w|s)}{P(w|d)}) \tag{15}$$

The weight of the sentence s (denoted as $Weight_s$) is inversely proportional to $KLD(s, d)$ [17] and is computed using Eq. 16.

$$Weight_s = \frac{1}{KLD(s, d)} \tag{16}$$

The sentences are arranged as per their weights in the final summary NL and this constitutes the *system generated summary* of the corpus C.

2.1   Generating Extractive Gold Summaries

Sentences in a document can be classified as "Important" or "Not-Important". Sentences that contain valuable information are ideally labeled as "Important", and the ones which do not carry any valuable information are labeled as "Not-Important". Only the sentences that are labeled as "Important" are eligible to be a part of the summary of that document. The steps mentioned below discussed how the extractive gold summary gets generated from the four human written summaries of DUC dataset C_{duc}.

i) Each document $d \in C_{duc}$ are parsed sentence by sentence. Natural Language Toolkit[4] is used for this purpose.

ii) All the words of the four human written gold summaries are stored in a list L. For every sentence $s \in d$, the number of common words (say r) between s and L is computed where r varies from sentence to sentence.

iii) The value of r determines the score for the sentence s. After the scores of each sentence $s \in d$ are obtained, the sentences are ranked based on these scores and stored in a new list L'.

iv) Top m sentences are selected from L' which generates the extractive gold summary of d. To conduct the experiment, m value is considered as 5. In this way every document of C_{duc} received an extractive gold summary of 5 sentences.

3   Experimental Framework

For experimental purposes, (DUC)[5] datasets are used and Table 1 shows the description of these datasets.

Table 1. DUC dataset

Datasets	No. of sets	No. of docs	Avg. no. of sent per doc	Length of summary	Data source
DUC-2001	30	298	28.1	100	TREC-9
DUC-2002	59	566	32.55	100	TREC-9
DUC-2006	50	1249	30.22	250	AQUAINT
DUC-2007	45	1124	37.51	250	AQUAINT

3.1   ROUGE-N Score Evaluation

Most extractive ATS researches use ROUGE [18] as the standard evaluation metric for measuring the correctness of summaries. ROUGE includes a set of metrics to evaluate extractive ATS. ROUGE metrics are designed to measure the similarity, i.e., the overlap of n-grams between the resulted (i.e., system generated summary) and reference summaries. Generally, researchers in the extractive ATS field compare their results against a reference summary. Generally, there are three main scores to evaluate the overlapping between words, which are Recall, Precision, and F1. Often, ATS researchers choose ROUGE-F1 to measure three ROUGE scores, which are ROUGE-1, to measure the overlap of unigrams, i.e., every single word, between the generated and reference summaries, ROUGE-2, to measure the overlap of bigrams, i.e., every two consecutive words, between the resulted and reference summaries, and ROUGE-SU4, an extension of ROUGE-S(Skip-Bigram co-occurrence statistics). For demonstration purposes, the cohesion scores (discussed in step 5 of Sect. 2) of 5 example sentences (randomly

---

[4] http://www.nltk.org/.

[5] http://www.duc.nist.gov.

selected) of a document of DUC-2002 dataset is shown in Table 2. The extractive and human-written summary scores on different DUC datasets are shown in Tables 3, 4, 5, 6, 7, 8, 9, 10, 11, 12, 13, 14, 15, 16, 17 and 18 respectively.

3.2   Performance Comparison on DUC-2002 Dataset

The ROUGE scores (average F-measure of extractive summary) using DUC-2002 dataset (on the entire 296 documents) are compared with the results of the five well established summary systems (*URANK* [19], *ILP* [20], *TGRAPH* [21], *NN_SE* [22], *TextRank* [23]). The ROUGE-1 and ROUGE-2 results are shown in the Figs. 2 and 3 respectively.

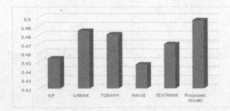

Fig. 2. ROUGE-1 (DUC-2002)   **Fig. 3.** ROUGE-2 (DUC-2002)

Table 2. D076B (DUC-2002)

Cohesion score	Sentence
0.47216	BEIJING, January 5 (Xinhua) A delegation from the Carter Center of the United States, led by Charles E Costello, director of the center's democracy program, arrived in Beijing this evening to observe the election of township level people's deputies
0.44545	Dr. Robert Pastor, who headed the center's two inspection delegations to China, said on his last trip, "Our entire delegation was impressed by what we saw and by the commitment of the villagers to have free and fair elections, by the competition, and by the sincerity with which the Chinese officials try to make this election successful"
0.43335	LAGOS, February 23 (Xinhua) Observers from the Organization of African Unity (OAU) and the European Union (EU) have commended the peaceful manner in Nigeria's National Assembly election and described the election as a qualified success, local press reported Tuesday
0.21524	That should be an instructive example for a youngish ex-president-to-be who is concerned about his own place in history
0.08779	Jimmy Carter, who was 52 when he was inaugurated in 1977, will turn 75 on Friday

Table 3. Extractive DUC-2001 (ROUGE-1)

Doc-no	Recall	Precision	F-measure
D01A	0.67470	0.16120	0.26022
D02A	0.77724	0.10197	0.18029
D03A	0.59951	0.29545	0.39583
D07B	0.50481	0.34426	0.40936
D09B	0.74463	0.08446	0.15171
D10B	0.53012	0.25611	0.34537
D16C	0.49412	0.39179	0.43704
D17C	0.54726	0.25287	0.34591
D18C	0.61071	0.32138	0.42114
D20D	0.55847	0.34412	0.42584
D21D	0.38517	0.44722	0.41388
D23D	0.56782	0.34306	0.42771
D25E	0.59268	0.15831	0.24987
D26E	0.42410	0.32001	0.36477
D29E	0.57518	0.33241	0.42133

Table 4. Human written DUC-2001 (ROUGE-1)

Doc-no	Recall	Precision	F-measure
D01A	0.44363	0.20841	0.28359
D02A	0.67545	0.23602	0.34981
D03A	0.49339	0.26794	0.34729
D07B	0.44161	0.19836	0.27376
D09B	0.66033	0.23525	0.34691
D10B	0.44467	0.25728	0.32596
D16C	0.46725	0.19963	0.27974
D17C	0.47535	0.15517	0.23397
D18C	0.59443	0.24584	0.34783
D20D	0.40270	0.21912	0.28381
D21D	0.31047	0.23889	0.27002
D23D	0.32176	0.19306	0.24132
D25E	0.67138	0.27818	0.39337
D26E	0.54741	0.23091	0.32481
D29E	0.50806	0.26069	0.34458

From the results, it can be seen that the proposed model is better compared to the above baseline models.

3.3 Performance Comparison on DUC-2006 Dataset

The ROUGE scores (average F-measure of extractive summary) of the proposed model on DUC-2006 dataset (on the entire 1250 documents) are compared with six of the well-known multi-document summarization techniques such as

Table 5. Extractive DUC-2002 (ROUGE-1)

Doc-no	Recall	Precision	F-measure
D070F	0.43272	0.74536	0.54756
D071F	0.44991	0.77818	0.57017
D072F	0.37161	0.86548	0.51996
D073B	0.47492	0.79913	0.59577
D074B	0.55002	0.75213	0.63539
D075B	0.20626	0.89594	0.33532
D076B	0.71322	0.72053	0.71686
D077B	0.74887	0.68652	0.71634
D078B	0.40891	0.85113	0.55243
D079A	0.33214	0.86333	0.47974
D080A	0.47538	0.74504	0.58042
D081A	0.78038	0.71554	0.74656
D082A	0.45230	0.75985	0.56706
D083A	0.47950	0.78655	0.59579
D084A	0.68774	0.68914	0.68844

Table 6. Human written DUC-2002 (ROUGE-1)

Doc-no	Recall	Precision	F-measure
D070F	0.46290	0.22784	0.30537
D071F	0.51104	0.26883	0.35233
D072F	0.47225	0.60595	0.53082
D073B	0.68564	0.32935	0.44496
D074B	0.59351	0.22409	0.32534
D075B	0.19081	0.64403	0.29438
D076B	0.76017	0.17863	0.28927
D077B	0.58570	0.13852	0.22404
D078B	0.54838	0.33602	0.41671
D079A	0.35295	0.57364	0.43702
D080A	0.51152	0.27371	0.35659
D081A	0.61164	0.13118	0.21603
D078A	0.54473	0.28927	0.37787
D083A	0.52238	0.22174	0.31133
D084A	0.57045	0.32260	0.41213

Table 7. Extractive DUC-2006 (ROUGE-1)

Doc-no	Recall	Precision	F-measure
D0601A	0.56146	0.23396	0.33029
D0602B	0.50803	0.18031	0.26616
D0603C	0.55950	0.20181	0.29662
D0605E	0.48726	0.16758	0.24939
D0607G	0.54989	0.20156	0.29499
D0608H	0.53110	0.18317	0.27239
D0609I	0.53791	0.26928	0.35889
D0610A	0.72646	0.16829	0.27327
D0611B	0.46495	0.07593	0.13053
D0612C	0.49941	0.22496	0.31019
D0613D	0.68871	0.13661	0.22801
D0615F	0.68379	0.18473	0.29088
D0617H	0.72119	0.29372	0.41743
D0618I	0.39050	0.19786	0.26264
D0619A	0.46398	0.25795	0.33157

Table 8. Human written DUC-2006 (ROUGE-1)

Doc-no	Recall	Precision	F-measure
D0601A	0.68898	0.08076	0.14457
D0602B	0.58103	0.11069	0.18596
D0603C	0.64528	0.10264	0.17711
D0605E	0.58635	0.07996	0.14072
D0607G	0.57143	0.10895	0.18301
D0608H	0.66805	0.08856	0.15639
D0609I	0.65432	0.18861	0.29282
D0610A	0.74118	0.05570	0.10362
D0611B	0.54801	0.05227	0.09544
D0612C	0.63095	0.08516	0.15007
D0613D	0.64876	0.08579	0.15154
D0615F	0.84362	0.05473	0.10278
D0617H	0.62948	0.11961	0.20102
D0618I	0.57769	0.19385	0.29029
D0619A	0.74104	0.10954	0.19087

Table 9. Extractive DUC-2007 (ROUGE-1)

Doc-no	Recall	Precision	F-measure
D0715A	0.54534	0.11413	0.18876
D0716A	0.58368	0.20607	0.30458
D0717A	0.51668	0.23307	0.32125
D0718A	0.55702	0.21626	0.31158
D0726B	0.49162	0.17401	0.25704
D0727B	0.30195	0.24291	0.26922
D0728B	0.51428	0.25863	0.34418
D0729B	0.79961	0.15010	0.25278
D0731C	0.38977	0.29898	0.33838
D0732C	0.67521	0.29780	0.41331
D0733C	0.46971	0.26006	0.33478
D0734C	0.47485	0.20707	0.28837
D0726D	0.44699	0.24967	0.32038
D0727D	0.59543	0.27757	0.37863
D0728D	0.54276	0.22413	0.31725

Table 10. Human written DUC-2007 (ROUGE-1)

Doc-no	Recall	Precision	F-measure
D0715A	0.73704	0.05486	0.10211
D0716A	0.67703	0.08787	0.15558
D0717A	0.44532	0.28572	0.34808
D0718A	0.71312	0.17921	0.28643
D0726B	0.61509	0.13159	0.21679
D0727B	0.48607	0.38487	0.42959
D0728B	0.49408	0.35921	0.41598
D0729B	0.76385	0.07789	0.14136
D0731C	0.60078	0.31341	0.41193
D0732C	0.76379	0.13692	0.23221
D0733C	0.63877	0.28189	0.39114
D0734C	0.62452	0.19246	0.29424
D0726D	0.67968	0.11084	0.19059
D0727D	0.58121	0.18062	0.27559
D0728D	0.61088	0.19124	0.29127

Table 11. Extractive DUC-2001 (ROUGE-2)

Doc-no	Recall	Precision	F-measure
D01A	0.12270	0.05760	0.07840
D02A	0.27298	0.09533	0.14131
D03A	0.16556	0.08982	0.11646
D07B	0.13553	0.06076	0.08390
D09B	0.20380	0.07257	0.10703
D10B	0.17137	0.09907	0.12555
D16C	0.14474	0.06168	0.08650
D17C	0.13428	0.04373	0.06597
D18C	0.21429	0.08846	0.12523
D20D	0.14363	0.07806	0.10115
D21D	0.09420	0.07242	0.08189
D23D	0.10441	0.06259	0.07826
D25E	0.26299	0.10887	0.15399
D26E	0.22944	0.09654	0.13590
D29E	0.17790	0.09116	0.12055

Table 12. Human written DUC-2001 (ROUGE-2)

Doc-no	Recall	Precision	F-measure
D01A	0.15676	0.03341	0.05508
D02A	0.27224	0.03209	0.05742
D03A	0.17473	0.07784	0.10771
D07B	0.08356	0.05090	0.06327
D09B	0.26738	0.02708	0.04918
D10B	0.14054	0.06061	0.08469
D16C	0.12533	0.08972	0.10458
D17C	0.13333	0.05524	0.07811
D18C	0.22554	0.10641	0.14460
D20D	0.17439	0.09426	0.12237
D21D	0.07219	0.07521	0.07367
D23D	0.14139	0.07650	0.09928
D25E	0.18733	0.04433	0.07169
D26E	0.06648	0.04372	0.05275
D29E	0.16757	0.08564	0.11335

Table 13. Extractive DUC-2002 (ROUGE-2)

Doc-no	Recall	Precision	F-measure
D070F	0.26547	0.45739	0.33596
D071F	0.30685	0.53083	0.38889
D072F	0.26915	0.62704	0.37662
D073B	0.34113	0.57411	0.42796
D074B	0.37892	0.51823	0.43775
D075B	0.17577	0.76434	0.28579
D076B	0.46162	0.46633	0.46396
D077B	0.50025	0.45861	0.47853
D078B	0.31702	0.66006	0.42831
D079A	0.26957	0.70093	0.38937
D080A	0.29129	0.45658	0.35567
D081A	0.57446	0.52674	0.54957
D082A	0.29048	0.48813	0.36422
D083A	0.32334	0.53046	0.40177
D084A	0.41051	0.41135	0.41092

Table 14. Human written DUC-2002 (ROUGE-2)

Doc-no	Recall	Precision	F-measure
D070F	0.11553	0.05652	0.07588
D071F	0.12378	0.06472	0.08498
D072F	0.13555	0.17273	0.15192
D073B	0.22112	0.10551	0.14287
D074B	0.17938	0.06728	0.09787
D075B	0.07698	0.25508	0.11705
D076B	0.30041	0.07012	0.11368
D077B	0.16445	0.03863	0.06254
D078B	0.15735	0.09581	0.11908
D079A	0.07857	0.12687	0.09704
D080A	0.09777	0.05197	0.06789
D081A	0.13406	0.02857	0.04708
D082A	0.11667	0.06157	0.08058
D083A	0.07638	0.03217	0.04529
D084A	0.12334	0.06923	0.08869

Table 15. Extractive DUC-2006 (ROUGE-2)

Doc-no	Recall	Precision	F-measure
D0601A	0.18404	0.07664	0.10821
D0602B	0.17105	0.06065	0.08955
D0603C	0.17573	0.06330	0.09307
D0605E	0.11324	0.03890	0.05791
D0607G	0.18511	0.06776	0.09920
D0608H	0.16933	0.05834	0.08678
D0609I	0.14252	0.07126	0.09501
D0610A	0.23057	0.05336	0.08667
D0611B	0.12881	0.02099	0.03610
D0612C	0.12857	0.05788	0.07982
D0613D	0.30387	0.06014	0.10041
D0615F	0.17606	0.04753	0.07485
D0617H	0.32030	0.13030	0.18525
D0618I	0.09788	0.04953	0.06578
D0619A	0.12301	0.06836	0.08788

Table 16. Human written DUC-2006 (ROUGE-2)

Doc-no	Recall	Precision	F-measure
D0601A	0.11489	0.01247	0.02249
D0602B	0.15319	0.02713	0.04609
D0603C	0.21032	0.03183	0.05529
D0605E	0.08155	0.01041	0.01846
D0607G	0.10684	0.01947	0.03294
D0608H	0.20524	0.02587	0.04594
D0609I	0.18103	0.04988	0.07821
D0610A	0.25103	0.01798	0.03356
D0611B	0.10612	0.00992	0.01815
D0612C	0.17031	0.02090	0.03723
D0613D	0.13974	0.01750	0.03110
D0615F	0.39316	0.02457	0.04624
D0617H	0.22222	0.03939	0.06692
D0618I	0.14768	0.04685	0.07114
D0619A	0.26582	0.03712	0.06515

Table 17. Extractive DUC-2007 (ROUGE-2)

Doc-no	Recall	Precision	F-measure
D0715A	0.15176	0.03174	0.05250
D0716A	0.17048	0.06014	0.08892
D0717A	0.18437	0.08290	0.11437
D0718A	0.18882	0.07321	0.10551
D0726B	0.20434	0.07221	0.10671
D0727B	0.07481	0.06012	0.06666
D0728B	0.18965	0.09511	0.12669
D0729B	0.36748	0.06886	0.11599
D0731C	0.13207	0.10125	0.11462
D0732C	0.25002	0.11016	0.15294
D0733C	0.18844	0.10421	0.13421
D0734C	0.12606	0.05489	0.07648
D0726D	0.13471	0.07520	0.09651
D0727D	0.23428	0.10905	0.14883
D0728D	0.18344	0.07560	0.10707

Table 18. Human written DUC-2007 (ROUGE-2)

Doc-no	Recall	Precision	F-measure
D0715A	0.28152	0.01986	0.03713
D0716A	0.16666	0.02073	0.03686
D0717A	0.17502	0.10554	0.13167
D0718A	0.22945	0.05465	0.08827
D0726B	0.16308	0.03228	0.05391
D0727B	0.12972	0.09811	0.11172
D0728B	0.14816	0.10376	0.12204
D0729B	0.22781	0.02222	0.04048
D0731C	0.18931	0.09505	0.12656
D0732C	0.24474	0.04097	0.07019
D0733C	0.22985	0.09581	0.13524
D0734C	0.21993	0.06464	0.09992
D0726D	0.22448	0.03506	0.06065
D0727D	0.21365	0.06251	0.09672
D0728D	0.23771	0.07074	0.10903

CTMSUM [24], IIITH-Sum [25], OnModer [26], TopicalN [27], SFU_v36 [28], and RMSUM [29]. The comparison details are shown in Figs. 4, 5 and 6 respectively. Results demonstrate that ROUGE-2 score of the proposed model is either comparable or less than CTMSUM and IIITH-sum model. ROUGE-1 and ROUGE-SU4 scores are better compared to all the models. This shows the effectiveness of the proposed approach.

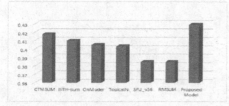

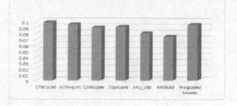

Fig. 4. ROUGE-1 (DUC-2006)   **Fig. 5.** ROUGE-2 (DUC-2006)

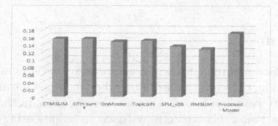

Fig. 6. ROUGE-SU4 (DUC-2006)

Table 19. Summary readability methods

Readability method	Formula
Flesch kincaid grade level (FKGL)	0.39 * (words/sentences) + 11.8 * (syllables/words) − 15.59
Coleman liau (CL)	5.89 * (characters/words) − 0.3 * (sentences/words) − 15.8
Automated readability index (ARI)	4.71 * (characters/words) + 0.5 * (words/sentences) − 21.43

3.1 Performance Comparisons Using Summary Readability

Summary readability says how better others can read and understand the system
generated summary, which is affected by many parameters like the density of a
sentence, length and weight of a sentence, number of title words in a sentence,
etc. [30]. Many statistical methods are available to compute the summary readability [31], and the proposed approach used some of them as shown in Table 19.
The high the score, the better is the system generated summary for easy reading
and understanding. Based on these statistical methods, the proposed approach
is compared with other baseline approaches using DUC2002 and 2006 datasets,
and the results are shown in Figs. 7 and 8 respectively.

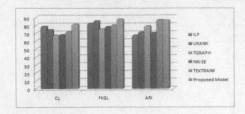
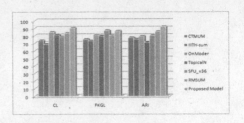

Fig. 7. Summary readability comparison (DUC-2002)

Fig. 8. Summary readbility comparison (DUC-2006)

4   Conclusion

This paper proposed a novel approach to summarize multi-documents of a given corpus by combining the word similarity based on modified harmonic mean with sentence similarity based on cohesion score. The sentences in the final summary are arranged based on a relative entropy-based technique using KL-divergence. The summarization technique is extractive in nature. The experimental work of the proposed approach is carried out using different DUC datasets. Empirical results on DUC-2002 and DUC-2006 datasets show the effectiveness of the proposed approach compared to the conventional approaches. This work can be improved further by achieving a more grammatically coherent and information-rich summary using the abstractive text summarization technique. A possible step towards achieving fully abstractive summarization would be to reduce the size of the summary units (sentences in the present case) to phrases that are smaller than sentences. It is possible to extract the key phrases using a similar technique. It can then connect these key phrases using a set of predefined grammar rules to form summaries that can be more dense content-wise compared to the ones generated by the proposed method.

References

1. Miller, G.A.: WordNet: a lexical database for English. Commun. ACM **38**(11), 39–41 (1995)
2. Gambhir, M., Gupta, V.: Recent automatic text summarization techniques: a survey. Artif. Intell. Rev. **47**(1), 1–66 (2016). https://doi.org/10.1007/s10462-016-9475-9
3. Roul, R.K., Arora, K.: A nifty review to text summarization-based recommendation system for electronic products. Soft. Comput. **23**(24), 13183–13204 (2019). https://doi.org/10.1007/s00500-019-03861-3
4. Wang, L., Yao, J., Tao, Y., Zhong, L., Liu, W., Du, Q.: Proceedings of the 27th International Joint Conference on Artificial Intelligence, IJCAI 2018, pp. 4453–4460 (2018)
5. Roul, R.K., Sahoo, J.K., Goel, R.: Deep learning in the domain of multi-document text summarization. In: Shankar, B.U., Ghosh, K., Mandal, D.P., Ray, S.S., Zhang, D., Pal, S.K. (eds.) PReMI 2017. LNCS, vol. 10597, pp. 575–581. Springer, Cham (2017). https://doi.org/10.1007/978-3-319-69900-4_73

6. Roul, R.K., Joshi, P.M., Sahoo, J.K.: Abstractive text summarization using enhanced attention model. In: Tiwary, U.S., Chaudhury, S. (eds.) IHCI 2019. LNCS, vol. 11886, pp. 63–76. Springer, Cham (2020). https://doi.org/10.1007/978-3-030-44689-5_6
7. Luhn, H.P.: The automatic creation of literature abstracts. IBM J. Res. Dev. **2**(2), 159–165 (1958)
8. Elbarougy, R., Behery, G., Khatib, A.E.: Graph-based extractive Arabic text summarization using multiple morphological analyzers. J. Inf. Sci. Eng. **36**(2), 347–367 (2020)
9. Wang, D., Zhu, S., Li, T., Chi, Y., Gong, Y.: Integrating document clustering and multidocument summarization. ACM Trans. Knowl. Discov. Data (TKDD) **5**(3), 1–26 (2011)
10. Abdi, A., Shamsuddin, S.M., Hasan, S., Piran, J.: Machine learning-based multi-documents sentiment-oriented summarization using linguistic treatment. Expert Syst. Appl. **109**, 66–85 (2018)
11. Suanmali, L., Salim, N., Binwahlan, M.S.: Feature-based sentence extraction using fuzzy inference rules. In: 2009 International Conference on Signal Processing Systems, pp. 511–515. IEEE (2009)
12. Roul, R.K.: Topic modeling combined with classification technique for extractive multi-document text summarization. Soft. Comput. **25**(2), 1113–1127 (2020). https://doi.org/10.1007/s00500-020-05207-w
13. Roul, R.K., Mehrotra, S., Pungaliya, Y., Sahoo, J.K.: A new automatic multi-document text summarization using topic modeling. In: Fahrnberger, G., Gopinathan, S., Parida, L. (eds.) ICDCIT 2019. LNCS, vol. 11319, pp. 212–221. Springer, Cham (2019). https://doi.org/10.1007/978-3-030-05366-6_17
14. Pedersen, T., Banerjee, S., Patwardhan, S.: Maximizing semantic relatedness to perform word sense disambiguation, vol. 25, p. 2005. Research report UMSI 2005/25. University of Minnesota Supercomputing Institute (2005)
15. Shepard, R.N.: Toward a universal law of generalization for psychological science. Science **237**(4820), 1317–1323 (1987)
16. Erkan, G., Radev, D.R.: LexRank. graph-based lexical centrality as salience in text summarization. J. Artif. Intell. Res. **22**, 457–479 (2004)
17. Kumar, C., Pingali, P., Varma, V.: A light-weight summarizer based on language model with relative entropy. In: Proceedings of the 2009 ACM Symposium on Applied Computing, pp. 1752–1753 (2009)
18. Lin, C.-Y.: ROUGE: a package for automatic evaluation of summaries. In: Text Summarization Branches Out: Proceedings of the ACL-2004 Workshop, vol. 8, pp. 74–81 (2004)
19. Wan, X.: Towards a unified approach to simultaneous single-document and multi-document summarizations. In: Proceedings of the 23rd International Conference on Computational Linguistics, pp. 1137–1145. Association for Computational Linguistics (2010)
20. Woodsend, K., Lapata, M.: Automatic generation of story highlights. In: Proceedings of the 48th Annual Meeting of the Association for Computational Linguistics, pp. 565–574. Association for Computational Linguistics (2010)
21. Parveen, D., Ramsl, H.-M., Strube, M.: Topical coherence for graph-based extractive summarization. In: Proceedings of the 2015 Conference on Empirical Methods in Natural Language Processing, pp. 1949–1954 (2015)
22. Cheng, J., Lapata, M.: Neural summarization by extracting sentences and words. In: Proceedings of the 54th Annual Meeting of the Association for Computational Linguistics, pp. 484–494 (2016)

23. Mihalcea, R., Tarau, P.: TextRank: bringing order into text. In: Proceedings of the 2004 Conference on Empirical Methods in Natural Language Processing, pp. 404–411 (2004)
24. Yang, G., Wen, D., Chen, N.-S., Sutinen, E., et al.: A novel contextual topic model for multi-document summarization. Expert Syst. Appl. **42**(3), 1340–1352 (2015)
25. Jagarlamudi, J., Pingali, P., Varma, V.: Query independent sentence scoring approach to DUC 2006. In: Proceeding of Document Understanding Conference (DUC-2006) (2006)
26. Ye, S., Chua, T.-S., Kan, M.-Y., Qiu, L.: Document concept lattice for text understanding and summarization. Inf. Process. Manag. **43**(6), 1643–1662 (2007)
27. Wang, X., McCallum, A., Wei, X.: Topical n-grams: phrase and topic discovery, with an application to information retrieval. In: Seventh IEEE International Conference on Data Mining (ICDM 2007), pp. 697–702. IEEE (2007)
28. Melli, G.: Description of SQUASH, the SFU question answering summary handler for the DUC-2006 summarization task. Safety **1**, 14345754 (2006)
29. Zhai, C., Lafferty, J.: A study of smoothing methods for language models applied to ad hoc information retrieval. In: ACM SIGIR Forum, vol. 51, no. 2, pp. 268–276. ACM (2017)
30. Zamanian, M., Heydari, P.: Readability of texts: state of the art. Theory Pract. Lang. Stud. **2**(1), 43–53 (2012)
31. Klare, G.R.: Assessing readability. Read. Res. Quarter. **10**(1), 62–102 (1975)

Multi-channel Deep Model for Classification of Alzheimer's Disease Using Transfer Learning

Sriram Dharwada, Jitendra Tembhurne[✉], and Tausif Diwan

Department of Computer Science and Engineering, Indian Institute of Information Technology, Nagpur 441108, India
jtembhurne@iiitn.ac.in

Abstract. In this paper, we perform the classification of Alzheimer's disease (AD) using 3D structural magnetic resonance imaging (sMRI) images through 2D convolutional neural networks (CNNs). Most existing methods that use 2D convolutional neural networks for AD classification, extract 2D image slices from each 3D MRI scan along the three anatomical planes of view of the brain. A CNN is trained separately on images from each plane of view. However, these methods only consider images from one plane of view at a time which leads to loss of 3D information. We address this issue by proposing a novel way of using an ensemble of multi-channel convolutional neural networks wherein, given a location in the brain, a multi-channel model looks at images from all three planes of view at a time around that location to obtain 3D information from 2D images. Multiple such locations from the brain are considered, and ensemble learning is used to give predictions at a subject level. Transfer learning is adopted wherein each channel in the multi-channel network utilizes state-of-the-art pre-trained CNNs, customized to the classification task. The proposed model obtains 98.33% accuracy for the Alzheimer's disease (AD) vs Cognitively Normal (CN) classification task, outperforming current state-of-the-art methods.

Keywords: Alzheimer's disease · Deep learning · Multi-channel model · Transfer learning · 2D CNN

1 Introduction

Alzheimer's disease is a chronic irreversible neurological disease that wreaks havoc on memory and other cognitive abilities [3, 4]. It is the most prevalent cause of dementia, which is characterized by a progressive loss of cognitive, behavioural, and social abilities that impairs a person's capacity to operate freely [3]. Although, it is not possible to undo the initial pathological changes, it is essential to give diagnosis as early and accurately as possible. In some cases, early diagnosis of the disease or risk of disease is beneficial so that the individual and their families have time to make decisions and plan for the future, as well as to provide access to medicines that can help manage symptoms [4].

Since the gradual deterioration of the brain structures and volume change in characteristic locations can be detected in Magnetic Resonance Imaging (MRI) scans, they

© Springer Nature Switzerland AG 2022
R. Bapi et al. (Eds.): ICDCIT 2022, LNCS 13145, pp. 245–259, 2022.
https://doi.org/10.1007/978-3-030-94876-4_17

have been used extensively for the early diagnosis of AD [5, 6]. Latest trends in the current literature show that the deep learning methods i.e. CNNs are very efficient in classifying subjects with Alzheimer's disease. Since neuroimaging provides 3D MRI scans, and there is information from all three views of the brain in a single scan, 3D CNNs have become quite mainstream. They take as input, either the whole 3D MRI scan, or a particular 3D Region-of-Interest (ROI). However, taking the whole scan as a single input, results in high feature dimensionality and makes training computationally expensive. Choosing predefined ROIs is not without issues. The abnormal tissue arising due to AD can take up a very small part of a pre-defined ROI, or it can span over multiple ROIs. Thus, leads to a loss of discriminative information [14].

2D CNNs are a great alternative to 3D CNNs for AD classification. They are computationally inexpensive to train and no requirement for ROI identification. Instead of the whole 3D MRI scan, they use 2D slices as an input. Thus, the resulting network is simplified, and consists of a very few number of parameters. But, by far the best advantage that they offer over 3D CNNs is Transfer Learning (TL) which caters specifically to 2D images. TL has demonstrated to be amazing for cross-domain classification problems, for example, networks which are trained on natural images utilized for classification of medical images. 2D CNNs that employ TL have extensively been used for AD detection and have been known to significantly decrease training time and improve accuracy compared to 3D CNNs [19].

Even though 2D CNNs are easier to train, and can support TL, they are not efficient in encoding the spatial information of the 3D images due to the absence of kernel sharing across the third dimension [27]. To overcome this limitation, in this paper, we propose the methodology – given a particular location in the brain, we take into consideration, in parallel, three perpendicular planes of view that pass through that point, before making a decision. These three planes of view are called Coronal (x-y plane), Axial (z-x plane) and Sagittal (y-z plane) planes in the MRI literature. Thus, we propose a multi-channel neural network with three channels – one for each of the brain's three planes of view. Projections from each one of the three planes about a point in the brain act as inputs for each of the three channels. First, each channel extracts features from its respective plane of view. These features are concatenated in parallel at some point, later, these features are passed to a softmax activation all within the same model. This lets the model not only learn information from the three planes of view about a point in the brain individually, but also learn the relationship between the three planes of view about that point. Multiple such multi-channel models are trained for multiple intersection points in the brain. These intersection points are selected intelligently so as to gain maximum information from the brain, using image entropy. An ensemble of all these multi-channel models, each trained to predict on one intersection point in the brain, utilized to finally offer good accuracy at a subject level.

Pre-trained models are employed as a base and customization is applied for all the three channels. A variety of popular and latest pre-trained CNN architectures such as InceptionV3 [7], ResNet50 [10], and DenseNet121 [8] have been used for this purpose. We have experimented with numerous combinations of these architectures on the three channels, as well as the optimal number of intersection points in the brain to maximize the accuracy for AD classification. We used sMRI scans provided by the Alzheimer's Disease Neuroimaging Institute (ADNI) [1].

Our main contributions are two folds:

1. A novel end-to-end multi-channel framework that factors in all three views of an MRI scan is proposed for the detection of AD.
2. Although, each channel has a different view of the brain as an input source, we show that through TL, and concatenating the feature maps from the three channels at the right time, the model is able to learn the relationship between the three planes of views very well.

The remainder of this paper is divided as follows: We review related work in Sect. 2. Then in Sect. 3, we provide a detailed explanation of our method. The results and their discussion are provided in Sect. 4. Section 5 summarizes and concludes our work.

2 Related Works

Many studies in the literature have made use of deep learning approaches to build classifiers using medical imaging data, primarily in the form of MRI, and clinical measures for the diagnosis of Alzheimer's Disease.

Korolev *et al.* [15] readapted the classical architectures VGGNet [9] and ResNet [10] to 3D MRI. Both of the readapted architectures obtained similar results, and set a baseline accuracy of 80% on the AD vs CN classification task using the ADNI dataset. Network attention areas for a CN subject were generated to find areas most affected by AD. Recently, 3D CNN was utilized by Xia *et al.* [16], used six layer 3D CNN to learn informative features, and then leveraged a 3D Convolutional Long Short Term Memory (3DCLSTM) layer to further extract the channel-wise higher-level information. Further, authors adopted Grad-CAM and plotted heatmaps to find out the regions with critical importance in diagnosing AD. Subsequently, Long Short Term Memory (LSTM) networks were applied for AD detection by Feng *et al.* [17] wherein a 3D CNN is employed to extract features from both MRI and Positron Emission Tomography (PET) modalities, and extracted high level semantic and spatial information from the output of the 3D CNN using fully stacked bi-directional LSTM. Oh *et al.* [18] developed an inception module based 3D convolutional autoencoder for the AD classification task. Unsupervised learning was first performed extract a sparse visual representation of neuroimaging data. Supervised fine-tuning was applied later to build the AD vs CN classifier. Unsupervised pre-training improved the accuracy by 10.85% compared to training from scratch for the AD vs CN task.

However, it should be noted that 3D CNN approaches are extremely cost intensive. Better results can be obtained by using 2D CNNs with reduced model complexity and reduced training time. For instance, Xing *et al.* [19] were able to improve the accuracy obtained by a baseline 3D CNN approach on the AD vs CN task by 9.5% and with only 20% of its training time by using a 2D CNN pre-trained on the ImageNet dataset [12] indicating the high effectiveness of 2D CNNs as compared to 3D CNNs. In [20], TL by pre-training on ImageNet was performed earlier, and adapted pre-trained VGG16

[9] and InceptionV4 [8] architectures to AD classification by using 2D image slices from the OASIS dataset [2]. The 32 most informative scans were taken from the axial plane of each 3D scan. The accuracy of 96.25% is reported on AD vs CN task, and demonstrated that even with a small training dataset, and without training the entire deep model from scratch, TL can help to achieve highly accurate classification of AD. On the same dataset, Maqsood *et al.* [21] fine-tuned an ImageNet pre-trained AlexNet [11] to perform multiclass AD classification tasks. The last three layers of AlexNet were replaced with a SoftMax, fully connected and output classification layer in order to extract class specific features of the OASIS dataset, and able to attain 92.8% multiclass accuracy.

Another TL method utilized 2D image slices is proposed by Islam *et al.* [22]. MRI scans were taken from the ADNI dataset, sliced into 2D images along the coronal planes, and passed to DenseNet architecture pre-trained on ImageNet dataset. Wang *et al.* [28] employed TL by first pretraining an expedited CNN on the OASIS dataset. This pre-trained model was then repurposed for the Mild Cognitive Impairment (MCI) vs CN classification task with subjects from the ADNI dataset. Pre-training on OASIS improved the accuracy by 9.2%. In addition, data augmentation is adopted to deal with limited training data.

Choi *et al.* [23] created an ensemble of 2D deep CNNs for AD detection where the weights of each deep CNN member were optimized by designing a deep ensemble generalization loss which takes into consideration the interaction and cooperation between the deep CNNs.

An ensemble of 2D CNNs for AD detection was also employed by Pan et al. [29]. For each view of the brain, authors created sets wherein each set composed of a single slice from that view of the brain from the training subjects. Multiple such sets corresponding to multiple slices from a particular view were created, and a 2D CNN classifier was trained on each set of each view. From each view, an ensemble classifier composed of the 5 best performing classifiers was created. Finally, another ensemble classifier was built on top of the three single-view ensemble classifiers using max-voting to give the final subject-level prediction.

Aderghal *et al.* [24] proposed a model to focus on only a few slices of the hippocampal region of the brain and combined features from sMRI and Diffusion Tensor Imaging (DTI) modalities using images from the ADNI dataset. Authors obtained an accuracy of 92.3% by using LeNet architecture, and a combination of two TL schemes: 1) cross-modal TL between sMRI and DTI brain images, and 2) cross-domain TL from MNIST dataset [13] to medical brain scans.

Nonetheless, it should be noted that 2D CNN approaches are limited to a single channel, i.e., a single view of the brain. They do not take into account the 3D information of the MRI scan. In contrary to all these approaches, we propose a multi-channel ensemble model that makes a decision on a subject after taking into account all three planes of view of the brain from intelligently selecting intersection points of the brain.

3   Methods and Materials

In this section, we present the methodology includes data collection, pre-processing, slice selection, multi-channel network architecture, and proposed ensemble of multi-channel networks.

3.1   Data Selection

For our work, we used sMRI data from [1]. Specifically, T1-weighted MRI data from the ADNI1: Annual 3 Yr 1.5T dataset is utilized. Within this dataset, MRI scans that are already reviewed for quality and Gradient inhomogeneity correction (Gradwarp), B1 non-uniformity corrected and N3 processed (to reduce residual intensity non-uniformity) are chosen. A total of 327 subjects (150 AD and 177 CN) are MRI scans that fit this criterion. Out of these 327 subjects, 300 subjects (150 AD and 150 CN) are randomly selected. Moreover, one MRI scan is utilized per subject.

3.2   Data Preprocessing

All the MRI scans belong to the ADNI database and go through three phases of preprocessing before being utilized as an input for the proposed deep model. Initially, all the scans are of dimensions $256 \times 256 \times 166$.

Phase 1: The raw scans contain non-brain areas such as the neck, nose, skull, etc. in which we are not interested. The first step is to remove these areas by performing cortical reconstruction using the recon-all-autorecon1 function provided by the Freesurfer tool. This function performs the following five transformations on the scans – 1) Motion Correction and Conform, 2) NU (Non-Uniform intensity normalization), 3) Talairach transform computation, 4) Intensity Normalization 1, and 5) Skull Strip. After this phase of pre-processing, skull-stripped MRI scans of dimensions $256 \times 256 \times 256$ are obtained.

Phase 2: Depending upon the position of the head of the subject, the type of scanner and coils used, there can be differences in size and how the images are aligned. Thus, affine registration is adopted to translate, rotate, zoom and shear one image to match it with another. All images are registered with the MNI152 T1 template MRI scan. Registration has been done using the "nibabel" and "dipy" libraries in Python. After this phase, scans are consistent in shape, position and alignment, with dimensions of $182 \times 218 \times 182$.

Phase 3: In order to save memory without compromising the classification, and retaining enough slices from each view, all the MRI scans are downsampled to $112 \times 112 \times 112$ as suggested by Suk et al. [30].

Because, the brain is a 3D structure, any location in the brain can be localized using three planes - Sagittal, Coronal and Axial. After preprocessing, each MRI scan is a 3D image of dimensions $112 \times 112 \times 112$. Thus, we have 112, 2D slices from each of the three planes of view.

3.3 Slice Selection

From each pre-processed scan, 'N' 2D slices are selected from each view, around the corresponding view's most informative slice. From a given view, the slice with the highest entropy has the most variation and can be considered the most informative slice of that view [20]. The Shannon entropy [31] of an image can be defined as:

$$H = - \sum_{i=1}^{n} p_i \times \log_2 p_i$$

where n is the number of gray levels and pi is the probability of a pixel in the image having gray level i.

For each subject, we first calculate the image entropy of every slice from all three views using Shannon entropy. For each view, the slice that has highest Shannon entropy the most number of times over all the subjects is selected as the most informative slice.

We call the most informative slice from the Sagittal view as MI_S, the most informative slice from the Coronal view as MI_C, and the most informative slice from the Axial view as MI_A. Ultimately, we select slices − 1) MI_S - $floor(N/2)$ to $MI_S + ceil(N/2) − 1$ from the Sagittal view, 2) MI_C - $floor(N/2)$ to $MI_C + ceil(N/2) − 1$ from the Coronal view, and 3) MI_A - $floor(N/2)$ to $MI_A + ceil(N/2) − 1$ from the Axial view. Here, $floor(x)$ represents the greatest integer $\leq x$, and $ceil(x)$ defines the greatest integer $\geq x$. This yields a total of N slices around each view's most informative slice. Figure 1 shows the image slices belonging to Sagittal, Coronal and Axial views of two MRI scans after preprocessing.

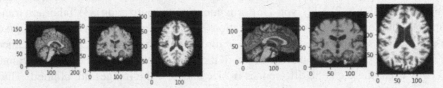

Fig. 1. Slices from the Sagittal, Coronal and Axial views of two MRI scans after pre-processing.

3.4 Multi-channel Network Architecture

Each channel utilizes a CNN pre-trained on the ImageNet dataset [12], initially. The input shapes for the Coronal, Axial and Sagittal base models are set to (142, 142, 3), (178, 142, 3) and (178, 142, 3), moreover, the topmost classification layer of each base model is removed. We define a 'BN-D-DP-BN' block as a sequence of a Batch Normalization layer, a Dense Layer of 64 units, a Dropout layer of 0.5 and another Batch Normalization layer (more details see Fig. 2).

Each pre-trained model is connected to a BN-D-DP-BN block. The outputs of each BN-D-DP-BN block are concatenated, and passed to another BN-D-DP-BN block before being passed to a softmax layer. The BN-D-DP-BN blocks are added to learn, to turn the old features of the pre-trained models into predictions on the current classification

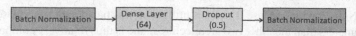

Fig. 2. A BN-D-DP-BN block.

task. Figure 3 show the architecture of the proposed multi-channel model for AD classification. By using this architecture, efficient features from Sagittal, Coronal and Axial are combined to perform the final classification task.

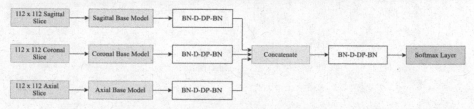

Fig. 3. Proposed multi-channel architecture for AD classification.

From Fig. 3, we depict that each channel learns 2D information of its respective plane of view for a particular location. When feature maps from all the three channels are concatenated, the network learns the relationship between the three views about a particular location. Essentially, the model learns 3D information from 2D slices.

The following three pre-trained networks are utilized as base CNN models corresponding to Sagittal, Coronal and Axial image slices features' extraction. In addition, we can depict the network architecture of InceptionV3, ResNet, and DenseNet in Fig. 4.

1. InceptionV3 [7] is a CNN network from the Inception family built by Google. It introduced a regularizing component called label smoothing to prevent overfitting, 7×7 convolutions that factorized into smaller symmetric and asymmetric convolutions, and Batch Normalization in the auxiliary classifiers.

2. The ResNet architecture [10] has won the ImageNet contest in 2015 and demonstrated the possibility to greatly improve the depth of the network while having fast convergence. Authors, observed that with an increase in network depth, accuracy gets saturated, and then degrades rapidly. To overcome this, residual or skip connections is introduced to provide an alternative pathway for data and gradients to flow. ResNet50 model consists of 5 stages with the last 4 stages consisting of a stack of residual blocks. Each residual block consists of a stack of layers where the activation from a previous layer gets added with the activation of a deeper layer in the block, through a skip connection.

3. When CNNs get deeper, the path between input and output becomes so big that information vanishes as it reaches the other side. DenseNet [9] is an architecture developed to solve this problem and provide maximum information flow in very deep neural networks, by using shorter connections. DenseNet121, Densenet160, and DenseNet210 are the different architectures in the DenseNet family. Each variant of the DenseNet architecture is composed of a stack of 'Dense Blocks' in which each layer adds features on top of existing feature maps through concatenation.

DenseNet121 with 4 Dense Blocks, is utilized in this paper as it has a lesser number of parameters than the other two architectures, and is thus relatively computationally inexpensive.

Moreover, Table 1 shows the number of parameters utilized in InceptionV3, ResNet50 and DenseNet121 at the time of model training.

For each multi-channel model, different combinations of these three pre-trained CNNs are utilized as base models to the three channels to maximize accuracy.

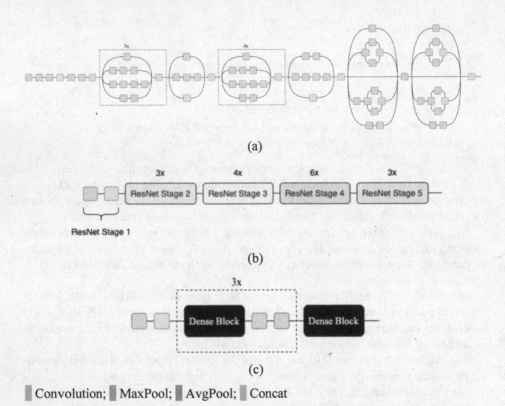

(a)

(b)

(c)

▌Convolution; ▌MaxPool; ▌AvgPool; ▌Concat

Fig. 4. Network architectures of the three base models - (a) InceptionV3, (b) ResNet50, (c) DenseNet121 with the topmost classification layers removed.

Table 1. Number of parameters for each base model

	InceptionV3	ResNet50	DenseNet121
Total parameters	21,802,784	23,564,800	7,037,504
Trainable parameters	21,768,352	23,519,360	6,953,856
Non-trainable parameters	34,432	45,440	83,648

3.5 Ensemble of Multi-channel Model

For any particular subject, there are N input features:

[(MI_S - $floor(N/2)$ + i)th Sagittal slice, (MI_C - $floor(N/2)$ + i)th Coronal slice, (MI_A − $floor(N/2)$ + i)th Axial slice], $0 \leq i < N$.

Every input feature is a location in the brain or an 'intersection point' that can be observed from three different views. The N such input features for one subject give such N locations or intersection points in that subject's brain. Each point is incrementally diagonal i.e. no two locations are on the same plane. This gives us three distinct planes of view for each intersection point.

Corresponding to each of N intersection points, N multi-channel models are first trained individually, and a max-voting ensemble of N models is composed to give predictions at a subject level.

Figure 5 shows an ensemble classifier is composed on top of N multi-channel models, each trained on its respective intersection point, to provide predictions for a single subject.

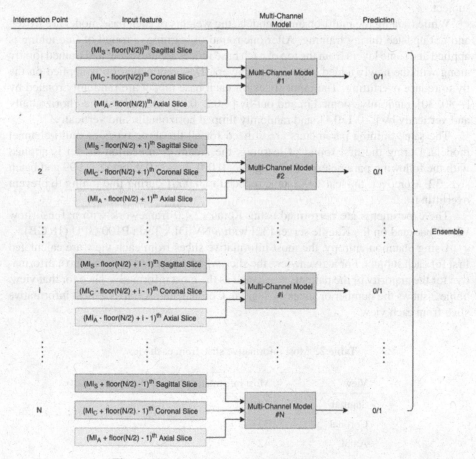

Fig. 5. Proposed framework of ensemble approach.

4   Results and Discussions

As aforementioned, 150 subjects with Alzheimer's Disease and 150 subjects who are Cognitively Normal are considered and N images from each of the three views are taken from each subject as one input feature. The hold-out method is applied to obtain the results, with 80% of the data used for training, and 20% of the data utilized for testing. The 10% of the training data is used as a validation dataset. The split is made at a subject level, and not at a slice/feature level, thus avoiding any data leakage.

The train-validation-test split yields, 108 train subjects, 12 validation subjects, and 30 test subjects. Corresponding to each of N intersection points, N datasets are created with each dataset containing 108 training features, 12 validation features, and 30 testing features, and a single multi-channel model is trained on each of N datasets. To give predictions at a subject level, predictions are made on each of N intersection points by the corresponding multi-channel model, and the predictions which we get from the majority of the models (max-voting ensemble) are utilized as the final prediction for that subject.

While training the multi-channel models, the weights of each base model are frozen and not updated during training. After one round of learning, a round of fine tuning is applied and some layers from the top of each base model are unfrozen, and trained jointly along with the newly added classification layers. Data augmentation is applied on the fly to reduce overfitting. The input slices for each base model are randomly rotated by $[-30, 30]$, randomly zoomed in and out by $[-0.2, 0.2]$, randomly shifted horizontally and vertically by $[-0.1, 0.1]$, and randomly flipped horizontally and vertically.

The same training parameters are utilized for all the three types of multi-channel models. During the first round of learning, the Adam optimization model is applied with the following parameters – learning rate: 0.001, beta1: 0.9, beta2: 0.999 and batch size: 32. Moreover, the learning rate is reduced to 0.0001 during fine tuning to prevent overfitting.

The experiments are performed using Keras v2.4.0 framework with a Tensorflow v2.4.2 backend on the Kaggle server [32] with a NVIDIA Tesla P100 GPU (16 GB).

Using Shannon entropy, the most informative slices from each view are calculated first for each subject. For a given view, the slice which happened to be the most informative for the majority of the patients is selected as the most informative slice for that view. Table 2 shows the number of slices of Sagittal, Coronal, and Axial as a most informative slice from each view.

Table 2. Most informative slice from each view.

View	Most informative slice
Sagittal	48
Coronal	73
Axial	42

4.1 Effect of Base Models and Optimal Value of N

We consider InceptionV3 (IV3), ResNet50 (R50) and DenseNet121 (D121) as base pre-trained models to the three channels. All possible combinations of these base models are experimented with various values of N (i.e. 3, 5, 10, 15, and 20), to determine the optimal number of intersection points, and the best combination of the pre-trained models.

Results obtained by the top 5 best performing multi-channel ensembles along with the 5 different values of N are shown in Table 3.

Table 3. Performance of top 5 multi-channel models with different values of N.

Coronal base model	Axial base model	Sagittal base model	No. of intersection points (N)	Accuracy	Precision	Recall	F1-Score
D121	R50	I3	3	91.66	91.71	91.66	91.66
			5	95.00	95.05	95.00	94.99
			10	91.66	91.71	91.66	91.66
			15	95.00	95.05	95.00	94.99
			20	95.00	95.05	95.00	94.99
R50	R50	I3	3	90.00	90.00	90.00	90.00
IRV2	D121	IRV2	5	96.66	96.87	96.66	96.66
IRV2	IRV2	D121	10	93.33	93.52	93.33	93.32
IRV2	D121	D121	15	95.00	95.05	95.00	94.99
IRV2	D121	IRV2	20	95.00	95.05	95.00	94.99
D121	D121	D121	3	91.66	91.71	91.66	91.66
			5	96.66	96.87	96.66	96.66
			10	95.00	95.45	95.00	94.98
			15	95.00	95.45	95.00	94.98
			20	95.00	95.45	95.00	94.98
R50	R50	D121	3	93.33	93.52	93.33	93.32
			5	96.66	96.87	96.66	96.66
			10	91.66	92.85	91.66	91.60
			15	96.66	96.87	96.66	96.66
			20	95.00	95.45	95.00	94.98
D121	R50	D121	3	96.66	96.87	96.66	96.66
			5	**98.33**	98.38	98.33	98.33
			10	96.66	96.87	96.66	96.66
			15	98.33	98.38	98.33	98.33
			20	96.66	96.87	96.66	96.66

The highest accuracy of 98.33% is obtained by setting the number of intersection points to 5, and applying DenseNet121, ResNet50, and DenseNet121 as the Sagittal, Coronal and Axial base models, respectively, and we choose this combination as our proposed model. Moreover, the training and validation of accuracy and loss for the proposed multi-channel model for its best performing intersection point is presented in Fig. 6.

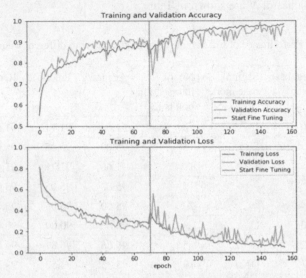

Fig. 6. Training and Validation Accuracy, and Loss for the best performing intersection point of the proposed model.

It is observed that the optimal number of intersection points as defined in Sect. 3.4 is 5. From Fig. 7, we can depict that the accuracy increases with an increase in N, peaks at $N = 5$, and does not increase with a further increase in N. Even though, a similar accuracy is achieved with $N = 15$ and $N = 20$, model training time for these is far greater than the training with $N = 5$ (4085 s), as 10 and 15 more multi-channel models need to be trained for $N = 15$ (12032 s) and $N = 20$ (16113 s) as compared to $N = 5$.

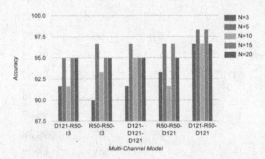

Fig. 7. Influence of N on top 5 best performing models.

The results of this model are compared with state-of-the-art methods [15–27]. From Table 4, we depict that our models outperforms the existing models based on the accuracy and other performance metrics, thus, shows the usefulness of our models.

Table 4. Comparison with existing models for AD *vs* CN classification.

Ref.	Dataset	Classifier	Accuracy (%)
[15]	ADNI	VoxResNet	80
[18]	ADNI	Inception module based CAE	86.60
[25]	ADNI	2D CNN SqueezeNet (TL) + LSTM	90.62
[19]	ADNI	2D CNN + Attention Mechanism	92
[26]	ADNI	LSTM	92.2
[24]	ADNI	Two level TL on 2D CNN (LeNet)	92.3
[21]	OASIS	2D CNN AlexNet (TL)	92.8
[27]	ADNI	Multi Modal 3D CNN	93.26
[23]	ADNI	Ensemble of 2D CNNs with optimal fusion weights	93.15
[16]	ADNI	3D CNN + 3D CLSTM	94.19
[17]	ADNI	3D CNN and FSBi LSTM	94.82
[22]	ADNI	2D CNN DenseNet121 (TL)	94.97
[20]	OASIS	2D CNN Inception V4 (TL)	96.25
Our	ADNI	Multi-Channel Ensemble of 2D CNNs	98.33

5 Conclusion

In this paper, using ADNI dataset, we proposed a novel multi-channel ensemble 2D CNN model for the diagnosis of AD wherein each channel takes as input images from one of the three views of the brain. Prior works employed 2D CNNs and failed in considering the fact of spatial relationship from 3D MRI scans. Given an intersection point in the brain, our proposed model takes into account all three views of the brain around that point, and efficiently learns the relationship between these three brain views and preserves this spatial relationship. The most informative 2D slices from each view are selected using image entropy. The number of intersection points and combination of base models are experimented extensively. The proposed model uses pre-trained DenseNet121, ResNet50, and DenseNet121 as a base models for the Sagittal, Coronal, and Axial channels, respectively and performing an ensemble over 5 intersection points of the brain. Our model outperforms state-of-the-art models for AD classification and reported the highest accuracy of 98.33%. In future work, we plan to integrate other modalities such as PET scans to construct multi-modal networks for AD classification, and take into account intermediate stages of AD for multiclass classification tasks.

References

1. http://adni.loni.usc.edu/. Accessed 21 Feb 2021
2. https://www.oasis-brains.org/. Accessed 21 Feb 2021
3. Alzheimer's disease - Symptoms and Causes. https://www.mayoclinic.org/diseases-condit ions/alzheimers-disease/symptoms-causes/syc-20350447. Accessed 10 Feb 2021
4. Jill, R., Langerman, H.: Alzheimer's disease - why we need early diagnosis. Degenerative Neurol. Neuromuscul. Dis. **9**, 123–130 (2019). https://doi.org/10.2147/DNND.S228939
5. Keith, A., et al.: Brain imaging in Alzheimer disease. Cold Spring Harb. Perspect. Med. **2**(4), a006213 (2012). https://doi.org/10.1101/cshperspect.a006213
6. Alzheimer Disease - Radiology Reference Article. https://radiopaedia.org/articles/alzheimer-disease-1. Accessed 10 Feb 2021
7. Szegedy, C., et al.: Inception-v4, Inception-ResNet and the Impact of Residual Connections on Learning, In: AAAI (2017)
8. Huang, G., Liu, Z., Weinberger, K.Q.: Densely connected convolutional networks. In: IEEE Conference on Computer Vision and Pattern Recognition (CVPR), pp. 2261–2269. IEEE (2017)
9. Simonyan K., Zisserman, A.: Very deep convolutional networks for large-scale image recognition. CoRR, abs/1409.1556 (2015)
10. He, K., et al.: Deep residual learning for image recognition. IEEE Conference on Computer Vision and Pattern Recognition (CVPR), pp. 770–778. IEEE (2016)
11. Krizhevsky, A., et al.: ImageNet classification with deep convolutional neural networks. Neural Information Processing Systems, 25, 1097−1105 (2012). https://doi.org/10.1145/306 5386
12. Deng, J., et al.: ImageNet: a large-scale hierarchical image database. In: IEEE conference on computer vision and pattern recognition, pp. 248–255, IEEE (2009). https://doi.org/10.1109/ CVPR.2009.5206848
13. LeCun, Y., Cortes, C.: MNIST handwritten digit database (2010)
14. Liu, M., et al.: Anatomical landmark based deep feature representation for MR images in brain disease diagnosis. IEEE J. Biomed. Health Inform. **22**(5), 1476–1485 (2018)
15. Korolev, S., et al.: Residual and plain convolutional neural networks for 3D brain MRI classification. In: IEEE 14th International Symposium on Biomedical Imaging (ISBI 2017), pp. 835–838. IEEE (2017)
16. Xia, Z., et al.: A novel end-to-end hybrid network for Alzheimer's disease detection using 3D CNN and 3D CLSTM. In: IEEE 17th International Symposium on Biomedical Imaging (ISBI), pp. 1–4. IEEE (2020). https://doi.org/10.1109/ISBI45749.2020.9098621
17. Feng, C., et al.: Deep learning framework for Alzheimer's disease diagnosis via 3D-CNN and FSBi-LSTM. IEEE Access **7**, 63605–63618 (2019). https://doi.org/10.1109/ACCESS.2019. 2913847
18. Oh, K., et al.: Classification and visualization of Alzheimer's disease using volumetric convolutional neural network and transfer learning. Sci. Rep. **9**, 18150 (2019). https://doi.org/10. 1038/s41598-019-54548-6
19. Xing, X., et al.: Dynamic Image for 3D MRI Image Alzheimer's Disease Classification. ArXiv, abs/2012.00119 (2020)
20. Hon, M., et al.: Towards Alzheimer's disease classification through transfer learning. In: IEEE International Conference on Bioinformatics and Biomedicine (BIBM), pp. 1166–1169. IEEE (2017)
21. Maqsood, M., et al.: Transfer learning assisted classification and detection of Alzheimer's disease stages using 3D MRI scans. Sensors (Basel, Switzerland) **19**(11), 2645 (2019). https:// doi.org/10.3390/s19112645

22. Islam, J., Zhang, Y.: Deep convolutional neural networks for automated diagnosis of Alzheimer's disease and mild cognitive impairment using 3D Brain MRI. In: Wang, S., et al. (eds.) BI 2018. LNCS (LNAI), vol. 11309, pp. 359–369. Springer, Cham (2018). https://doi.org/10.1007/978-3-030-05587-5_34

23. Choi, J.Y., Lee, B.: Combining of multiple deep networks via ensemble generalization loss, based on MRI images, for Alzheimer's disease classification. IEEE Signal Process. Lett. **27**, 206–210 (2020). https://doi.org/10.1109/LSP.2020.2964161

24. Karim, A., et al.: Improving Alzheimer's stage categorization with Convolutional Neural Network using transfer learning and different magnetic resonance imaging modalities. Heliyon **6**(12), e05652 (2020). https://doi.org/10.1016/j.heliyon.2020.e05652

25. Ebrahimi-Ghahnavieh, A., Luo, S., Chiong, R.: Transfer Learning for Alzheimer's Disease Detection on MRI Images. In: IEEE International Conference on Industry 4.0, Artificial Intelligence, and Communications Technology (IAICT), pp. 133–138. IEEE, (2019). https://doi.org/10.1109/ICIAICT.2019.8784845

26. Hong, X., et al.: Predicting Alzheimer's Disease Using LSTM. IEEE Access **7**, 80893–80901 (2019). https://doi.org/10.1109/ACCESS.2019.2919385

27. Liu, M., et al.: Multimodality cascaded convolutional neural networks for Alzheimer's disease diagnosis. Neuroinformatics **16**, 295–308 (2018)

28. Wang, S., Shen, Y., Chen, W., Xiao, T., Hu, J.: Automatic recognition of mild cognitive impairment from MRI images using expedited convolutional neural networks. In: Lintas, A., Rovetta, S., Verschure, P.F.M.J., Villa, A.E.P. (eds.) ICANN 2017. LNCS, vol. 10613, pp. 373–380. Springer, Cham (2017). https://doi.org/10.1007/978-3-319-68600-4_43

29. Pan, D., et al.: Early detection of Alzheimer's disease using magnetic resonance imaging: a novel approach combining convolutional neural networks and ensemble learning. Front. Neurosci. **14**, 259 (2020)

30. Suk, H.I., et al.: Hierarchical feature representation and multimodal fusion with deep learning for AD/MCI diagnosis. Neuroimage **101**, 569–582 (2014)

31. Shannon, C.E.: A mathematical theory of communication. Bell Syst. Tech. J. **27**(3), 379–423 (1948)

32. Kaggle: Your Home for Data Science. https://www.kaggle.com/. Accessed 08 Jul 2021

Deep Learning and Linguistic Feature Based Automatic Multiple Choice Question Generation from Text

Rajat Agarwal[1]([✉]), Vaishnav Negi[2], Akshat Kalra[3], and Ankush Mittal[4]

[1] Indraprastha Institute of Information Technology, Delhi, India
rajata@iiitd.ac.in
[2] Graphic Era University, Clement Town, Dehradun 248002, India
[3] College of Engineering Roorkee, Roorkee, India
[4] Raman Classes, Roorkee 247667, India

Abstract. Multiple Choice Questions (MCQs) feature more and more in modern-day assessments due to more straightforward exams and faster checking. However, with this comes the challenge of creating a diverse pool of MCQs specific to a given subject matter. This work proposes an MCQ generation system that uses linguistic features and Deep Learning techniques to create MCQs from a given text. The entire process has three steps: i) The pre-trained DL state-of-the-art model summarizes a text paragraph to get relevant information. ii) Linguistic features generate question (stem) and answer (key) pairs. iii) Distractor generation using the key or correct answer. DL-based paraphrasing models are used to augment the MCQs dataset with questions of similar type and difficulty level.

Keywords: MCQ generation · Question answer system · Deep learning · Text linguistic features

1 Introduction

The rise of e-learning technologies has immensely facilitated education, but also poses a challenge for the people involved in assessment due to the compounded effect of a large number of examinees to be assessed at once; a lack of variation in the questions compared to prior assessments; and finally, it being a tedious task to manually delve into subject literature to formulate a sufficient number of questions. All these factors led to the research in computer-aided systems to generate questions.

Natural Language Processing (NLP) has been the obvious choice to tackle the problem of Automatic Question Generation (AQG). However, with the popularisation and increased accessibility of Machine Learning and Deep Learning,

---

V. Negi and A. Kalra—Equal contribution.

R. Bapi et al. (Eds.): ICDCIT 2022, LNCS 13145, pp. 260–264, 2022.
https://doi.org/10.1007/978-3-030-94876-4_18

these are being employed to gain novel perspectives in AQG. Still many challenges persist [7], making this problem riveting and one worth exploring.

Moving on, MCQs are easier to administer and evaluate than essay-type questions, and are thus explicitly used in mass and online testing scenarios. This work also focuses on auto generation of MCQs for a given text. Some important terminologies regarding MCQs are:

1. **Stem/Question-Sentence**: precedent that the question relies on, containing sufficient information for an examinee to figure out the correct answer.
2. **Key**: correct answer to the question posed by the stem.
3. **Distractors**: set of alternatives present with the key, contextually and semantically close to the key to deter guessing by the examinee while also being unambiguously wrong.

This paper aims at outlining a pipeline for the generation of interrogative type MCQ questions and proposes a method to increase the obtained question pool by leveraging paraphrasing techniques.

2 Related Work

One of the best, most comprehensive, and recent survey papers is [5]. Some other essential survey papers that we came across are [6] and [7]. [5] discusses not only the prominent research done in the field but also outlines a generic workflow for how MCQs are to be generated from a text.

Dhole et al. [4] have developed a rule-dependent framework SynQG, for producing questions by outlining brief answers using dependency trees, semantic roles identified for predicates' verb arguments, named entities, state of various actors over time, and by verb-specific semantic-roles assigned to the participants.

Bhatia et al. [8] creates a reference set of sentences by replacing the 'Wh phrases' with the first option in existing MCQs, which is used to find potential stems and keys, for a given text input. For distractor generation, an attribute set is created using tabular data on Wikipedia, for a key. Wikipedia is again searched for related candidates from the same category as the key using modifiers from the attribute set.

Majumder et al. [1] improve the sentence selection used by [8] using various preprocessing techniques. The parse trees in the reference set and the parse trees of input text are compared for finding stems, identifying the key in a candidate stem, question formation from the stem, and the generation of distractors.

Santhanavijayan et al. [3] devise a system to collect relevant text for a user-specified domain. A fireflies-based preference learning summarization is applied to the collected text, to filter informative sentences. Keys are found using POS tagging and a preference mechanism for identified POS tags. Distractors are produced using metrics of similarity (hyponyms and hypernyms).

3 Methodology

The MCQ generation system, is compartmentalized to perform various sub-tasks associated with the system. Figure 1 depicts its workflow.

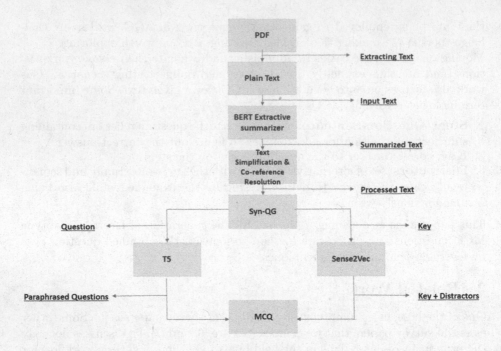

Fig. 1. Basic workflow for the MCQ generation process used in this paper.

3.1   Extraction

At first, the user provides a pdf file as input from which text is extracted using Pypdf. It is a pure-Python library built as a PDF toolkit. Some of its capabilities that are required for a question generation system are extracting document information and splitting documents page by page.

3.2   Summarization

The system utilizes BERT Extractive Summarizer [11] to summarize the text. It parses the meaning by consolidating the relevant sentences, as well as reduces the number of irrelevant sentences.

Coreference resolution and sentence simplification are applied to the sentences extracted by BERT, as it extracts complex and compound sentences, that are inappropriate for further processes. NeuralCoref, a pipeline extension for spaCy based on [13], is employed for coreference resolution while Multilingual Unsupervised Sentence Simplification (MUSS) [9] is used for sentence simplification.

3.3   SynQG

The SynQG framework by Dhole et al. [4] generates numerous question-answer pairs from a single statement using universal dependencies, shallow semantic parsing, lexical resources, and custom rules. SynQG modifies the argument of each predicate into the form of semantic roles, according to a predefined set of rules. It also identifies the named entity and other generic entities that are part of the statement.

3.4 Distractor Generation

In MCQs, distractors are incorrect answers that obfuscate the correct answer to make the examinee think about the study material. This is done by finding words that are conceptually close or belong to the same category as the key. Sense2Vec [10] (with automatically compiled lexicons from a text corpus) is used for the generation of distractors.

3.5 Paraphrasing

Sometimes it is advantageous to use paraphrased questions to have a set of similar questions with equal difficulty. We are using the text to text transfer transformer (T5) [12] model to achieve this. Unlike BERT models that only either produce a class label or a span of an input, T5 input and output are always text strings.

4 Experiments and Results

Regarding human evaluation, two predominant approaches exist. [8] uses domain relevance, quality of the selected key, question formation, level of information provided by the question, 'distractors' closeness to key, etc. as parameters. On the other hand, [1] only asked the evaluators if the questions were 'good' or 'not good'.

For this paper, evaluators are only asked to mark questions as 'pass' or 'fail' based on their understanding of the passage provided while being mindful of factors like grammar, semantics, contextual closeness to input text, distractor quality, the difficulty of the questions, and naturalness (if questions look human enough). Evaluators' response is collected via Google forms and success rate is calculated for each assessor as follows:

$$Success\,percentage = \frac{Number\,of\,questions\,passed}{Total\,number\,of\,questions} \tag{1}$$

50 human assessors participated in the evaluation, wherein they are provided a text from a high school history textbook, followed by 25 MCQs from the same text. The average success rate for the aforementioned text is **77.14** %, as per Eq. 1.

5   Conclusion

Most of the prior works used blank question types as they are easier to generate and yield higher accuracy, but we target generating simple interrogative questions or 'Wh' question type MCQs. First input text is summarized. Coreference resolution and sentence simplification are applied to the obtained summary to get stems. SynQG took these stems as input to yield question-answer couplets, for which distractors were generated using Sens2vec. Some of these questions were paraphrased using a T5 Transformer to augment the question pool. Human evaluators then evaluated the system using high school history texts. After a thorough analysis of the evaluation results, it can be concluded that the accuracy of the model can be improved by better pre-processing of the input texts and enhancing the SynQG model to recognize a variety of sentence structures. Summarization can also be improved to recognize more informative and complete sentences.

References

1. Majumder, M., Saha, S.K.: A system for generating multiple choice questions: with a novel approach for sentence selection. In: Proceedings of the 2nd Workshop on Natural Language Processing Techniques for Educational Applications (2015)
2. Faizan, A., Lohmann S.: Automatic generation of multiple choice questions from slide content using linked data. In: Proceedings of the 8th International Conference on Web Intelligence, Mining and Semantics (2018)
3. Santhanavijayan, A., et al.: Automatic generation of multiple choice questions for e-assessment. Int. J. Sig. Imag. Syst. Eng. **10**(1–2), 54–62 (2017)
4. Dhole, K.D., Manning, C.D.: Syn-QG: syntactic and shallow semantic rules for question generation. arXiv preprint arXiv:2004.08694 (2020)
5. Ch, D.R., Saha, S.K.: Automatic multiple choice question generation from text: a survey. IEEE Trans. Learn. Technol. **13**(1), 14–25 (2018)
6. Kurdi, G., et al.: A systematic review of automatic question generation for educational purposes. Int. J. Artif. Intell. Educ. **30**, 121–204 (2020)
7. Das, B., Majumder, M., Phadikar, S., Sekh, A.A.: Automatic question generation and answer assessment: a survey. Res. Pract. Technol. Enhan. Learn. **16**(1), 1–15 (2021). https://doi.org/10.1186/s41039-021-00151-1
8. Singh Bhatia, A., Kirti, M., Saha, S.K.: Automatic generation of multiple choice questions using wikipedia. In: Maji, P., Ghosh, A., Murty, M.N., Ghosh, K., Pal, S.K. (eds.) PReMI 2013. LNCS, vol. 8251, pp. 733–738. Springer, Heidelberg (2013). https://doi.org/10.1007/978-3-642-45062-4_104
9. Martin, L., et al.: MUSS: multilingual unsupervised sentence simplification by mining paraphrases. arXiv preprint arXiv:2005.00352 (2020)
10. Trask, A., Michalak, P., Liu, J.: sense2vec - A Fast and Accurate Method for Word Sense Disambiguation In Neural Word Embeddings. arXiv eprint arxiv:1511.06388 (2015)
11. Miller, D.: Leveraging BERT for extractive text summarization on lectures. CoRR abs/1906.04165 (2019)
12. Raffel, C., et al.: Exploring the limits of transfer learning with a unified text-to-text transformer. arXiv eprint arxiv:1910.10683 (2020)
13. Clark, K., Manning, C.D.: Deep reinforcement learning for mention-ranking coreference models. arXiv eprint arXiv:1609.08667 (2016)

A Deep Multi-kernel Uniform Capsule Approach for Hate Speech Detection

Vipul Shah[1]([✉]), Amey Bhole[2], Sandeep S. Udmale[1], and Vijay Sambhe[1]

[1] Department of Computer Engineering and Information Technology,
Veermata Jijabai Technological Institute (VJTI), Mumbai 400019, Maharashtra, India
vpshah_m19@ce.vjti.ac.in, {ssudmale,vksambhe}@it.vjti.ac.in
[2] Faculty of Science and Engineering, University of Groningen, Bernoulliborg,
Nijenborgh 9, 9747AG Groningen, The Netherlands

Abstract. Hate Speech is an expression that expresses hatred towards people of a specific ethnic group or nationality and incites hatred. Even though many countries have anti-hate speech legislation, hate speech can spread in the native language on social media platforms, resulting in violent riots and protests that spiral out of control and result in anti-social events. Hence, hate speech has caused a crucial social issue. Thus, various intelligent mechanisms have been employed to classify hate speech, depending on the category. A deep learning model has certain limitations for providing n-gram features for text classification of the native language. As a result, in this paper, the Multi-kernel uniform capsule network for multilingual languages is proposed. The proposed method employs a Multi-kernel uniform capsule network to improve feature selection performance by utilizing the capsule network routing algorithm. The experiments were carried out on political, COVID-19 and vaccination, lockdown, and multilingual dataset. The experimental results demonstrate that the proposed methods achieve adequate results when compared with other machine learning models for hate speech detection.

Keywords: Capsule network · COVID-19 · Hate speech · Lockdown · Multilingual · US election · Vaccination

1 Introduction

The popularity and the user's growth on social websites are increasing day by day. Social networking websites provide a platform for every user to express their sentiments and share readily attainable comments through the Internet [4,7]. There are numerous advantages to utilizing social media to unite people, bring people together, and serve businesses which are developing faster every day. Nevertheless, it has drawbacks; this technology increases cyberhate and hateful content about a particular group or a person which spread rapidly [6]. Recently, we have also been able to post on social media sites in our native language. As the usage of social networking websites grows in each country, cyberhate attracts the attention of researchers and those working in multilingual domain. Thus, we need

© Springer Nature Switzerland AG 2022
R. Bapi et al. (Eds.): ICDCIT 2022, LNCS 13145, pp. 265–271, 2022.
https://doi.org/10.1007/978-3-030-94876-4_19

to stop hate speech in all native languages around the world. According to the research literature, biased people can spread hatred content, who have negative sentiments toward some communities, minority groups, characteristics, women, etc. Hence, these hateful messages directly impact the victims and their families [6]. Certain events, such as cyberhate propaganda, racist communications, and comment threads on social networking websites, are usually enough to start a chain reaction [1,4,7]. Therefore hate speech detection is essential in order to stop hate crimes.

2   Related Work

In 2021, a BERT code mixed algorithm was proposed to effectively detect hate speech. It focuses on code-mixed multilingual language and classifies with the help of the BERT model, in which necessary features have been selected for the BERT embedding approach [11]. After that, transformers and their variants method have originated to detect the ambiguous nature of data. Also, a Multi-channel uses BERT for English and Chinese language datasets with a multi-channel BERT model and illustrated trustworthy accuracy for hate speech classification [10]. Some researchers have offered a unique method of one-class type and focus on rumor detection over social media, as rumor can cause and propagate hate [3]. Hana et al. have created and developed a multi-label classification of Indonesian Hate speech with a support vector machine (SVM) to help identity and detection online public shaming. The SVM concept has been used to attain better results and simultaneously reduce computational time [5]. The code-switched text messages approach compares different feature word embedding techniques with word-level and character-level n-gram to check the accuracy of various multilingual languages [8]. Patricia et al. have classified English and French language abuse tweets using an attention mechanism using sentence embedding with bi-directional long short-term memory (LSTM) [2]. The proposed paradigm identifies the ambiguity in the sentence for a more reliable classification. Recently, researchers and developers have been employing the autoencoder (AE) to detect hate speech. Thus, deep learning AE-based hate speech detection has been performed to handle the ambiguous data for enhancing the performance [14]. Based on the above discussion, we can conclude that a single deep learning model cannot provide n-gram features for native language text classification. As a result, in this paper a the Multi-kernel capsule network for multilingual languages is proposed and evaluated on various datasets.

3   Methods

In this section, we describe the dataset and the proposed model in detail.

3.1   Data Sets

We use three types of data sets in this paper for hate speech detection. The monolingual data sets contain topics related to the 2020 US election (DS1),

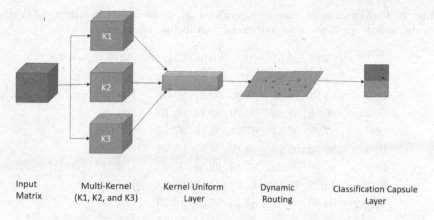

Fig. 1. Multi-Kernel uniform CapsNet

Indian Farms Act protest (DS2), Lockdown 2020 (DS3), Lockdown 2021 (DS4), and COVID-19 vaccinations (DS5) [9]. We use the three data sets published by Hate Speech and Offensive Content Identification in Indo-European Languages (HASOC 2019) [4,12,13] with Hindi (MDS1), English (MSD2), and German (MSD3) languages. To add another language, we also use a data set in the Korean (MSD4) language[1]. Besides, the mixture of three multilingual data sets, namely English-Hindi (CMSD1), English-German (CMSD2), and English-Korean (CMSD3), are created using the above-mentioned MDS1, MDS2, MDS3, and MDS4 datasets. To remove unwanted noise from the datasets, we use lemmatization from the nltk library [9].

3.2 Classification Model

In this section, we describe the proposed method for hate speech detection. This paper proposed a Multi-kernel capsule network (MKU-CapsNet) method, as shown in Fig. 1. A single kernel of a capsule network (CapsNet) can exhibit bias towards a specific class. To overcome the bias towards a particular class, MKU-CapsNet employs three different kernel uniforms: GLOROT, HE, and NORMAL uniform. Furthermore, the model combines three different kernels k by calculating the square root of the summation of three kernels based on individual kernel weights given in Eq. (1). As a result, the proposed method has been used to derive a generalized fit from an independent kernel uniform.

$$k_n = \sqrt{k1^2 + k2^2 + k3^2} \tag{1}$$

In text classification, a large dimensional corpus is built because each unique word is a feature. Thus, the proposed MKU-CapsNet method helps when a

---

[1] https://www.kaggle.com/junbumlee/lgbt-hatespeech-comments-at-naver-news-korean.

Table 1. Performance of various algorithms on monolingual political, COVID-19 datasets, multilingual, and composition of multilingual datasets.

	SVM	LSTM	CNN	GRU	CapsNet	MKU-CapsNet
DS1	77.02	88.71	94.35	91.69	93.46	97.92
DS2	95.57	99.35	98.95	99.31	99.01	99.34
DS3	96.55	99.80	99.72	99.73	99.10	99.38
DS4	97.27	97.34	97.27	98.52	97.13	97.69
DS5	88.50	99.13	99.10	99.09	97.03	98.47
DS6	85.19	99.30	99.42	99.33	97.28	98.81
MDS1	78.32	73.51	73.85	74.93	66.33	74.78
MDS2	88.88	86.07	81.25	85.63	86.73	88.37
MDS3	65.95	63.44	62.94	63.44	61.65	65.66
MDS4	72.49	82.75	80.34	82.21	83.80	84.08
CMDS1	70.29	69.82	68.32	68.47	65.89	69.09
CMDS2	72.88	73.24	68.35	71.29	72.07	75.10
CMDS3	72.22	78.08	76.14	75.52	72.69	76.47

single kernel extracts and performs dynamic routing on each unique feature. The CapsNet network can't understand the word's feature meaning and actual ground truth, as the single word feature may contain different contexts based on the sentence. For a broad feature set, a single kernel fails to pass the test. The CapsNet for text classification uses a single kernel and performs dynamic routing depending on the features selected from the embedding layer. So the CapsNet is legged for large and complex datasets and cannot understand the ground truth of a word in dynamic routing; if a single kernel with a large feature matrix is applied. So, we have used the MKU-CapsNet for vital feature selection and, those features pass to the network for dynamic routing for better performance. Once we get the ground truth of each feature word, it is easy for the CapsNet to perform dynamic routing to overcome the issue of a large-scale feature set, where a single kernel does not identify the relationship between words in a sentence.

4   Experiments

This section describes the experiments and comparative analysis of the results obtained from different models.

4.1   Experimental Setup

We investigate in six models namely SVM, LSTM, Convolutional Neural Networks (CNN), Gated recurrent unit (GRU), CapsNet and the proposed MKU-CapsNet on the datasets mentioned in Sect. 3.1. We use binary-cross entropy loss function and report the accuracy on the test set. The hyperparameters of the proposed model are convolution filters: 100, numbers of capsules: 10, routing: 05, dimensions of capsule: 16. All the experiments were implemented using standard Python library.

4.2 Results

In Table 1, the testing performed for the DS1 dataset ranges from 88.0% to 94.0% for the individual deep learning model. The varying skills of the deep learning model to specify the input data contribute to this difference within the outcome. Among competing deep learning models, CNN has a worthy performance of 94.35%. However, the proposed MKU-CapsNet model in the DS1 dataset performs 97.92% and outperforms other models. The proposed technique outperformed the other architectures by 99.34%. Besides, the LSTM model attained the highest accuracy of 99.35% for data set DS2, which is slightly higher than the MKU-CapsNet model. The best result was obtained for the monolingual data set DS3 with 99.38%. Aside from that, the proposed MKU-CapsNet model delivers good results and outperforms single kernel CapsNet on all datasets. Still, GRU obtains more accuracy of 0.1% to 0.5% for the DS4, DS5, and DS6 than the proposed MKU-CapsNet Model.

For the Multilingual datasets MDS1, MDS2, and MDS3, the proposed model achieves higher accuracy than the single kernel uniform CapsNet and lower accuracy than the GRU for MDS1, SVM for MDS1, MDS2, and MDS3. Also, the proposed MKU-CapsNet performance better and increased accuracy ranges from 0.01% to 10.00% for other deep learning models. The performance of the proposed method for MDS4 is 84.08%, which is higher than the performance of all models. For the composition of multilingual dataset CMDS1 and CMDS3, the proposed model achieves better accuracy than the single kernel uniform CapsNet and lower than the LSTM for CMDS1 and CMDS3, SVM for CMDS1. Also, the performance is decent than the other deep learning models, ranging from 0.01% to 5.00%. For CMDS2, the proposed method outperformed all models and the single kernel CapsNet approach by 75.10%. Observations for other data sets are also noted with the effect of the uncertainty of the text, overcoming the limitations of using a single uniform CapsNet learning method. Overall, the outcomes show that the proposed strategy can efficiently deal with the text uncertainty effect, overcoming the constraints of most deep learning models and single kernel uniform methods.

5 Conclusion

This paper proposes a Multi-Kernel Uniform Capsule Network approach for English, multilingual, and composition of English multilingual dataset for hate speech text classification. The main contribution is fusing the three different uniform kernels to improve generalization and decrease bias. The proposed approach achieves better or comparable results than other baseline models and outperforms CapsNet on all datasets. Multi-kernel dynamic routing has excellent capabilities while working with a multilingual feature set compared to traditional methods. Capsule networks perform well on image datasets. Thus in our future study, we will look into hybrid models to comprehend feature heterogeneity using image hate speech datasets. It will further improve the detection of hate speech.

References

1. Alorainy, W., Burnap, P., Liu, H., Williams, M.L.: "The enemy among us": detecting cyber hate speech with threats-based othering language embeddings. ACM Trans. Web **13**(3), 1–26 (2019)
2. Chiril, P., Benamara Zitoune, F., Moriceau, V., Coulomb-Gully, M., Kumar, A.: Multilingual and multitarget hate speech detection in tweets. In: Actes de la Conférence sur le Traitement Automatique des Langues Naturelles (TALN) PFIA 2019. Volume II: Articles courts, pp. 351–360. ATALA, Toulouse, July 2019. https://aclanthology.org/2019.jeptalnrecital-court.21
3. Ebrahimi Fard, A., Mohammadi, M., Chen, Y., Van de Walle, B.: Computational rumor detection without non-rumor: a one-class classification approach. IEEE Trans. Comput. Soc. Syst. **6**(5), 830–846 (2019)
4. Fortuna, P., Nunes, S.: A survey on automatic detection of hate speech in text. ACM Comput. Surv. **51**(4), 1–30 (2018)
5. Hana, K.M., Adiwijaya, Faraby, S.A., Bramantoro, A.: Multi-label classification of Indonesian hate speech on twitter using support vector machines. In: 2020 International Conference on Data Science and Its Applications (ICoDSA), pp. 1–7 (2020). https://doi.org/10.1109/ICoDSA50139.2020.9212992
6. Liu, H., Burnap, P., Alorainy, W., Williams, M.L.: A fuzzy approach to text classification with two-stage training for ambiguous instances. IEEE Trans. Comput. Soc. Syst. **6**(2), 227–240 (2019)
7. Naseem, U., Razzak, I., Eklund, P.W.: A survey of pre-processing techniques to improve short-text quality: a case study on hate speech detection on twitter. Multimedia Tools Appl., 1–28 (2020). https://doi.org/10.1007/s11042-020-10082-6
8. Ombui, E., Muchemi, L., Wagacha, P.: Hate speech detection in code-switched text messages. In: 2019 3rd International Symposium on Multidisciplinary Studies and Innovative Technologies (ISMSIT), pp. 1–6 (2019). https://doi.org/10.1109/ISMSIT.2019.8932845
9. Shah, V., Udmale, S.S., Sambhe, V., Bhole, A.: A deep hybrid approach for hate speech analysis. In: Tsapatsoulis, N., Panayides, A., Theocharides, T., Lanitis, A., Pattichis, C., Vento, M. (eds.) CAIP 2021. LNCS, vol. 13052, pp. 424–433. Springer, Cham (2021). https://doi.org/10.1007/978-3-030-89128-2_41
10. Sohn, H., Lee, H.: MC-BERT4HATE: hate speech detection using multi-channel BERT for different languages and translations. In: 2019 International Conference on Data Mining Workshops (ICDMW), pp. 551–559 (2019). https://doi.org/10.1109/ICDMW.2019.00084
11. Vashistha, N., Zubiaga, A.: Online multilingual hate speech detection: experimenting with Hindi and English social media. Information **12**(1) (2021). https://doi.org/10.3390/info12010005. https://www.mdpi.com/2078-2489/12/1/5
12. Wiegand, M., Siegel, M.: Overview of the GermEval 2018 shared task on the identification of offensive language (2018)

13. Zampieri, M., Malmasi, S., Nakov, P., Rosenthal, S., Farra, N., Kumar, R.: SemEval-2019 task 6: identifying and categorizing offensive language in social media (OffensEval). In: Proceedings of the 13th International Workshop on Semantic Evaluation, pp. 75–86. Association for Computational Linguistics, Minneapolis (2019). https://doi.org/10.18653/v1/S19-2010. https://aclanthology.org/S19-2010
14. Zhao, R., Mao, K.: Cyberbullying detection based on semantic-enhanced marginalized denoising auto-encoder. IEEE Trans. Affect. Comput. 8(3), 328–339 (2017)

Author Index

Printed in the United States
by Baker & Taylor Publisher Services